TOTEM
VOICES

TOTEM VOICES

PLAYS
FROM THE
BLACK WORLD
REPERTORY

Edited and with an introduction by

PAUL CARTER HARRISON

Grove Press
New York

Published by Grove Press
a division of Wheatland Corporation
841 Broadway
New York, N.Y. 10003

Library of Congress Cataloging-in-Publication Data

Totem voices: plays from the Black world repertory/edited with an
introduction by Paul Carter Harrison. —1st ed. p.   cm.
Contents: Mother/word/Paul Carter Harrison—The strong breed/Wole
Soyinka—Shango de Ima/Pepe Carril—Ti-Jean and his brothers/
Derek Walcott—A new song/Zakes Mofokeng—For colored girls who
have considered suicide/when the rainbow is enuf/Ntozake Shange—
Zooman and the sign/Charles Fuller—Ma Rainey's black bottom/August
Wilson—Ameri/Cain Gothic/Paul Carter Harrison.
ISBN 0-8021-1053-3
ISBN 0-8021-3126-3 (pbk.)
1. American drama—Afro-American authors.   2. English drama—Black
authors.   3. Afro-Americans—Drama.   4. Blacks—Drama.
I. Harrison, Paul Carter, 1931–
PS628.N4T68   1988
812'.54'080896—dc19   88-21420
CIP

Designed by Irving Perkins Associates

Manufactured in the United States of America

This book is printed on acid-free paper.

First Edition 1989

10   9   8   7   6   5   4   3   2   1

CONTENTS

ACKNOWLEDGMENTS

The Strong Breed. Copyright © 1964 by Oxford University Press. Reprinted from Wole Soyinka's *Collected Plays 1* (1973) by permission of Oxford University Press.

Shango de Ima: A Yoruba Mystery Play by Pepe Carril. English adaptation by Susan Sherman. Translation copyright © 1970 by Susan Sherman. Reprinted by permission of Doubleday & Company, Inc. Information about the availability of the music used in *Shango de Ima* can be supplied to serious researchers or people interested in doing the play by writing the adapter, Susan Sherman, c/o Doubleday, 277 Park Avenue, New York, NY 10017.

Ti-Jean and His Brothers, from *Dream on Monkey Mountain* by Derek Walcott. Copyright © 1970 by Derek Walcott. Reprinted by permission of Farrar, Straus and Giroux, Inc.

A New Song. Copyright © 1989 by Zakes Mofokeng. All rights reserved. Reprinted by permission. For inquiries, contact the author c/o Grove Press, 841 Broadway, New York, NY 10003.

the United States and Canada) should be directed to John Breglio, Paul, Weiss, Rifkind, Wharton & Garrison, 345 Park Avenue, New York, NY 10154. All inquiries concerning stock and amateur stage performance rights in the United States and Canada should be addressed to Samuel French, Inc., 25 West 45th Street, New York, NY 10036. For information on royalty terms and lead sheets for the following songs, apply to Samuel French, Inc.: "Ma Rainey's Black Bottom" by Ma Rainey, published by MCA Music, A Division of MCA Inc.; "See See Rider" by Ma Rainey, published by Northern Music Company (MCA); "Hear Me Talkin' to You" by Louis Armstrong, published by MCA Music, A Division of MCA Inc.; "Trust No Man" by Lillian Hardeway Henderson, published by Northern Music Company (MCA); "Doctor Jazz" by Joseph Oliver and Walter Melrose, published by MCA Music, A Division of MCA Inc., and Edwin H. Morris & Company, A Division of MPL Communications, Inc.

MOTHER/WORD*

BLACK THEATRE
IN THE
AFRICAN CONTINUUM:
WORD/SONG AS METHOD

When you go into any culture, I don't care what the culture is, you have to go with some humility. You have to understand the language, and by that I do not mean what we speak, you've got to understand the language, the interior language of the people. You've got to be able to enter their philosophy, their world view. You've got to speak both the spoken language and the metalanguage of the people.
— WOLE SOYINKA

In the small hours of a Bahia night, a group of black American writers was summoned to the hotel room of Verta Mae Grosvenor by the insistent persuasion of a young Bahian poet who zealously wished to share his poems with the American visitors. Verta Mae knew intuitively it wouldn't work as the Americans listened politely to the young Brazilian's efforts to communicate the interior values of his poetry in halting, albeit passionate, English. Suddenly, with an alarming sense of inhospitality, Verta Mae interrupted the proceedings and exhorted the young poet to render the poems in his native language. He hesitated at first, since no one in the room spoke Portuguese, particularly Afro-Brazilian Portuguese. However, prompted by the consensus of the American visitors, the poet began his narrative with the familiar word/song

---

* Mother/word as in fore/word or first/word or *the* word as in *truth*.

generic to storytelling in most black cultures, his incantations invoking images shaped by polyrhythm, repetition, and occasional vamps that onomatopoetically awakened the spirit of consanguinity, sweeping the American visitors along as willing participants in a ritualistic mode allowing access to the deeper significations of the poet's experience. The very immanence of the poet's word/song transcended the artificial barrier of alien-tongue and gave the visitors a sense of having shared in a narrative ritual that had peeled away layers of cultural distance. And in response to its beneficence, *we* smiled gratefully.

Word!

Mother/word!!

Ritual is the affective technique common to most theatrical exercises in the black world. Within these exercises, the word is not simply a mechanism of discourse. It is, rather, a creative elixir—Nommo force—that activates the dramatic mode (context of experience) and reveals the symbolic gesture of the Mask (characterization). Embedded in this mode are references to common experience, myths and significations that define the collective moral universe. The lessons of myth are secured in the inner world of experience, what Wole Soyinka describes as the "psychic substructure and temporal subsidence, the cumulative history and empirical observations of the community,"[1] which often requires strong rituals to reconcile past knowledge with contemporary realities. In his essay "Desire's Design, Vision's Resonance,"[2] Jay Wright notes that in traditional societies, ritual "challenges the creative and critical faculties of a historical community. What it provides is the invested life; it reveals the communal significance of experience. To understand what we mean by historical experience you must understand the necessity for desire, the rage of vision in Afro-America." The word, then, must have the power to reach beyond objective reality, to touch the spirit and awaken the soul—a necessary condition for the affirmation of existence—or to uncover what Soyinka calls the "quintessence of inner being."

The study of African philosophical systems is crucial to an understanding of the aesthetics of black cultures (including the black cultures of the New World, which are essentially Afrocentric in their aesthetic sensibility). That which is defined as beautiful in blackness requires the supportive foundation of ontology, a conception of the nature of the world and oneself in it. In recent years, many black scholars have turned their attention to the Dogon and Akan systems of thought for insight into the social and spiritual organizing principles that influence the aesthetics of blacks. Prominent among such scholars is W. E. Abrahams, whose study of the Akan in *The Mind of Africa*[3] reminds us that man/woman is an "encapsulated spirit," the materialization of the nonmaterial; and since spirit is a constant element in the nature of man/ woman, it is irreducible, though it is often manipulated or profaned by the conceits and caprices of the material world. "The physical world," observes Jay Wright in his analysis of J. B. Danquah's *The Akan Doctrine of God*,[4] "seems valuable only as spirit's exemplification or repository. And spirit subtly becomes intelligence, or mind. . . . Danquah's philosophico-theological *historia* is an aesthetic one, one in which he seeks terms for the arrangement and synthesis of experience derived from perception." Close inspection of language in the African diaspora—save, perhaps, the hybrid form of nine-teenth-century European speech retained in Liberia—reveals the common verbal impulse to make the word sing, irrespective of alien-tongue or corruptions of original syntax. What is most important here, as much so as for the Dogon, is that the resulting actions of language—spoken or gesticulated—have meaningful correspondences in both the physical and spiri-tual worlds. It is not uncommon, then, to discover in the art forms of the black world a language that is mythopoetic and intensified or amplified by an orphic sonority. A scat song, for example, is a rhythmic elaboration of language that, much like "talkin' in tongues," probes the "numinous shadow" for light and the meaning of objective reality, and produces, as Wilson Harris has noted in *The Womb of Space*,[5] "metaphoric

imagery that intricately conveys music as the shadow of vanished but visualized presences."

As evidenced by the storyteller's resistance to static exposition and fixity of conclusion, language in the black world is a
creative process with a plurality of meaning, its significance
changing as the experiential context shifts. Perhaps such a
tendency can be attributed directly to the Akan world view,
which, as Wright suggests, "sees experience and knowledge
as cumulative, the cosmos as creatively and harmonically
ordered, the social and physical world as a unitary system of
infinite complexity and correspondences. . . .What is necessary is terms to control experience. Ritual understands and
accomplishes this." If language has as its function the reaffir-
mation of collective consciousness and the codification of
myth that "embraces knowledge and feelings at the highest
level," ritual forms must be able to withstand objective contradictions that might inhibit acquisition of "reverence and com-
passion, visual and auditory rigor, emotional and intellectual
rigor (what we may call discipline of imagination, the freedom
of rule), respect for history and memory, respect for vision and
desire, and finally [the ability] to face up to the seriousness of
life and to the inevitability of death." The power of the ritual
should lead not only to cognitive enlightenment but also
transformation born out of spiritual revelation. To probe the
metaphysical world for symbolic correspondences to objective
reality, the contemporary black theatre artist requires an unre-
lenting discipline, the rigor of the traditional African carver,
whose apparently naturalistic forms are intensely potent
expressions imparting, as Isidore Okpewho[6] says, "tangible
meaning to those visible and spiritual presences which give
context to his daily life and thought"—in much the same way
that the music of Ellington, Monk, and Mingus produces what
the late poet Larry Neal called an "acoustic iconography" tran-
scending sociological explication or prosaic identification with
the stereotypic references commonly associated with the
blues. Rather than the duplication of experience, which invites
uncritical response to the mundane, we discover in their musi-

cal forms a rigorous excavation of significant communal values and an illumination of hidden impulses.

Until recently, black theatre in the United States, unlike the culturally informed ritual exercises of Africa, was merely the reproduction of material life, with little content beyond obvious protestation or abject solicitation of the dominant culture for recognition—and even authentication—of the black experience. In "Black Theatre in Search of a Source," an introductory essay to the anthology *Kuntu Drama,* I sought to identify the formal/ritualistic style of the black church as a paradigm for Afro-American dramaturgy, an alternative to the reigning theatrical form. Exploring the sacred experience for aesthetic reference seemed more than reasonable, since most people of African descent are first and foremost respon-sive to spiritual values, even when they are not affiliated with organized religion. Few blacks in the Americas are able to resist the groundswell of feeling and transport when the spirit is aroused in the formal exercises called church. Irre-spective of affiliation—Holiness, African Methodist Episco-pal, Baptist, Pentecostal in Puerto Rico, Candomble in Brazil, Macumba in Cuba, Pocomania in Jamaica, even Catholic or conservative Presbyterian—profound spiritual feelings can-not be suppressed "when the Saints come marchin' in"! And while the church experience may appear to be unchanged in form, the execution of the ritual is never static or otherwise predictable, largely due to the irrepressible magical incanta-tions of the preacher's performance style.

Secular rituals—even one as spiritually rousing as *The Gos-pel at Colonus*—cannot generate as much power as the orga-nized church experience, where word/song becomes the force that brings order to the congregation's collective vision, inspiring a sense of transformation of mind/body that leads, potentially, to productive action. Still, such an exercise, at least in form, should be a natural source of inspiration for the secular ritual we call theatre. In a recent interview,[7] Amiri Baraka (LeRoi Jones) examined the cultural implications of a religiously or spiritually informed aesthetic:

You'll find [a] contrast between say, the dionysian mode which is African, a complete emotional outlet, whether it's Black church or Black art . . . as opposed to the apollonian kind of Post-Greek, European approach where it's restraint. Nietzsche goes so far as to say life has to be kept separate from art because you might get too excited, it might stop you from being able to think. We look at them as two extremes, in that sense. I think that what the Afro-American has always been trying to evolve is an art that comes out of the basically dionysian, basic African spirit possession, because the Black church has always been about spirit possession. You know, they say the spirit will not descend without song. So you got to have music to make the spirit come down, and you gotta get the spirit, you gotta actually get the frenzy, you gotta get happy like they say, to actually have participated in that religious experience.

Further liberation from realism, with its static appraisal of the black experience, required a reexamination of black folk life for the sound and rhythms of the oral tradition—an inquiry that led to a new appreciation for the liturgical sophistication and resilience of sacred folk music—and a studied reacquaintance with the improvisational system of contemporary black classical music (so-called jazz). The poets, seminally influenced by Baraka, turned their ears toward the spontaneity of Charlie "Yardbird" Parker, the lyricism of Smokey Robinson, the tonal shifts and modulations of a Betty "Bebop" Carter scat song, the driving force of utterance and rhythmic repetition produced by James Brown, and the sustained, relentless, incantatory power generated by John Coltrane. Secular evocation of spirit was clearly apparent in black music, paving the way for the poets of the sixties—such as Baraka, Larry Neal, Ted Joans, Henry Dumas, Sonia Sanchez, and the original Last Poets—to explore the use of musical techniques in language. These same techniques would later appear in the new dramaturgy of black playwrights, finally rescuing black theatre from the predictable, facile presentation of the black experience held hostage by realism.

Lorraine Hansberry's *A Raisin in the Sun* (1959) represents the apotheosis of achievement in an aesthetic appropriated from the traditions of the American theatre, yet for black artists it signaled an end to realism and the beginning of expressionism. New black music and poetry, emerging out of a sixties social climate that demanded self-determination of thought and action, projected an aesthetic outside the social world of Hansberry and her peers and her black predecessors, a world that seemed tailored for realism. Hansberry, after all, was an integrationist who, having gone for the fake to the left, projected herself as a humanist, preferring the broad stroke of human aspiration to the specificity of objectives determined by black culture. That she crafted the form masterfully cannot be denied, but humanism, by its own admission, is an arresting challenge to spiritualism, for it is hell-bent on establishing through empirical verification the Aristotelian notion that man is a rational animal. The ensuing atomization and analysis of experience, which allows human behavior to assume some measure of predictability, sets the aesthetic posture of realism that leads to the stagnation of the imaginative impulse. W. E. Abrahams has noted that "the essence of humanism consists in the replacement of God the creator with man the creator." Hansberry's dramaturgy, then, was wholly consistent with the social posture of her period, a spirit of egalitarianism that leveled her experience. She embraced the distant vision of Everyman, as if uncertain about, perhaps even insecure with, the idea that black life and its attendant aesthetic point of view could be the veritable source of universal postulation. As a dramaturgical form, realism seldom illuminates the black experience in a manner that inspires a transformation of spirit or otherwise galvanizes the audience/congregation to action. It merely produces self-conscious entertainments that by and large arrest the spirit. Adrienne Kennedy, who had abandoned playwriting until Hansberry's success gave her a renewed sense of encouragement, recalls in her autobiography[8] the need to disavow the constraints of realism in order to exert the power of her language:

After I read and saw [Garcia Lorca's] *Blood Wedding*, I changed my idea about what a play was. Ibsen, Chekhov, O'Neill, and even Williams fell away. Never again would I try to set a play in a "living room," never again would I be afraid to have my characters talk in a nonrealistic way, and I would abandon the realistic set for a greater dream setting. It was a turning point.

In the new theatre, the word would sing and make visible the true nature of the human experience hidden behind the familiar mask of social realism.

Though there is an apparent affinity between black music and black language, Jay Wright cautioned against facile equations:

Todo poesía se acerca a lo sagrado (Ramon Xirau). We have been arguing for what you might call a distributive law of the sacred in Afro-American life and poetry. Spirit's distribution indicates why it is appropriate to correlate ritual and poetic forms. It is necessary to insist again that ritual song or chant is poetry of a special kind. One does not comfortably become the other, though both, written or not, must be spoken. We have to make this distinction and assert so much because too much has been made of contemporary black poetry's oral character as opposed to Homer, Chaucer, Dante, Milton, Goethe, Shakespeare. One wonders what the troubadors and Garcia Lorca and his friends were doing in those gardens and cafes. We know Pound's claim that all poetry must approach, even become, music. With few exceptions, our critics have failed us. We hear much about blues poetry and jazz poetry. No one tells us that they, the blues and black music, are only other distributive forms, if the reader will allow the formulation, and subordinate in practice and significance to the primary distributive form, the sacred, or, if that term frightens you, the spirit. We realize that putting things this way may do away with the trivia which have assertively passed in disguise as poetry. "The history of an art is the history of masterwork, not of failures, or mediocrity" (Pound). You have not necessarily

composed a masterwork in poetry by telling us the poem
has something to do with music.

Still, it is the musical ear that most informs the language
forged by poets and dramatists of the eighties, as if in
response to the South African poet Keorapetse Kgositsile's
exhortation of his contemporaries in the United States to
"celebrate in song" rather than simply words:[9]

> The word, then, in the service of the poet's vision, proposes
> certain relationships in whatever area of experience the
> poet has isolated to explore or celebrate in song.

Song, here, does not mean a tune or song per se but rather
denotes the intrinsic value of heightened language. Thus, in
Tales, Baraka recalls listening to Jay McNeely, whose "horn
spat enraged sociologies," and Aimé Césaire reflects on the
"bouquet of songs" enveloping the worshipers at a Martinque
church service in his epic poem *Return to My Native Land:*[10]

> Not only the mouths are singing, hands too, feet,
> buttocks, genitals, the whole fellow creature flowing in
> sound, voice and rhythm.
> When the joy reaches the highest point of its ascent, it
> bursts like a cloud. The songs do not stop, but anxious
> and heavy they roll now along valleys of fear and tunnels
> of anguish, through the fires of hell.

And within the threnodic voice of Jane Cortez's *Song for
Kwame,*[11] we hear the intonations of a scat-song riff:

> You are fallen
> You are gone
> and like grain inside rivermouths
> of our nostrils we grow you
> in the poolroom thought of our blackskins like
> a ceremony of secret alleys
> > beneath lips of cork

ears of omen
eyes of coin
scarification of sacred rouges
muscatels of rocking sadnesses
    you are growin under the gin-head-mask
    of beer breaths like a love shout from
    the black-belt of broken nipples
    dominating madness
you have fallen
you are gone
you are ancestral placenta
reassembled on the fifth day
of the flatted fifth scream
spreading like fire
    through isolated profiles of sanctified
    invalids

Implicit in poetic language is song, the heightened expression of the word, which dredges the invisible world for symbols that nurture our mythic and corporeal reality. Song penetrates this invisible world of nonrational forces to resurrect our totemic relationship to the ancestors. A totem is normally configured by an animal or object force that spiritually relates to members of a clan. Father Tempels[12] explains that an "animal or tree is often identified with a clan through the common ancestor whose life is then made known through a totemic or astral myth." It is not merely romantic speculation that one contemplates ancestral voices in the music of Bird, Hawk, Cannonball, Jug, or Trane, and astral myths in the totemic masks of the Art Ensemble of Chicago.

"The purpose of such identification with totem," continues Tempels, "is the appropriation of the psychic force associated with the particular totem." Analysis of Léopold Senghor's poem *Le Totem* leads Austin J. Shelton[13] to the conclusion that the "totem in the poem suggests the real self of the poet, as distinct from the artificial, Europeanised surface of the acculturated African." Black poets in the past, compelled by the force of ancestral totems—as opposed to muses—were designated *songsters*, bearers of words that illuminate our experience; and contemporary musicians have often been referred to as *magicians* because of their capacity to mediate our invisible and objective realities, gripping the spirit of common experience with what novelist Wilson Harris[14] might call a "phantom limb," urging to the surface intense feelings that were formerly submerged.

As Nathaniel Mackey points out, the concept of music as a "phantom limb" in many ways parallels Victor Zuckerkandl's observation that "music bears witness to what's left out of [our] concept of reality, or if not exactly what, to the fact that something *is* left out. The world, music reminds us, inhabits while extending beyond what meets the eye, resides in but rises above what's apprehensible to the senses." Reflecting on this convergence of immanence and transcendence, Mackey notes:

> Music as phantom limb arises from a capacity for feeling which holds itself apart from numb contingency. The phantom limb haunts or critiques a condition in which feeling, consciousness itself, would seem to have been cut off. It's this condition, the non-objective character of reality, to which Michael Taussig applies the expression "phantom objectivity," by which he means the veil by way of which a social order renders its role in the construction of reality invisible. . . . "Phantom," then, is a relative, relativizing term which cuts both ways, occasioning a shift in perspective between real and unreal, an exchange of attributes between the two.

The mediating properties of word/song, long a common feature in black diaspora literature, reveal what Richard Wright once termed "forms of things unknown." Such language often aspires to orphic insinuation, as in Jean Toomer's elegiac prose song, *Cane*,[15] where Kabnis, a spiritually alienated Northern schoolteacher, responds apprehensively to the wind blowing through the cracks of his Southern shack:

KABNIS: The walls, unpainted, are seasoned a rosin yellow.
And cracks between the boards are black. These cracks
are the lips the night winds use for whispering. Night
winds in Georgia are vagrant poets, whispering. . . .
Night winds whisper in the eves. Sing weirdly in the
ceiling cracks.

Mediation is also possible through the identification of characters with mystic powers, such as Legba, one of the most powerful *orishas* of Haitian vodun—he who presides over the crossroads and, though deformed, is the master of "polyrhythmicity and heterogeneity." Legba becomes incarnate in the person of Lebert Joseph in Paule Marshall's *Praisesong for the Widow,*[16] where allusion to a sort of "phantom limb" paradoxically becomes a testament of potency:

Out of his stooped and winnowed body had come the
illusion of height, femininity, and power. Even his fore-
shortened left leg has appeared to straighten itself out and
grow longer as he danced.

And the convergence of immanence and transcendence is quite apparent in Ralph Ellison's *Invisible Man,*[17] which exploits the potential of music to penetrate the invisible for metaphysical reference, allowing the protagonist to contemplate Louis Armstrong as a totemic source of vitality in an otherwise amorphous reality:

Invisibility, let me explain, gives one a slightly different
sense of time, you're never quite on the beat. Sometimes
you're ahead and sometimes behind. Instead of the swift
and imperceptible flowing of time, you are aware of its
nodes, those points where time stands still or from which it
leaps ahead. And you slip into the breaks and look around.
That's what you hear vaguely in Louis' music.

In his examination of Akan oral literature, W. E. Abrahams identified four categories of oral expression that are found throughout the black world: (1) the "purely oral literature which was recited and not sung," a form of oratory used to praise leaders or revered members of the community; (2) the "recitative which was half-spoken and half-sung"—dirges and folk-inspired raps of celebration that, much like the blues, address the fortunes and misfortunes of individuals or families; (3) "lyric poetry where song was used as a vehicle for poetry," a "stylized exhortation," as in spirituals or anthems for occasions of ceremony or worship, or for other "didactic purposes"; and (4) the "messages of the horns and drums which by their pitch, turn of phrase, and economy of expression, were literary." Each of these categories, with only minor variations of intention, is recognizable in the work of black poets; and the identification of musical instruments as extensions of voice has long been acknowledged as a source of iconographic reference. For example, in Larry Neal's play, *The Glorious Monster in the Bell of a Horn*, the musician's instrument becomes the mimesis of human tragedy, emitting sounds that fracture the continuity of time and space with coded improvisations, much like the mock-voicing of Paul Blackburn's poem *Listening to Sonny Rollins at the Five Spot*,[18] which graphically describes the sound of a Rollins performance:

> There will be many other nights like
> me standing here with someone, some
> one
> someone
> someone
> some
> some
> some
> some
> some
> some
> one
> there will be other songs
> a-nother fall, another_____ spring, but
> there will never be a-noth, noth
> a-noth
> noth

```
anoth-er
noth-er
noth-er
            other lips that I may kiss,
but they won't thrill me like
            thrill me like
                    like yours
used to
            dream a million dreams.
but how can they come
when there          never be
a-noth_____
```

The poet Quincy Troupe noted in the introduction to *Giant Talk*, an anthology of Third World literature, that writing "about musicians and their instruments gives the illusion of oneness with the aspirations of music, and studying the techniques of these musicians gives the writer new ideas for their own art. . . . From jazz, poets have learned the improvisation of all levels of linguistic expression. Words lose their traditional spelling, assume new shapes with different spellings, and create sounds that have never before been put onto the written page." One of the principal initiators of this new poetic style was Amiri Baraka, who underscored the possibilities of music in *Leadbelly Gives an Autograph:*[19]

The possibilities of music. First
that it does exist. And that we do,
in the scripture of rhythms. The earth,
I mean the soil, as melody. The fit you need,
the throes. To pick it up and cut
away what does not singularly express.

Need.
Motive.
The delay of language.

A strength to be handled by giants.

The aesthetic logic of black music improvisation, with its vamps, breaks, and "tradin' fours," has had an enormous impact on the language of the poets—at home and abroad—and given new impetus to the aesthetic implementation of very specific storytelling devices in the contemporary theatre of both old and new worlds. Thus, in the process of constructing a story that reveals the imperatives of communal myth while shedding light on objective reality, the storyteller achieves verbal virtuosity through his/her command of those vital communicative techniques, rhythm, repetition, and call and response.

To begin with, rhythm is vital to all processes of communication and action, from the casual conversation of communal recreation to the efficient execution of team athletics to the formal discourse of social organization. Léopold Senghor, the Senegalese poet-philosopher-statesman who, along with Aimé Césaire, promoted the cultural concept of *negritude*, viewed rhythm as the creative catalyst of black cultural style:[20]

> Rhythm is the architecture of being, the inner-dynamic that gives form, the pure expression of the life force. Rhythm is the vibratory shock, the force which, through our senses, grips us at the root of our being. It is expressed through corporeal and sensual means; through lines, surfaces, colours, and volumes in architecture, sculpture, or painting; through accents in poetry and music, through movements in dance. But, doing this, rhythm turns all these concrete things towards the light of the spirit. In the degree to which rhythm is sensuously embodied, it illuminates the spirit.

Rhythm, both emotionally and cognitively, becomes a generative force that galvanizes the spirit toward a highly intuitive sense of creation. However, as James A. Snead appropriately reminds us in his most illuminating essay "On Repetition in Black Culture":[21]

Without an organizing principle of repetition, true improvisation would be impossible, as an improvisor relies upon the ongoing recurrence of the beat. . . . That the beat is there to pick up does not mean that it must have been metronomic, but merely that it must have been at one point begun and that it must be at any point "social"— i.e., amenable to re-starting, interruption, or entry by a second or third player or to response by an additional musician.

As a cultural phenomenon, the black world, due to its cyclical view of experience, welcomes repetition, which is perceived as an opportunity to revitalize a shared cosmogony through social and sacred rituals. Continuity of experience is dependent upon the inextricable relationship between the worlds of the ancestors, the living, and the unborn. Such cyclical transitions are evident in Pepe Carril's *Shango de Ima*, a ritual drama inspired by *santería*, a Cuban form of Yoruba religion. Here the powerful *orisha* Shango symbolizes man struggling for self-awareness; owing to his many indiscretions, he is bound by Obatala, Mother of Earth—a procreative force represented by the male principle in traditional Yoruba religion—to recurring cycles of death and rebirth until he gains understanding of his true nature:

OBATALA: And this compliance will be your punishment, Shango de Ima. The joy which makes suffering possible, the birth which leads to death will be your punishment and the punishment of all men. . . . You are, by the designation of Olofi, eternal keeper of fire, of the sun's ray, of thunder, of the flame, but your followers must then also know the shadow that extinguishes these great lights. And this is your punishment also. If the eyes of your sons, your lights, become extinguished, light them again if you can, Shango de Ima, *orisha* of the flames, and see them extinguished again and again in the eternal cycle which follows your battles without end. And see if death gives way one inch. Iku is also the son of Olofi and thus life is followed by death and light by darkness in that endless cycle until

all the paths of the road turn toward their inevitable
end in the quiet of the cemeteries . . .

Conversely, in Western culture—at least as defined by Hegel,
who contradicts an earlier world view that had kinship with
black culture—repetition is not cyclical and is thus experienced as disquieting unless perceived as a progression, a
development toward a goal. Snead draws an analogy with the
economic system of capitalism:

> In black culture, repetition means the thing circulates
> (exactly in the manner of any flow, including capital flows),
> there is an equilibrium. In European culture, repetition
> must be seen to be not just circulation and flow, but accu-
> mulation and growth.

On such a view, the cyclical chaos and human sacrifices of
war must be appraised as a continuing refinement of the
means of destruction.

Further, repetition in black music or language is sometimes
characterized by a *vamp* that sustains the focus of the central
idea with subtle, unanticipated, yet imminent shifts in the
voicing, thereby intensifying the relentless power of the beat
and revealing nuances that enliven the experience with a
sense of renewal. Snead observes that "the thing (the ritual,
the dance, the beat) is *there for you to pick it up when you come
back to it*. If there is a goal (*Zweck*) in such a culture, it is always
deferred; it continually *cuts* back to the start, in the musical
meaning of *cut* as an abrupt, seemingly unmotivated break
(an accidental da capo) with a series already in progress and a
willed return to a prior series." Contrary to such a preinclina-
tion, we find in the classical European aesthetic canons for
music and literature—excepting, perhaps, the Baroque
fugues, the percussive sonority of Beethoven, the folk ethos
of Orff's *Carmina Burana*, the twelve-tone serialism fashioned
by Schoenberg, or the narratives of Yeats, Joyce, and Dos-
toyevsky in modern letters—that rhythm is used as a method
of denotation to advance the exposition of an idea, while

repetition becomes a device subordinated to construction and development. The resultant organization of tidy beginnings, suspended middle tensions, and resounding climactic resolutions is not paramount for the African sensibility, which instead values the capacity of word/song to immerse the soul in an expressive mode, continually pressing the familiar for new responses that assure revelation, rather than presenting inert ideas powered by dogma.

A vivid case in point is provided by a scene from the New York City Opera Company's 1987 production of the contemporary opera *X*—composed by jazz pianist Anthony Davis and written by poet Thulani Davis—which depicts Malcolm X's initial pilgrimage to Mecca. Departing from the usual Eurocentric conventions of story development, which demand quickly paced exposition and variation of action, the scene unfolded as a tableau of repetitive communal chants and genuflection. This allowed Malcolm time to become absorbed in the Islamic ritual, a slow, arduous, even burdensome process that ultimately infused him with a sense of redemption, thereby strengthening his commitment to Islam both spiritually and politically. The very rigor of the scene demanded that the audience suspend its usual need for mechanical plot advancement and participate in the visceral experience of the event. The animation of the scene, without adherence to the conventions of linear continuity, gave the audience a sense of relief, but also a new illumination of character that could not have been achieved by the kind of bombastic verbal rhetoric normally associated with Malcolm. The unanticipated yet imminent break or cut in the repetitive pattern served to heighten the potential for greater revelations in the rhythmic mode.

In popular music, James Brown has distinguished himself as the master of the break/cut device, which "overtly insists on the repetitive nature of the music by abruptly skipping it back to another beginning which we have already heard," notes Snead. In this case, repetition is not perceived as redundancy or the kind of negative feedback that retards acquisition of information, but rather as revitalization of an idea, much as in the improvisations of black classical music (so-called jazz), where the break/cut "is the unexpectedness with which the soloist will depart from the 'head' or the theme and from its normal harmonic sequence, or the drummer from the tune's accepted and familiar primary beat," exposing nuances in the musical mode that were earlier submerged.

Repetition, advanced through vamps and breaks, clearly plays a role in the performance style of the traditional black folk preacher:

Bretheren, and sisteren, my discourse dis even am gwine to be on the beautifulness of heav'n, and de horrifulness of hell, and one or de other of dem two things ought to reach every man, woman, and child in this vast assembliment.

I wishes to further say, dat I sees in dis congregation, a big flock of black sheep without a sheperd: one in which de bline am temptin' to lead de bline. De very openin' song dat you has just sung show dat you am followin' after false doctrine.

Now hear me, people, and give your ears over to under-standin'. De Bible specifies dat all flesh am not de same; dat dare am one kine of flesh of men; another kine of birds; and still another kine for fish and fowls; and it mought have further said dat all flesh of men am not de same kine of meat, for we has de flesh of de white folks; de flesh of the blacks; de flesh of de Injun; and at last, de flesh of de Chinaman, all differin' in glory de same as one star differs from another star in glory.

Listen now, and hear me, people. All heavens and all hells am not duh same kine, either.

Listen now, and hear me . . . (I am gwine to ax de brother dat is settin' de closest to dat dawg to please kick him out of dis sanctuary 'fore I proceeds any further, and I wants to agin call de attention to all of you to dat scripture dat says, "Cast not your pearls before a hawg, nor feed holy things to er dawg." Dat am de third time now dat I has seed dat same dawg tryin' to lif' dat kiver from off dat Sacrament board, and I am going to ax you once more to leave dem

dawgs at home in de future. . . . Thank you, my brother,
be seated).
   Now hear me, people, and harken unto my voice . . .[22]

The narrative here is amplified by a well-placed break that
seems incongruous to the text yet serves to reaffirm, almost
providentially, the urgency of the idea. In a blues narrative,
the break in the repeated phrases might take the form of a
random speculation outside the text, or a personal appraisal
of one's ability to render the deeper meaning of the song, or
simply a few open bars as a space to be filled without words,
each device creating tension in the performance. Though a
recapitulated phrase may seem redundant, its cumulative
resonance verifies the interior meaning of the statement, as
demonstrated by the strident, anaphoric incantation of the
distraught city dweller perched on top of a tenement building
in Melvin Van Peeble's musico-ritual *Ain't Supposed to Die a
Natural Death*:

         Take your hands off me Mister
         I ain't jumping. I'm leaning over
            picking up some of this breeze
            this is the coolest place in town
         Take your hands off me Mister
            If I didn't jump when sister got busted
            or junior boy started switching round
            take your hands off me Jim
            you know I ain't gonna jump now
         Take your hands off me Buddy
         Besides he'd just think it was 'cause I miss him so
            an you know you shouldn't talk bad about people
            after they go
            so he's gone—good—I suppose
         Take your hands off me mother
            If I didn't leap when Medgar got your message
            or Malcolm, or Martin Luther King
            Take your hands off me Jim
            You know I ain't gonna do it now

A similiar effort to restrain encroaching nihilism is apparent in Derek Walcott's epic poem *Another Life*,[23] where the spirit of resistance is forcefully expressed through the selective patterning of repeated words:

> I am pounding the faces of gods back into the red clay they
> leapt from with the mattock of heel after heel as if heel
> after heel were my thumbs that once gouged out as sacred
> vessels for women the sockets of eyes, the deaf howl
> of their mouths and I have wept less for them dead than I
>   did
> they leapt from my thumbs into birth, than my
> heels which have never hurt horses that now pound them
> back into what they should never have sprung from,
> staying unnamed and un-praised where I found them—
> in the god-breeding, god-devouring earth!

The emotional experience that fuels the above linguistic strategies is often recognized to be the same that underlies the blues, sometimes sad, sometimes glad, but never maudlin. Rather than indulging in self-pity or sentimentality, the blues purges the soul in order to open it to the critical insights required to deal with profound feelings of alienation. The blues does not solicit sympathy: it searches for answers while provoking the incongruous posture of lachrymose mirth evinced in August Wilson's *Ma Rainey's Black Bottom* when a group of musicians engages in the ritual aggression of "signifyin' " as a means of suspending their private hostilities:

> LEVEE: Damn, Slow Drag! Watch them big-ass shoes you
>   got.
>
> SLOW DRAG (*crosses and sits on the crates, holding his bass*): Boy,
>   ain't nobody done nothing to you.
>
> LEVEE (*crosses to bench, takes a rag out of his horn case, and
>   wipes his shoe*): You done stepped on my shoes.

SLOW DRAG: Move them the hell out the way then. You was in my way . . . I wasn't in your way. (*Stretches one foot out toward Levee; mockingly:*) You can shine these when you get done, Levee. (*All laugh except Levee.*)

CUTLER (*leans his trombone against the piano, takes another reefer and a box of matches out of his pocket, and lights the reefer*): If I had them shoes Levee got, I could buy me a whole suit of clothes.

LEVEE (*tosses the rag back into the horn case and sits on the bench*): What kind of difference it make what kind of shoes I got? Ain't nothing wrong with having nice shoes. I ain't said nothing about your shoes. Why you wanna talk about me and my Florsheims?

CUTLER (*puts the matchbox in his pocket*): Any man . . . who takes a whole week's pay . . . and puts it on some shoes—you understand what I mean, what you walk around on the ground with—is a fool! And I don't mind telling him.

LEVEE: What difference it make to you, Cutler!

SLOW DRAG: The man ain't said nothing about your shoes. Ain't nothing wrong with having nice shoes. Look at Toledo.

TOLEDO: What about Toledo?

SLOW DRAG: I said ain't nothing wrong with having nice shoes.

LEVEE: Nigger got them clodhoppers! Old brogans! He ain't nothing but a sharecropper. (*Levee and Slow Drag laugh.*)

The blues is also embodied in the ascendant melancholy of Ellington's *In a Sentimental Mood:* its melodic lyricism, however, should not be confused with sentimentality or prettiness. Rather, the sound is word—*mother/word*—and is by no means intended to represent the adorned sense of beauty that strives for perfection by Eurocentric standards. The blues, like folk language, is often irregular yet captures the imagination like the intensity of a black pearl or the alluring seductiveness of gapped teeth in the mouth of a potential paramour. The beauty of black language, as manifested by the blues, is not prettiness of speech but potency, as Kabnis discovers in *Cane:*

> KABNIS: The form thats burned int my soul is some twisted awful thing that crept in from a dream, a godam nightmare, an wont stay still unless I feed it. An it lives on words. Not beautiful words. God Almighty no. Misshapen, split-gut, tortured, twisted words.

As a storytelling vehicle—vocally and instrumentally—the blues produces in language an effect very much like that of traditional African art, which, as W. E. Abrahams describes it, is "direct, magical, attempting a sort of plastic analogue of onomatopoeia, to evince and evoke feeling." It is *feeling*, rather than strict adherence to form, that allows the storyteller—be it Leadbelly or Coltrane—to adorn the bare facts of his recitation. The improvisational character of these recitations, or rather, public testimonies, is best realized when the blues mediator—preacher, orator, poet, musician, rap master, reggae-calypso praise singer—is able to tap into the emotional flow of the audience, thereby producing the effect of public participation in a communal drama. The popular rap group Run-DMC, though musically impoverished, works in a rhythmic mode potent enough to transport a massive throng of teenagers on a wave of lusty exuberance, their inner turbulence channeled collectively through ritual call and response to both testimonial raps and dance movements, in an invocative process that has many of the vestiges, at least in form, of the oral tradition.

In traditional societies, as well as in contemporary communities throughout the diaspora, music has often been used as a method of securing communal participation in both sacred and secular ceremonies. Abrahams notes that the "need to adapt musical aids to the proceedings without submerging the verbal account forced the raconteur to seek musical qualities in his words. Thus there was a public exploitation of sound and semantic value for aesthetic effect. When this was successful, the sound of the word and its association, and so its evocative power, were deeply enriched by the musical accompaniment." On the other hand, while poets tend to emulate musicians, black musicians, observes Snead, tend "to imitate the human voice, and the tendency to *stretch* the limits of the instruments may have been there already since the wail of the first blues guitar, the whisper of the first muted jazz trumpet, or the growl of the first jazz trombone." Thus, whether speaking in tongues during a sacred ceremony or issuing the word nonverbally through instruments—as exemplified by the concertized version of Julius Hemphill's *Long Tongues: A Saxophone Opera*, performed at New York's Alice Tully Hall with six saxophonists as principal voices, supported by a conventional orchestra of strings and brass—the storyteller must be cognizant of modifications in rhythm, pitch, and tonality, significance of motival intention implied by repetition, and the transcendental potential of word/song elicited through call and response.

Call and response is deeply embedded in the traditional modes of communication in the black world. Typically, early folk storytellers in the rural South would initiate a story with a brief preamble:

> STORYTELLER: I'm gonna tell a story.
>
> RESPONDENTS: Uh-huh.
>
> STORYTELLER: Yawl ain't got to believe this story, but it's true.
>
> RESPONDENTS: Uh-huh.
>
> STORYTELLER: It's a story about a rabbit.
>
> RESPONDENTS: Uh-huh.

STORYTELLER: Yawl know this story?

RESPONDENTS: Uh-huh.

STORYTELLER: What's his name?

RESPONDENTS: Brer' Rabbit!

STORYTELLER: Yawl gonna believe it?

RESPONDENTS: Uh-huh!

In Trinidad, the traditional folk story is initiated by a codified form of call and response known as *cric-crac*, a form Derek Walcott exploits symbolically in his ritual excavation of the folk wisdom embedded in his fable *Ti-Jean and His Brothers:*

FROG:
Greek-croak, Greek-croak.

CRICKET:
Greek-croak, Greek-croak.

(*The others join.*)

FROG (*sneezing*):
Aeschylus me!
All that rain and no moon tonight.

CRICKET:
The moon always there even fighting the rain
Creek-crak, it is cold, but the moon always there
And Ti-Jean in the moon just like the story.

(*Bird passes.*)

CRICKET:
Before you fly home, listen,
The cricket cracking a story
A story about the moon.

FROG:
If you look in the moon,
Though no moon is here tonight,
There is a man, no, a boy,
Bent by a weight of faggots

He carried on his shoulder,
A small dog trotting with him.
That is Ti-Jean the hunter,
He got the heap of sticks
From the old man of the forest
They calling Papa Bois,
Because he beat the devil,
God put him in that height
To be the sun's right hand
And light the evil dark,
But as the bird so ignorant,
I will start the tale truly.

And Ti-Jean too, under the choric guidance of the totemic community, will discover the cycle of birth, death, and rebirth.

As a device for communal participation, call and response is most often associated with sacred ceremonies, the preacher calling his flock to testify—or at times with the hue and cry of politicians exhorting their constituents during rallies. However, the technique can also be found in the communal response to the high pitch of talking drums in Nigeria or to the deep resonances of the Candomble drums in Brazil, or even in Max Roach's shimmering vibrato on the high-hat cymbals in response to the tom-tom, or in the "tradin' fours" (exchanging of four bars) that extends the musicians' improvisational exploration of a tune, an objective also of interest to the griot and rapster storytellers, whose voices may slide up and down in various pitches and timbres to execute the call and response of multiple personas in a single voice. Nor should we overlook the sometimes intricate elaboration of questions and answers in children's games, or the coded, nonsensical utterances exchanged by men and women in that public display of propriety called "signifyin'." Significantly, signifyin', or ritual teasing—a verbal or at times nonverbal strategy of critical insinuation—is a social art form that serves to suspend the objective consequences of flawed behavior. In

many traditional African societies, signifyin' is a device used
to publicly address the social or political transgressions of
leaders without fear of retaliation, as in the Praise Singer's
marketplace confrontation with Elesin in Soyinka's *Death and
the King's Horseman*.[24] As Soyinka orchestrates their lines in a
sterling exhibition of call and response, the Praise Singer, his
voice emanating from the invisible world to project the dead
King's spirit, reminds the Horseman, who has enjoyed a
wealth of worldly benefits, that it is his communal responsibility to join the King beyond the veil:

> PRAISE SINGER:
> Elesin Alafin, can you hear my voice?
>
> ELESIN:
> Faintly, my friend, faintly.
>
> PRAISE SINGER:
> Elesin Alafin, can you hear my call?
>
> ELESIN:
> Faintly, my king, faintly.
>
> PRAISE SINGER:
> Is your memory sound Elesin?
> Shall my voice be a blade of grass and
> Tickle the armpit of the past?
>
> ELESIN:
> My memory needs no prodding but
> What do you wish to say to me?
>
> PRAISE SINGER:
> Only what has been spoken. Only what
>   concerns
> The dying wish of the father of all.
>
> ELESIN:
> It is buried like seed-yam in my mind.
> This is the season of quick rains, the harvest
> Is this moment due for gathering.

PRAISE SINGER:
If you cannot come, I said, swear
You'll tell my favourite horse. I shall
Ride on through the gates alone.

ELESIN:
Elesin's message will be read
Only when his loyal heart no longer beats.

PRAISE SINGER:
If you cannot come Elesin, tell my dog
I cannot stay the keeper too long
At the gate.

ELESIN:
A dog does not out run the hand
That feeds it meat. A horse that
    throws its rider
Slows down to a stop. Elesin Alafin
Trusts no beast with messages between
A king and his companion.

The semantic density and acoustic iconography of Soyinka's language produce the cosmic intensity of a Cecil Taylor piano solo and reaffirm the astral myths available to race memory. While there is no attempt here to conflate the many diverse applications of culture in the black world, it should be apparent that Soyinka and Taylor share an aesthetic posture that is informed by an Afrocentric perception of reality, irrespective of the specific influence of European culture on the means and modes of artistic expression. No matter how we decorate the African persona, the creative impulse invariably reflects race memory, which should not be construed as nostalgia or sentimental atavism. In spite of our cultural uniqueness, our kindred reactions to the history of colonialism and racial oppression reveal a commonly shared open wound on our consciousness. However, as Robert Elliot Fox observes:[25]

Art is a healing medium. Though it may sometimes take its inspiration from disturbances in society or the individual, its final effect is to meld the fissures of consciousness through its affirmation of continuity, its testimonial to imagination's procreative powers.

The artifacts forged out of specific histories reflect the particular urgencies of each culture, although we share a common sensibility. While Soyinka may resist oppression wherever it exists in the black world, the issue of neocolonial totalitarianism among corrupt and despotic African leaders may be more compelling for him than the racial policy of apartheid confronted by South African writers such as Mbongeni Ngema and Zakes Mofokeng, or the more subtle plight of the Caribbean mulatto, alienated and adrift on the shoals of race memory in the poems of Derek Walcott. Soyinka has complained, without malice, that Afro-Americans are too preoccupied with "the Man," unaware, no doubt, that the psychic intimacy blacks share with whites in the United States produces a peculiarly ambivalent symbiotic relationship that is totally absorbing. Clearly, the colonized black whose culture, however modified, supports his stance against the occupying alien legions manages to interface with the stranger due to a sense of cultural sovereignty that somehow must make the violation tolerable. This attitude is certainly unlike the vituperation expressed by blacks in America and South Africa in response to the doctrines and institutions of racial supremacy. Consider, for example, the impatience of Manana, the wife of Sello, a desultory trumpet player in Zakes Mofokeng's *A New Song,* who urges her husband to rid their home/nation of the uninvited visitor who had cajoled Sello's grandfather/ancestor out of the house where they now live as servants:

> MANANA: Life is not easy Sello. It is not easy for a woman to give birth. It's pain, not easy. I am a woman Sello, ask me. When I was in pain, delivering your son, you were taking it easy with your friends drinking beers and celebrating "I'm going to be a father!" You became a

father without even feeling any change. Now Sello, getting John out of here is not like becoming a father. It's like giving birth, it's painful, because you'll be giving birth to a new life.

If dignity is to be restored to life, the Man simply has to go, and by any means necessary, save the subtle subterfuge of passive aggression, the sort that leads to appropriation of the oppressor's values or cultivation of the intruder's style and manner. This strategy may win the privilege of elevated discourse for the victimized, perhaps even following Soyinka's recommendation that "when we borrow an alien language to sculpt or paint in, we must begin by co-opting the entire properties of that language as correspondences to properties in our matrix of thought and expression."[26] But appropriation of language, one of the principal indices of culture, is very difficult for the South African or Afro-American who seeks liberation from the psychic hegemony of the dominant culture. In fact, for the Afro-American, the "correspondences to properties in our matrix of thought and expression" are few when one considers that America is a land of processed foods and the sort of synthetic religiosity that has polyester television ministries offering a toll-free call to Jesus, a country where from the ramparts we watch a curious sense of euphoria overtake a large segment of the dominant culture during the unrestrained demolition of cars in a crash derby, a nation where the power of the presidency and its implied authority have been demystified by allowing men of questionable integrity to occupy the office, an illusory place where the canned image of Max Headroom, an electronically conceived characterization of the Anglo-Saxon mythic hero, is listed among mortals as one of the ten sexiest men in America. Indeed, as Soyinka himself has observed,[27] blacks in the United States are American in form but substantively Afro-Americans who have developed a language style that unquestionably has been appropriated by the dominant culture:

Now *soul* is a language of one proletariat that we know, recognize, and identify as one of many regional proletariats in need of socio-economic liberation. It is a community that has a very distinct culture—very palpable, almost quantifiable in all its complex structures and their social correlations. I will not sentimentalize this society, which is at once violent and tender, at once cynical, acquisitive, and millennial; I will content myself with asserting that it exists, that it is part of a larger society whose capitalistic philosophy it shares. This micro-society has its own bourgeoisie which, to some extent, also appropriates the language of the black proletariat . . . not only within the large American continent but also in much of the Caribbean, particularly Jamaica. Soul has its own mythologies too, and it is highly marketable; nevertheless, it is a summation of music to this very specific socio-polity, and it resists outright appropriation, being woven tightly into the interstices of daily social interaction—in short, into a vocabulary of a socially replete existence.

Many of the mythologies of soul, however, have been trivialized within the dominant culture for the sole purpose of popular entertainment. Self-appropriation without illumination, as in minstrelsy, is tantamount to self-mockery. During slavery in the United States, blacks improvised a spontaneous form of entertainment that consisted of storytelling, songs, dances, and virtuoso renderings on makeshift instruments. The elements were appropriated by the landowners and formalized into a structured entertainment performed in corked blackface and known as minstrelsy. In the mid-nineteenth century, blacks were allowed to adorn the minstrel stage— in blackface—to perform mock parodies of their reality. Today the world of entertainment continues to use blacks to exploit the iconographic stereotypes that trivialize, even profane, the integrity of soul: one can easily conclude that Oprah Winfrey's mammyism and Whoopi Goldberg's piccaninnyism are arrested states of negroidness, a *pigment* of the dominant culture's imagination. Moms Mabley, on the other hand, was an authentic voice, an icon "woven tightly into the interstices of daily social interaction—in short, into a vocabulary of a socially replete existence."

When memory serves us, we achieve the timeless tapestry of Romare Bearden's *Quilting Time*, which employs the plastic gesture of collage in a seemingly improvisational manner to rhythmically orchestrate apparently discordant images into a seamless communal signification, exposing the event to a new inspection of its mythic resonance. It is a nonlinear achievement in image-making that conforms to W. E. Abrahams' description of the ideal objectives in traditional African art, an aesthetic that seems applicable to the contemporary black theatre as well:

> The superlative achievement of African art probably lies in the control achieved over deformity and its associated feelings in their societies. Thus in the relevant works, there is near-vigor, but not vigor *à la Japan*, near-hideousness but not hideousness, near-distortion which is not complete, the complex of attributes which does not quite scarify, but leaves a ponderous aura of dark forces, of massive unreleased potency, of the unknown and the indeterminate, almost a hushed version of the ventriloquist ubiquity of the rattle-snake, the sense of mesmerized helplessness, still, cold, silent, enchantedly forlorn, and an aura of the numinous presence of primeval spirit. African art was testamental . . .

Black theatre too, when aesthetically uncluttered by realism, is testamental. The inclination to testimony is the direct outgrowth of blacks attempting to overcome the rifts of consciousness created by regionalism and elitism so as to identify the tracings of a collective ethos, a sense of common purpose. Thus, archetypal characters are more vital for public testimony than individuated characters pursuing their personal assessment of reality. Like the blues singer, archetypes provide potent communal references that illuminate the social landscape. Commitment to the communal vision by no means suggests inhibition of individualism, as the improvisation of musical ensembles demonstrates. Individualism, with its fullest complement of personal expression, is simply subordinated to collective goals. In Akan society, as Abrahams notes, the relationship between the individual, the community, and the spiritual world is a social contract that does not produce a literature preoccupied with the individual as the primary source of reference—an idea that is "nonsensical, for, even before man was born, his spiritual factors belonged to specific ethnic groups. . . . Their central concern was with particular, stylised expressions, whose repeated occurrence never failed to be applauded." Testimony, used in the black church to illuminate the collective experience, is a technique that prevails in black theatre, as made evident by the parade of archetypes in George Wolfe's *The Colored Museum* and Ntozake Shange's choreopoem *for colored girls who have considered suicide/when the rainbow is enuf:*

> *lady in brown*
> dark phrases of womanhood
> of never havin been a girl
> half-notes scattered
> without rhythm/no tune
> distraught laughter fallin
> over a black girl's shoulder
> it's funny/it's hysterical
> the melody-less-ness of her dance
>
> don't tell nobody don't tell a soul
> she's dancin on beer cans & shingles
>
> this must be the spook house
> another song with no singers
> lyrics/no voices
> & interrupted solos
> unseen performances
>
> are we ghouls?
> children of horror?
> the joke?

don't tell nobody don't tell a soul
are we animals? have we gone crazy?

The conscious legitimation of testimony in the work of
contemporary black dramatists signaled a departure from
Ibsen, O'Neill, and Williams that was as aesthetically liberat-
ing as the distance created by contemporary black musicians
from the constraints of Stephen Foster, George Gershwin,
and Francis Scott Key. In an effort to locate a specific culturally derived voice, Afro-Americans began to shape an aesthetic that reflected both the African legacy and their
cumulative experience in a highly technological society. The
aesthetic formulations seemed crude in the beginning, song-
dance-drum—those civilizing forces of ritual—appearing
quaint and exotic next to the formal canons of Western dramaturgy. However, after the discovery of oral and literary
traditions among the Yoruba and the Akan, and of the
ontological system of the Dogon, the rudimentary apprehension of drum as iconographic reference—the rhythmical analogue to the human voice—was elaborated into a more
sophisticated aesthetic principle. The urgency to formulate an
aesthetic based upon the American experience but informed
by the ethical sensibilities of Africa led Larry Neal to identify
the common objectives of art and politics in his now famous
1968 manifesto "The Black Arts Movement":[28]

The Black Arts Movement is radically opposed to any concept of the artist that alienates him from his community.
Black Art is the aesthetic and spiritual sister of the Black
Power concept. As such, it envisions an art that speaks
directly to the needs and aspirations of Black America. In
order to perform this task, the Black Arts Movement proposes a radical reordering of the western cultural aesthetic.
It proposes a separate symbolism, mythology, critique, and
iconology. The Black Arts and the Black Power concept
both relate broadly to the Afro-American's desire for self-
determination and nationhood. Both concepts are nation-

alistic. One is concerned with the relationship between art
and politics; the other with the art of politics.

Neal's prophetic mandate reflected a social and political
tenor of the period, prompting an inward search into the
reservoir of black experience for the authentic symbols,
myths, and icons that would sharpen critical focus. However,
the intoxication of revolutionary zeal offered many facile configurations of black iconography and its associated myths,
which led to predictable, noncritical conclusions regarding
the black experience. The commitment to social change
sparked a plethora of agitation-propaganda theatrical exercises erected upon the foundations of a Western morality that
pursues a linear, causally determined response to confrontation based upon the notion "Do unto others what you would
have them do unto you," as opposed to the moral wisdom
apprehended in most black communities that suggests the
cyclical imperative of adversary relationships: "What goes
around comes around." Fortunately, sobriety soon prevailed,
and the latter sensibility became apparent in the new dramaturgy, which produced enlightened views of social commitment, engaging our consciousness with icons seldom
confronted on stage—such as the disturbing spectre and
testimony of Zooman, the volatile street-tough of Charles
Fuller's *Zooman and the Sign*, whose moral universe, circum-
scribed by a life of abandonment and social insularity, challenges us to impugn the validity of his judgment:

ZOOMAN: They call me, Zoo-man! That's right. Z-O-O-
M-A-N! From the Bottom! I'm the runner down thea'.
When I knuck with a dude, I fight like a panther. Strike
like a cobra! Stomp on mothafuckas' like a whole herd
of bi-son! Zooman! . . . What am I doing here now? I
just killed somebody. Little girl, I think. Me and Stockholm turned the corner of this street?—and there's
Gustav and them jive mothafuckas' from uptown, and
this little bitch has to be sitting on her front steps

playing jacks—or some ole' kid shit! But I had tol'
Gustav if I eva' saw his ass around the Avenue, I'd blow
him away. (*Shrugs.*) So I started shootin' and she jes'
got hit by one of the strays, that's all. She ain't had no
business bein' out there. That street is a war zone—
ain' nobody see her, we was runnin'—shit! And in that
neighborhood you supposed to stay indoors, anyway!
(*Pause.*) She was in the wrong place at the wrong
time—how am I supposed to feel guilty over somethin' like that? Shiiit, I don't know the little bitch,
anyway.

Initially, Zooman provokes our wrath: his final demise, however, as if he were offered to the flames of malevolent spirits
like a sacrificial lamb, causes us to suspend our indignation to
attend the wisdom realized by his victim's mother, who seizes
upon the fact that Zooman—like all the Zoomen of the
world—is *still* some mother's child in the community, and
worthy of redemption. Perhaps Zooman's death, like so
many senseless killings in America, is what Soyinka would
call "the tragic prelude" to greater acquisition of the truth.
Still, the apparent ritual sacrifice of Zooman is a hard lesson,
though he is spared the arbitrary judgment of a morality
fueled by a puritanical sense of retribution. Zooman is not a
tragic hero but rather a demonic force inviting a social critique. His story is a revelation of the contradictions that must
be negotiated in the black experience, as opposed to simplis-
tic analysis of good versus evil.

Edward James[29] notes that sacrifice "may take the form of a
personal commitment to refrain from a social act, an item of
food, an attitude, or it may take the form of an offering to an
orisha of fruits or cooked food. Man learns by these acts of
sacrifice that life is a balance—one item or act is given up in
order to obtain another of greater depth. Sacrifice is never a
punishment, indeed, it is always a way to attain something
greater, to achieve a greater integration of one's self in order to
better understand one's way in life." In Wole Soyinka's *The
Strong Breed*, we discover ritual sacrifice to be an essential

aspect of Yoruba religiosity. Eman, a schoolteacher in an alien village, is inadvertently drawn into an annual ritual that requires him to commit himself to being the sacrificial "carrier." Human sacrifice is often viewed by Western standards of reality as a tragedy. Soyinka would have us understand that sacrifice represents a commitment to transition and transformation of communal objectives; what is tragic is the use of rituals that fail to yield new consequences. "It is a poor beginning for a year," laments Jaguna, "when our own curses remain hovering over our homes because the carrier refused to take them." Eman rejects the inevitablility of a bloodline that offers him as involuntary carrier for a failed cyclical ritual, and is pursued by Jaguna, who leads the anxiety-ridden villagers in their quest to cleanse their community of a persistent curse. But then the genealogy of his fate is revealed to him through a hallucination of his dead father, a former carrier:

> OLD MAN: I meant to wait until after my journey to the river, but my mind is so burdened with my own grief and yours I could not delay it. You know I must have all my strength. But I sit here, feeling it all eaten slowly away by my unspoken grief. It helps to say it out. It even helps to cry sometimes. (*He signals to the attendant to leave them.*) Come nearer . . . we will never meet again son. Not on this side of the flesh. What I do not know is whether you will return to take my place.

> EMAN: I will never come back.

> OLD MAN: Do you know what you are saying? Ours is a strong breed my son. It is only a strong breed that can take this boat to the river year after year and wax stronger on it. I have taken down each year's evils for over twenty years. I hoped you would follow me.

Goaded by ancestral imperative and temporal vexation, Eman retreats into the shadows of the river in pursuit of his father, his flight portending resignation rather than transfor-

mation. Death is senseless, even tragic, when the human
spirit is not renewed by revelation.

The appropriate rituals are required to assure transformation of the spirit even for Black Junior, the junkie of Archie
Shepp's testimony in his poem *The Wedding*.[30] Black Junior
had "vounced" on Panamanian Red or "good coke when he
could get it," then OD'd, the potentially procreative rites of
marriage ironically suspended by the rites of dark passage
beyond the veil:

> Black Junior
>   seemed to soar past the preacher
>   in his metal casket
>   straight through the gleaming eye
>   of God
> "I said, Thank you, Jesus"
>   Sista Beatrice said.
> Pearly Mae screamed
>   and clutched her groin
> In that instant of death
>   she had given life
>   and I
>   became a man
>   with the slippery future
>   of a fish.
> I had bellowed Harlem
>   inside her
>   and she swelled into loaves
>   of yeasty cities
>   like bread
>   on a poisoned river
> "You poisoned the river"
>   she said.
> Then retrieved me with the
>   songs of Damballah
>   and Engels
>   on her lips.

The enumeration of social causes and effects cannot ade-
quately address the tragedy of Black Junior; the appropriate

ritual, however, should reveal, once again, the *tragic prelude*, an investment of the tragic experience with illumination. Without illumination, tragedy becomes hopeless voyeurism and leads to cynical appraisals of the event.

How, for example, does one evaluate the loss of Martin Luther King, Jr., to the assassin's bullet: tragedy or sacrifice? Certainly, King's death glaringly illuminated the social conflict gripping the nation, revealing a shocking predisposition to violence. King had placed himself in the middle of the malevolent storm of hostilities that had claimed the lives of men, women, and children—black and white, good and evil—with blind ferocity. Perhaps the tragedy can be found in the inability of the black community to protect King from the strife of black-white confrontation in America, as I attempt to suggest in *Ameri/Cain Gothic*. Here I. W. Harper, a black private investigator responsible for reconnoitering Memphis before King's arrival, is distracted by Cass, a white recluse living in the rooming house from which the fatal bullet is ultimately fired. Cass is suffering from a grave sense of imminent violence and solicits his help:

> CASS: I was leaving that department store on Main Street where the old Gayoso Hotel used to be. And I thought to myself, what a shame that so much garbage should be heaped upon the spot where the finest hotel between New Orleans and Chicago used to be. It was the pride of the Cotton Kings. I passed through the debris and made my way to Beale Street, where my ears were assaulted by that wretched race music. And right there on the corner of Beale and Main was an old colored woman selling love potions. She seemed quite agitated, whooping and hollering as she talked to a large peacock called Juno that fanned out its tail in a mass of evil eyes. The woman turned toward me with her eyes rolled back in her head. I thought she was having a seizure, but she extended her hand to make an offering. I wanted that love potion dearly, but I was frightened by so many evil eyes. I turned away and ran

home, leaving a five-block trail of rubbish behind me.
And on my heels was a shadow. It followed me up the
stairs. I dashed into my room, bolted the door, and
being weary from the whole ordeal, took off my
clothes and went to bed. When I awoke, a man's hand
was around my throat.

Harper becomes ritualistically absorbed in an effort to trace
this elusive shadow. The process forces him to dredge the
depths of his subconscious and unearth a deeply submerged
experience with domestic violence that reveals the patholog-
ical symbiosis between racism and sexism, and its corrosive
effects on the victim.

HARPER: I mean it, Cass. You have no sense of urgency.
Home used to say, if somebody is on your trail, and you
don't know who it is, you've gotta stay way out in front
of him. Home knows all about survival. There'll be no
slippin' up on Home. He stays on the move. Even an
unknown assailant has got to keep movin'. In a funny
way, the assailant gets caught up in his own momentum. As long as he stalks his prey down some dark
corridor on Beale Street, he's okay. But as soon as he
turns down Main Street, he takes a chance of blowin'
his cover. He must move quickly and decisively on his
momentum before the prey turns around for an unguarded glimpse and simply asks . . . "Haven't we met
somewhere before?" The prey never had a chance,
catching only a brief peek at the sudden stroke of
horror.

Harper's personal intimacy with violence, however, cannot
avert the grim denouement that overtakes King.
    Out of the ashes of such human despair, there is a lesson to
be learned, some new insight into the frailty of human
nature, some glimmer of understanding that is regenerative
rather than corrosive. Tragedy is often compelling to the
senses, particularly when the experience comes to conscious-

ness on a scale that is unfathomable, the spectacle achieving the heightened effects of poetry. As Soyinka aptly declares:[31]

> If tragedy enforces its own music, its own poetry, if this *tragic grandeur* can be expressed only in beautiful tomes of sublime music, or the particular sound and orchestration of words which we call poetic, what is wrong with that? That is part of the property of experience, and that is part of the richness of art and literature.

Both Larry Neal and Charles Fuller, who received the 1982 Pulitzer Prize for *A Soldier's Play*, have often argued that a black theatre aesthetic cannot survive without an attendant literature. The dramaturgy of early black authors in the United States, such as William Branch, Alice Childress, Loften Mitchell, and Langston Hughes, conformed to the melodramatic standard popularized by the American stage. With the exception of Hughes, perhaps, word/song testimonies in the literature were conspicuously absent. Since the mid-sixties, however, a literature defined by a black aesthetic has developed through several tributaries, including commercial and regional theatres, traditional American as well as black theatre repertories, Equity showcases, professional workshops, and university productions. Under the guidance of Douglas Turner Ward, the Negro Ensemble Company undertook the most significant cultivation of the literature. Ironically enough, the 1967 inaugural season of NEC—created following the successful commercial production of Ward's *A Day of Absence*, which satirized the socioeconomic interdependence between blacks and whites—opened auspiciously with *The Song of the Lusitanian Bogey*, a ritual denunciation of Portugal's colonization of Angola, with songs and verse scripted by the German writer Peter Weiss, who had won international acclaim for his *Marat/Sade*. Weiss's poetic testimony of brutal oppression gained force through the music of Coleridge-Taylor Perkinson, a collaboration that enabled the newly formed company to exploit the play's nonlinear form and demonstrate their ensemble-style technique. In the same season, however, Ward introduced Wole Soyinka's *Kongi's Harvest*, initiating a commitment to bring plays from the black world into the repertory, which later included Derek Walcott's *Dream on Monkey Mountain*, and Lennox Brown's *A Ballet Behind the Bridge*, out of Trinidad, and from Jamaica, Trevor Rhone's *Two Can Play*. The plays developed by Ward over the past twenty years have won every coveted award from Obie to Pulitzer and represent some of the best works produced in the United States. A partial list of those works might begin with Lonne Elder III's *Ceremonies in Dark Old Men*, Phillip Hayes Dean's *Sty of the Blind Pig*, Joseph Walker's *River Niger*, Gus Edwards' *The Offering*, Steve Carter's *Eden*, Leslie Lee's *The First Breeze of Summer*, Larry Neal's *In an Upstate Motel*, Pearl Cleage's *Puppet Play*, Samm-Art Williams' *Home*, Charles Fuller's *A Soldier's Play*, and my own *The Great MacDaddy*.

Woodie King's New Federal Theatre has also contributed vastly to the exposure and development of contemporary black playwrights through Equity showcase formats. A partial list of distinguished work introduced by King includes Bill Gunn's *Black Picture Show*, Ron Milner's *What the Wine Sellers Buy* (and the recent national tour of Milner's *Check Mates*), J. E. Franklin's *Black Girl*, Amiri Baraka's *Slave Ship*, P. J. Gibson's *Long Time Since Yesterday*, Ed Bullins' *The Taking of Miss Janie*, Vincent D. Smith's *Williams and Walker*, and Ntozake Shange's *for colored girls*.

Among the significant plays developed and produced by traditional American theatre institutions are Baraka's *Dutchman* and Adrienne Kennedy's *Funnyhouse of a Negro* (Barr-Albee Workshop), Milner's *Who's Got His Own* (American Place Theatre), Archie Shepp's *Junebug Graduates Tonight* and Aishah Rahman's *Lady Day: A Musical Tragedy* (Chelsea Theatre), Ray Aranha's *My Sister, My Sister* (Hartford Stage), James Baldwin's *Blues for Mister Charlie* (Actors Studio), Richard Wesley's *Black Terror* and Charles Gordone's *No Place to Be Somebody*, the first black play to be awarded a Pulitzer Prize, in

1970 (New York Shakespeare Festival). The universities have contributed also, particularly with the work of the 1987 Pulitzer Prize recipient, August Wilson (*Fences*), who has benefited greatly from the nurturing of director Lloyd Richards, dean of the Yale School of Drama and director of the Eugene O'Neill Festival Workshop. And recently Columbia College in Chicago initiated the Theodore Ward Prize for Afro-American playwriting. Its first two recipients, following a national search, were Silas Jones for *John Doe Variations* and Christopher Moore for *The Last Season*.

Black theatre literature, by definition, includes plays written by black authors about the black experience and thus excludes dramatizations that simply document the experience, such as Martin Duberman's *In White America* or Howard Sackler's Pulitzer Prize work, *The Great White Hope;* even DuBose Heyward's folk homily *Porgy and Bess* does not qualify, and certainly not the insipid depiction of Negro religiosity in Marc Connelly's *The Green Pastures*, which lacks even the slightest redeeming virtue. By definition, even Athol Fugard's *Boesman and Lena*, with its cogent exposition of the social forces that impact on an itinerant black South African couple's relationship, might be only marginally acceptable, though *The Island* and *Sizwe Bansi Is Dead*, highly acclaimed works resulting from Fugard's collaboration with two black South African actors, John Kani and Winston Ntshona, fully qualify as part of the growing black world theatre literature. The definition does not preclude enlightenment from genuine expositions of the black experience by white authors, though Edward Albee's allegory *The Death of Bessie Smith* provides fewer opportunities for incandescence than Barney Simon's edifying *Born in the RSA* (Republic of South Africa).

Recently, in response to the feminist movement worldwide, the literature has been splintered by a gender-focal sensitivity that separates female issues from ethnic objectives. While gender issues in America have allowed black female playwrights a wider basis for discourse, there is little need to cavil over whether their output should be viewed as a reflection of a gender experience specifically or the black experience generally. The special insights that women share among themselves does indeed accord them a unique focus, such as is expressed in the dying mother's confession to her daughter in Pearl Cleage's *The Hospice*[32] . . .

> ALICE: I did not see my future as the dedicated wife of the charismatic leader, dabbling in a little poetry, being indulged at cultural conferences and urged to read that one about the beautiful brothers and sisters in Soweto, or Watts, or Montgomery, Alabama. I couldn't just be that. The world is bigger than that. The world inside my head is bigger than that. Even now . . . I used to watch your father at rallies and in church on Sunday morning, and he'd be so strong and beautiful it was all I could do to sit still and look prim in my pew. But he was committed to "the movement." He didn't have time anymore to lay in bed with me and improvise. I'd been a wife since I was seventeen and here I was almost thirty, with a ten-year-old daughter, trying to convince your father to let me publish some love poems! But he couldn't. Or he wouldn't. The kind of love he had to give me now didn't allow for that. And I couldn't do without it. So I left. Not much of a story is it?

. . . or in recriminations born of disillusionment as Jet confronts her musician boyfriend in Alexis De Veaux's *The Tapestry:*[33]

> JET:
> you been seeing somebody else
> behind my back
> i can smell it
>
> AXIS (*trying to be calm*):
> jet
> you sound like you getting ready to go off
> on me and i dont want to deal with it
> no more from you

JET (*inching closer*):
i bet you been sleeping with her
did you before you came waltzing over here
tonight? sweet talking and breathing hard
one minute and saying so long baby im
leaving the next

AXIS:
watch yourself
you dishing out more than
your ears can eat

JET (*insistent*):
you tell her the same things you tell me
when you fall on top of her at night?
groping for the wonderland
between her legs? do you?
do you make her feel like shes more
than a good piece of gimme-some-tonight
but i dont know if ill be around tomorrow?
dont count on me for nothing
sis   tah?

(*they stand face-to-face confrontation and are nearly screaming
at each other*)

AXIS:
i sure was wrong about you baby
you aint nothing but a goddamn kid
youre as far away from being a woman
as a pygmy is from heaven

JET:
do you pretend with her too?
huh axis?
do you tell her how much you going to crack the world
open with that pawn-shop horn you stick
under your arm all the time?
or do you just leave the sound of your

(*she illustrates the following words in melodic voice and
quick body movements*)

mu   sic getting mol   dy
in her head like stick leftovers
in the garbage can as you can make it
to the next bed
do you tell her you love her too?

Undoubtedly, gender perception is a vital barometer of reality, and black women are reliable articulators of the total
experience, the vitiating effects of oppression having affec-
ted/infected them so profoundly. Thus, Margaret Wilkerson's
collection *Nine Plays by Black Women* is a welcome addition to
black theatre literature, which can ill afford to ignore women's
point of view.

But to whom do these totem voices speak, these male and
female dramatists at home and abroad? Larry Neal would
insist that the black theatre first be directed to the ears and
hearts of black people, then to the world. Implicit here is the
supposition that those outside the experience will gain access
to universal values only when the black theatre has cultivated
an authentic cultural point of view, in the manner of the
Habimah Theatre of Israel, the Abbey Players of Ireland, the
Kabuki theatre of Japan, or the Moscow Arts Theatre of
the Soviet Union. However, it is not always easy to sustain a
theatre for an indigenous population, as was demonstrated by
the demise of Living Newspaper in Harlem during the forties,
Spirit House in Newark, the Free Southern Theatre in New
Orleans, and the New Lafayette Theatre during the sixties. Derek Walcott recollects his efforts to cultivate an indigenous audience for the Trinidad Theatre Workshop, an
effort that failed when support from the local gentry was
withdrawn:[34]

When one began twenty years ago it was in the faith that
one was creating not merely a play, but a theatre, and not
merely a theatre, but its environment. . . . We, the actors
and poets, would strut like new Adams in a nakedness
where sets, costumes, dimmers, all the "dirty devices" of

theatre were unnecessary or inaccessible. Poverty seemed a gift to the imagination, necessity was truly a virtue, so we set our plays in the open, in natural, unphased light, and our subjects bare, "unaccommodated man." Today one writes this with more exhaustion than pride, for that innocence has corrupted and society has taken the old direction. In these new nations art is a luxury, and the theatre the most superfluous of amenities.

Commercialization has taken its toll of the "unaccommodated man" in the United States, forcing many black artists to dress up the "native experience" in a convoluted critique of society that sometimes approaches self-flagellation, while others entrench themselves in a posture of parochial inertia and resist higher standards of accomplishment. Few black theatres in the Western Hemisphere have developed along the lines of South Africa's township theatre movement, which began in the twenties and creatively exploited its forced isolation by building a repertory without the patronage of white audiences. As a result, it is not always clear who is listening to the totem voices and for what purpose. Neither is it uncommon for American critics, resisting a need to be better informed, to favor conventional forms of black theatre and exhibit contempt for nonlinear exercises inspired by an aesthetic that seems remote, even culturally subversive, as Wole Soyinka recently discovered after the New York premiere of his *Death and the King's Horseman*. Soyinka, Nobel laureate, a universalist who proffers Proteus as a creative principle in one breath and Ogun in the next, conjoined classical Greek and traditional Yoruba metaphors into a tragic mode for his august and bountiful ritual drama, which was rudely greeted by the obtuse, even insulting, estimations of the New York critics. Ensconced in their characteristically smug philistine insularity, they dismissed the work as so much hocus-pocus, much ado about nothing other than an abstruse ritual suicide: one respected pundit even ventured an indecent comparison with a King Kong film before concluding, "Is this what's meant by beating a dead horse?" Grounded in Babylon, Soyinka responded:[35]

> There is definitely an overtone of racism in some of the language used. The very idea that someone from Africa, from the ex-colonial world, should come and challenge their theatrical ideas in such a serious, direct way . . . We have problems with the critics I think because they feel threatened. They feel that they're the intellectual luminaries, the intellectual guides of this nation, and they're lazy, very lazy. They prefer plays where they do not come to exercise any stretch of the imagination, any stretch of the intellect, where they do not have to exercise their innate sensibilities. They resent it, they say, "How dare! How dare! Who is this individual? Who is this alien who dares come and pose serious challenges to us?"

On the other hand, Johannesburg's Market Theatre, spawned from the tradition of the township theatre movement, arrived in New York flexing its vocal and torso muscles with an exuberance redolent of the black church, their performance of Mbongeni Ngema's *Asinamali!* revealing a rigorous style that subordinated the props to the creative physicality of the actors. *Asinamali!* garnered wide acclaim from both black and white audiences, and unanimous applause from the critics. However, one can easily surmise that this tolerance for one of the most compelling stylistic experiences in the contemporary theatre was due to the rhetorical remoteness of the testimonies: apartheid, not in America this time, but in South Africa.

For a style of work with the potential to galvanize the ensemble performances of black theatre in the United States, one need look no further than the Market Theatre. Mbongeni Ngema, one of the leading exponents of and trainers in the new style, is a former member of the influential Gibson Kente township theatre traveling troupe, which uses popular music and dance rhythms to inform their improvisational acting techniques. The style was highly visible in *Asinamali!*,[36] which was performed at the New Heritage Theatre in Harlem before highlighting the Woza Afrika Festival at New York's Lincoln Center Theatre. It is a style that demands high energy and disciplined physicality in the service of storytelling. The drama is punctuated with a capella singing, somewhat like that of the Persuasions, but executed with greater spontaneity and precision; and the insinuations of gesture effectively create mimesis through body movements, as in the performances of Ladysmith Black Mambazo, the South African ensemble singers of the Graceland tour, whose blood-surging body orchestrations make the gesticulations of the Temptations seem as anemic as synchronized swimming. In addition, time and place are projected in an environment where less is more: the absence of grand sets, a veritable blessing for the "unaccommodated man," allows the space to be magically defined by six chairs and a few objects suspended from a wooden frame. In this style of work, very much as in the improvisational system of black classical music, invention is at a premium in the process of constructing word/song testimonies that assume an almost incantatory quality:

> BHEKI (*jumps up mid-song and moves downstage on top of the music*): I come from Zululand. I got a place to stay in Lamontville township, near the white city of Durban. During that time this man (*he points to his T-shirt which has the picture of a man*) Msizi Dube, a very strong leader and a powerful voice for our people, was killed. They killed him. The government spies killed him. The reason for his death was that he maintained that we have no money. A-SI-NA-MA-LI! So we cannot afford to pay the government's high rent increase. People took up this call: "AAASSSIIINNNAAAMMMAAALLLIII!" and the police went to work. Many of us died and many of us went to jail, and it is still happening outside.

The stylizations of the Market Theatre might very well become an important influence on the new musical forms that are currently being developed in the black theatre. These new developments were born of a need to provide a frame for the elaboration of language by black poets who were inspired by the cosmic inventions of black classical music (so-called jazz). A formal structure was needed to contain and thereby focus a language style unconstrained by fixed rhymes or rhythms, as well as a music iconography that had lost its usual dance cadences since the arrival of bebop in the forties. The new collaboration of playwrights, poets, plastic artists, and musicians has encouraged the formal manipulation of word/song and black classical music improvisations on an operatic scale. The spirit of the enterprise is clearly recorded in Baraka's enthusiasm:

> Music expands, extends the words, see, it gives the words another kind of impact, another kind of penetration. That's why I like those kind of collaborations. Now I am writing mostly plays with music. I don't think I'll write the other anymore because I think plays are supposed to have music.

These new works eschew the song-and-dance routines and other trivializations of black experience that are usually identified with black musicals. The breadth and scale of the opera form—or *bopera*, as Baraka would call it—provides the collaborators an opportunity to explore the mythic range of word/song in a ritual mode that exploits the natural affinity between European twentieth-century harmony, with its twelve-tone serializations, and the improvisational system of black classical music, with its African-inspired tonal configurations.

As yet, the new form has not been named, though *jazz opera* is often used as a convenient handle to distinguish these works from conventional musicals. Whether Thulani Davis and Anthony Davis's *X* and Julius Hemphill's *Long Tongues: A Saxophone Opera* are truly operas by purist standards is not nearly as important as their emergence as signs of revitalized possibilities of a new musical theatre form. In addition to the aforementioned, other major collaborations include Archie Shepp and Aishah Rahman (*Lady Day: A Musical Tragedy*); Cecil Taylor and Adrienne Kennedy (*Rat's Mass*); David Murray and Baraka (*A Primitive World*); Max Roach and Baraka (*Bumpy: A Bopera*); Max Roach and Larry Neal (*The Glorious Monster in the Bell of a Horn*); Olu Dara and Dianne McIntyre's adaptation of Zora Neale Hurston's work (*A Dance Adventure in Southern Blues*); Hugh Masekela and Mbongeni Ngema (*Sarafina*); and my own collaborations with Eric Gravatt (*Tabernacle*), Archie Shepp (*Tophat*), Gladyce DeJesus (*The Death of Boogie Woogie*), Henry Threadgill (*Return to My Native Land*), and Julius Hemphill (*Anchorman*).

In conclusion, deep in the recesses of black life throughout the world, one discovers in word/song a common semantic iconography that suggests a consanguinity of spirit and stands as a testament to the resilience of race memory. Still, race memory reveals the collective unconscious, not the specifics of the diaspora experience, as Robert Fox cautions:

> History is not true collective memory; it is selective, hierarchical for the most part. Ancestral memory is enshrined archetypically in myth, which has always proved more valuable to art than the most acute historical sense—and individual memory can hope to link up with origins only when it consciously eschews the weight of history. As for modern mass memory, it is, when not amnesia, mostly nostalgia, which is one of history's agonized offsprings.

While we in the New World—Afro-Latins, Afro-Caribbeans, and Afro-Americans—look toward Africa for ontological charity that might strengthen our aesthetic sensibilities, we are reminded that the black experience at home and abroad is quite complex and cannot be subsumed, or otherwise appropriated, by the standards of a singular experience. The resilience of memory can only be gauged by the specific assessments of experience, whereby history is evaluated without sentimental attachment, so that the products of artis-

tic creation show evidence of having evolved from the particular to the larger world view, the veritable repository of universal truth.

PAUL CARTER HARRISON
Leeds, Massachusetts

Notes

1. Wole Soyinka, *Myth, Literature and the African World* (Cambridge: Cambridge University Press, 1976).
2. Jay Wright, "Desire's Design, Vision's Resonance," *Callaloo 27* 9, no. 2
   (Spring 1986).
3. W. E. Abrahams, *The Mind of Africa* (Chicago: University of Chicago
   Press, 1962).
4. J. B. Danquah, *The Akan Doctrine of God*, Africana Modern Library no.
   2, second ed. (London: Frank Cass and Company Ltd., 1968).
5. Wilson Harris, *The Womb of Space: The Cross-Cultural Imagination* (West-
   port, Conn.: Greenwood Press, 1983).
6. Isidore Okpewho, "The Principles of Traditional African Art," *Journal of
   Aesthetics and Art Criticism* 35 (1977).
7. Amiri Baraka interview, *The Drum* 16–17, no. 1–2 (May 1987).
8. Adrienne Kennedy, *People Who Led to My Plays* (New York: Alfred A.
   Knopf, 1987).
9. Keorapetse Kgositsile, *The Word Is Here: Poetry from Modern Africa* (New
   York: Doubleday, 1973).
10. Aimé Césaire, *Return to My Native Land* (Harmondsworth, England:
    Penguin Books, 1969).
11. In Quincy Troupe and Rainer Schulte, eds., *Giant Talk: An Anthology of
    Third World Writing* (New York: Random House, 1975).
12. Placide Tempels, *Bantu Philosophy* (Paris: Presence Africaine, 1959).
13. Austin J. Shelton, *The African Assertion* (New York: Odyssey Press,
    1968).
14. Quoted in Nathaniel Mackey, "Sound and Sentiment, Sound and Sym-
    bol," *Callaloo 30* 10, no. 1 (Winter 1987).
15. Jean Toomer, *Cane* (New York: Harper and Row, 1969).
16. Paule Marshall, *Praisesong for the Widow* (New York: Dutton, 1984).
17. Ralph Ellison, *Invisible Man* (New York: Signet Books, New American
    Library, 1952).
18. Paul Blackburn, *Listening to Sonny Rollins at the Five Spot*, on *New Jazz
    Poets*, Broadside Records, BR461.
19. In Troupe and Schulte, *Giant Talk*.

20. Léopold Senghor, 'L'esprit de la civilisation ou les lois de la culture negro-africaine," *Presence Africaine* 8 (Paris, 1956).

21. James A. Snead, "On Repetition in Black Culture," *Black American Literary Forum* 15, no. 4 (Winter 1981).

22. J. Mason Brewer, ed., *American Negro Folklore* (Chicago: Quadrangle Books, 1968).

23. Derek Walcott, *Another Life* (New York: Farrar, Straus and Giroux, 1973).

24. Wole Soyinka, *Death and the King's Horseman,* in *Collected Plays* (New York: Oxford University Press, 1973–74).

25. Robert Elliot Fox, "Derek Walcott: History as Dis-Ease," *Callaloo* 27 9, no. 2 (Spring 1986).

26. Quoted in "The New Culture: Nigeria," *New York Post,* Feb. 17, 1987.

27. Wole Soyinka, "The Critic and Society: Barthes, Leftocracy, and Other Mythologies," *Black American Literary Forum* 15, no. 4 (Winter 1981).

28. Larry Neal, "The Black Arts Movement", *TDR/The Drama Review: Black Theatre,* T/40 (New York University, 1968).

29. Edward James, introduction to *Shango de Ima* (New York: Doubleday, 1970).

30. Archie Shepp, *The Wedding,* on *Live in San Francisco* Impulse Records, 1966.

31. Wole Soyinka, introduction to *Soyinka: Six Plays* (London: Methuen, 1984).

32. Pearl Cleage, *The Hospice, Callaloo 30* 10, no. 1 (Winter 1987).

33. Alexis De Veaux, *The Tapestry,* in *Nine Plays by Black Women,* Margaret B. Wilkerson, ed. (New York: New American Library, 1986).

34. Derek Walcott, "What the Twilight Says: An Overture," introduction to *Dream on Monkey Mountain* (New York: Farrar, Straus and Giroux, 1970).

35. Wole Soyinka interview, *The New Theatre Review* 1, no. 2 (Summer 1987).

36. In Duma Ndlovu, ed., *Woza Afrika! An Anthology of South African Plays* (New York: George Braziller, 1986).

THE
STRONG
BREED

WOLE SOYINKA

The Strong Breed, presented by Farris-Belgrave Productions in association with Afolabi Ajayi, opened at the Greenwich Mews Theatre in New York City on November 9, 1967, with the following cast:

EMAN	Harold Scott
SUNMA	Mary Alice
IFADA	Edward Lius Espinosa
GIRL	Yvette Hawkins
JAGUNA	James Spruill
OROGE	Dennis Tate
ATTENDANT STALWARTS AND VILLAGERS	Peggy Kirkpatrick, Afolabi Ajayi, Yvonne Worden, Tom Hawkins, Austin Briggs Hall, Jr.

Directed by Cynthia Belgrave; setting and lighting by Jack Blackman; music composed and arranged by Pat Patrick; costumes by Edward Wolrond; stage manager, Bernard Ward.

CHARACTERS

EMAN   a stranger
SUNMA   Jaguna's daughter
IFADA   an idiot
A GIRL
JAGUNA
OROGE
ATTENDANT STALWARTS
VILLAGERS

from Eman's past—

OLD MAN   his father
OMAE   his betrothed
TUTOR
PRIEST
ATTENDANTS
VILLAGERS

The scenes are described briefly, but very often a darkened stage with lit areas will not only suffice but is necessary. Except for the one indicated place, there can be no break in the action. A distracting scene-change would be ruinous.

A mud house, with space in front of it. Eman, in light buba and trousers, stands at the window, looking out. Inside, Sunma is clearing the table of what looks like a modest clinic, putting the things away in a cupboard. Another rough table in the room is piled with exercise books, two or three worn text-books, etc. Sunma appears agitated. Outside, just below the window, crouches Ifada. He looks up with a shy smile from time to time, waiting for Eman to notice him.

SUNMA (*hesitant*): You will have to make up your mind soon Eman. The lorry leaves very shortly.

(*As Eman does not answer, Sunma continues her work, more nervously. Two villagers, obvious travellers, pass hurriedly in front of the house. The man has a small raffia sack, the woman a cloth-covered basket. The man enters first, turns, and urges the woman who is just emerging to hurry.*)

SUNMA (*seeing them, her tone is more intense*): Eman, are we going or aren't we? You will leave it till too late.

EMAN (*quietly*): There is still time—if you want to go.

SUNMA: If I want to go . . . and you?

(*Eman makes no reply.*)

SUNMA (*bitterly*): You don't really want to leave here. You never want to go away—even for a minute.

(*Ifada continues his antics. Eman eventually pats him on the head and the boy grins happily. Leaps up suddenly and returns with a basket of oranges which he offers to Eman.*)

EMAN: My gift for today's festival enh?

(*Ifada nods, grinning.*)

They look ripe—that's a change.

SUNMA (*she has gone inside the room; looks round the door*): Did you call me?

EMAN: No. (*She goes back.*) And what will you do tonight Ifada? Will you take part in the dancing? Or perhaps you will mount your own masquerade?

(*Ifada shakes his head, regretfully.*)

You won't? So you haven't any? But you would like to own one.

(*Ifada nods eagerly.*)

Then why don't you make your own?

(*Ifada stares, puzzled by this idea.*)

Sunma will let you have some cloth you know. And bits of wool . . .

SUNMA (*coming out*): Who are you talking to Eman?

EMAN: Ifada. I am trying to persuade him to join the young maskers.

SUNMA (*losing control*): What does he want here? Why is he hanging round us?

EMAN (*amazed*): What . . . ? I said Ifada, Ifada.

SUNMA: Just tell him to go away. Let him go and play somewhere else!

EMAN: What is this? Hasn't he always played here?

SUNMA: I don't want him here. (*Rushes to the window.*) Get away idiot. Don't bring your foolish face here any more, do you hear? Go on, go away from here . . .

EMAN (*restraining her*): Control yourself Sunma. What on earth has got into you?

(*Ifada, hurt and bewildered, backs slowly away.*)

SUNMA: He comes crawling round here like some horrible insect. I never want to lay my eyes on him again.

EMAN: I don't understand. It *is* Ifada you know. Ifada! The unfortunate one who runs errands for you and doesn't hurt a soul.

SUNMA: I cannot bear the sight of him.

EMAN: You can't do what? It can't be two days since he last fetched water for you.

SUNMA: What else can he do except that? He is useless. Just because we have been kind to him . . . Others would have put him in an asylum.

EMAN: You are not making sense. He is not a madman, he is just a little more unlucky than other children. (*Looks keenly at her.*) But what is the matter?

SUNMA: It's nothing. I only wish we had sent him off to one of those places for creatures like him.

EMAN: He is quite happy here. He doesn't bother anyone and he makes himself useful.

SUNMA: Useful! Is that one of any use to anybody? Boys of his age are already earning a living but all he can do is hang around and drool at the mouth.

EMAN: But he does work. You know he does a lot for you.

SUNMA: Does he? And what about the farm you started for him! Does he ever work on it? Or have you forgotten that it was really for Ifada you cleared that bush. Now you have to go and work it yourself. You spend all your time on it and you have no room for anything else.

EMAN: That wasn't his fault. I should first have asked him if he was fond of farming.

SUNMA: Oh, so he can choose? As if he shouldn't be thankful for being allowed to live.

EMAN: Sunma!

SUNMA: He does not like farming but he knows how to feast his dumb mouth on the fruits.

EMAN: But I want him to. I encourage him.

SUNMA: Well keep him. I don't want to see him any more.

EMAN (*after some moments*): But why? You cannot be telling all the truth. What has he done?

SUNMA: The sight of him fills me with revulsion.

EMAN (*goes to her and holds her*): What really is it? (*Sunma avoids his eyes.*) It is almost as if you are forcing yourself to hate him. Why?

SUNMA: That is not true. Why should I?

EMAN: Then what is the secret? You've even played with him before.

SUNMA: I have always merely tolerated him. But I cannot any more. Suddenly my disgust won't take him any more. Perhaps . . . perhaps it is the new year. Yes, yes, it must be the new year.

EMAN: I don't believe that.

SUNMA: It must be. I am a woman, and these things matter. I don't want a mis-shape near me. Surely for one day in the year, I may demand some wholesomeness.

EMAN: I do not understand you. (*Sunma is silent.*) It was cruel of you. And to Ifada who is so helpless and alone. We are the only friends he has.

SUNMA: No, just you. I have told you, with me it has always been only an act of kindness. And now I haven't any pity left for him.

EMAN: No. He is not a wholesome being. (*He turns back to looking through the window.*)

SUNMA (*half-pleading*): Ifada can rouse your pity. And yet if anything, I need more kindness from you. Every time my weakness betrays me, you close your mind against me . . . Eman . . . Eman . . .

(*A Girl comes in view, dragging an effigy by a rope attached to one of its legs. She stands for a while gazing at Eman. Ifada, who has crept back shyly to his accustomed position, becomes somewhat excited when he sees the effigy. The Girl is unsmiling. She possesses, in fact, a kind of inscrutability that does not make her hard but is unsettling.*)

GIRL: Is the teacher in?

EMAN (*smiling*): No.

GIRL: Where is he gone?

EMAN: I don't really know. Shall I ask?

GIRL: Yes, do.

EMAN (*turning slightly*): Sunma, a girl outside wants to know
. . . (*Sunma turns away, goes into the inside room.*) Oh.
(*Returns to the Girl, but his slight gaiety is lost.*) There is no
one at home who can tell me.

GIRL: Why are you not in?

EMAN: I don't really know. Maybe I went somewhere.

GIRL: All right. I will wait until you get back. (*She pulls the
effigy to her, sits down.*)

EMAN (*slowly regaining his amusement*): So you are all ready for
the new year.

GIRL (*without turning round*): I am not going to the festival.

EMAN: Then why have you got that?

GIRL: Do you mean my carrier? I am unwell you know. My
mother says it will take away my sickness with the old
year.

EMAN: Won't you share the carrier with your playmates?

GIRL: Oh, no. Don't you know I play alone? The other children
won't come near me. Their mothers would beat them.

EMAN: But I have never seen you here. Why don't you come to
the clinic?

GIRL: My mother said No. (*Gets up, begins to move off.*)

EMAN: You are not going away?

GIRL: I must not stay talking to you. If my mother caught
me . . .

EMAN: All right, tell me what you want before you go.

GIRL (*stops; for some moments she remains silent*): I must have some clothes for my carrier.

EMAN: Is that all? You wait a moment.

(*Sunma comes out as he takes down a buba from the wall. She goes to the window and glares almost with hatred at the Girl. The Girl retreats hastily, still impassive.*)

By the way Sunma, do you know who that girl is?

SUNMA: I hope you don't really mean to give her that.

EMAN: Why not? I hardly ever use it.

SUNMA: Just the same don't give it to her. She is not a child. She is as evil as the rest of them.

EMAN: What has got into you today?

SUNMA: All right, all right. Do what you wish.

(*She withdraws. Baffled, Eman returns to the window.*)

EMAN: Here . . . will this do? Come and look at it.

GIRL: Throw it.

EMAN: What is the matter? I am not going to eat you.

GIRL: No one lets me come near them.

EMAN: But I am not afraid of catching your disease.

GIRL: Throw it.

(*Eman shrugs and tosses the buba. She takes it without a word and slips it on the effigy, completely absorbed in the task. Eman watches for a while, then joins Sunma in the inner room.*)

GIRL (*after a long, cool survey of Ifada*): You have a head like a spider's egg, and your mouth dribbles like a roof. But there is no one else. Would you like to play?

(*Ifada nods eagerly, quite excited.*)

You will have to get a stick.

(*Ifada rushes around, finds a big stick, and whirls it aloft, bearing down on the carrier.*)

Wait. I don't want you to spoil it. If it gets torn I shall drive you away. Now, let me see how you are going to beat it.

(*Ifada hits it gently.*)

You may hit harder than that. As long as there is something left to hang at the end. (*She appraises him up and down.*) You are not very tall . . . will you be able to hang it from a tree?

(*Ifada nods, grinning happily.*)

You will hang it up and I will set fire to it. (*Then, with surprising venom:*) But just because you are helping me, don't think it is going to cure you. I am the one who will get well at midnight, do you understand? It is my carrier and it is for me alone. (*She pulls at the rope to make sure that it is well attached to the leg.*) Well don't stand there drooling. Let's go.

(*She begins to walk off, dragging the effigy in the dust. Ifada remains where he is for some moments, seemingly puzzled. Then his face breaks into a large grin and he leaps after the procession, belabouring the effigy with all his strength. The stage remains empty for some moments. Then the horn of a lorry is sounded and Sunma rushes out. The hooting continues for some time with a rhythmic pattern. Eman comes out.*)

EMAN: I am going to the village . . . I shan't be back before nightfall.

SUNMA (*blankly*): Yes.

EMAN (*hesitates*): Well what do you want me to do?

SUNMA: The lorry was hooting just now.

EMAN: I didn't hear it.

SUNMA: It will leave in a few minutes. And you did promise we could go away.

EMAN: I promised nothing. Will you go home by yourself or shall I come back for you?

SUNMA: You don't even want me here?

EMAN: But you have to go home haven't you?

SUNMA: I had hoped we would watch the new year together— in some other place.

EMAN: Why do you continue to distress yourself?

SUNMA: Because you will not listen to me. Why do you continue to stay where nobody wants you?

EMAN: That is not true.

SUNMA: It is. You are wasting your life on people who really want you out of their way.

EMAN: You don't know what you are saying.

SUNMA: You think they love you? Do you think they care at all for what you—or I—do for them?

EMAN: *Them?* These are your own people. Sometimes you talk as if you were a stranger too.

SUNMA: I wonder if I really sprang from here. I know they are evil and I am not. From the oldest to the smallest child, they are nourished in evil and unwholesomeness in which I have no part.

EMAN: You knew this when you returned?

SUNMA: You reproach me then for trying at all?

EMAN: I reproach you with nothing. But you must leave me out of your plans. I can have no part in them.

SUNMA (*nearly pleading*): Once I could have run away. I would have gone and never looked back.

EMAN: I cannot listen when you talk like that.

SUNMA: I swear to you, I do not mind what happens afterwards. But you must help me tear myself away from here. I can no longer do it by myself. . . . It is only a little thing. And we have worked so hard this past year . . . surely we can go away for a week . . . even a few days would be enough.

EMAN: I have told you Sunma . . .

SUNMA (*desperately*): Two days Eman. Only two days.

EMAN (*distressed*): But I tell you I have no wish to go.

SUNMA (*suddenly angry*): Are you so afraid then?

EMAN: Me? Afraid of what?

SUNMA: You think you will not want to come back.

EMAN (*pitying*): You cannot dare me that way.

SUNMA: Then why won't you leave here, even for an hour? If you are so sure that your life is settled here, why are you afraid to do this thing for me? What is so wrong that you will not go into the next town for a day or two?

EMAN: I don't want to. I do not have to persuade you, or myself, about anything. I simply have no desire to go away.

SUNMA (*his quiet confidence appears to incense her*): You are afraid. You accuse me of losing my sense of mission, but you are afraid to put yours to the test.

EMAN: You are wrong Sunma. I have no sense of mission. But I have found peace here and I am content with that.

SUNMA: I haven't. For a while I thought that too, but I found there could be no peace in the midst of so much cruelty. Eman, tonight at least, the last night of the old year . . .

EMAN: No Sunma. I find this too distressing; you should go home now.

SUNMA: It is the time for making changes in one's life Eman. Let's breathe in the new year away from here.

EMAN: You are hurting yourself.

SUNMA: Tonight. Only tonight. We will come back tomorrow, as early as you like. But let us go away for this one night. Don't let another year break on me in this place . . . You don't know how important it is to me, but I will tell you, I will tell you on the way . . . but we must not be here today, Eman, do this one thing for me.

EMAN (*sadly*): I cannot.

SUNMA (*suddenly calm*): I was a fool to think it would be otherwise. The whole village may use you as they will but for me there is nothing. Sometimes I think you believe that doing anything for me makes you unfaithful to some part of your life. If it was a woman then I pity her for what she must have suffered. (*Eman winces and hardens slowly. Sunma notices nothing.*) Keeping faith with so much is slowly making you inhuman. (*Seeing the change in Eman:*) Eman. Eman. What is it? (*As she goes towards him, Eman goes into the house. Sunma, apprehensive, follows him.*) What did I say? Eman, forgive me, forgive me please. (*Eman remains facing into the slow darkness of the room. Sunma, distressed, cannot decide what to do.*) I swear I didn't know . . . I would not have said it for all the world.

(*A lorry is heard taking off somewhere nearby. The sound comes up and slowly fades away into the distance. Sunma starts visibly, goes slowly to the window.*)

SUNMA (*as the sound dies off, to herself*): What happens now?

EMAN (*joining her at the window.*): What did you say?

SUNMA: Nothing.

EMAN: Was that not the lorry going off?

SUNMA: It was.

EMAN: I am sorry I couldn't help you.

(*Sunma, about to speak, changes her mind.*)

I think you ought to go home now.

SUNMA: No, don't send me away. It's the least you can do for me. Let me stay here until all the noise is over.

EMAN: But are you not needed at home? You have a part in the festival.

SUNMA: I have renounced it; I am Jaguna's eldest daughter only in name.

EMAN: Renouncing one's self is not so easy—surely you know that.

SUNMA: I don't want to talk about it. Will you at least let us be together tonight?

EMAN: But . . .

SUNMA: Unless you are afraid my father will accuse you of harbouring me.

EMAN: All right, we will go out together.

SUNMA: Go out? I want us to stay here.

EMAN: When there is so much going on outside?

SUNMA: Some day you will wish that you went away when I tried to make you.

EMAN: Are we going back to that?

SUNMA: No. I promise you I will not recall it again. But you must know that it was also for your sake that I tried to get us away.

EMAN: For me? How?

SUNMA: By yourself you can do nothing here. Have you not noticed how tightly we shut out strangers? Even if you lived here for a lifetime, you would remain a stranger.

EMAN: Perhaps that is what I like. There is peace in being a stranger.

SUNMA: For a while perhaps. But they would reject you in the end. I tell you it is only I who stand between you and contempt. And because of this you have earned their hatred. I don't know why I say this now, except that somehow, I feel that it no longer matters. It is only I who have stood between you and much humiliation.

EMAN: Think carefully before you say any more. I am incapable of feeling indebted to you. This will make no difference at all.

SUNMA: I ask for nothing. But you must know it all the same. It is true I hadn't the strength to go by myself. And I must confess this now, if you had come with me, I would have done everything to keep you from returning.

EMAN: I know that.

SUNMA: You see, I bare myself to you. For days I had thought it over, this was to be a new beginning for us. And I placed my fate wholly in your hands. Now the thought will not leave me, I have a feeling which will not be shaken off, that in some way, you have tonight totally destroyed my life.

EMAN: You are depressed, you don't know what you are saying.

SUNMA: Don't think I am accusing you. I say all this only because I cannot help it.

EMAN: We must not remain shut up here. Let us go and be part of the living.

SUNMA: No. Leave them alone.

EMAN: Surely you don't want to stay indoors when the whole town is alive with rejoicing.

SUNMA: Rejoicing! Is that what it seems to you? No, let us remain here. Whatever happens I must not go out until all this is over.

(*There is silence. It has grown much darker.*)

EMAN: I shall light the lamp.

SUNMA (*eager to do something*): No, let me do it. (*She goes into the inner room.*)

(*Eman paces the room, stops by a shelf, and toys with the seeds in an ayo board, takes down the whole board and places it on a table, playing by himself.*

The Girl is now seen coming back, still dragging her carrier. Ifada brings up the rear as before. As he comes round the corner of the house two men emerge from the shadows. A sack is thrown over Ifada's head, the rope is pulled tight, rendering him instantly helpless. The Girl has reached the front of the house before she turns round at the sound of scuffle. She is in time to see Ifada thrown over the shoulders and borne away. Her face betraying no emotion at all, the girl backs slowly away, turns, and flees, leaving the carrier behind. Sunma enters, carrying two kerosene lamps. She hangs one up from the wall.)

EMAN: One is enough.

SUNMA: I want to leave one outside.

(*She goes out, hangs the lamp from a nail just above the door. As she turns she sees the effigy and gasps. Eman rushes out.*)

EMAN: What is it? Oh, is that what frightened you?

SUNMA: I thought . . . I didn't really see it properly.

EMAN (*goes towards the object, stoops to pick it up*): It must belong to that sick girl.

SUNMA: Don't touch it.

EMAN: Let's keep it for her.

SUNMA: Leave it alone. Don't touch it Eman.

EMAN (*shrugs and goes back*): You are very nervous.

SUNMA: Let's go in.

EMAN: Wait. (*He detains her by the door, under the lamp.*) I know there is something more than you've told me. What are you afraid of tonight?

SUNMA: I was only scared by that thing. There is nothing else.

EMAN: I am not blind Sunma. It is true I would not run away when you wanted me to, but that doesn't mean I do not feel things. What does tonight really mean that it makes you so helpless?

SUNMA: It is only a mood. And your indifference to me . . . let's go in.

(*Eman moves aside and she enters; he remains there for a moment and then follows.*
  She fiddles with the lamp, looks vaguely round the room, then goes and shuts the door, bolting it. When she turns, it is to meet Eman's eyes, questioning.)

SUNMA: There is a cold wind coming in. (*Eman keeps his gaze on her.*) It *was* getting cold.

(*She moves guiltily to the table and stands by the ayo board, rearranging the seeds. Eman remains where he is a few moments, then brings a stool and sits opposite her. She sits down also and they begin to play in silence.*)

What brought you here at all, Eman? And what makes you stay? (*There is another silence.*) I am not trying to share your life. I know you too well by now. But at least we have worked together since you came. Is there nothing at all I deserve to know?

EMAN: Let me continue a stranger—especially to you. Those who have much to give fulfill themselves only in total loneliness.

SUNMA: Then there is no love in what you do.

EMAN: There is. Love comes to me more easily with strangers.

SUNMA: That is unnatural.

EMAN: Not for me. I know I find consummation only when I have spent myself for a total stranger.

SUNMA: It seems unnatural to me. But then I am a woman. I have a woman's longings and weaknesses. And the ties of blood are very strong in me.

EMAN (*smiling*): You think I have cut loose from all these—ties of blood.

SUNMA: Sometimes you are so inhuman.

EMAN: I don't know what that means. But I am very much my father's son. (*They play in silence. Suddenly Eman pauses, listening.*) Did you hear that?

SUNMA (*quickly*): I heard nothing . . . it's your turn.

EMAN: Perhaps some of the mummers are coming this way. (*Eman, about to play, leaps up suddenly.*)

SUNMA: What is it? Don't you want to play any more? (*Eman moves to the door.*) No. Don't go out Eman.

EMAN: If it's the dancers I want to ask them to stay. At least we won't have to miss everything.

SUNMA: No, no. Don't open the door. Let us keep out everything tonight.

(*A terrified and disordered figure bursts suddenly round the corner, past the window, and begins hammering at the door. It is Ifada. Desperate with terror, he pounds madly at the door, dumb-moaning all the while.*)

EMAN: Isn't that Ifada?

SUNMA: They are only fooling about. Don't pay any attention.

EMAN (*looks round the window*): That is Ifada. (*Begins to unbolt the door.*)

SUNMA (*pulling at his hands*): It is only a trick they are playing on you. Don't take any notice Eman.

EMAN: What are you saying? The boy is out of his senses with fear.

SUNMA: No, no. Don't interfere Eman. For God's sake don't interfere.

EMAN: Do you know something of this then?

SUNMA: You are a stranger here Eman. Just leave us alone and go your own way. There is nothing you can do.

EMAN (*he tries to push her out of the way but she clings fiercely to him*): Have you gone mad? I tell you the boy must come in.

SUNMA: Why won't you listen to me Eman? I tell you it's none of your business. For your own sake do as I say.

(*Eman pushes her off, unbolts the door. Ifada rushes in, clasps Eman round the knees, dumb-moaning against his legs.*)

EMAN (*manages to re-bolt the door*): What is it Ifada? What is the matter?

(*Shouts and voices are heard coming nearer the house.*)

SUNMA: Before it's too late, let him go. For once Eman, believe what I tell you. Don't harbour him or you will regret it all your life.

(*Eman tries to calm Ifada who becomes more and more abject as the outside voices get nearer.*)

EMAN: What have they done to him? At least tell me that. What is going on Sunma?

SUNMA (*with sudden venom*): Monster! Could you not take yourself somewhere else?

EMAN: Stop talking like that.

SUNMA: He could have run into the bush couldn't he? Toad! Why must he follow us with his own disasters!

VOICES (*outside*): It's here . . . Round the back . . . Spread, spread . . . this way . . . no, head him off . . . use the bush path and head him off . . . get some more lights . . .

(*Eman listens. Lifts Ifada bodily and carries him into the inner room. Returns at once, shutting the door behind him.*)

SUNMA (*slumps into a chair, resigned*): You always follow your own way.

JAGUNA (*comes round the corner followed by Oroge and three men, one bearing a torch*): I knew he would come here.

OROGE: I hope our friend won't make trouble.

JAGUNA: He had better not. You, recall all the men and tell them to surround the house.

OROGE: But he may not be in the house after all.

JAGUNA: I know he is here . . . (*To the men:*) Go on, do as I say. (*He bangs on the door.*) Teacher, open your door . . . you two stay by the door. If I need you I will call you.

(*Eman opens the door. Jaguna speaks as he enters.*)

We know he is here.

EMAN: Who?

JAGUNA: Don't let us waste time. We are grown men, teacher. You understand me and I understand you. But we must take back the boy.

EMAN: This is my house.

JAGUNA: Daughter, you'd better tell your friend. I don't think he quite knows our ways. Tell him why he must give up the boy.

SUNMA: Father, I . . .

JAGUNA: Are you going to tell him or aren't you?

SUNMA: Father, I beg you, leave us alone tonight . . .

JAGUNA: I thought you might be a hindrance. Go home then if you will not use your sense.

SUNMA: But there are other ways . . .

JAGUNA (*turning to the men*): See that she gets home. I no longer trust her. If she gives trouble carry her. And see that the women stay with her until all this is over.

(*Sunma departs, accompanied by one of the men.*)

Now teacher . . .

OROGE (*restrains him*): You see, Mister Eman, it is like this. Right now, nobody knows that Ifada has taken refuge here. No one except us and our men—and they know how to keep their mouths shut. We don't want to have to burn down the house you see, but if the word gets around, we would have no choice.

JAGUNA: In fact, it may be too late already. A carrier should end up in the bush, not in a house. Anyone who doesn't guard his door when the carrier goes by has himself to blame. A contaminated house should be burnt down.

OROGE: But we are willing to let it pass. Only, you must bring him out quickly.

EMAN: All right. But at least you will let me ask you something.

JAGUNA: What is there to ask? Don't you understand what we have told you?

EMAN: Yes. But why did you pick on a helpless boy. Obviously he is not willing.

JAGUNA: What is the man talking about? Ifada is a godsend. Does he have to be willing?

EMAN: In my home, we believe that a man should be willing.

OROGE: Mister Eman, I don't think you quite understand. This is not a simple matter at all. I don't know what you do, but here, it is not a cheap task for anybody. No one in his senses would do such a job. Why do you think we give refuge to idiots like him? We don't know where he came from. One morning, he is simply there, just like that. From nowhere at all. You see, there is a purpose in that.

JAGUNA: We only waste time.

OROGE: Jaguna, be patient. After all, the man has been with us for some time now and deserves to know. The evil of the old year is no light thing to load on any man's head.

EMAN: I know something about that.

OROGE: You do? (*Turns to Jaguna who snorts impatiently.*) You see I told you so didn't I? From the moment you came I saw you were one of the knowing ones.

JAGUNA: Then let him behave like a man and give back the boy.

EMAN: It is you who are not behaving like men.

JAGUNA (*advances aggressively*): That is a quick mouth you have . . .

OROGE: Patience Jaguna . . . if you want the new year to cushion the land there must be no deeds of anger. What did you mean my friend?

EMAN: It is a simple thing. A village which cannot produce its own carrier contains no men.

JAGUNA: Enough. Let there be no more talk or this business will be ruined by some rashness. You . . . come inside. Bring the boy out, he must be in the room there.

EMAN: Wait.

(*The men hesitate.*)

JAGUNA (*hitting the nearer one and propelling him forward*): Go on. Have you changed masters now that you listen to what he says?

OROGE (*sadly*): I am sorry you would not understand Mister Eman. But you ought to know that no carrier may return to the village. If he does, the people will stone him to death. It has happened before. Surely it is too much to ask a man to give up his own soil.

EMAN: I know others who have done more.

(*Ifada is brought out, abjectly dumb-moaning.*)

You can see him with your own eyes. Does it really have meaning to use one as unwilling as that.

OROGE (*smiling*): He shall be willing. Not only willing but actually joyous. I am the one who prepares them all, and I have seen worse. This one escaped before I began to prepare him for the event. But you will see him later tonight, the most joyous creature in the festival. Then perhaps you will understand.

EMAN: Then it is only a deceit. Do you believe the spirit of a new year is so easily fooled?

JAGUNA: Take him out. (*The men carry Ifada.*) You see, it is so easy to talk. You say there are no men in this village because they cannot provide a willing carrier. And yet I heard Oroge tell you we only use strangers. There is only one other stranger in the village, but I have not heard him offer himself. (*Spits.*) It is so easy to talk is it not?

(*He turns his back on Eman. They go off, taking Ifada with them, limp and silent. The only sign of life is that he strains his neck to keep his eyes on Eman till the very moment that he disappears from sight. Eman remains where they left him, staring after the group.*)

A black-out lasting no more than a minute. The lights come up slowly and Ifada is seen returning to the house. He stops at the window and looks in. Seeing no one, he bangs on the sill. Appears surprised that there is no response. He slithers down on his favourite spot, then sees the effigy still lying where the Girl had dropped it in her flight. After some hesitation, he goes towards it, begins to strip it of the clothing. Just then the Girl comes in.

GIRL: Hey, leave that alone. You know it's mine.

(Ifada pauses, then speeds up his action.)

I said it is mine. Leave it where you found it.

(She rushes at him and begins to struggle for possession of the carrier.)

Thief! Thief! Let it go, it is mine. Let it go. You animal, just because I let you play with it. Idiot! Idiot!

(The struggle becomes quite violent. The Girl is hanging to the effigy and Ifada lifts her with it, flinging her all about. The Girl hangs on grimly.)

You are spoiling it . . . why don't you get your own? Thief! Let it go you thief!

(Sunma comes in walking very fast, throwing apprehensive glances over her shoulder. Seeing the two children, she becomes immediately angry. Advances on them.)

SUNMA: So you've made this place your playground. Get away you untrained pigs. Get out of here.

(Ifada flees at once. The Girl retreats also, retaining possession of the carrier. Sunma goes to the door. She has her hand on the door when the significance of Ifada's presence strikes her for the first time. She stands rooted to the spot, then turns slowly round.)

Ifada! What are you doing here?

(Ifada turns back, bewildered. Sunma turns suddenly and rushes into the house, flying into the inner room and out again.)

Eman! Eman! Eman! *(She rushes outside.)* Where did he go? Where did they take him?

(Ifada, distressed, points. Sunma seizes him by the arm, drags him off.)

Take me there at once. God help you if we are too late.
You loathsome thing, if you have let him suffer . . .

(*Her voice fades into other shouts, running footsteps, banged tins,
bells, dogs, etc., rising in volume.*)

*It is a narrow passage-way between two mud-houses. At the far end
one man after another is seen running across the entry, the noise
dying off gradually.*

    *About half-way down the passage, Eman is crouching against the
wall, tense with apprehension. As the noise dies off, he seems to
relax, but the alert hunted look is still in his eyes which are ringed in
a reddish colour. The rest of his body has been whitened with a floury
substance. He is naked down to the waist, wears a baggy pair of
trousers, calf-length, and around both feet are bangles.*

EMAN: I will simply stay here till dawn. I have done enough.

(*A window is thrown open and a woman empties some slop from a
pail. With a startled cry, Eman leaps aside to avoid it and the
woman puts out her head.*)

WOMAN: Oh, my head. What have I done! Forgive me neigh-
    bour . . . Eh, it's the carrier! (*Very rapidly she clears her
    throat and spits on him, flings the pail at him, and runs off,
    shouting:*) He's here. The carrier is hiding in the passage.
    Quickly, I have found the carrier!

(*The cry is taken up and Eman flees down the passage. Shortly
afterwards his pursuers come pouring down the passage in full cry.
After the last of them come Jaguna and Oroge.*)

OROGE: Wait, wait. I cannot go so fast.

JAGUNA: We will rest a little then. We can do nothing anyway.

OROGE: If only he had let me prepare him.

JAGUNA: They are the ones who break first, these fools who
    think they were born to carry suffering like a hat. What
    are we to do now?

OROGE: When they catch him I must prepare him.

JAGUNA: He? It will be impossible now. There can be no joy left in that one.

OROGE: Still, it took him by surprise. He was not expecting what he met.

JAGUNA: Why then did he refuse to listen? Did he think he was coming to sit down to a feast. He had not even gone through one compound before he bolted. Did he think he was taken round the people to be blessed? A woman, that is all he is.

OROGE: No, no. He took the beating well enough. I think he is the kind who would let himself be beaten from night till dawn and not utter a sound. He would let himself be stoned until he dropped dead.

JAGUNA: Then what made him run like a coward?

OROGE: I don't know. I don't really know. It is a night of curses Jaguna. It is not many unprepared minds will remain unhinged under the load.

JAGUNA: We must find him. It is a poor beginning for a year when our own curses remain hovering over our homes because the carrier refused to take them.

(*They go.*)

The scene changes. Eman is crouching beside some shrubs, torn and bleeding.

EMAN: They are even guarding my house . . . as if I would go there, but I need water . . . they could at least grant me that . . . I can be thirsty too . . . (*He pricks his ears.*) . . . there must be a stream nearby . . . (*As he looks round him, his eyes widen at a scene he encounters.*)

(*An Old Man, short and vigorous looking, is seated on a stool. He also is wearing calf-length baggy trousers, white. On his head, a white cap. An Attendant is engaged in rubbing his body with oil. Round his eyes, two white rings have already been marked.)*

OLD MAN: Have they prepared the boat?

ATTENDANT: They are making the last sacrifice.

OLD MAN: Good. Did you send for my son?

ATTENDANT: He's on his way.

OLD MAN: I have never met the carrying of the boat with such a heavy heart. I hope nothing comes of it.

ATTENDANT: The gods will not desert us on that account.

OLD MAN: A man should be at his strongest when he takes the boat my friend. To be weighed down inside and out is not a wise thing. I hope when the moment comes I shall have found my strength.

(Enter Eman, a wrapper round his waist and a danski* over it.)

I meant to wait until after my journey to the river, but my mind is so burdened with my own grief and yours I could not delay it. You know I must have all my strength. But I sit here, feeling it all eaten slowly away by my unspoken grief. It helps to say it out. It even helps to cry sometimes. *(He signals to the Attendant to leave them.)* Come nearer . . . we will never meet again son. Not on this side of the flesh. What I do not know is whether you will return to take my place.

EMAN: I will never come back.

OLD MAN: Do you know what you are saying? Ours is a strong breed my son. It is only a strong breed that can take this boat to the river year after year and wax stronger on it. I have taken down each year's evils for over twenty years. I hoped you would follow me.

EMAN: My life here died with Omae.

*A brief Yoruba attire.

OLD MAN: Omae died giving birth to your child and you think the world is ended. Eman, my pain did not begin when Omae died. Since you sent her to stay with me son, I lived with the burden of knowing that this child would die bearing your son.

EMAN: Father . . .

OLD MAN: Don't you know it was the same with you? And me? No woman survives the bearing of the strong ones. Son, it is not the mouth of the boaster that says he belongs to the strong breed. It is the tongue that is red with pain and black with sorrow. Twelve years you were away my son, and for those twelve years I knew the love of an old man for his daughter and the pain of a man helplessly awaiting his loss.

EMAN: I wish I had stayed away. I wish I never came back to meet her.

OLD MAN: It had to be. But you know now what slowly ate away my strength. I awaited your return with love and fear. Forgive me then if I say that your grief is light. It will pass. This grief may drive you now from home. But you must return.

EMAN: You do not understand. It is not grief alone.

OLD MAN: What is it then? Tell me, I can still learn.

EMAN: I was away twelve years. I changed much in that time.

OLD MAN: I am listening.

EMAN: I am unfitted for your work father. I wish to say no more. But I am totally unfitted for your call.

OLD MAN: It is only time you need son. Stay longer and you will answer the urge of your blood.

EMAN: That I stayed at all was because of Omae. I did not expect to find her waiting. I would have taken her away, but hard as you claim to be, it would have killed you.

And I was a tired man. I needed peace. Because Omae
was peace, I stayed. Now nothing holds me here.

OLD MAN: Other men would rot and die doing this task year
after year. It is strong medicine which only we can take.
Our blood is strong like no other. Anything you do in life
must be less than this, son.

EMAN: That is not true father.

OLD MAN: I tell you it is true. Your own blood will betray you
son, because you cannot hold it back. If you make it do
less than this, it will rush to your head and burst it open.
I say what I know my son.

EMAN: There are other tasks in life father. This one is not for
me. There are even greater things you know nothing of.

OLD MAN: I am very sad. You only go to give to others what
rightly belongs to us. You will use your strength among
thieves. They are thieves because they take what is ours,
they have no claim of blood to it. They will even lack the
knowledge to use it wisely. Truth is my companion at
this moment my son. I know everything I say will surely
bring the sadness of truth.

EMAN: I am going father.

OLD MAN: Call my attendant. And be with me in your
strength for this last journey. A-ah, did you hear that? It
came out without my knowing it; this is indeed my last
journey. But I am not afraid.

(*Eman goes out. A few moments later, the Attendant enters.*)

ATTENDANT: The boat is ready.

OLD MAN: So am I.

(*He sits perfectly still for several moments. Drumming begins somewhere in the distance, and the Old Man sways his head almost
imperceptibly. Two men come in bearing a miniature boat, contain-
ing an indefinable mound. They rush it in and set it briskly down*

near the Old Man, and stand well back. The Old Man gets up slowly, the Attendant watching him keenly. He signs to the men, who lift the boat quickly onto the Old Man's head. As soon as it touches his head, he holds it down with both hands and runs off, the men give him a start, then follow at a trot.

As the last man disappears Oroge limps in and comes face to face with Eman—as carrier—who is now seen still standing beside the shrubs, staring into the scene he has just witnessed. Oroge, struck by the look on Eman's face, looks anxiously behind him to see what has engaged Eman's attention. Eman notices him then, and the pair stare at each other. Jaguna enters, sees him, and shouts, "Here he is," rushes at Eman who is whipped back to the immediate and flees, Jaguna in pursuit. Three or four others enter and follow them. Oroge remains where he is, thoughtful.)

JAGUNA (*re-enters*): They have closed in on him now, we'll get him this time.

OROGE: It is nearly midnight.

JAGUNA: You were standing there looking at him as if he was some strange spirit. Why didn't you shout?

OROGE: You shouted didn't you? Did that catch him?

JAGUNA: Don't worry. We have him now. But things have taken a bad turn. It is no longer enough to drive him past every house. There is too much contamination about already.

OROGE (*not listening*): He saw something. Why may I not know what it was?

JAGUNA: What are you talking about?

OROGE: Hm. What is it?

JAGUNA: I said there is too much harm done already. The year will demand more from this carrier than we thought.

OROGE: What do you mean?

JAGUNA: Do we have to talk with the full mouth?

OROGE: S-sh . . . look!

(*Jaguna turns just in time to see Sunma fly at him, clawing at his face like a crazed tigress.*)

SUNMA: Murderer! What are you doing to him. Murderer! Murderer!

(*Jaguna finds himself struggling really hard to keep off his daughter; he succeeds in pushing her off and striking her so hard on the face that she falls to her knees. He moves on her to hit her again.*)

OROGE (*comes between*): Think what you are doing Jaguna, she is your daughter.

JAGUNA: My daughter! Does this one look like my daughter? Let me cripple the harlot for life.

OROGE: That is a wicked thought Jaguna.

JAGUNA: Don't come between me and her.

OROGE: Nothing in anger—do you forget what tonight is?

JAGUNA: Can you blame me for forgetting? (*Draws his hand across his cheek—it is covered with blood.*)

OROGE: This is an unhappy night for us all. I fear what is to come of it.

JAGUNA: Let's go. I cannot restrain myself in this creature's presence. My own daughter . . . and for a stranger . . .

(*They go off. Ifada, who came in with Sunma and had stood apart, horror-stricken, comes shyly forward. He helps Sunma up. They go off, he holding Sunma bent and sobbing.*)

Enter Eman—as carrier. He is physically present in the bounds of this next scene, a side of a round thatched hut. A young girl, about fourteen, runs in, stops beside the hut. She looks carefully to see that she is not observed, puts her mouth to a little hole in the wall.

OMAE: Eman . . . Eman . . .

(*Eman—as carrier—responds, as he does throughout the scene, but they are unaware of him.*)

EMAN (*from inside*): Who is it?

OMAE: It is me, Omae.

EMAN: How dare you come here!

(*Two hands appear at the hole and pushing outwards, create a much larger hole through which Eman puts out his head. It is Eman as a boy, the same age as the girl.*)

Go away at once. Are you trying to get me into trouble!

OMAE: What is the matter?

EMAN: You. Go away.

OMAE: But I came to see you.

EMAN: Are you deaf? I say I don't want to see you. Now go before my tutor catches you.

OMAE: All right. Come out.

EMAN: Do what!

OMAE: Come out.

EMAN: You must be mad.

OMAE (*sits on the ground*): All right, if you don't come out I shall simply stay here until your tutor arrives.

EMAN (*about to explode, thinks better of it and the head disappears; a moment later he emerges from behind the hut*): What sort of a devil has got into you?

OMAE: None. I just wanted to see you.

EMAN (*his mimicry is nearly hysterical*): "None. I just wanted to see you." Do you think this place is the stream where you can go and molest innocent people?

OMAE (*coyly*): Aren't you glad to see me?

EMAN: I am not.

OMAE: Why?

EMAN: Why? Do you really ask me why? Because you are a woman and a most troublesome woman. Don't you know anything about this at all. We are not meant to see any woman. So go away before more harm is done.

OMAE (*flirtatious*): What is so secret about it anyway? What do they teach you.

EMAN: Nothing any woman can understand.

OMAE: Ha ha. You think we don't know eh? You've all come to be circumcised.

EMAN: Shut up. You don't know anything.

OMAE: Just think, all this time you haven't been circumcised, and you dared make eyes at us women.

EMAN: Thank you—woman. Now go.

OMAE: Do they give you enough to eat?

EMAN (*testily*): No. We are so hungry that when silly girls like you turn up, we eat them.

OMAE (*feigning tears*): Oh, oh, oh, he's abusing me. He's abusing me.

EMAN (*alarmed*): Don't try that here. Go quickly if you are going to cry.

OMAE: All right, I won't cry.

EMAN: Cry or no cry, go away and leave me alone. What do you think will happen if my tutor turns up now.

OMAE: He won't.

EMAN (*mimicking*): "He won't." I suppose you are his wife and he tells you where he goes. In fact this is just the time he comes round to our huts. He could be at the next hut this very moment.

OMAE: Ha-ha. You're lying. I left him by the stream, pinching the girls' bottoms. Is that the sort of thing he teaches you?

EMAN: Don't say anything against him or I shall beat you. Isn't it you loose girls who tease him, wiggling your bottoms under his nose?

OMAE (*going tearful again*): A-ah, so I am one of the loose girls eh?

EMAN: Now don't start accusing me of things I didn't say.

OMAE: But you said it. You said it.

EMAN: I didn't. Look Omae, someone will hear you and I'll be in disgrace. Why don't you go before anything happens.

OMAE: It's all right. My friends have promised to hold your old rascal tutor till I get back.

EMAN: Then you go back right now. I have work to do. (*Going in.*)

OMAE (*runs after and tries to hold him; Eman leaps back, genuinely scared*): What is the matter? I was not going to bite you.

EMAN: Do you know what you nearly did? You almost touched me!

OMAE: Well?

EMAN: Well! Isn't it enough that you let me set my eyes on you? Must you now totally pollute me with your touch? Don't you understand anything?

OMAE: Oh, that.

EMAN (*nearly screaming*): It is not "oh, that." Do you think this is only a joke or a little visit like spending the night with your grandmother? This is an important period of my life. Look, these huts, we built them with our own hands. Every boy builds his own. We learn things, do you understand? And we spend much time just think- ing. At least, I do. It is the first time I have had nothing to do except think. Don't you see, I am becoming a man. For the first time, I understand that I have a life to fulfil. Has that thought ever worried you?

OMAE: You are frightening me.

EMAN: There. That is all you can say. And what use will that be when a man finds himself alone—like that? (*Points to the hut.*) A man must go on his own, go where no one can help him, and test his strength. Because he may find himself one day sitting alone in a wall as round as that. In there, my mind could hold no other thought. I may never have such moments again to myself. Don't dare to come and steal any more of it.

OMAE (*this time, genuinely tearful*): Oh, I know you hate me. You only want to drive me away.

EMAN (*impatiently*): Yes, yes, I know I hate you—but go.

OMAE (*going, all tears; wipes her eyes, suddenly all mischief*): Eman.

EMAN: What now?

OMAE: I only want to ask one thing . . . do you promise to tell me?

EMAN: Well, what is it?

OMAE (*gleefully*): Does it hurt?

(*She turns instantly and flees, landing straight into the arms of the returning Tutor.*)

TUTOR: Te-he-he . . . what have we here? What little mouse leaps straight into the beak of the wise old owl eh?

(*Omae struggles to free herself, flies to the opposite side, grimacing with distaste.*)

I suppose you merely came to pick some fruits eh? You did not sneak here to see any of my children.

OMAE: Yes, I came to steal your fruits.

TUTOR: Te-he-he . . . I thought so. And that dutiful son of mine over there. He saw you and came to chase you off my fruit trees didn't he? Te-he-he . . . I'm sure he did, isn't that so my young Eman?

EMAN: I was talking to her.

TUTOR: Indeed you were. Now be good enough to go into your hut until I decide your punishment. (*Eman withdraws.*) Te-he-he . . . now now my little daughter, you need not be afraid of me.

OMAE (*spiritedly*): I am not.

TUTOR: Good. Very good. We ought to be friendly. (*His voice becomes leering.*) Now this is nothing to worry you my daughter . . . a very small thing indeed. Although of course if I were to let it slip that your young Eman had broken a strong taboo, it might go hard on him you know. I am sure you would not like that to happen, would you?

OMAE: No.

TUTOR: Good. You are sensible my girl. Can you wash clothes?

OMAE: Yes.

TUTOR: Good. If you will come with me now to my hut, I shall give you some clothes to wash, and then we will forget all about this matter eh? Well, come on.

OMAE: I shall wait here. You go and bring the clothes.

TUTOR: Eh? What is that? Now now, don't make me angry. You should know better than to talk back at your elders. Come now. (*He takes her by the arm, and tries to drag her off.*)

OMAE: No no, I won't come to your hut. Leave me. Leave me alone you shameless old man.

TUTOR: If you don't come I shall disgrace the whole family of Eman, and yours too.

EMAN (*re-enters with a small bundle*): Leave her alone. Let us go Omae.

TUTOR: And where do you think you are going?

EMAN: Home.

TUTOR: Te-he-he . . . As easy as that eh? You think you can leave here any time you please? Get right back inside that hut!

(*Eman takes Omae by the arm and begins to walk off.*)

Come back at once.

(*He goes after him and raises his stick. Eman catches it, wrenches it from him, and throws it away.*)

OMAE (*hopping delightedly*): Kill him. Beat him to death.

TUTOR: Help! Help! He is killing me! Help!

EMAN (*alarmed, clamps his hand over his mouth*): Old tutor, I don't mean you any harm, but you mustn't try to harm me either. (*He removes his hand.*)

TUTOR: You think you can get away with your crime. My report shall reach the elders before you ever get into town.

EMAN: You are afraid of what I will say about you? Don't worry. Only if you try to shame me, then I will speak. I am not going back to the village anyway. Just tell them I have gone, no more. If you say one word more than that I shall hear of it the same day and I shall come back.

TUTOR: You are telling me what to do? But don't think to come back next year because I will drive you away. Don't think to come back here even ten years from now. And don't send your children. (*Goes off with threatening gestures.*)

EMAN: I won't come back.

OMAE: Smoked vulture! But Eman, he says you cannot return next year. What will you do?

EMAN: It is a small thing one can do in the big towns.

OMAE: I thought you were going to beat him that time. Why didn't you crack his dirty hide?

EMAN: Listen carefully Omae . . . I am going on a journey.

OMAE: Come on. Tell me about it on the way.

EMAN: No, I go that way. I cannot return to the village.

OMAE: Because of that wretched man? Anyway you will first talk to your father.

EMAN: Go and see him for me. Tell him I have gone away for some time. I think he will know.

OMAE: But Eman . . .

EMAN: I haven't finished. You will go and live with him till I get back. I have spoken to him about you. Look after him!

OMAE: But what is this journey? When will you come back?

EMAN: I don't know. But this is a good moment to go. Nothing ties me down.

OMAE: But Eman, you want to leave me.

EMAN: Don't forget all I said. I don't know how long I will be. Stay in my father's house as long as you remember me. When you become tired of waiting, you must do as you please. You understand? You must do as you please.

OMAE: I cannot understand anything Eman. I don't know where you are going or why. Suppose you never came back! Don't go Eman. Don't leave me by myself.

EMAN: I must go. Now let me see you on your way.

OMAE: I shall come with you.

EMAN: Come with me! And who will look after you? Me? You will only be in my way, you know that! You will hold me back and I shall desert you in a strange place. Go home and do as I say. Take care of my father and let him take care of you. (*He starts going but Omae clings to him.*)

OMAE: But Eman, stay the night at least. You will only lose your way. Your father Eman, what will he say? I won't remember what you said . . . come back to the village . . . I cannot return alone Eman . . . come with me as far as the crossroads.

(*His face set, Eman strides off and Omae loses balance as he increases his pace. Falling, she quickly wraps her arms around his ankle, but Eman continues unchecked, dragging her along.*)

Don't go Eman . . . Eman, don't leave me, don't leave me . . . don't leave your Omae . . . don't go Eman . . . don't leave your Omae . . .

(*Eman—as carrier—makes a nervous move as if he intends to go after the vanished pair. He stops but continues to stare at the point where he last saw them. There is stillness for a while. Then the Girl enters from the same place and remains looking at Eman. Startled, Eman looks apprehensively round him. The Girl goes nearer but keeps beyond arm's length.*)

GIRL: Are you the carrier?

EMAN: Yes. I am Eman.

GIRL: Why are you hiding?

EMAN: I really came for a drink of water . . . er . . . is there anyone in front of the house?

GIRL: No.

EMAN: But there might be people in the house. Did you hear voices?

GIRL: There is no one here.

EMAN: Good. Thank you. (*He is about to go, stops suddenly.*) Er . . . would you . . . you will find a cup on the table. Could you bring me the water out here? The water-pot is in a corner.

(*The Girl goes. She enters the house, then, watching Eman carefully, slips out and runs off. Eman sits.*)

Perhaps they have all gone home. It will be good to rest. (*He hears voices and listens hard.*) Too late. (*Moves cautiously nearer the house.*) Quickly girl, I can hear people coming. Hurry up. (*Looks through the window.*) Where are you? Where is she? (*The truth dawns on him suddenly and he moves off, sadly.*)

(*Enter Jaguna and Oroge, led by the Girl.*)

GIRL (*pointing*): He was there.

JAGUNA: Ay, he's gone now. He is a sly one is your friend. But it won't save him for ever.

OROGE: What was he doing when you saw him?

GIRL: He asked me for a drink of water.

JAGUNA and OROGE (*together*): Ah! (*They look at each other.*)

OROGE: We should have thought of that.

JAGUNA: He is surely finished now. If only we had thought of it earlier.

OROGE: It is not too late. There is still an hour before midnight.

JAGUNA: We must call back all the men. Now we need only wait for him—in the right place.

OROGE: Everyone must be told. We don't want anyone heading him off again.

JAGUNA: And it works so well. This is surely the help of the gods themselves Oroge. Don't you know at once what is on the path to the stream?

OROGE: The sacred trees.

JAGUNA: I tell you it is the very hand of the gods. Let us go.

An overgrown part of the village. Eman wanders in, aimlessly, seemingly uncaring of discovery. Beyond him, an area lights up, revealing a group of people clustered round a spot, all the heads are bowed. One figure stands away and separate from them. Even as Eman looks, the group breaks up and the people disperse, coming down and past him. Only three people are left, a man (Eman) whose back is turned, the village Priest, and the isolated one. They stand on opposite sides of the grave, the man on the mound of earth. The Priest walks round to the man's side and lays a hand on his shoulder.

PRIEST: Come.

EMAN: I will. Give me a few moments here alone.

PRIEST: Be comforted.

(They fall silent.)

EMAN: I was gone twelve years but she waited. She whom I thought had too much of the laughing child in her. Twelve years I was a pilgrim, seeking the vain shrine of secret strength. And all the time, strange knowledge, this silent strength of my child-woman.

PRIEST: We all saw it. It was a lesson to us; we did not know that such goodness could be found among us.

EMAN: Then why? Why the wasted years if she had to perish giving birth to my child? *(They are both silent.)* I do not really know for what great meaning I searched. When I returned, I could not be certain I had found it. Until I reached my home and I found her a full-grown woman, still a child at heart. When I grew to believe it, I thought, this, after all, is what I sought. It was here all the time. And I threw away my new-gained knowledge. I buried the part of me that was formed in strange places. I made a home in my birthplace.

PRIEST: That was as it should be.

EMAN: Any truth of that was killed in the cruelty of her brief happiness.

PRIEST (*looks up and sees the figure standing away from them, the child in his arms; he is totally still*): Your father—he is over there.

EMAN: I knew he would come. Has he my son with him?

PRIEST: Yes.

EMAN: He will let no one take the child. Go and comfort him Priest. He loved Omae like a daughter, and you all know how well she looked after him. You see how strong we really are. In his heart of hearts the old man's love really awaited a daughter. Go and comfort him. His grief is more than mine.

(*The Priest goes. The Old Man has stood well away from the burial group. His face is hard and his gaze unswerving from the grave. The Priest goes to him, pauses, but sees that he can make no dent in the man's grief. Bowed, he goes on his way.*

Eman, as carrier, walks towards the graveside, the other Eman having gone. His feet sink into the mound and he breaks slowly on to his knees, scooping up the sand in his hands, and pouring it on his head. The scene blacks out slowly.)

Enter Jaguna and Oroge.

OROGE: We have only a little time.

JAGUNA: He will come. All the wells are guarded. There is only the stream left him. The animal must come to drink.

OROGE: You are sure it will not fail—the trap I mean.

JAGUNA: When Jaguna sets the trap, even elephants pay hom-
    age—their trunks downwards and one leg up in the sky.
    When the carrier steps on the fallen twigs, it is up in the
    sacred trees with him.

OROGE: I shall breathe again when this long night is over.

(*They go out. Enter Eman—as carrier—from the same direction as
the last two entered. In front of him is a still figure, the Old Man as
he was, carrying the dwarf boat.*)

EMAN (*joyfully*): Father. (*The figure does not turn round.*) It is
    your son. Eman. (*He moves nearer.*) Don't you want to
    look at me? It is I, Eman. (*He moves nearer still.*)

OLD MAN: You are coming too close. Don't you know what I
    carry on my head?

EMAN: But father, I am your son.

OLD MAN: Then go back. We cannot give the two of us.

EMAN: Tell me first where you are going.

OLD MAN: Do *you* ask that? Where else but to the river?

EMAN (*visibly relieved*): I only wanted to be sure. My throat is
    burning. I have been looking for the stream all night.

OLD MAN: It is the other way.

EMAN: But you said . . .

OLD MAN: I take the longer way, you know how I must do this.
    It is quicker if you take the other way. Go now.

EMAN: No, I will only get lost again. I shall go with you.

OLD MAN: Go back my son. Go back.

EMAN: Why? Won't you even look at me?

OLD MAN: Listen to your father. Go back.

EMAN: But father!

(*He makes to hold him. Instantly the Old Man breaks into a rapid
trot. Eman hesitates, then follows, his strength nearly gone.*)

Wait father. I am coming with you . . . wait . . . wait for me father . . .

(*There is a sound of twigs breaking, of a sudden trembling in the branches. Then silence.*)

The front of Eman's house. The effigy is hanging from the sheaves. Enter Sunma, still supported by Ifada. She stands transfixed as she sees the hanging figure. Ifada appears to go mad, rushes at the object, and tears it down. Sunma, her last bit of will gone, crumbles against the wall. Some distance away from them, partly hidden, stands the Girl, impassively watching. Ifada hugs the effigy to him, stands above Sunma. The Girl remains where she is, observing.

Almost at once, the villagers begin to return, subdued and guilty. They walk across the front, skirting the house as widely as they can. No word is exchanged. Jaguna and Oroge eventually appear. Jaguna, who is leading, sees Sunma as soon as he comes in view. He stops at once, retreating slightly.

OROGE (*almost whispering*): What is it?

JAGUNA: The viper.

OROGE (*looks cautiously at the woman*): I don't think she will even see you.

JAGUNA: Are you sure? I am in no frame of mind for another meeting with her.

OROGE: Let's go home.

JAGUNA: I am sick to the heart of the cowardice I have seen tonight.

OROGE: That is the nature of men.

JAGUNA: Then it is a sorry world to live in. We did it for them. It was all for their own common good. What did it benefit me whether the man lived or died. But did you see them? One and all they looked up at the man and words died in their throats.

OROGE: It was no common sight.

JAGUNA: Women could not have behaved so shamefully. One by one they crept off like sick dogs. Not one could raise a curse.

OROGE: It was not only him they fled. Do you see how unattended we are?

JAGUNA: There are those who will pay for this night's work!

OROGE: Ay, let us go home.

(*They go off. Sunma, Ifada, and the Girl remain as they are, the light fading slowly on them.*)

CURTAIN

SHANGO DE IMA

A YORUBA
MYSTERY PLAY

PEPE CARRIL

The original Spanish version of *Shango de Ima* was first presented by the Teatro Guiñol, Consejo Nacional de Culture, Havana, Cuba, with the following cast:

OBATALA-MADRE	Zenaida Elizalde
SHANGO	Ulises Garcia
IKU, LA MUERTE	Luis Brunet
AGAYU SOLA	Armando Morales
OSHUN	Xiomara Palacio
OYA	Isabel Cancio
OLOFI	Nelson Toledo
YEMAYA-MADRE	Regina Rossie
OBBA	Mabel Rivero, Carucha Camejo
OGUN ARERE	Ernesto Briel, Mario Gonzalez

Artistic director, Pepe Carril; assistant director, Pedro Camejo; adviser on folklore, singer, music for flute, Rogelio Martínez Furé; bata drums, Conjunto Isupo Iawo; choreography by Iván Tenorio; puppets by Guiñol Workshop.

The English adaptation of *Shango de Ima* was first presented by the La Mama Dance Drama Theatre on January 1, 1970, with the following cast:

OGUN	Asaman Byron
IKU	Ric Larson
YEMAYA	Myra Lee
OBATALA	Vicky Miller
OLOFI	Fernley A. Murray
SHANGO	Ray Ramirez*
AGAYU SOLA	Ozzie Rodriguez
OYA	June Segál
OBBA	Lea Scott*
OSHUN	Grenna Whitaker
DANCERS	Scott Adams (Ogun II), Florence Bowe, Dolores Floyd, Ivey Harris (Ogun III), Cookie Holmes (Cana Cana Bird), La Vern Jamison, Madupe, Laura Slater
DRUMMERS	John Amira, Michael Fraiser, John Mason

Directed by Josef Bush; dances by Betty Barney, Larl Becham; arrangement of chants by John Amira; additional material by Asaman Byron, Cookie Holmes.

* Performed courtesy of Actors Equity.

49

AUTHOR'S NOTE

The pronunciation of the Yoruba chants in this play is written according to Spanish usage. Therefore in the chants and Yoruba phrases, *i* is pronounced as long *e*, etc., as in normal Spanish pronunciation.

Many thanks to Nancy Colin, without whose research the English adaptation would not have been possible, and to Ed James for his advice and continuous help in the authentication of Yoruba ritual for the English version, and special thanks to Ellen Stewart and the La Mama Dance Drama Workshop for their dedication to the performance of this work in New York.

Costumes should be made according to the colors used to represent each Orisha (see below). Since this is a religious play, certain conventions must be followed as closely as possible.

ELEGUA:	black and red
OBATALA-MOTHER:	white
SHANGO:	red and white
IKU:	white
AGAYU SOLA:	deep purple
OSHUN:	yellow
OYA:	maroon
YEMAYA-MOTHER:	blue
OGUN ARERE:	green and black

CHARACTERS

ELEGUA*   Orisha of the Paths and
           Crossroads; Mediator and
           Opener of the Doors

OBATALA-MOTHER Mother of Earth and of Man; The
           Law-giver; Father-Mother; King
           and Queen

SHANGO   Orisha of Fire, Thunder, and
           Lightning, of the Intellect and
           of Life

IKU   The Spirit of Death

AGAYU SOLA   Ferryman of all the Rivers; the
           one who cares for the Waters

OSHUN   Orisha of Love, the Sweet Waters,
           and Coquetry

OYA   Queen of the Cemetery,
           Lightning, and the Whirlwind

OLOFI   The Supreme Father, the Sun

YEMAYA-MOTHER Supreme Goddess of the Oceans
           and of Motherhood

OBBA   Shango's Wife

OGUN ARERE   Orisha of Power who descends
           from the Mountains

---

* Although Elegua is not personified in this play, he is mentioned many times, and as the mediator between the gods and man, all sacred ceremonies must begin with a chant to him.

SCENE ONE

Obatala, Mother of Earth and of Man, of Justice and of Purity, recalls how she came to give birth to Shango de Ima, King of Lightning and of Fire.

As darkness encloses her, she sings to Elegua, Orisha of the Paths and Crossroads, so that he might initiate the ceremony.

VOICE, CHORUS, and DRUMS:
>Barasuayo . . .
>o moni ara guana
>ma ma quena iraguo e
>Barasuayo . . .
>o moni ara guana
>ma ma quena iraguo e
>O barauayo
>e . . . Kee . . .
>Echuodara . . .
>o moni ara guana
>ma ma quena iraguo e . . .

(*The illuminated altar of Obatala appears, carried by her children.*)

VOICE, CHORUS, and DRUMS:
>Enu aye mimosheo
>enu aye mi baba . . . (*Repeat.*)
>Obatala ta wini wini
>se e kure
>bobo la ina fere . . . (*Repeat.*)

OBATALA: I, Orishanla, am born of Olodummare, Uan Mariqueno, Olofi made me father and mother of the sky and of the earth. I was always sanctified and old. I was never able to be a child, to live the life of an ordinary woman . . . But I have my sixteen roads. I have humility. I am loving, vengeful, voluptuous, and simple. I am father, mother, king, and queen. I am wise and serene. I am the mistress of destiny. (*She laughs.*) And I am also nothing.

Father, Son, and Holy Spirit . . . this white hair of mine reflects all mysteries. I have the power of all minds, and I

53

bring retribution to those whose minds are evil. One day
the clear eyes of providence will be mine and then I will
watch over everyone—the good as well as the bad. I will
give to each what he deserves, the ones who create and
those who destroy. And also, and this will come soon, I
will give to all the forgiveness I have never refused my
own children.

VOICE, CHORUS, and DRUMS:
>   *Baba oba oma seye*
>   *Oma baba oma seye . . . (Repeat.)*
>   *Oma seye ee . . .*
>   *Oma seye . . . (Repeat.)*

OBATALA: There came a time when it was necessary for me to
cross the waters. The dark and turbulent waters that
warned me of death. I don't know if it was a fear of death
or if it was the terror of submerging myself in the solitary
house of the water, but I begged Agayu to let me cross in
his boat. Agayu Sola, the boatman who is also beautiful.
Agayu Sola who cares for the waters. How many promises I made him, if only I could cross in the protection of
his oars, of his boat. How many promises I made him!
And when we had reached the other side of the river, he
said to me, "*Omorde*, woman, pay me what you have
promised." I stood as if ignorant of what I had said. I
stood as if dumb. And then I took off all my clothes and
laid myself naked on the grass.

And then Agayu, the strongest of the boatmen, who
alone knew the cool motion of the boat in the water,
mounted me and lay with me without knowing who I
was. Afterward I said to him, "Boatman, do you know
who I am? I am Obatala." How I surprised him! (*She
laughs.*) I transformed myself into a man, proud and
indignant, and I went to my house. And as I walked
along the path, I sang. (*She sings:*) "*Yaku yogbi . . .*"

CHORUS: *Olori efa . . .*

OBATALA: *Yaku yogbi* . . .

CHORUS: *Olori efa* . . .

(*While singing, Obatala transforms herself into a man, and then into a white dove in flight.*)

SCENE TWO

Shango de Ima, from the time he is a little boy, pesters his mother for the name of his father. One day, Obatala, overwhelmed by his insistent questioning, answers, "Your father's name is Agayu Sola, go and search for him, and when you find him—stay with him!"

(*Obatala's house, which contains the echoes of bells and the rattles of snakes.*)

SHANGO: Mother, I want to know my name . . .

OBATALA (*indifferent*): Call yourself anything you please. There are as many names for a man as there are pebbles in a mountain.

SHANGO: I also want to know your name, so I can know where I came from.

OBATALA: You can call me "woman," or "the lie" . . . You can call yourself "man," or "the question" . . . Or you can take the name of "Black," which is like our condition and our blood. Perhaps, though, it is best for you to have the name that is yours alone. I am Obatala, queen and mother of the Black child. You can call yourself Shango.

SHANGO: Shango . . . I like my name! . . .

(*The sounds of tambourines are heard, continuing until they reach a violent crescendo. Shango and his mother dance. Soon exhausted, they fall silent.*)

SHANGO: Obatala, I want to know the name of my father . . .

OBATALA: Child, don't pester me.

SHANGO: I want to know who my father is.

OBATALA: There is not enough time in all eternity to answer your questions.

SHANGO: And I, everyday, from dawn until sunset, will ask you the same thing. Again and again. Until I drive you crazy!

OBATALA: And just how is this father of yours to mean anything to you when he is so unworthy of me?

SHANGO: I don't care. I want to know who my father is. I want to see my father! I WANT MY FATHER!!

VOICES: I want to see my father . . . I want to see my father . . .

OBATALA (*over the voices which multiply in number and in volume*): Someday when you no longer wish to see or to hear the name of the one who came to my side as justice, then what will you say? Your father's name is Agayu Sola, go and search for him. Go and look for him upon the rivers, and when you find him, STAY WITH HIM!

(*Shango withdraws, and Obatala, furious, erases the light.*)

SCENE THREE

Iku, White Spirit of Death, potential enemy of Shango and eternal threat to life, appears with sinister countenance, announcing his unending pursuit of Shango.

VOICES, CHORUS, and DRUMS:
  Chon, chon, chon,
  como la lame fami chobode . . .
  chon, chon, chon,
  como la lame fami chobode . . .

IKU: Do you hear it? The desperate voice of the son who begs to know his father. I have heard the harsh tones, and they

ring like music in my ears. Joyfully they sing, into the
very hollows of my face. The great mother who denies
him his father knows well the confusion of paths that
Elegua can prepare for him. I go now to his father's house
to play with death, as a child plays with toys . . . (*Three
voices whistle*.) *Iku on bo lo tiwao* . . . (*He exits*.)

SCENE FOUR

*Agayu Sola in the solitude of his boat remembers his fleeting
moment of love with Obatala.*

(*Agayu draws near with his boat to the shore of the river.*)

AGAYU: Every afternoon I evoke you and long for you. Every
afternoon I return to you, woman, who crossed the river
that night and paid me with your body. Since then, each
night, I call to you in my dreams, "*Obatala, yaguatima,
tanimbe.*" The road I walk, looking for you, is a hurricane
of trees, of cries, and of echoes that pursue me without
end . . . *Obatala, yaguatima* . . . *Obatala, yaguatima* . . .

(*His voice multiplies into thousands of voices and is mixed with the
voice of the child Shango, who calls to his father over all the roads.*)

SHANGO: Agayu Sola . . . Agayu Sola . . . (*He appears before
Agayu.*)

AGAYU: Who are you looking for, child?

SHANGO: I'm looking for my father.

AGAYU: Who is your father?

SHANGO: Agayu Sola, ferryman of all the rivers.

AGAYU: Who told you that?

SHANGO: My mother, Obatala.

AGAYU: That's a lie! I am Agayu Sola, but I'm no father of any
son of Obatala!

SHANGO: My mother doesn't lie. You are my father. You are!

AGAYU: I'm very hungry right now. I'm thinking of my dinner and I can't be bothered listening to such foolishness.

SHANGO: You *are* my father.

AGAYU: Be quiet.

SHANGO: I won't be quiet. I drove my mother to distraction so I could force her to say your name. You are my father. I know it's true. You are my father. You are!!

AGAYU: If you won't shut up, I'll kill you. I'll roast you and eat you for my dinner.

SHANGO: I don't care. You are my father.

(*Iku, who has been the invisible witness of these events, arranges for a thick beam of wood to appear within the reach of Agayu.*)

AGAYU: Agayu Sola does not back down. Agayu Sola stands by his word. If you repeat once again that I am your father . . . *Iku aina* . . . death by fire . . .

SHANGO: You are my father . . . Agayu Sola is my father . . . He is my father . . . My father . . . MY FATHER!

(*Agayu Sola hits his son with the thick beam of death. Shango's body twists and falls. Agayu Sola contemplates the wounded body of his son. Iku laughs with pleasure.*)

AGAYU: Obatala, you lied. Liar is your name, and a lie is this son of Agayu Sola. Today I remain alone with my grief, as I have each day since we lay together. But today I will eat this son of yours, this lie of yours, whoever his father might be . . .

SCENE FIVE

Agayu Sola leaves Shango to burn in the bonfire. Iku frightens away Cana Cana, the sacred bird, so that he cannot carry the news of what has happened to Olofi, the Supreme Father.

Two children—Oya, Queen of the Cemetery, Lightning, and the Whirlwind, and Oshun, Orisha of Love, the Sweet Waters, and Coquetry, witness the funeral ceremony of Iku before the bonfire and promptly go to Olofi for aid.

VOICE, CHORUS, and DRUMS:
*Chon, chon, chon . . .
como la lame fami chobode . . .
chon, chon, chon,
como la lame fami chobode . . .*

IKU: Cana Cana, bird of Olofi's heavens, who always eats the dead first and carries the news of death to the supreme father. Whatever you peck turns to blood. But this death belongs to the fire. In the ashes of Shango there will be no meal for the bird of death. Silent you are and silent you will remain eternally about this death.

(The bird cries and withdraws. Iku draws close to Shango.)

IKU: Who threw your body into the scalding flames?

SHANGO: Agayu Sola.

IKU: Who shrank back from your plaintive cry of "father"?

SHANGO: Agayu Sola.

IKU: Who has committed this crime?

CHORUS: His father.

IKU: Evil one! Evil one! This father who denies his own son.

CHORUS: Agayu Sola.

IKU: He deserves the worst of deaths.

CHORUS: Agayu Sola.

IKU: All his people, together, acting as one, should rise and strike him dead.

CHORUS: He has lost himself in the palms. He has no people. Another punishment is necessary.

IKU: I am his death. I am his other and better punishment.

OSHUN and OYA: The wisest thing to do is to advise Olofi of what has happened.

OTHER VOICES: Go to Olofi! To Olofi! Olofi!

SCENE SIX

The two children, Oya and Oshun, enter into the bright presence of Olofi, the Sun. They tell him what has happened to Shango. Olofi arms Oya with lightning and orders her and Oshun to return to Shango and bring the child back to life.

A VOICE (*sings*):
    Osun duro madubule
    buruganaga la bosi . . .
    Osun duro madubule
    buruganga
    la bosi alardo . . .

OYA and OSHUN: *Maferefun, Olofi.* We ask your benediction. We place ourselves in the presence of your light. We place ourselves in your hands. The Sun. Olofi. The Light.

OSHUN: The voices of the mountain say the father of Shango is guilty.

OYA: He kindled the fire to burn Shango. He kindled the fire to roast Shango and afterward to eat him.

OSHUN: The fire has consumed the flesh of Shango. His flesh is dried up, his blood is flame.

OYA: And his father is deaf to his pleas.

OLOFI: Don't be so generous with your words. When somebody knows nothing about anything, his tongue always boasts of great knowledge.

OSHUN: Tell us the truth then, Sun Father.

OLOFI: The truth is not the sister, but can often be the neighbor of the lie. Go to the mountain, my children, and perform rituals for me. I will remain here, in my home, in the heavens. I already grow tired of so much confusion. Soon I will be silent. But before that, it is necessary for me to know that all below remains in good hands. You, Oya, take the lightning in your hands. With it, you will light the darkness. When the desire comes to you, live in the cemetery and there receive the visions that will come to you.

    Both of you now, return to the fire of Shango de Ima and bring the child back in your arms.

A VOICE (sings):
Osun duro madubule
buruganga
la bosi . . .

SCENE SEVEN

The fire can no longer destroy the body of Shango because now he rests under the benediction of Olofi. Agayu waits eagerly to watch him die in the flames.

SHANGO: The fire has charred my skin, but I'm not really wounded, father. If you were to destroy me, it wouldn't matter to me, because you are my father.

AGAYU: You are a chatterer and a boaster, but the flames will soon silence your words, conceited child. Your body and your tongue will soon be ashes.

SHANGO: *Iku busi si an!*

(*Oya and Oshun appear.*)

OYA: Before, Agayu Sola, when the Father, Olofi, was ignorant of your crime, you were able to throw Shango into the flames of death. But now, the child is in our hands. We will protect him from your rage.

AGAYU: Your hands are not strong enough to force me to leave this place.

OYA: The Father, Olofi, put his lightning into my hands, so that I might protect the child, Shango. (*Flashes of lightning.*) Depart, Agayu Sola. Olofi's commandments are fulfilled; the child is saved.

AGAYU: Agayu respects the Father that put lightning into your hands. I will go now and take refuge in the palms. But one day I will come down again, and on that day I will defend my honor.

(*Oya and Oshun come close to Shango.*)

OSHUN: Whoever my hand protects will walk the better path.

OYA: Whoever is illumined by my hands will arrive finally in the heavens of Olofi.

SCENE EIGHT

Oshun and Oya bring the child back to life. They carry him to the presence of Olofi, who gives to Shango the absolute power of fire, thunder, and lightning.

A VOICE (*sings*):
> *Osun duro madubule*
> *buruganga*
> *la bosi . . .*
> *Osun duro madubule*
> *buruganga*
> *la bosi alardo . . .*

OSHUN: Father and Master, Olofi, the Sun, the child Shango has been returned to life.

OYA: We have brought the child here to your presence as you commanded.

OLOFI: From the rock comes pebbles and from the moon, stars. You, Shango, will become, by my grace, master of the fire and you will hold this sacred office forever.

(*The child Shango crosses the rays of the sun and is changed into a man.*)

SHANGO: *Toto jun, toti ori olori . . .*

OLOFI: You, Oya, will remain the mistress of lightning.

OSHUN: And what about me, Master?

OLOFI: You, Oshun, will retain the natural graces you already have. Another day I will give you something more. Today I have conceded many attributes.

(*The girls cross the rays of the sun and appear as two beautiful women.*)

OSHUN: Thank you, Father. Now it is time for me to go home and look after my gourds.

OLOFI: Yes, each *orisha* has his home. Shango, Obatala expects you to return to yours.

SCENE NINE

Obatala receives Shango and asks him for an account of his adventure. She asks him if he has had a good time with his father, reminding him that the mother judges all truth and punishes all trickery.

VOICE, CHORUS, and DRUMS:
Enu aye mimosheo
enu aye mi baba . . . (Repeat.)
Obatala ta wini wini
se e kure
bobo la ina fere . . . (Repeat.)

(*Shango appears in the house of Obatala.*)

SHANGO: Mother, I have returned to you and to my home, and I am content. I have satisfied my desire for knowledge. I am the happiest of men. I have been close to my father.

OBATALA: That will be the day.

SHANGO: But it's true. I had a very good time.

OBATALA: Really? Why didn't you stay with him then?

SHANGO: I wanted to come and give you the news. My father has taught me many things. Look. (*He passes his body through a burning flame.*) The fire is now my natural element.

OBATALA: And who gave you this ability?

SHANGO: My father.

OBATALA: You lie!

SHANGO: No, it's the truth, *iya*. It was my good father who brought me before Olofi and said to him, "Give my son a power." And Olofi responded by making me the *orisha* of fire.

OBATALA: Liar! All your father has taught you is the ability to lie!

SHANGO: I see! It's becoming very clear to me that you hate my father very much!

OBATALA: You are a lying brat. You deserve only my punishment. (*She strikes him with a white tail whip that is the same whiteness as her hair.*) This is so you will never again talk to me of your father.

SHANGO (*weeping*): Hear me now, Olofi, Great Father who has blessed me. Transform the words of my mother to fire and ashes.

OBATALA: You go too far! You want to destroy my life and my home, but before you can do that I would rather bury you in the ground with my own hands. I give you that future rather than the one you wish. OUT! (*Shango leaves.*) Now you can be as ill-tempered and noisy as you wish, but far away from me, Shango.

(*Snakes' rattles and bells echo as Obatala waves her white whip furiously in the air.*)

SCENE TEN

Yemaya, Supreme Goddess of the Oceans and of Motherhood, dances with stateliness in expectation of the adopted son that Father Olofi has promised her. Shango, now transformed into a bolt of fire, whirls violently in the sky until he arrives, finally, as a man, on the blue waters of Yemaya, who receives him with open arms and heart.

VOICE, CHORUS, and DRUMS:
> Yemaya asesu . . .
> asesu Yemaya . . . (*Repeat.*)
> Yemaya olodo . . .
> olodo Yemaya . . . (*Repeat.*)

(*A peal of thunder interrupts Yemaya's dance. She quickly shelters herself in the waters. Suddenly, in the dark sky, Shango de Ima appears, transformed into a bolt of fire.*)

VOICE, CHORUS, and DRUMS:
> Omorde o mo titi o
> eyolarde . . . (*Repeat.*)
> Oluwa chiki ni oluwa
> Eda wi we omio yanya o
> omo lomio de . . . (*Repeat.*)

VOICE: *Iya chiki ni . . .*

CHORUS: *. . . a la mogdanza . . .* (*Repeat.*)

VOICE, CHORUS:
> *Omorde o mo titi o*
> *eyolarde . . .* (*Repeat.*)
> *Emi ode omo de*
> *Omo de emi ode*
> *Ca chu mama*
> *Iya onbe leo . . .* (*Repeat.*)

SCENE ELEVEN

Yemaya receives Shango and offers him the gift of mastery of all drums. She begs him to protect her from Ogun Arere, a warlike hermit who is stealing her lands.

(*Shango discovers Yemaya, smiling and radiant.*)

YEMAYA: *Mokenken,* what do you want?

SHANGO: Alas, my true mother has hurled me to the heavens in her wrath.

YEMAYA: Whose son are you?

SHANGO: I am the son of Obatala.

YEMAYA: And what is your name?

SHANGO: I am Shango.

YEMAYA: Ah, Shango, surely you are the present Olofi has deigned to send me. I will give you a careful upbringing.

SHANGO: That sounds good to me.

YEMAYA: I will make you master of all the drums.

SHANGO: I will be master of the drums!

YEMAYA: You will be the courageous one who defends me and
my home, threatened as they are always by Ogun, the
coarsest and fattest man on this earth. He has an inaccessible dwelling in the middle of the mountain and ven-
tures forth alone to measure his strength against that of
the soldiers who pass by.

SHANGO: I will go to the center of the mountain to battle this
man! I pledge you my knife with his blood on it!

YEMAYA: Words come easily, conceited boy. You'd better be
more careful than that. This is not that kind of war.

SHANGO: I will prove my skill to you. (*He laughs.*) Who does
not tremble at the sound of thunder?

YEMAYA: I will marry you to Obba, a faithful and industrious
woman who will look after you. She will nourish you to
strength and aggressiveness. I will send my little sisters
Oya and Oshun to the battle to act as my witnesses and
tell me what takes place. (*She gives him the Eddu ax.*) This
is the weapon you must carry. If you need anything else,
tell my sisters and it will be delivered to you. (*Shango
takes the weapon and prepares to depart.*) The battle begins at
the waning of the moon. Where are you going now?

SHANGO: Didn't you make me master of the drums?

YEMAYA: Yes.

SHANGO: Then I shall gather together my drums and prepare
the feast of Guemilere. It will have such force that all the
fires of the mountain will be lit. I want to feast and
afterward . . . afterward I will go to battle. (*He laughs and
leaves.*)

YEMAYA: Ah, Shango, Shango de Ima. I see your destiny. I see it in the whirlpool. I see it in that water that brings the tempest. And the fury I see destined for you is followed by death. That death in which everything dissolves and is transformed.

SCENE TWELVE

In the middle of the feast, Shango pauses to throw the divining shells on the Ifa board. He throws the shells and then throws them again. Each time they foretell death. But whose?

VOICE, CHORUS, and DRUMS:
Didilaro . . .
ara fo wo . . .
didilaro . . .
ara fo wo . . . (Repeat.)

SHANGO: How quiet the feast of Guemilere is. (*Absolute silence.*) How silent the big drum is and . . . look! It is changing into the divining board of *Ifa!!!*

(*The tablet and divining shells appear in the air.*)

VOICES: *Eboda!*

SHANGO (*taking the shells*): Now I'll know the fortune of each one present.

VOICES: *Kaguo . . . Kabiosile . . .*

SHANGO: Shells onto the tablet. Onto the tablet of *Ifa!!* (*He throws.*) *Oguani lariche? Okana sorde efun!* Damn it! The hour of the shadow! Yes!! I've turned up death. Death without recourse or remedy! Have hope, Shango. (*He throws again.*) Be happy you who will remain alive, but who is it that will die! Who will die? You? Or you? (*He throws again.*) DEATH!!! BUT WHOSE?!?

VOICES: Oh, Shango. It is your death you see before you.

(*Iku appears as the White Spirit of Death. He wails at Shango's back.*)

VOICES: Oh, Shango, it is your death you see before you in the shells.

(*Shango sees Iku and runs away. All withdraw. The enclosure darkens and Iku remains at the center of the stage.*)

SCENE THIRTEEN

Iku, dominating the scene, predicts Shango's eternal persecution and announces the curse of the women who have known him and of the ones he has yet to know.

VOICE, CHORUS, and DRUMS:
   Chon, chon, chon,
   como la lame fami chobode . . .
   chon, chon, chon,
   como la lame fami chobode . . .

IKU: I, Iku, have come from the cemetery to confront you with your destiny, Shango de Ima, thief of sky and of earth. A curse to every woman you have ever known or has known you! Shango de Ima, boastful and wicked to a father who did not recognize you as his son, you will be cursed and destroyed by the Father Olofi. This bone without meat, this food without sustenance I leave you, Shango de Ima, to remind you always of who I am, I, Iku, who pursues you and watches you. When you are guilty of evil or treason, you will remember me and be filled with dread, because when you betray any person on this earth, you betray me. Cana Cana, the bird of the sky of Olofi will fly over you from now on in my name, hoping eagerly to satisfy his hunger with your body. *Iku guanada ronoko lo ochako ni guo guo.*

VOICE, CHORUS, and DRUMS:
Chon, chon, chon . . .
como la lame fami chobode . . .

(*The chant is repeated until it crescendos to a loud climax.*)

SCENE FOURTEEN

Oshun, when she dances, resembles a fan of peacock feathers, sunflowers, and honey. A vision of the air, her clothing is of brilliant gold.

Oya, with her black hair, resembles the rainbow. Her gown is multi-colored and floats like the air.

Oya and Oshun appear to Shango, who views them with ecstasy. He does not recognize them immediately and flatters and courts them. He feels he is received unkindly by Oya and with coquetry by Oshun.

VOICE, CHORUS, and DRUMS:
yeye bi obi tosuo
yeye bi obi tosuo
yeye tani bakua
lubo legue o . . .
yeye tani bakua
lubo legue o . . .
yeye yeye o . . .
yeye tani bakua
lubo legue o . . .

VOICE:
che cu che

CHORUS:
ekue mile

VOICE:
ti ti le ko

CHORUS:
> *ekue mile*

VOICE:
> *eri olu*

CHORUS:
> *ekue mile iya mio*
> *ekue mile*

(*While the chant is being sung, Oya and Oshun dance.*)

OYA: When flowers dance, they dance for the dead. They dance for the sin that sleeps, the blood that is in repose. These flowers are the flowers of my desire. I wish to place them in the moon of my cemeteries.

(*Shango stops to observe the two women.*)

SHANGO: I think I know them, but who are they? How beautiful they are.

OSHUN: I salute the passing of the kings . . .

SHANGO: They are the daughters of Ile Gelefun . . .

OSHUN: You have a short memory, Shango. We are Oya and Oshun, the same women who went to the throne of Olofi to beg him for your redemption from the fire.

SHANGO: Now I remember! I had forgotten the terrible denial of my father when I was a child, but I will never forget the beautiful children who helped me that day.

OSHUN: You, Shango, of all men, appear to be the most gallant . . . and also the most presumptuous!

SHANGO: You're absolutely right about Shango . . . when he was a child. I was able to see how beautiful you were when you were only children, but now that the children have grown to women!

(*Oshun laughs.*)

OYA: Let's go, Oshun, we're not traveling the best road . . .

OSHUN: No, no, little sister. I think I will stay . . . I wish to ask Shango with all his great knowledge if he thinks he presumes to know how to light *my* hands with that sacred fire he possesses . . .

(*Oya, disturbed, withdraws.*)

SHANGO: No, Oshun, it is necessary for you to go with your sister now. I must go without delay to the center of the mountain to battle Ogun.

OSHUN: Ogun will be the winner of your battle if I do not put my hands on the great weapon you prepare . . . (*She leaves.*) Wait for me, Oya!

SHANGO (*calling after her*): I'll think about it! And tell that sister of yours that she doesn't know anything at all about my road and the only reason she calls hers best is because it's the only one she knows! (*He laughs.*)

(*He turns to look for his weapons and encounters Obba.*)

SCENE FIFTEEN

Obba humbly offers Shango her body and her life.

SHANGO (*sees Obba*): And you? Who are you?

OBBA: I am Obba, chosen by your adopted mother Yemaya to be your wife and companion. Whenever you wish, I will be at your side. I will be there always, as you desire.

SHANGO (*looking at her attentively*): My mother has good judgment, picking for me the most handsome woman in all the kingdom . . .

OBBA: Don't play with the truth, Shango. Obba is not the most beautiful of women, but she is the woman most able to love and serve the man Shango. The man that Olodummare has appointed her to. Under any circumstances my body is yours, but I think the most precious gift is what my house contains for my husband . . . What do you desire of me?

(*Shango draws close to her. She reaches to kiss him, but he turns aside. She steps back.*)

SHANGO: You will be to me as Yemaya commanded, my most faithful companion. The woman who will serve to me the best and most nourishing of food so I will be strong when I go to battle against Ogun. *Amala,* corn with the best and choicest of meats—that is the food that pleases me the most.

OBBA: I am a poor woman, but I swear to you that you will always eat what you desire. I swear you will eat only the best and choicest of foods.

SHANGO: Now I will go to the center of the mountain to battle Ogun. A woman belongs in the home. A man needs a woman in the home and not in combat. I will come to you when I am ready for my meal.

OBBA: But my hands are your food, your strength. My body is your house, your love.

(*Shango leaves. Obba stands for a moment alone, then Oya and Oshun appear on the stage opposite her.*)

SCENE SIXTEEN

Oshun and Oya draw close to Obba. They have come to counsel her how best to hold Shango and in that way to destroy the relationship imposed upon her by Yemaya.

OSHUN and OYA: Obba will be married. Let us dance. At the marriage of Obba let us dance. Obba is the wife of Shango. Let us dance. Obba is the wife of Shango.

OSHUN: Yemaya-Mother proclaims the happiness of her son and his wife to every corner of the earth.

OYA: The Proud One is at the side of her son.

OBBA: And Obba will not fail in her pledge of faithfulness to him, even though sometimes he may not be too faithful to her and due to the heat of his passion, he might find his way to the door of some other woman's house.

OYA: He will go to another woman's entrance only when he doesn't find what he wants at yours . . .

OSHUN: A woman is truly married only when she knows how to keep her husband in *her* house.

OYA: Listen, be careful of the entrance that your husband comes in and goes out of, and if by a higher will all goes well, your husband will never leave your walls . . .

OSHUN: Not if you spray your room with perfumed waters . . .

OYA: And remember, never raise your voice above the dust on the ground. The woman of Shango must not have a mouth, only ears with which to talk to her husband.

OBBA: My sisters know very well I will not listen to them. Although Shango would come with nothing but scorn for me, I would never ask advice, for I know very well what my duty is—to serve and honor him and nothing else.

OYA: And what do you know besides that? Does Obba know how to laugh? Can Obba offer Shango the pleasure that any man needs?

OSHUN: Shango, the man, will look for the most pleasing among all of the women.

OYA: Obba would be a happy woman indeed if she could hear the voices of the ancient women in the cemetery, women who loved until their very blood was drained from them.

OSHUN: Those deep secrets only Oya can repeat from out of the dark silence.

OBBA: Secrets?

OYA: Yes, secrets. Secrets of how to hold your man, of how to make him feel that there is only one blood beneath both skins, one blood alone which flows beneath the skin of the man and the woman who love.

OBBA: I need those secrets.

(*Oshun laughs and withdraws.*)

OYA: Time is running out, Obba. Let us go to the cemetery now to seek the best counsel. A piece of your body . . . the same body the man covers at night with love.

(*The music of rattles drowns out the voice of Oya as she exits, twirling her horse-tail whip around Obba's head.*)

SCENE SEVENTEEN

In a clearing in the mountain, Shango prepares for battle. Oshun appears. She offers Shango the benediction of her body. They join in love.

SHANGO:
> *Fire from the depths*
> *Fire from the lightning*
> *Fire from the stone*
> *Fire in my mouth*
> *In my clenched fist*
> *Ogun has traps on the paths of the mountain*
> *Dry grass hide the wrath of Ogun*
> *Fire from above*
> *And fire from below*

I will arrive at the center of the mountain
I will arrive at the house of Ogun
I will be the most courageous of all warriors
Yemaya will have peace from the traps of Ogun
Fire from above
Fire from below

In my words, in my fists,
in the earth, in the sky
Fire in all things
In the songs of Shango

SHANGO and DRUMS:
Kaguo e
Ye kaguo e
Ye kaguo e
Kabio sile o

CHORUS:
Kaguo e
Ye kaguo e
Ye kaguo e
Kabio sile o

SHANGO:
Kaguo e
Ye kaguo e
Ye kaguo e
Kabio sile o

CHORUS: (*Repeat.*)

SHANGO: And I will be the most courageous of all.

OSHUN (*entering*): You will be the most courageous, yes, but only if I have the chance to place my hands on the best of weapons that you will carry into combat.

SHANGO: And your sister?

OSHUN: She is at home. I have come alone to bless the courage and strength of your "arms." (*Oshun laughs and exits.*)

(In the distance Oshun opens her cape. She is naked. Oshun and Shango embrace passionately.)

SHANGO: You smell like the honey of flowers.

OSHUN: What you smell is the perfume of my breasts . . .

SCENE EIGHTEEN

Shango and Ogun confront each other in the center of the mountain.

(Ogun appears. He dominates the center of the stage. Shango enters.)

SHANGO: I have been searching for you.

OGUN: What for?

SHANGO: To teach you my abilities in war.

OGUN: Why?

SHANGO: Because you are a selfish man, master of the center of the mountains. Because my mother, Yemaya, wishes to live in peace.

OGUN: And how did you get here? No one travels my lands and escapes from my traps.

SHANGO: My white horse traveled with great care along your roads and none of your traps detained me.

OGUN: Then you are doubly guilty. First for having offended the dignity of my lands, and second for confronting me without having asked my permission. Your body, subdued by my machete, will be delivered to the throne of Olofi, to prove to him that I, Ogun, am the most warlike and skillful of all his warriors.

SHANGO: It is for this reason also I have come. Are you ready?

Pepe Carril

OGUN: I am ready!!!!

SHANGO: Then . . . TO COMBAT!!!!!

VOICE, CHORUS, and DRUMS:
> A . . . Oggun Meye A . . .
> Meye, meye . . .
> A . . . Oggun Meye A . . .
> Meye, meye . . .

SCENE NINETEEN

The sound of battle. Sounds of Shango's ax and Ogun's machete ring through the heavens. Hundreds of axes and machetes cover the trees, razing everything that lives. Ogun's machetes increase. Shango's axes, intimidated, diminish. Shango screams and flees.

VOICE, CHORUS, and DRUMS:
> A . . . Oggun Meye A . . .
> Meye, meye . . .
> A . . . Oggun Meye A . . .
> Meye, meye . . .

(*The song repeats indefinitely until the moment when Shango cries and escapes.*)

SCENE TWENTY

In a secluded corner of the mountain, Shango throws himself on the ground to rest.

(*At his side Oya looks at Shango attentively. Shango, not seeing her face, takes hold of her skirt.*)

SHANGO: Ah, Obba has arrived just in time with my dinner.

OYA: I have brought you no dinner and I am not your wife. I am Oya.

SHANGO: Why are you here?

OYA: I wished to come and witness you in your defeat, to convince myself you are as much a coward in war as you are passionate in love . . . Iku has taught me the correct road . . .

SHANGO: I am not a man who knows defeat. I came to confront Ogun, and I can always do battle with him. (*Pause.*) Have you seen him?

OYA: No.

SHANGO: Well . . . when I do confront him, he will learn the invincibility of my arms.

OYA: Will those be the same arms with which you conquered my sister Oshun?

SHANGO: No, another kind of arms. You do not harm a woman. You kindle her body with a softer kind of weapon, with a flame that burns but does not wound.

OYA: And what about the times you have caused pain without causing blood to flow . . . Shango de Ima, you are weak and you are a coward. You can conquer women with your weapons but when it comes to men who equal you in strength, then the great Shango de Ima is afraid of battle.

SHANGO: It seems to me you don't like me very much. Why? My hands have never touched you.

OYA: But your eyes have. And the love my sisters feel for you has given me much pain.

SHANGO: Oshun filled me with courage for my battle. Obba is faithful in love and attentiveness. I need what they give me . . . and always I need more. You also can help me.

OYA: You have never asked me for any help.

SHANGO: I need you to change clothes with me.

OYA: What for?

SHANGO: So I can return to combat. If I am clothed like a woman I can get close enough to Ogun Arere to give him a mortal blow.

OYA: You are as tricky as you are domineering, Shango.

(*Shango takes her by the shoulders affectionately.*)

VOICE:
> *Iye iyekua*
> *Iye iyekua*
> *oyansire confooya*
> *otaguere ala jeru . . .*
> *maribo oyarde . . . (Repeat.)*

SHANGO: Come . . .

OYA: And if I don't want to . . .

SHANGO: Come . . .

(*Shango gently removes her blouse and begins to remove all of her clothes. The song ends in darkness.*)

SCENE TWENTY-ONE

Dressed like a woman, Shango arrives to battle Ogun.

(*Drums beat, accenting Ogun's dance.*)

OGUN (*dancing with his machete in the air*): Ogun does not want defeated men. Ogun plays at the game of war, plays to the finish of the game, plays till the dread of war overcomes war, till war is defeated by war.

Ogun refuses to see the defeated crying out their loss.

(*Shango enters dressed like a woman, strutting, swinging his hips. He lies on his back provocatively.*)

OGUN: Who are you looking for, woman? You are very beautiful. You have the dark and toughened skin of the warriors who come to do battle with me.

(*Shango laughs like a woman.*)

You will be discovered with that gracious laugh of yours. All eyes will be turned toward you. Who is your husband?

SHANGO (*drawing close to him*): I am only looking for . . . THE HEAD OF OGUN ARERE . . . !!!!!!! (*He reveals himself armed.*) *SHANGO PALADA SURU!!!*

(*A struggle begins. Ogun holds Shango on the ground, his machete to his neck.*)

OGUN: FALSE ONE! SHAM!! DECEITFUL WARRIOR!! Your deceit turns you into a small leaf on the point of my machete. (*He raises the machete.*) Now let us see it through to the end . . . this dangerous game of war!!!!!

(*Drumbeat—the beat changes from the rhythm for Ogun into a "meta-meta" quick-quick rhythm for Shango. He breaks away from Ogun's grasp and as they continue to fight, exiting.*)

SCENE TWENTY-TWO

Obba, in her anxiety to retain Shango, has cut off her ears for Shango's meal. With her hands cupped over her ears to stop the flow of blood, Obba provokes her husband's curiosity.

(*Obba appears, whirling crazily next to Shango, who is eating his dinner in a sloppy and gluttonous manner. Obba holds her hands to both sides of her face to stop the flow of blood from her wounds.*)

VOICES and DRUMS:
Mala amala kalalu u u . . .
mala amala kalalu . . .

mala amala kalalu u u . . .
mala amala kalalu . . .
obbi misha
efu Shango
mala amala kalalu . . . (Repeat.)

(*Continues in a soft whisper under the first speech.*)

OBBA: Ay, Shango, being a married woman must have more pleasant moments than the pain your scorn has given me. I have never received from you the good I have extended. I couldn't find any meat for you. I looked all over the mountain and could find nothing other than what I was told at the cemetery to use for your supper. I cannot rob because Yemaya has taught me to be honest. Honest both within my house and outside of it. I could find nothing for your meal . . . so I cut off my ears.

(*Shango looks at her, astonished.*)

The food you eat is part of my own body. The same body your ardent flame should look to at night. For you, to hold you, the pain wouldn't matter. For you I would give my whole body to exalt you over all the gods.

(*Shango draws close to her and takes her by the arms.*)

SHANGO: Let me see!!

OBBA: You see me.

SHANGO: I want to see your ears!!

OBBA: I don't have any!

SHANGO: I WANT TO SEE YOUR EARS!

OBBA: I told you already, I don't have them. They are in your supper.

SHANGO: I want to see you without ears!

(*Obba removes her hands.*)

OBBA (*bleeding*): The fresh blood keeps flowing from my wounds.

SHANGO: And fresh blood will flow for a much longer time than that. Blood from your eyes and from your mouth. Blood from your shoulders and from your hands. You will remain ugly, bloody, without ears and . . . without a husband! Because I don't want a mutilated woman!! Earless!!!!! Earless!!!!!

(*Obba screams. Ogun appears, fully armed. Obba exits.*)

OGUN: Shango, warrior to man, curse to women. I have frightened your white horse and it will never return to you. Now you will wage your last battle. Iku already searches the mountain for you. Death who pardons all has put his mark on the point of my machete.

(*Shango removes his gown and reveals his sex, taunting Ogun.*)

SHANGO: *EMI OGORDO KUAMI!!!*

(*Ogun advances with his machete raised and Shango escapes. Drum—"meta"—for Shango.*)

SCENE TWENTY-THREE

Shango, after fierce combat, seeks counsel from the Father Olofi and is ordered to maintain himself in perpetual combat with Ogun Arere.

(*Father Olofi appears as the round sun with sixteen rays.*)

VOICE (*sings*):
Osun duro madubule
buruganga
la bosi . . .
Osun duro madubule

buruganga
la bosi alardo . . .

(*Shango enters and falls submissively before Olofi.*)

SHANGO: Great Father, giver of the fire that consumed me, I am cast down. I have been here since dawn, in front of the sacred cotton silk tree, fighting an endless battle with Ogun the warrior. Ogun who is so boastful of his courage and skill in combat . . .

OLOFI: Ogun is a warrior of strong reputation. I know of your battle and that as yet there is no victor.

SHANGO: I have resolved to maintain myself in this battle until final victory, but I have lost my weapons and my white horse, my courage, has escaped to the hills.

OLOFI: Then it is now necessary for you to depend on your cunning rather than on your strength of arms. You must face this battle, Shango, win or lose, and then and only then you will receive the reward or the punishment you have earned.

CHORUS: *Osun duro . . .*

SCENE TWENTY-FOUR

Iku and all of Shango de Ima's women parade to the kingdom of Obatala to demand justice.

VOICE, CHORUS, and DRUMS:
Chon, chon, chon,
como la lame fami chobode . . .
chon, chon, chon,
como la lame fami chobode . . . (*Repeat.*)

(*Enter Oya, goddess of the cemetery, raising her hand to Iku, white spirit of death.*)

Oya: Let us go to Shango. The man who fears you as no other man has ever feared you. (*Iku laughs in a sinister manner.*) The man who forgets that your shadow is the only shadow that follows him. Today we will discover him, oppressed by his guilt, anguished by his treason, his lies increasing by the moment. (*Iku wails.*) His body subdues the bodies of the women he comes near. His body is a passionate flame that I want you to extinguish. (*Iku laughs.*) With the permission of Olofi and the approval of all my sisters, I want his flame dampened until it resembles the dark earth of the cemeteries . . .

(*They exit. Oshun enters.*)

Oshun: I also wish to condemn him . . . I have to bear within me the love burden of his throbbing body. I knew when I handed myself over to him, as I had never done to any man before, in the fullness and depth of my desire, all I would get in exchange was his scorn and abuse in my ears . . . "You are good for nothing. You are unworthy of my bed. You don't know how to make love to a man." I, also, with all my heart, condemn him . . . However, I wish to ask Olofi to permit him the benefit of my consolation when he collapses and is consumed by pain.

(*Oshun exits and Obba enters.*)

Obba: Ay, the pain in my blood and in my spirit for the love I have given to my husband! Father Olofi, if only my husband, Shango, could be pardoned of that guilt, I would wish, for the sake of my love for him, to bring upon myself the weight of his punishment. My eyes dried of their tears, my body dried of its blood, I wish now to entomb my body and my pain in the healing water of some cool river.

(*She exits. Shango enters, his hands waving in the air, and dances to the rattles of the snake.*)

SCENE TWENTY-FIVE

Shango turns to Yemaya for help. Lying in her bed, he tells her about his wanderings.

(*Music for flute and rattles. Yemaya is lying on her mat, and lying next to her is Shango, her adopted son. She begins to stroke him tenderly.*)

SHANGO: Your bed is soft and warm, mother. How I wish I could rest sometimes like I used to, but now it seems I'm always fighting somewhere for your tranquillity.

YEMAYA: For the moment at least all is calm, so be at ease, Shango. No one can enter my house without my invitation. Tell me now of yourself and your adventures since leaving my house.

SHANGO: I don't have to relate to you the history of the battles I have fought. The history of war is the history of mankind. I will tell you instead of love, of those activities which have consumed at least as much of my time as war.

YEMAYA: Yes, I know that also. That you have loved for good as well as for evil.

SHANGO: I have known soft arms, tender bodies, firm breasts, as well as dull and reserved embraces. I have known much tenderness and also I have known an embrace as strong as if it came from the arms of a man. These embraces pleased me—all of them—only to feel life palpitating in my hands.

YEMAYA: Coquettish Oshun, tyrannical Oya, faithful Obba— all these devoted women are yours . . .

SHANGO: All? No, mother. I have also known Okute, a beautiful woman like no other whose bed I've been in. At times I think it was a dream of love. I can make love even as I dream, true? Okute, Okute, how like you she is, beautiful and full of expectant life. Her waist is the same as yours, slender as a ray of light crossing the water.

YEMAYA: Now I can see how your body is able to seduce and kill. We have different paths, Shango.

SHANGO: No, no . . . think about the pleasure in a mother's body. *Iya*, mine, I desire you.

YEMAYA: Embrace me then and . . . hush . . .

(*They embrace, trembling.*)

VOICE, CHORUS, and DRUMS:
   Chon, chon, chon . . .
   como la lame fami chobode . . . (Repeat.)

(*Iku appears carrying a bunch of tall white reeds which he uses to hide their bed.*)

IKU: This act of sainted mother and sainted son will never be seen. It is the sin of sacred life and I am one who denies such life. One who hates all life and that which makes life possible, the seed of love.

(*He begins to shake his rattle to cover the love-making of Yemaya and Shango. The sound of his rattle continues into the next scene.*)

SCENE TWENTY-SIX

Everyone assembles in the house of Obatala for the judgment of Shango. Obatala closes the ceremony of this sacred legend with the Yoruba phrase "Orunla ibo su boya."

(*Oya, Oshun, Yemaya, and Obba are seated in front. In the background many women sit shrouded in white. Iku talks to them in a low tone. Shango is silent. Obatala enters.*)

OBATALA (*over a general murmur*): SILENCE! (*There is total silence.*) Women, although you are saints, you must learn how to be quiet. And how to gather your speech together as one so that Obatala will pay heed.

ALL: *Maferefun, Olofi.*

OBATALA: Olofi will not come. Olofi is silent. Olofi will always be in his home, in the heavens, but he has turned away from listening to the petitions of man. Now he speaks to me alone and his justice will be dispensed by me and no one else.

ALL: *Maferefun, Obatala.*

OBATALA: Of all the women here is there one who can speak for all of you?

OYA: The oldest!!!

OSHUN: No woman is the oldest.

YEMAYA: She who has been hurt most is the one who should speak.

(*All eyes turn to Obba. After a moment of silence she rises.*)

OBBA: I was blind and dumb when I encountered Shango de Ima. I submitted to him in silence so as not to annoy him, and I wish to remain silent so I will continue to be both a pure and a faithful woman to my husband.

(*A sound of loud murmuring of all voices.*)

OBATALA: Silence! You have chosen Obba to speak and she has said what she had to say. Now we will listen to the man.

SHANGO: I am, Obatala, what I am . . . Obba is what she is . . . Each woman of the sky or of the earth is also what they are . . . I want every woman in my kingdom to understand and experience this supreme and perfect gift that Olofi has given to man. If I was not the receptacle of this gift I would be someone else, not the Shango you know. The air would be different, the fire and the skies would remain dark eternally. This gift of light, of birth, of fire and flame is as it is and if Olofi orders my punishment for using what he himself has given me, then I reject that punishment . . .

OBATALA: Don't blaspheme, Shango. Blasphemy smells badly on the breath of a saint.

IKU: I request punishment for Shango de Ima. Oh that Olofi would ordain his punishment!

OBATALA: The punishment of man is already out of the hands of Olofi. From now on man's punishment will be found in his own condition.

SHANGO: And I, Great Mother, comply with this word . . .

OBATALA: And this compliance will be your punishment, Shango de Ima. The joy which makes suffering possible, the birth which leads to death will be your punishment and the punishment of all men . . . You are, by the designation of Olofi, eternal keeper of fire, of the sun's ray, of thunder, of the flame, but your followers must then also know the shadow that extinguishes these great lights. And this is your punishment also. If the eyes of your sons, your lights, become extinguished, light them again if you can, Shango de Ima, *orisha* of the flames, and see them extinguished again and again in the eternal cycle which follows your battles without end. And see if death gives way one inch. Iku is also the son of Olofi and thus life is followed by death and light by darkness in the endless cycle until all the paths of the road turn toward their inevitable end in the quiet of the cemeteries . . .
ORUNLA IBO SU BOYA

(*The* orishas *part and the drums appear initiating the rites of* Guemilere.)

VOICE, CHORUS, and DRUMS:
Shango de Ima kulenkue . . .
jere mi takua jere mi ya
ogordo Ima kulenkue . . .
jere mi takua jere mi ya

jere mi jere oguo
jere mi takua jere mi ya
jere mi jere oguo
jere mi takua jere mi ya
Ure ure kore iroko iroko rokeke
araba ra ina kore abagna
abagna ni kiki . . .
olu koso lo le ke sa guo . . .
Aina bukanka . . .
kamaguo . . .
Aina bukanka . . .

(*The closing chant to Elegua signals the end of the sacred legend. It is followed traditionally by the performers celebrating to a rhumba beat.*)

VOICE, CHORUS, and DRUMS:
Elegua ni kua laroye so kuo
e . . . e . . . elegua ni kua laroye
so kuo e

(THE CELEBRATION)

TI-JEAN
AND HIS
BROTHERS

DEREK WALCOTT

For Peter Walcott

Ti-Jean and His Brothers was first performed at the Little Carib Theatre, Port of Spain, Trinidad, in 1958, with the following cast:

GROS JEAN	William Webb
MI-JEAN	Horace James
TI-JEAN	Freddie Kissoon
MOTHER	Jean Herbert, Veronica Jenkin
BOLOM	Russell Winston
PAPA BOIS	
PLANTER	} Errol Jones
DEVIL	
FROG	Bertrand Henry
MUSICIANS	John Henderson, Gene Lawrence, Colin Laird, Michael Warren

Ti-Jean and His Brothers was revived by the Trinidad Theatre Workshop in June 1970 at the Town Hall, Port of Spain, with original music by Andre Tanker and with the following cast:

CRICKET	Adele Bynoe
FROG	Hamilton Parris
BIRD	Roslyn Rappaport
GROS JEAN	Claude Reid
MI-JEAN	Stanley Marshall
BOLOM	Belinda Barnes
TI-JEAN	Ellsworth Primus
MOTHER	Ormine Wright
PAPA BOIS	
PLANTER	} Albert LeVeau
DEVIL	

CHARACTERS

CRICKET
FROG
FIREFLY
BIRD
GROS JEAN
MI-JEAN
TI-JEAN
MOTHER
BOLOM
OLD MAN, or PAPA BOIS
PLANTER
DEVIL

PROLOGUE

*Evening. Rain. The heights of a forest. A Cricket, a Frog, a Firefly, a
Bird. Left, a hut with bare table, an empty bowl, stools. The Mother
waiting.*

FROG:
>   Greek-croak, Greek-croak.

CRICKET:
>   Greek-croak, Greek-croak.

(*The others join.*)

FROG (*sneezing*):
>   Aeschylus me!
>   All that rain and no moon tonight.

CRICKET:
>   The moon always there even fighting the rain
>   Creek-crak, it is cold, but the moon always there
>   And Ti-Jean in the moon just like the story.

(*Bird passes.*)

CRICKET:
>   Before you fly home, listen,
>   The cricket cracking a story
>   A story about the moon.

FROG:
>   If you look in the moon,
>   Though no moon is here tonight,
>   There is a man, no, a boy,
>   Bent by a weight of faggots
>   He carried on his shoulder,
>   A small dog trotting with him.
>   That is Ti-Jean the hunter,
>   He got the heap of sticks
>   From the old man of the forest
>   They calling Papa Bois,
>   Because he beat the devil,

95

God put him in that height
To be the sun's right hand
And light the evil dark,
But as the bird so ignorant
I will start the tale truly.

(*Music.*)

Well, one time it had a mother,
That mother had three sons.
The first son was Gros Jean.
That son he was the biggest,
His arm was hard as iron,
But he was very stupid.

(*Enter Gros Jean, a bundle of faggots in one hand, an axe over his shoulder, moving in an exaggerated march to music. The creatures laugh.*)

FROG:
The name of the second son,
They was calling him Mi-Jean,
In size, the second biggest,
So only half as stupid; now,
He was a fisherman, but
Always studying book, and
What a fisherman; for
When he going and fish,
Always forgetting the bait,
So between de bait and debate . . .

CRICKET:
Mi boug qui tait cooyon!
(Look man who was a fool!)

(*Roll of drums. Comic quatro, martial. Enter Mi-Jean from the opposite side, carrying a book in one hand and a fishing net over his shoulder. Halfway across the stage he flings the net casually, still reading.*)

BIRD:

How poor their mother was?

(*Sad music on flute.*)

FROG:

Oh that was poverty, bird!
Old hands dried up like claws
Heaping old sticks on sticks,
too weak to protect her nest.
Look, the four of that family

(*Light shows the hut.*)

Lived in a little house,
Made up of wood and thatch,
On the forehead of the mountain,
Where night and day was rain,
Mist, cloud white as cotton
Caught in the dripping branches;
Where sometimes it was so cold
The frog would stop its singing

(*The Frog stops. Five beats. Resumes.*)

The cricket would stop rattling
And the wandering firefly
That lights the tired woodsman
Home through the raining trees
Could not strike a damp light
To star the wanderer home!

(*The music stops. The brothers Gros Jean and Mi-Jean put their arms
around each other, and to heavy drums tramp home.*)

CRICKET:

I damned sorry for that mother.

FROG:

Aie, cricket, you croak the truth!
The life of an old woman
With her husband cold in earth,
Where the bamboo leaves lie lightly,

And smell of mouldering flesh,
How well I know that story!
Near where the mother was,
Across the wet and melancholy
Mountain where her hut was, O God,
The Devil used to live!

(*Crash of cymbals. Shrieks, thunder. The animals cower as the Devil with his troop of fiends, the Werewolf, the Diablesse, the Bolom, somersault and dance across the stage. The sky is red.*)

DEVIL:

> *Bai Diable-là manger un 'ti mamaille!*
> (Give the Devil a child for dinner!)

DEVILS:

> *Un, deux, trois 'ti mamaille!*
> (One, two, three little children!)

(*They whirl around the stage, leaping, chanting, then as suddenly go off.*)

BIRD:

> Wow!
> Were they frightened of him?

FROG:

> If they were frightened?
> They were frightened of his skin,
> Powdery as leprosy,
> Like the pock-marked moon,
> Afraid of his dead eye,
> That had no fire in it . . .

CRICKET:

> Of the terrible thunder
> In his wood-shaking throat!

(*Roar of devils off-stage.*)

FROG:

> Just hear them in the hut . . .

(Sad flute, as the light comes up on the three sons around the knees of the old woman.)

GROS JEAN:

> One time again it have nothing to eat,
> But one dry bread to break;
> I went out to chop some wood
> To make a nice fire,
> But the wood was too damp,
> So I didn't use the axe
> As I didn't want it to get wet;
> If it get wet it get rusty.

MI-JEAN:

> Sense!
> I went out to do fishing
> For crayfish by the cold stones,
> In the cold spring in the ferns,
> But when I get there so,
> I find I lack bait,

(Rising solemnly.)

> Now for man to catch fish,
> That man must have bait,
> But the best bait is fish,
> Yet I cannot catch no fish
> Without I first have bait,
> As the best bait for fish
> Is to catch fish with fish,
> So I . . .

GROS JEAN:

> Mi-Jean is a fool,
> Reading too much damn book.

MOTHER:

> My sons, do not quarrel,
> Here all of us are starving,
> While the planter is eating

From plates painted golden,
Forks with silver tongues,
The brown flesh of birds,
And the white flesh of fish,
What did you do today,
My last son Ti-Jean?

TI-JEAN:
  Maman, m'a fait un rien.
  (Mama, I didn't do a thing.)

GROS JEAN:
  We do all the damned work.

MI-JEAN:
  We do all the damn thinking.

GROS JEAN:
  And he sits there like a prince.

MI-JEAN:
  As useless as a bone.

GROS JEAN and MI-JEAN (*jeering*):
  Maman, m'a fait un rien!
  Maman, m'a fait un rien!

MOTHER:
  Wait, and God will send us something.

GROS JEAN:
  God forget where he put us.

MI-JEAN:
  God too irresponsible.

MOTHER:
  Children!

(*Weird music. The Bolom or Foetus rolls in unheard, somersaults around the hut, then waits. Sound of wind, rain, shriek of insects.*)

Children, listen,
There is something listening
Outside of the door!

GROS JEAN:
I don't hear nothing.

MI-JEAN:
I hear only the rain,
Falling hard on the leaves,
And the wind down the throat
Of the gorge with the spring,
The crickets and the bull-frog,
And maybe one frightened bird.

MOTHER (*standing*):
I tell you there is something
Outside of the door,
I tell you from experience
I know when evil comes.
It is not the wind, listen!

(*The Bolom imitates a child crying.*)

MI-JEAN:
A young child out in the forest.

GROS JEAN:
Looking for its mother.

MOTHER:
The Devil has sent us
Another of his angels!
I prayed to God all day,
While I scrubbed the hut bare,
On the knuckles of my knees
All day in the hungry house;
Now God has sent me evil,
Who can understand it?
Death, death is coming nearer.

GROS JEAN:
>Line the step with fine sand
>To keep the evil out!

MI-JEAN:
>Turn over, Mother, the hem of your skirt!

GROS JEAN and MI-JEAN:
>Let two of our fingers form in one crucifix!

(*Ti-Jean steps outside.*)

MOTHER:
>Spirit that is outside,
>With the voice of a child
>Crying out in the rain,
>What do you want from the poor?

(*Ti-Jean searches carefully.*)

BOLOM:
>I have a message for a woman with three sons.

MOTHER:
>Child of the Devil, what is your message?

BOLOM:
>Send the first of your sons outside for it,
>They must die in that order. And let the youngest
>Return into the hut.

(*Ti-Jean steps back into the hut.*)

MOTHER:
>We can hear you in the wind,
>What do you want of me?

(*A weird light shows the Bolom. Shrieks.*)

ALL:
>Where are you? Where is it?
>Hit it! There! Where is it?

BOLOM (*leaping, hiding*):
> Here, in the bowl!
> Here, sitting on a stool!
> Here, turning in a cup!
> Here, crawling up your skirt!

MOTHER:
> I have done you no harm, child.

BOLOM:
> A woman did me harm,
> Called herself mother,
> The fear of her hatred
> A cord round my throat!

MOTHER (*turning, searching*):
> Look, perhaps it is luckiest
> Never to be born,
> To the horror of this life
> Crowded with shadows,
> Never to have known
> That the sun will go out,
> The green leaf rust,
> The strong tree be stricken
> And the roaring spring quail;
> Peace to you, unborn,
> You can find comfort here.
> Let a mother touch you,
> For the sake of her kind.

BOLOM (*shrieks, dancing back*):
> Whatever flesh touches me,
> Withers me into mortality;
> Not till your sons die, Mother,
> Shall this shape feel this life.

GROS JEAN (*seizes axe*):
> Kill it, then, kill it.

MI-JEAN:
>Curse it back to the womb.

DEMON'S VOICE:
>*Faire ca mwen di ous!*
>(Do what I commanded!)

BOLOM:
>I hear the voice of my master.

DEMON'S VOICE:
>*Bolom, faire tout ça mwen dire ous!*
>(Child, do all that I ordered you!)

BOLOM:
>Listen, creature of gentleness,
>Old tree face marked with scars,
>And the wounds of bearing children,
>Whom the earth womb will swallow,
>This is the shriek
>Of a child which was strangled,
>Who never saw the earth light
>Through the hinge of the womb,
>Strangled by a woman,
>Who hated my birth,
>Twisted out of shape,
>Deformed past recognition,
>Tell me then, Mother,
>Would you care to see it?

(Bolom moves out of the light, shrieking.)

GROS JEAN:
>Let us see you!

MOTHER:
>The sight of such horror, though you are brave,
>Would turn you to stone, my strong son, Gros Jean.

MI-JEAN:
>Let us reason with you.

MOTHER:
> My son, the thing may be a ball of moving fire,
> A white horse in the leaves, or a clothful of skin,
> Found under a tree, you cannot explain that!

BOLOM:
> Save your understanding for the living,
> Save your pity for the dead,
> I am neither living nor dead,
> A puny body, a misshapen head.

MOTHER:
> What does your white master
> The Devil want from us?

BOLOM:
> The house looks warm, old woman,
> Love keeps the house warm,
> From the cold wind and cold rain;
> Though you bar up the door,
> I can enter the house.

(*Thunder.*)

MOTHER:
> Enter! You are welcome.

(*She flings open the door.*)

GROS JEAN and MI-JEAN:
> Shut the door, shut the door!

(*Crash of cymbals. The Bolom rolls in a blue light towards the hut, then enters; all freeze in fear.*)

BOLOM:
> The Devil my master
> Who owns half the world,
> In the kingdom of night,
> Has done all that is evil
> Butchered thousands in war,
> Whispered his diseases

In the ears of great statesmen,
Invented human justice,
Made anger, pride, jealousy,
And weakened prayer;
Still cannot enjoy
Those vices he created.
He is dying to be human.
So he sends you this challenge!
To all three of your sons,
He says through my voice,
That if anyone on earth

(*Devils' voices chanting.*)

Anyone human
Can make him feel anger,
Rage, and human weakness,
He will reward them,
He will fill that bowl,
With a shower of sovereigns,
You shall never more know hunger,
But fulfillment, wealth, peace.

(*Increased drum roll to climax.*)

But if any of your sons
Fails to give him these feelings,
For he never was human,
Then his flesh shall be eaten,
For he is weary of the flesh
Of the fowls of the air,
And the fishes in the sea,
But whichever of your sons
Is brave enough to do this,
Then that one shall inherit
The wealth of my prince.
And once they are dead, woman,
I too shall feel life!

(*Exits.*)

DEVILS' VOICES (*off*):
Bai Diable-là manger un 'ti mamaille,
Un, deux, trois 'ti mamaille!
Bai Diable-là manger un 'ti mamaille,
Un,
> *deux,*
>> *trois . . .*

(Give the Devil a child for dinner,
One, two, three little children!
Give the Devil a child for dinner,
One,
> two,
>> three . . .)

(*Fadeout.*)

SCENE ONE

Daybreak. The hut. The Mother and her sons asleep. Gros Jean rises, packs a bundle. His Mother stirs and watches. He opens the door.

MOTHER:
You will leave me just so,
My eldest son?

GROS JEAN:
Is best you didn't know.

MOTHER:
Woman life is so. Watching and losing.

GROS JEAN: *Maman,* the time obliged to come I was to leave the house, go down the tall forest, come out on the high road, and find what is man work. Is big man I reach now, not no little boy again. Look, feel this arm, but to split trees is nothing. I have an arm of iron, and have nothing I fraid.

MOTHER:
> The arm which digs a grave
> Is the strongest arm of all.
> Your grandfather, your father,
> Their muscles like brown rivers
> Rolling over rocks.
> Now, they bury in small grass,
> Just the jaws of the ant
> Stronger than them now.

GROS JEAN:
> I not even fraid that. You see,
> Is best you still was sleeping?
> I don't want to wake my brothers.
> Ti-Jean love me and will frighten.
> Mi-Jean will argue and make me remain.
> The sun tapping me on my shoulder.

MOTHER:
> When you go down the tall forest, Gros Jean,
> Praise God who make all things; ask direction
> Of the bird, and the insects, imitate them;
> But be careful of the hidden nets of the Devil,
> Beware of a wise man called Father of the Forest,
> The Devil can hide in several features,
> A woman, a white gentleman, even a bishop.
> Strength, *ça pas tout*, there is patience besides;
> There always is something stronger than you.
> If is not man, animal, is God or demon.

GROS JEAN:
> *Maman*, I know all that already.

MOTHER:
> Then God bless you, Gros Jean.

GROS JEAN:
> The world not the same it was in your time,
> Tell my brothers I gone. A man have to go.

(*Marches from hut. Martial flute, quatro, drum.*)

GROS JEAN (*sings*):
> There's a time for every man
> To leave his mother and father
> To leave everybody he know
> And march to the grave he one!

(*Enter the animals, hopping around him.*)

> So the time has come for me
> To leave me mother and father
> To add my force to the world
> And go to the grave me one!

(*The Frog is in his path. He aims a kick.*)

> Get out of my way, you slimy bastard! How God could
> make such things? Jump out under my foot, cricket, you
> know you have no bones! *Gibier! Gibier, montrez-moi sortir!*
> Bird-o, bird-o, show me a good short-cut, be quick!

(*Suddenly the Bird, Cricket and the Frog all scurry shrieking,
croaking. The Old Man enters limping and rests a bundle of faggots
down. Gros Jean watches. The Old Man lifts a corner of his robe to
scratch a cloven, hairy hoof. Gros Jean emerges.*)

GROS JEAN:
> Bon jour, vieux papa.

OLD MAN:
> Bon matin, Gros Jean.

GROS JEAN:
> What you have with your foot?

OLD MAN:
> Fleas, fleas, boy.

(*Covers it quickly.*)

GROS JEAN:
> Is man I am now. Chiggers in your flesh?
> Is man I am, papa, and looking for success.

OLD MAN:
> The flesh of the earth is rotting. Worms.

GROS JEAN:
> Which way, papa?

OLD MAN:
> I cannot tell you the way to success;
> I can only show you, Gros Jean,
> One path through the forest.

GROS JEAN:
> I have no time to waste. I have an arm of iron,
> It have nothing, I fraid, man, beast, or beast-man,
> And more quick I get what I want, more better.

OLD MAN:
> I think strength should have patience. Look at me today.
> I was a strong woodman, now I burn coals,
> I'm as weak as ashes. And nearly deaf. Come nearer.

GROS JEAN (*advances calmly*):
> What you would say is the quickest way?

OLD MAN:
> The quickest way to what?

GROS JEAN:
> To what counts in this world.

OLD MAN:
> What counts in this world is money and power.

GROS JEAN:
> I have an arm of iron, only money I missing.

OLD MAN:
> Then I can't advise you.

GROS JEAN:
> You old and you have experience.

So don't be selfish with it.
Or you know what I'll do.

(*Grabs him, hurls him down, axe uplifted.*)

Chop you and bury you in the bamboo leaves!

OLD MAN:
With your arm of iron, the first thing to kill is wisdom?

GROS JEAN:
That's right, papa.

OLD MAN:
Well, the Devil always wants help.

GROS JEAN:
The Devil boasts that he never get vex.

OLD MAN (*rising*):
Easy, easy son, I'll help you if you wait,
Just let me adjust the edge of my skirt.
Well, I was coming through the forest now
And I passed by the white spring, and I saw
Some poor souls going to work for the white planter.
He'll work you like the devil, but that's what you want,
You and your impatience and arm cast in iron,
So turn to the right, go through the bamboo forest,
Over the black rocks, then the forest will open,
And you will see the sky, below that a valley,
And smoke, and a white house that is empty,
The old fellow is hiring harvesters today.
Remember an iron arm may rust, flesh is deciduous.
There's your short-cut, Gros Jean, make the most of it.

GROS JEAN:
Next time don't be so selfish.

(*Exit Gros Jean, marching.*)

OLD MAN (*sings, gathering bundle*):
Who is the man who can speak to the strong?

Where is the fool who can talk to the wise?
Men who are dead now have learnt this long,
Bitter is wisdom that fails when it tries.

(*To the audience:*)

Ah well, there's wood to cut, fires to light, smoke to
wrinkle an old man's eyes, and a shrivelling skin to keep
warm. There went the spirit of war: an iron arm and a
clear explanation, and might is still right, thank God, for
God is the stronger. But get old father forest from the path
of the fable, for there's wood to cut, a nest of twittering
beaks to feed with world-eating worms. Oh, oh, oh.

(*The creatures creep after him timidly.*)

For they all eat each other, and that's natural law,
So remember the old man in the middle of the forest.

(*He turns suddenly, then hobbles after them.*)

Eat and eat one another! It's another day. Ha, ha! Wah!
Wah!

(*They flee. He goes out.*)

GROS JEAN (*in another part of the wood*): I have an arm of iron,
and that's true, but I here since the last two days working
for this damn white man, and I don't give a damn if he
watching me. You know what I doing here with this bag
and this piece of stick? Well, I go tell you. While I smoke
a pipe. Let me just sit down, and I won't lose my
patience. (*He sits on a log.*) Well, you remember how I
leave home, and then bounce up this old man who put
me on to a work? Remember what the old son of a leaf-
gathering beggar said? He said that working for the Devil
was the shortest way to success. Well, I walked up
through the bush then I come onto a large field. Estate-
like, you know. Sugar, tobacco, and a hell of a big white
house where they say the Devil lives. Ay-ay.

So two next black fellers bring me up to him. Big white
man, his hand cold as an axe blade and his mind twice as

sharp. So he say, "Gros Jean, we has a deal to make, right?" So I say, "Sure, boss!" He say the one that get the other one vex, the one who show the first sign of anger will be eaten rrruuunnnhhh, just like that, right? You think I stupid? I strong, I have some sense and my name not Gros Jean for nothing. That was two days ago. Well, Jesus, a man ain't rest since then! The first job I had, I had was to stand up in a sugar-cane field and count all the leaves of the cane. That take me up till four o'clock. I count all the leaves and then divide by the number of stalks. I must tell you there had times when I was getting vex but the old iron arm fix me, because there is patience in strength. The Devil ain't say anything. About seven o'clock, he tell me to go and catch about seventy fireflies. Well, you must try and catch fireflies! Is not easy. Had a time when I do so once, one whap with the hand! thinking was a bunch but was nothing, only stars! So in the middle of all that, this man come up to me and say, what's the matter, Joe, he always like he don't know my name, but I is me, Gros Jean, the strongest! And if you ain't know my name, you best don't call me nothing. Say, "What's matter, Mac? You vex or sumpin?" So I say, "No, I ain't vex!" Well, is two days now, and I ain't get a cent. I so tired I giddy. But I giving the old iron arm a rest from cramp, and breaking a little smoke. After all! If was only sensible work, if a man could get the work that suit him, cotton or sugar or something important! Plus he getting eighty-five percent of the profit? Shucks, man, that ain't fair. Besides I could just bust his face, you know. But me mother ain't bring me up so. After all, man, after all, a man have to rest man. Shime!

(*Enter Devil masked as a Planter.*)

PLANTER: Well, how's it progressing, Joe, tired?

GROS JEAN: From where you was and now you come you hear me say I fagged? (*Slowly:*) And Gros Jean is the name, boss.

PLANTER: Tobacco break? Whistle's blown past lunch, boy.

GROS JEAN: I taking a five here, chief. Black people have to rest too, and once I rest, chief, I do more work than most, right?

PLANTER: That's right, Mac.

GROS JEAN (*gritting his teeth*): Gros Jean . . . Gros . . . Jean . . . chief . . . !

PLANTER: You sound a bit annoyed to me.

GROS JEAN (*with a painful, fixed grin from now on*): Have your fun. I know I ain't nobody yet, chief, but an old man tell me to have patience. And I ain't let you down yet, chief, hasn't I?

PLANTER: That's right, Gros Chien, Gros Jean, Gros Jean, sorry. Can't tell one face from the next out here. How's the work then? (*Pacing up and down.*)

GROS JEAN: Chief, why you don't take a rest too somewhat? You have all this land, all this big house and so forth, people working for you as if is ants self, but is only work, work, work in your mind, ent you has enough?

PLANTER (*looking at his watch*): Other people want what I have, Charley, and other people have more. Can't help myself, Joe, it's some sort of disease, and it spreads right down to the common man.

GROS JEAN: I not no common man, boss. People going hear about Gros Jean. Because I come from that mountain forest, don't mean I can't come like you, or because I black. One day all this could be mine!

PLANTER: Yes, yes. Well anyway, Horace, time is flying, and I want these leaves checked, counted, filed, and classified by weight and texture, and then stacked . . . What's the matter, Francis?

GROS JEAN (*to audience*): You see how he provoking me, you don't think I should curse his . . . (*Turns, bites hard on pipe, grinning.*) Look, I haven't let you down yet, boss, have I? I mean to say I take two three hours to catch your goat you send me to catch. I mean not so? Wait, chief, wait, listen . . . I ain't vex, boss. Ha-ha!

PLANTER: Sit down, Joe, relax, you can't take it with you, they say, only time is money, and the heights that great men reached, etc., and genius is ninety per cent perspiration and so forth . . . So, sit down, waste time, but I thought you were in a hurry . . . Henry.

GROS JEAN: Boss. (*Smiling.*) You really impatianate, yes. Ha-ha! I mean I don't follow you, chief. After I count and carry all the cane leaves for you, ain't I, and look—when the wind blow them wrong side I ain't say nothing, and I'm smiling ain't I? (*Relaxes his expression, then resumes.*) I'm smiling because I got confidence in the old iron arm, ain't it? And if I do it and have time to spare is the work and pay that matter, and is all you worried about, *big shot!* Ain't it? Excuse me, I mean to say, I'm smiling ain't I?

PLANTER: Sorry, sorry, Gros Jean, sometimes we people in charge of industry forget that you people aren't machines. I mean people like you, Hubert . . .

(*Gros Jean is about to sit.*)

GROS JEAN (*rising*): Gros Jean, chief, Gros Jean . . . Ha-ha!

PLANTER: Gros Jean, very well . . . (*Pause.*) Have your smoke. (*Pause.*) Plenty of time. It might rain, people may be stealing from me now. The market is unsteady this year. (*Pause.*) But we're human. (*Pause.*) You don't know what it means to work hard, to have to employ hundreds of people. (*Embracing him.*) You're worth more to me, Benton, than fifty men. So you should smoke, after all. (*Pause.*) And such a pleasant disposition, always smiling. (*Pause, steps back.*) Just like a skull. (*Long pause.*) But remember, Mervin, I'd like you to try and finish this, you see I have a contract and the harder you work the more I . . .

GROS JEAN (*exploding, smashing pipe in anger*): Jesus Christ
what this damn country coming to a man cyant even get
a goddamned smoke? (*He tries to grin.*) I ent vex, I ent
vex, chief. Joke, joke, boss . . .

(*Explosion. When the smoke clears, the Devil, his Planter's mask
removed, is sitting on the log, calmly nibbling the flesh from a bone.*)

DEVILS' VOICES (*off*):
    Bai Diable-là manger un 'ti mamaille
      Un!
    (Give the Devil a child for dinner
      One! . . .)

(*Blackout.*)

SCENE TWO

*Music. Dawn. The forest. A cross marked "Gros Jean." The creatures
foraging. Enter Mi-Jean walking fast and reading, a net slung over
his shoulder.*

BIRD (*to flute*):
    Mi-Jean, Mi-Jean, *bon jour,* M'sieu Mi-Jean.

(*The creatures dance.*)

MI-JEAN (*closes the book*):
    Bird, you disturbing me!
    Too much whistling without sense,
    Is animal you are, so please know your place.

CRICKET:
    Where you going, Mi-Jean?

MI-JEAN (*to the audience*):
    But see my cross, *oui,* ay-ay!
    Since from what time cricket
    Does ask big man their business?

FROG:

> You going to join your brother?
> You are a man's size now.

MI-JEAN (*again to the audience*):

> Well, confusion on earth, frog could talk!
> Gros Jean was one man, I is a next. Frog,
> You ever study your face in
> The mirror of a pool?

BIRD:

> Mi-Jean, Mi-Jean,
> Your brother is a little heap
> Of white under the bamboo leaves,
> Every morning the black beetles
> More serious than a hundred priests,
> Frowning like fifty undertakers
> Come and bear a piece away
> To build a chapel from his bones. Look, look!

(*Bird shows the cross. Mi-Jean kneels and peers through his spectacles.*)

CRICKET:

> Every morning I sit here,
> And see the relics of success,
> An arm of iron turned to rust,
> Not strong enough to stir the dirt.

FROG:

> Gros Jean was strong, but had no sense.

MI-JEAN (*rising and dusting his clothes*):

> He had the sin called over-confidence!
> Listen, I . . .

BIRD:

> Run, run, Papa Bois, Papa Bois . . .

(*All run off.*)

OLD MAN:
> *Bon jour*, Mi-Jean, Mi-Jean, *le philosophe*.

MI-JEAN (*to the audience*):
> When my mother told me goodbye in tears,
> She said, no one can know what the Devil wears.

(*To the Old Man:*)

> *Bon jour*, Papa Bois, how come you know my name?

OLD MAN: Who in the heights, in any small hut hidden in the ferns, where the trees are always weeping, or any two men are ploughing on a wet day, wrapped in old cloaks, or down in the villages among the smoke and rum, has not heard of Mi-Jean the jurist, and the gift of his tongue, his prowess in argument, Mi-Jean, the *avocat*, the fisherman, the litigant? Come, come, sir, don't be modest! I've been sitting there on the cold, crusty log, rough as the armoured bark of a frog, waiting to exchange knowledge with you. Ah, your brother's grave! How simple he was! Well, I'm half-blind, but I see you have one virtue more than your brother, fear. Nothing lives longer than brute strength, sir, except it is human cowardice. Come nearer, come nearer, and tell us why you left home? Sit down, you're among equals.

MI-JEAN:
> I good just where I am.
> I on my way to the sea
> To become a rich captain,
> The land work too hard.
> Then to become a lawyer.

OLD MAN (*softly singing*):
> *On land on sea no man is free,*
> *All meet death, the enemy.* I see,
> Hence the net, the net and the book.

MI-JEAN:
> What?

OLD MAN:
> I say hence the book,
> Hence the net, and the book.

MI-JEAN:
> *Ça c'est* hence?
> (What is "hence"?)

OLD MAN:
> Same as whereas, and hereunto affixed.
> These are terms used in tautology and law.

MI-JEAN (*nodding blankly; pause; then*):
> I see you have a cow-foot. Ain't that so?

OLD MAN:
> Yes, yes. A cow's foot. You have an eye for detail!
> Born with it, actually. Source of embarrassment.
> Would you like some tobacco? What are you reading?

MI-JEAN (*opens the book*):
> This book have every knowledge it have;
> I checking up on man with cow-foot, boss,
> In the section call religion, and tropical superstition.
> *Bos* . . . *Bovis* . . . Cow . . . foot . . . foot, boss? Boss foot?
> > *Bovis?*

OLD MAN:
> Outside in the world they are wiser now, Mi-Jean;
> They don't believe in evil or the prevalence of devils,
> Believe me, philosopher, nobody listens to old men;
> Sit down next to me and have a bit of tobacco.
> And since you need knowledge, I'll give you advice . . .

MI-JEAN (*still reading*):
> I don't smoke and I don't drink,
> I keep my head clear, and advice,
> I don't need none, but will listen.

(*Shuts the book.*)

This book is Latin mainly.
It have *bos*, meaning cow,
and *pes*, meaning foot,
Boss' foot, *bospes*, cow-heel perhaps,
It have plenty recipe
But it don't give the source! (*Sighs loudly.*) So!
Yes, apart from wisdom, I have no vices.

OLD MAN:
Life without sin. How about women?

MI-JEAN:
The downfall of man! I don't care for women,
Women don't have no brain. Their foot just like yours.

OLD MAN:
You believe in the Devil?
Oh, why don't you sit nearer,
Haven't you ever seen a cow-heel before?

MI-JEAN:
Not under a skirt, no. (*Sighs loudly.*) Yes!
I believe in the Devil, yes,
Or so my mother make me,
And is either that, papa,
Or not believe in God.
And when I meet this devil,
Whatever shape he taking,
And I know he is not you,
Since he would never expose
His identity so early,
I will do all that he commands,
But you know how I will beat him,

(*Sits near the Old Man.*)

With silence, and a smile.

(*He smiles.*)

Too besides when I meet him,

I will know if God exist,
We calling that in philosophy

(*Checks in the book.*)

We calling that in big knowledge,
Ah, polarities of belief,
When the existence of one object
Compels that of the other,
Bon Dieu, what terms, what terms!

(*Sighs loudly, rests the book down.*)

Yes. Silence shall be my defence.

(*He sings "The Song of Silence":*)

I

Within this book of wisdom
Hear what the wise man say:
The man who is wise is dumb
And lives another day,
You cannot beat the system
Debate is just a hook,
Open your mouth, de bait in!
And is you they going to juck

Chorus:
So when things dark, go blind
When nothing left, go deaf
When the blows come, be dumb
And hum, hum.

II

In Chapter Five from para-
Graph three, page 79,
This book opines how Socra-
Tes would have been better off blind.
God gave him eyes like all of we,
But he, he had to look.

The next thing, friends, was jail, *oui!*
Hemlock and him lock up!

Chorus:
So when things dark, go blind, etc.

III

The third set of instruction
This self-said book declares
Is that the wise man's function
Is how to shut his ears
Against riot and ruction
That try to climb upstairs.
If you can hear, don't listen!
If you can see, don't look!
If you must talk, be quiet!
Or your mouth will dig your grave.

(*While he sings his song, the Old Man goes behind a grove of bamboo, leisurely removes his robe and his mask, under which is the mask of the Devil; then he changes into the mask and clothes of the Planter.*)

PLANTER (*he sits on the log, legs crossed, smiling throughout the scene*): Ah, finished all the work I gave you, Mi-Jean? (*Mi-Jean nods.*) And menial work didn't bore you, a thinker? (*Mi-Jean nods.*) You're not one for small-talk, are you? (*Mi-Jean nods.*) Did you catch the wild goat? (*Mi-Jean nods yes.*) Frisky little bugger, wasn't he? Yes, sir, that's one hell of a goat. Some kid, what? Clever, however. How many canes were there on the estate? (*Mi-Jean uses ten fingers repeatedly.*)

Don't waste words, eh? All right, all right. Look, you don't mind a little chat while we work, do you? A bit of a gaff lightens labour. Good Lord, man, you've been here for over two days and haven't had the common decency to even pass the time of day. Where did you get your reputation as a bush lawyer, I mean it's only manners, blast it. (*Mi-Jean cocks his head at the Planter.*)

Oh, don't flatter yourself, young man, I'm not annoyed. It takes two to make a quarrel. Shut up, by all means. (*Rises.*) Now, before it gets dark, I want you to come up to the house, check and polish the silver, rearrange my library and . . . (*The goat bleats. Mi-Jean frowns.*)

Aha, looks like the old goat's broken loose again, son. Better drop what you're not doing and catch it before it's dark. (*Mi-Jean rises rapidly, runs off, returns.*) Ah, now you're smiling again, fixed him this time, haven't you? (*The goat bleats.*) Not quite, cunning animal, that goat, couldn't have tied him. (*Mi-Jean dashes out, annoyed, returns.*) Fast worker! (*The goat bleats.*)

Look, before you dash off, I'd like to say here and now . . . (*the goat bleating as Mi-Jean, mumbling, smiling, points off*) that I do admire your cheery persistence, your resigned nonchalance, so let me demonstrate something. There's a special kind of knot, and there's an end to that. Hence you take the rope thus, and whereas the goat being hereto affixed to the . . . (*goat bleating, Mi-Jean raging inside*) but if that doesn't fix him, then my recommendation is . . .

MI-JEAN: Look!

PLANTER: Yes?

MI-JEAN: I think I know what I'm doing . . . sir . . .

PLANTER (*above the sound of bleating*): Oh, sure, sure. But I was simply trying to explain just to help you out, that . . . (*Goat bleats.*) . . . You see? He's gone off again! Just a little more patience . . . (*Mi-Jean is about to run off.*) It's simply a question of how you tie this knot, don't you see? (*Mi-Jean, collecting himself, nods, then tiredly smiles.*) I mean, I've seen dumber men, not you, fail at this knot you know, it's just a matter of know-how, not really knowledge, just plain skill . . . (*Mi-Jean nodding, nodding.*) You look the kind of fellow who doesn't mind a bit of expert advice. (*Goat bleats furiously.*) And you'd better hurry up before it gets dark. Wait, remember how to tie the knot.

MI-JEAN (*under control, nods*): Yes, I remember. (*Runs off, crosses the stage several times in a chase.*)

PLANTER (*walks up and down in a rage*): Well, what the hell, I thought I had him there, he's no fool, that's certain, for the Devil comes in through apertures. He doesn't know right from wrong, and he's not interested. The only entrance I could have got through his mouth, I tried to leave ajar, but the fool bolted it completely. There he goes chasing the bloody goat like a simpleton, and not even shouting at it. Good old Master Speak No Evil. I hope he breaks his God-supported neck, the dummy! (*He sits.*) Here comes the comedy again, an eloquent goat and a tongueless biped!

(*The goat cavorts across and around the stage to merry music, with Mi-Jean behind him waving a rope and the net. Mi-Jean collapses.*)

PLANTER: Tough life, eh? (*Mi-Jean groans, nodding.*) Don't let it get you down. (*Goat bleats.*)

MI-JEAN: That goat certainly making a plethora of cacophony.

PLANTER: It's only a poor animal, in its own rut.

MI-JEAN (*smiling*): Men are lustiferous animals also, but at least they have souls.

PLANTER: Ah, the philosopher! The contemplative! An opinion at last! A man is no better than an animal. The one with two legs makes more noise and that makes him believe he can think. It is talk that makes men think they have souls. There's no difference, only in degree. No animal, but man, dear boy, savours such a variety of vices. He knows no season for lust, he is a kneeling hypocrite, who on four legs, like a penitent capriped, prays to his maker, but is calculating the next vice. That's my case!

MI-JEAN: Nonsensical verbiage! *Bettise!*

PLANTER: It's not, you know, and you're getting annoyed.

MI-JEAN (*shakes his head*): You can't get me into no argument! I have brains, but won't talk. (*Long pause.*) All I say is that man is divine!

PLANTER: You're more intelligent than the goat, you think?

MI-JEAN: I not arguing! Anything you want.

PLANTER (*rises*): Honestly, I'd like to hear what you think. You're the kind of chap I like to talk to. Your brother was a sort of politician, but you're a thinker. (*Mi-Jean, rising, is about to lecture. The goat bleats.*) Steady-on. For all we know, that may be poetry. Which Greek scholar contends in his theory of metempsychosis that the souls of men may return into animals?

MI-JEAN: I never study Greek, but I . . . (*Goat bleats. Mi-Jean pauses.*) I was saying that I never study no Greek but I'd . . . (*Goat bleats.*) It getting on like to have sense, eh?

PLANTER: Why not?

MI-JEAN: Listen, I ent mind doing what you proposed, any-thing physical, because that's ostentatious, but when you start theorising that there's an equality of importance in the creatures of this earth, when you animadvertently imbue mere animals with an animus or soul, I have to call you a crooked-minded pantheist . . . (*Goat bleats, sounding like "Hear, hear!"*) Oh, shut up, you can't hear two people talking? No, I'm not vexed, you know, but . . . (*Goat bleats.*)

PLANTER (*advancing towards him*): Your argument interests me. It's nice to see ideas getting you excited. But logically now. The goat, I contend, may be a genius in its own right. For all we know, this may be the supreme goat, the apogee of capripeds, the voice of human tragedy, the Greek . . .

MI-JEAN: Exaggerated hypothesis! Unsubstantiated!

PLANTER: Since the goat is mine, and if you allow me, for argument's sake, to pursue my premise, then if you get vexed at the goat, who represents my view, then you are vexed with me, and the contract must be fulfilled.

MI-JEAN: I don't mind talking to you, but don't insult me, telling me a goat have more sense than I, than me. Than both of we!

PLANTER (*embracing him*): Descendant of the ape, how eloquent you have become! How assured in logic! How marvellous in invention! And yet, poor shaving monkey, the animal in you is still in evidence, that goat . . . (*Goat sustains its bleating.*)

MI-JEAN: Oh, shut you damn mouth, both o'all you! I ain't care who right who wrong! I talking now! What you ever study? I ain't even finish making my points and all two of you interrupting, breach of legal practice! O God, I not vex, I not vex . . .

(*Planter removes his mask, and the Devil advances on Mi-Jean. Explosion. Blackout. The goat bleats once.*)

DEVILS' VOICES (*off*):
  Bai Diable-là manger un 'ti mamaille
  (Give the Devil a child for dinner)
      Un!
    (One!)
        Deux!
      (Two! . . .)

SCENE THREE

Dawn. The forest. Two crosses marked "Gros Jean," "Mi-Jean." The Old Man sits on the log, the creatures huddle near him. Ti-Jean, Mother, in the hut.

Devils' Voices (*off*):
> *Bai Diable-là manger un 'ti mamaille,*
> *Un, deux, trois 'ti mamaille!*
> *Bai Diable-là manger un 'ti mamaille,*
> *Un, deux, trois 'ti mamaille.*

Old Man:
> Aie! Feed the Devil the third, feed the Devil the third. Power is knowledge, knowledge is power, and the Devil devours them on the hour!

Devils:
> *Bai Diable-là manger un 'ti mamaille,*
> *Un, deux, trois 'ti mamaille!*

Old Man (*to audience*): Well, that's two good meals finished with a calm temper, and if all goes mortally, one more is to come. (*Shrieks, points to where Ti-Jean is consoling his Mother.*) Aie, ya, yie, a chicken is to come, a calf, a veal-witted young man, tender in flesh, soft in the head and bones, tenderer than old muscle power, and simpler than that net-empty atheist. For the next dish is man-wit, common sense. But I can wait, I can wait, gathering damp rotting faggots, aie!

Mother (*to flute*):
> If you leave me, my son,
> I have empty hands left,
> Nothing to grieve for.
> You are hardly a man,
> A stalk, bending in wind
> With no will of its own,
> Never proven your self
> In battle or in wisdom,
> I have kept you to my breast,
> As the last of my chickens,
> Not to feed the blind jaws
> Of the carnivorous grave.

TI-JEAN:

> You have told me yourself
> Our lives are not ours,
> That no one's life is theirs
> Husband or wife,
> Father or son,
> That our life is God's own.

MOTHER:

> You are hard, hard, Ti-Jean,
> O what can I tell you?
> I have never learnt enough.

TI-JEAN:

> You have taught me this strength,
> To do whatever we will
> And love God is enough.

MOTHER:

> I feel I shall never see you again.

TI-JEAN:

> To return what we love is our glory, our pain.

OLD MAN:

> Oh, enough of these sentiments, I'm hungry, and I'm
> cold!

TI-JEAN:

> Now pray for me, *maman*,
> The sun is in the leaves.

MOTHER:

> The first of my children
> Never asked for my strength,
> The second of my children
> Thought little of my knowledge,
> The last of my sons, now,
> Kneels down at my feet,
> Instinct be your shield,

> It is wiser than reason,
> Conscience be your cause
> And plain sense your sword.

(*The Bolom rolls towards the hut. Drums.*)

BOLOM:

> Old tree shaken of fruit,
> This green one must die.

MOTHER:

> Aie, I hear it, I hear it,
> The cry of the unborn!
> But then have I not given
> Birth and death to the dead?

(*The Bolom dances off, shrieking. Ti-Jean rises.*)

> Oh, Ti-Jean, you are so small,
> So small.

(*Exits.*)

TI-JEAN:

> Yes, I small, *maman*, I small,
> And I never learn from book,
> But, like the small boy, David.

(*Sings:*)

> I go bring down, bring down Goliath,
> Bring down below.
> Bring down, bring down Goliath,
> Bring down below.

(*He enters the forest.*)

TI-JEAN:

> Ah, *bon matin, compère Crapaud,*
> Still in your dressing-gown?

FROG:

> Ti-Jean, like your brothers you're making fun of me.

TI-JEAN:
Why should I laugh at the frog and his fine bass voice?

FROG:
You wouldn't call me handsome, would you?

TI-JEAN (*kneels among the creatures*):
Oh, I don't know, you have your own beauty.
Like the castanet music of the cricket over there.

CRICKET:
Crak, crak. Now say something nice to the firefly.

FIREFLY:
How can he? I don't look so hot in the daytime.

TI-JEAN:
But I have often mistaken you at night for a star.

(*Rises.*)

Now friends, which way is shortest to the Devil's estate?

FROG:
Beware of an old man whose name is wordly wisdom.

FIREFLY:
With a pile of sticks on his back.

CRICKET:
. . . and a foot cloven like a beast.

TI-JEAN:
If he is an old man, and mortal,
He will judge everything on earth
By his own sad experience.
God bless you, small things.
It's a hard life you have,
Living in the forest.

FIREFLY:
God preserve you for that.
Bird, take the tree and cry

If the old man comes through
That grove of dry bamboo.

(*Bird flies off.*)

CRICKET:
Crashing through the thicket
With the cleft hoof of a beast.

FIREFLY:
For though we eat each other,
I can't tempt that frog too close,
And we never see each other for dinner,
We do not do it from evil.

FROG:
True. Is a long time I never eat a firefly.

FIREFLY:
Watch it, watch it, brother,
You don't want heartburn, do you?

TI-JEAN:
No, it is not from evil.
What are these crosses?

CRICKET:
Nothing. Do not look, Ti-Jean.
Why must you fight the Devil?

TI-JEAN:
To know evil early, life will be simpler.

FROG:
Not so, Ti-Jean, not so. Go back.

(*Ti-Jean goes to the crosses, weeps.*)

BIRD:
Weep-weep-weep-weep-quick,
The old man is coming, quick.

FROG:
> If you need us, call us, brother, but
> You understand we must move.

(*Ti-Jean stands over the crosses.*)

OLD MAN: Ah, good morning, youngster! It's a damp, mournful walk through the forest, isn't it, and only the cheep of a bird to warm one. Makes old bones creak. Now it's drizzling. Damn it.

TI-JEAN: *Bon jou, vieux cor'*, I find the world pleasant in the early light.

OLD MAN: They say, the people of the forest, when the sun and rain contend for mastery, they say that the Devil is beating his wife. Know what I say? I say it brings rheumatism, I don't believe in the Devil. Eighty-eight years, and never seen his face.

TI-JEAN: Could you, being behind it?

OLD MAN: Eh? Eh? I'm deaf, come nearer. Come here and shelter. Good. Some people find me ugly, monstrous ugly. Even the small insects sometimes. The snake moves from me, and this makes me sad. I was a woodsman once, but look now. I burn wood into ashes. Let me sit on this log awhile. Tobacco?

TI-JEAN: No, thanks, sir.

OLD MAN: Tell me, boy, is your father living? Or your mother perhaps? You look frail as an orphan.

TI-JEAN: I think nothing dies. My brothers are dead but they live in the memory of my mother.

OLD MAN: You're very young, boy, to be talking so subtly. So you lost two brothers?

TI-JEAN: I said I had brothers, I never said how many. May I see that foot, father?

OLD MAN: In a while, in a while. No, I saw you looking at the two graves, so I presumed there were two. There were two, weren't there? Ah well, none can escape that evil that men call death.

TI-JEAN: Whatever God made, we must consider blessed. I'm going to look at your foot.

OLD MAN: Hold on, son. Whatever God made, we must consider blessed? Like the death of your mother?

TI-JEAN: Like the death of my mother.

OLD MAN: Like the vileness of the frog?

TI-JEAN (*advancing*): Like the vileness of the frog.

OLD MAN: Like the froth of the constrictor?

TI-JEAN: Like the froth of the constrictor. (*He is above the Old Man.*)

OLD MAN: Like the cloven cow's foot under an old man's skirt? (*Ti-Jean sweeps up the skirt, then drops it.*) What did you hope to find, but an old man's weary feet? You're a forward little fool! Now, do you want some advice? Tell me how you'll face the Devil, and I'll give you advice.

TI-JEAN: O help me, my brothers, help me to win. (*He retreats to the crosses.*)

OLD MAN:
Getting frightened, aren't you? Don't be a coward, son.
I gather twigs all day, in the darkness of the forest,
And never feared man nor beast these eighty-eight years.
I think you owe me some sort of apology.

(*The Bird runs out and begins to peck at the rope, untying the faggots with his beak. The Old Man jumps up, enraged.*)

Leave that alone, you damned . . .

TI-JEAN:
I'll help you, father.

(*Instead, he loosens the bundle.*)

OLD MAN:

> I'll kill that bird. Why did you loosen my sticks?
> Haven't you any respect for the weariness of the old?
> You've had your little prank, now help me collect them.
> If you had a father you'd know what hard work was,
> In the dark of the forest, lighting damp faggots . . .

(*Ti-Jean pretends to be assisting the Old Man, but carefully he lifts his skirt and sees that below the sackcloth robe he has a forked tail.*)

TI-JEAN:

> My mother always told me, my spirits were too merry,
> Now, here we are, old father, all in one rotten bundle.

OLD MAN:

> What's come over you, you were frightened a while back?

TI-JEAN:

> Which way to the Devil? Oh, you've never seen him.
> Tell me, does the Devil wear a hard, stiff tail?

OLD MAN: How would I know. (*Feels his rear, realises.*) Mm.
> Well, you go through that track, and you'll find a short-
> cut through the bamboo. It's a wet, leaf-rotting path, then
> you come to the springs of sulphur, where the damned
> souls are cooking . . .

TI-JEAN:

> You sure you not lying?

OLD MAN:

> It's too early in the morning to answer shallow questions,
> That's a fine hat you're wearing, so I'll bid you goodbye.

(*Ti-Jean lifts up a stick.*)

TI-JEAN:

> Not until I know who you are, papa!
> Look, I'm in a great hurry, or I'll brain you with this;

If evil exists, let it come forward.
Human, or beast, let me see it plain.

(*The stage darkens. Drums. The Old Man rises.*)

OLD MAN:
Very well then, look!

(*He unmasks: the Devil's face. Howls, cymbals clash.*)

DEVIL:
Had you not gotten me, fool,
Just a trifle angry,
I might have played the Old Man
In fairness to our bargain,
But this is no play, son.
For here is the Devil,
You asked for him early,
Impatient as the young.
Now remember our bargain,
The one who wastes his temper,
Will be eaten! Remember that!
Now, you will work!

TI-JEAN:
Cover your face, the wrinkled face of wisdom,
Twisted with memory of human pain,
Is easier to bear; this is like looking
At the blinding gaze of God.

DEVIL (*replacing Old Man's mask, and changing*):
It is hard to distinguish us,
Combat to fair combat, then I cover my face.
And the sun comes out of the rain, and the clouds.
Now these are the conditions, and the work you must do.

TI-JEAN:
Wait, old man, if is anything stupid,
I don't have your patience, so you wasting time.

OLD MAN:
> Then you must pay the penalty.
> These are your orders:
> I have an ass of a goat
> That will not stay tied.
> I want you to catch it
> Tonight before sundown.
> Over hill and valley
> Wherever it gallops.
> Then tie it good and hard.
> And if it escapes
> You must catch it again
> As often as it gets loose
> You try as many times.
> If you should lose your temper . . .

TI-JEAN:
> Where the hell is this goat?

OLD MAN:
> Over there by the . . . wait.
> The fool has run off.
> He won't last very long.

(*Exit Ti-Jean. The Old Man sits down, rocking back and forth with laughter. Ti-Jean runs back.*)

OLD MAN:
> Finished already?

TI-JEAN:
> That's right. Anything else?

OLD MAN:
> Ahm. Yes, yes, yes. Best I've seen, though.
> Now I want you to go down to the edge of the cane-
> field . . .

(*The goat bleats.*)

> Looks like you didn't tie him?

TI-JEAN:
> I tied the damned thing up.
> Something is wrong here.
> I tied the thing up properly.

(*The Old Man laughs. Ti-Jean runs off. The Old Man dances with joy. Goat bleats, then stops suddenly. Ti-Jean returns with something wrapped in a banana leaf and sits down quietly. The Old Man watches him. Pause. No bleat.*)

OLD MAN:
> What's that in your hands?

TI-JEAN (*proffers the leaf*):
> Goat seed.

(*The goat bleats girlishly.*)

OLD MAN:
> His voice is changing.
> I don't get you. Goat-seed?

TI-JEAN:
> I tied the damn thing.
> Then made it a eunuch.

(*The goat bleats weakly.*)

> Sounds much nicer.

OLD MAN:
> You er . . . fixed my one goat?
> Then you must have been angry.

TI-JEAN:
> No, I just couldn't see myself
> Chasing the damned thing all night.
> And anyhow, where I tied it,
> She'll never move again.

OLD MAN (*walking around stage*):
> You sit there calm as hell
> And tell me you er . . . altered Emilia?

TI-JEAN:
>Funny goat, with a girl's name,
>It's there by the plantain tree,
>Just by the stones.

OLD MAN:
>Boy, you have a hell of a nerve.

TI-JEAN:
>It look like you vex.

OLD MAN:
>Angry? I'm not angry. I'm not vexed at all.
>You see? Look! I'm smiling.
>What's an old goat anyhow?
>Just the only goat I had.
>Gave sour milk anyway.

TI-JEAN (*rising, rubbing his hands*):
>Fine. Now, what's next on the agenda?

OLD MAN:
>What? Yes, yes . . . Fixed the goat . . .

TI-JEAN:
>Now look here, life is . . .

OLD MAN:
>Enough of your catechism!

TI-JEAN:
>Temper, temper. Or you might lose something. Now what next?

OLD MAN:
>Now, listen to this, boy.
>Go down to the cane-fields
>And before the next cloud
>Start checking every blade,
>Count each leaf on the stalk,
>File them away properly

As fast as you can
Before the night comes,
Then report back to me.
Well, what are you waiting for?

TI-JEAN:

I got a bit tired chasing the goat,
I'm human you know.

OLD MAN:

I'm going back to the house,
I'll be back at dawn to check on your progress.

(*Exits.*)

TI-JEAN (*goes to the edge of the cane-field*):
Count all the canes, what a waste of time!

(*Cups his hands.*)

Hey, all you niggers sweating there in the canes!
Hey, all you people working hard in the fields!

VOICES (*far off*):
'Ayti? What happen? What you calling us for?

TI-JEAN:

You are poor damned souls working for the Devil?

VOICES:

Yes! Yes! What you want?

TI-JEAN:

Listen, I'm the new foreman! Listen to this:
The Devil say you must burn everything, now.
Burn the cane, burn the cotton! Burn everything now!

VOICES:

Burn everything now? Okay, boss!

(*Drums. Cries. Cane-burners' chorus.*)

TI-JEAN:

The man say Burn, burn, burn de cane!

CHORUS:
> Burn, burn, burn de cane!

TI-JEAN:
> You tired work for de man in vain!

CHORUS:
> Burn, burn, burn de cane!

(*Exeunt. The Frog enters.*)

FROG (*sings*):
> And all night the night burned
> Turning on its spit,
> Until in the valley, the grid
> Of the cane-field glowed like coals,
> When the devil, as lit as the dawn returned,
> Dead drunk, and singing his song of lost souls.

(*Enter Devil, drunk, with a bottle, singing.*)

DEVIL:
> Down deep in hell, where it black like ink,
> Where de oil does boil and the sulphur stink,
> It ain't have no ice, no refrigerator
> If you want water, and you ask the waiter,
> He go bring brimstone with a saltpetre chaser,
> While de devils bawling.

(*He is carrying the Old Man's mask. Now he puts it on.*)

> Oh, if only the little creatures of this world could understand, but they have no evil in them . . . so how the hell can they? (*The Cricket passes.*) Cricket, cricket, it's the old man.

CRICKET:
> Crek, crek, boo!

CHORUS:
> Fire one! Fire one
> Till the place burn down,
> Fire one! Fire one.

Devil (*flings the mask away*): I'll be what I am, so to hell with you. I'll be what I am. I drink, and I drink, and I feel nothing. Oh, I lack heart to enjoy the brevity of the world! (*The Firefly passes, dancing.*) Get out of my way, you burning backside, I'm the prince of obscurity and I won't brook interruption! Trying to mislead me, because I been drinking. Behave, behave. That youngster is having terrible effect on me. Since he came to the estate, I've felt like a fool. First time in me life, too. Look, just a while ago I nearly got angry at an insect that's just a half-arsed imitation of a star. It's wonderful! An insect brushes my dragonish hand, and my scales tighten with fear. Delightful! So this is what it means! I'm drunk, and hungry. (*The Frog, his eyes gleaming, hops across his path.*) O God, O God, a monster! Jesus, help! Now that for one second was the knowledge of death. O Christ, how weary it is to be immortal. (*Sits down on log.*) Another drink for confidence. (*Sings:*)

When I was the Son of the Morning,
When I was the Prince of Light.

(*He picks up the mask.*)

Oh, to hell with that! You lose a job, you lose a job. Ambition. Yet we were one light once up there, the old man and I, till even today some can't tell us apart. (*He holds the mask up. Sings:*)

And so I fell for forty days,
Passing the stars in the endless pit.

Come here, frog, I'll give you a blessing. (*The Frog hops back, hissing.*) Why do you spit at me? Oh, nobody loves me, nobody loves me. No children of my own, no worries of my own. To hell with . . . (*Stands.*) To hell with every stinking one of you, fish, flesh, fowl . . . I had the only love of God once (*Sits.*) but I lost that, I lost even that. (*Sings:*)

Leaning, leaning,
Leaning on the everlasting arms . . .

To hell with dependence and the second-lieutenancy! I had a host of burnished helmets once, and a forest of soldiery waited on my cough, on my very belch. Firefly, firefly, you have a bit of hell behind you, so light me home. (*Roars at the creatures:*) Get out, get out, all of you . . . Oh, and yet this is fine, this is what they must call despondency, weakness. It's strange, but suddenly the world has got bright, I can see ahead of me and yet I hope to die. I can make out the leaves, and . . . wait, the boy's coming. Back into the Planter. (*Wears the Planter's mask.*)

TI-JEAN (*enters, also with a bottle*): Oh, it's you, you're back late. Had a good dinner?

DEVIL: You nearly scared me. How long you been hiding there?

TI-JEAN: Oh, I just came through. Drunk as a fish.

DEVIL: Finished the work?

TI-JEAN: Yes, sir. All you told me. Cleaned the silver, made up the fifty rooms, skinned and ate curried goat for supper, and I had quite a bit of the wine.

DEVIL: Somehow I like you, little man. You have courage. Your brothers had it too, but you are somehow different. Curried goat? . . .

TI-JEAN: They began by doing what you suggested. Dangerous. So naturally when the whole thing tired them, they got angry with themselves. The one way to annoy you is rank disobedience. Curried goat, yes.

DEVIL: We'll discuss all that in the morning. I'm a little drunk, and I am particularly tired. A nice bathtub of coals, and a pair of cool sheets, and sleep. You win for tonight. Tomorrow I'll think of something. Show me the way to go home.

TI-JEAN (*his arms around the Devil*):
Oh, show me the way to go home,
I'm tired and I want to go to bed,
I had a little drink half an hour ago . . .

DEVIL (*removing his arm*): Wait a minute, wait a minute . . . I
don't smell liquor on you. What were you drinking?

TI-JEAN: Wine, wine. You know, suspicion will be the end of
you. That's why you don't have friends.

DEVIL: You have a fine brain to be drunk. Listen, I'll help you.
You must have a vice, just whisper it in my ear and I
won't tell the old fellow with the big notebook.

TI-JEAN (*holds up bottle*): This is my weakness. Got another
drink in there?

DEVIL (*passing the bottle*): This is powerful stuff, friend, liquid
brimstone. May I call you friend?

TI-JEAN: You may, you may. I have pity for all power. That's
why I love the old man with the windy beard. He never
wastes it. He could finish you off, like that . . .

DEVIL: Let's not argue religion, son. Politics and religion . . .
You know, I'll confess to you. You nearly had me vexed
several times today.

TI-JEAN: How did my two brothers taste?

DEVIL: Oh, let's forget it! Tonight we're all friends. It gets dull
in that big house. Sometimes I wish I couldn't have
everything I wanted. He spoiled me, you know, when I
was his bright, starry lieutenant. Gave me everything I
desired. I was God's spoiled son. Result: ingratitude. But
he had it coming to him. Drink deep, boy, and let's take a
rest from argument. Sleep, that's what I want, a nice
clean bed. Tired as hell. Tired as hell. And I'm getting
what I suspect is a hell of a headache. (*A blaze lightens the
wood.*) I think I'll be going up to the house. Why don't

you come in, it's damp and cold out here. It's got suddenly bright. Is that fire?

TI-JEAN: Looks like fire, yes.

DEVIL: What do you think it is, friend?

TI-JEAN: I think it's your house.

DEVIL: I don't quite understand . . .

TI-JEAN: Sit down. Have a drink. In fact, I'm pretty certain it's your home. I left a few things on fire in it.

DEVIL: It's the only house I had, boy.

TI-JEAN: My mother had three sons, she didn't get vexed. Why not smile and take a drink like a man?

DEVIL (*removing the Planter's mask*): What the hell do you think I care about your mother? The poor withered fool who thinks it's holy to be poor, who scraped her knees to the knuckle praying to an old beard that's been deaf since noise began? Or your two damned fools of brothers, the man of strength and the rhetorician? Come! Filambo! Azaz! Cacarat! You've burnt property that belongs to me.

(*Assistant Devils appear and surround Ti-Jean.*)

TI-JEAN: You're not smiling, friend.

DEVIL: Smiling? You expect me to smile? Listen to him! (*The Devils laugh.*) You share my liquor, eat out my 'fridge, I treat you like a guest, tell you my troubles. I invite you to my house and you burn it!

TI-JEAN (*sings*):
Who with the Devil tries to play fair,
Weaves the net of his own despair.
Oh, smile; what's a house between drunkards?

DEVIL: I've been watching you, you little nowhere nigger! You little squirt, you hackneyed cough between two immortalities, who do you think you are? You're dirt, and that's where you'll be when I'm finished with you. Burn my house, my receipts, all my papers, all my bloody triumphs.

TI-JEAN (*to the Devils*): Does your master sound vexed to you?

DEVIL: Seize him!

(*The Bolom enters and stands between Ti-Jean and the Devil.*)

BOLOM: Master, be fair!

DEVIL:
He who would with the devil play fair,
Weaves the net of his own despair.
This shall be a magnificent ending:
A supper cooked by lightning and thunder.

(*Raises fork.*)

MOTHER (*in a white light in the hut*):
Have mercy on my son,
Protect him from fear,
Protect him from despair,
And if he must die,
Let him die as a man,
Even as your Own Son
Fought the Devil and died.

DEVIL: I never keep bargains. Now, tell me, you little fool, if you aren't afraid.

TI-JEAN: I'm as scared as Christ.

DEVIL: Burnt my house, poisoned the devotion of my servants, small things all of them, dependent on me.

TI-JEAN:
You must now keep
Your part of the bargain.
You must restore
My brothers to life.

DEVIL:
>What a waste, you know yourself
>I can never be destroyed.
>They are dead. Dead, look!

(*The brothers pass.*)

>There are your two brothers,
>In the agony where I put them,
>One moaning from weakness,
>Turning a mill-wheel
>For the rest of his life,
>The other blind as a bat,
>Shrieking in doubt.

(*The two brothers pass behind a red curtain of flame.*)

TI-JEAN: O God.

DEVIL (*laughing*): Seize him! Throw him into the fire.

TI-JEAN (*with a child's cry*): Mama!

DEVIL: She can't hear you, boy.

TI-JEAN:
>Well, then, you pay her what you owe me!
>I make you laugh, and I make you vex,
>That was the bet. You have to play fair.

DEVIL:
>Who with the devil tries to play fair . . .

TI-JEAN (*angrily*): I say you vex and you lose, man! Gimme me
>money!

DEVIL: Go back, Bolom!

BOLOM:
>Yes, he seems vexed,
>But he shrieked with delight
>When a mother strangled me
>Before the world light.

DEVIL: Be grateful, you would have amounted to nothing, child, a man. You would have suffered and returned to dirt.

BOLOM: No, I would have known life, rain on my skin, sunlight on my forehead. Master, you have lost. Pay him! Reward him!

DEVIL: For cruelty's sake I could wish you were born. Very well then, Ti-Jean. Look there, towards the hut, what do you see?

TI-JEAN: I see my mother sleeping.

DEVIL:
> And look down at your feet,
> Falling here, like leaves,
> What do you see? Filling this vessel?

TI-JEAN:
> The shower of sovereigns,
> Just as you promised me.
> But something is wrong.
> Since when you play fair?

BOLOM:
> Look, look, there in the hut,
> Look there, Ti-Jean, the walls,
> The walls are glowing with gold.
> Ti-Jean, you can't see it?
> You have won, you have won!

TI-JEAN:
> It is only the golden
> Light of the sun, on
> My mother asleep.

(*Light comes up on the hut.*)

DEVIL:
> Not asleep, but dying, Ti-Jean.
> But don't blame me for that.

TI-JEAN:
Mama!

DEVIL:
She cannot hear you, child.
Now, can you still sing?

FROG:
Sing, Ti-Jean, sing!
Show him you could win!
Show him what a man is!
Sing Ti-Jean . . . Listen,
All around you, nature
Still singing. The frog's
Croak doesn't stop for the dead;
The cricket is still merry,
The bird still plays its flute,
Every dawn, little Ti-Jean . . .

TI-JEAN (*sings, at first falteringly*):
To the door of breath you gave the key,
Thank you, Lord,
The door is open, and I step free,
Amen, Lord . . .
Cloud after cloud like a silver stair
My lost ones waiting to greet me there
With their silent faces, and starlit hair
Amen, Lord.

(*Weeps.*)

DEVIL:
What is this cooling my face, washing it like a
Wind of morning. Tears! Tears! Then is this the
Magnificence I have heard of, of
Man, the chink in his armour, the destruction of the
Self? Is this the strange, strange wonder that is
Sorrow? You have earned your gift, Ti-Jean, ask!

BOLOM:

> Ask him for my life!
> O God, I want all this
> To happen to me!

TI-JEAN:

> Is life you want, child?
> You don't see what it bring?

BOLOM:

> Yes, yes, Ti-Jean, life!

TI-JEAN:

> Don't blame me when you suffering,
> When you lose everything,
> And when the time come
> To put two cold coins
> On your eyes. Sir, can you give him life.

DEVIL:

> Just look!

BOLOM (*being born*):

> I am born, I shall die! I am born, I shall die!
> O the wonder, and pride of it! I shall be man!
> Ti-Jean, my brother!

DEVIL:

> Farewell, little fool! Come, then,
> Stretch your wings and soar, pass over the fields
> Like the last shadow of night, imps, devils, bats,
> Eazaz, Beelzebub, Cacarat, soar! Quick, quick the sun!
> We shall meet again, Ti-Jean. You, and your new brother!
> The features will change, but the fight is still on.

(*Exeunt.*)

TI-JEAN:

> Come then, little brother. And you, little creatures.
> Ti-Jean must go on. Here's a bundle of sticks that
> Old wisdom has forgotten. Together they are strong,

Apart, they are all rotten.
God look after the wise, and look after the strong,
But the fool in his folly will always live long.

(*Sings:*)
Sunday morning I went to the chapel
Ring down below!
I met the devil with the book and the Bible.
Ring down below!
Ask him what he will have for dinner.

CHORUS:
Ring down below!

TI-JEAN:
Cricket leg and a frog with water.

CHORUS:
Ring down below!

TI-JEAN:
I leaving home and I have one mission!

CHORUS:
Ring down below!

TI-JEAN:
You come to me by your own decision.

CHORUS:
Ring down below!

TI-JEAN:
Down in hell you await your vision.

CHORUS:
Ring down below!

TI-JEAN:
I go bring down, bring down Goliath.

CHORUS:
Bring down below!

(Exeunt. The creatures gather as before.)

FROG: And so it was that Ti-Jean, a fool like all heroes, passed through the tangled opinions of this life, loosening the rotting faggots of knowledge from old men to bear them safely on his shoulder, brother met brother on his way, that God made him the clarity of the moon to lighten the doubt of all travellers through the shadowy wood of life. And bird, the rain is over, the moon is rising through the leaves. Messieurs, creek. Crack.

CURTAIN

A
NEW
SONG

ZAKES MOFOKENG

A New Song opened at the Laager Market Theatre, Johannesburg, South Africa, in the summer of 1982, with the following cast:

SELLO	Zakes Mofokeng
MANANA	Brenda Ngubane
JOHN	Owen Sajake

CHARACTERS

MANANA   a black woman
SELLO   a black man
JOHN   a white man

SCENE ONE

A well-equipped kitchen. The whole play takes place here.

MANANA: Thanks God!

SELLO: John is a funny man.

MANANA: Thanks God he's gone. He's a pain in the neck.

SELLO: I heard him clearly yesterday saying he likes tea in the morning and coffee for the rest of the day; today he has changed, it's the other way round, coffee in the morning.

MANANA: Is that what you were fighting for?

SELLO (*imitating John*): Yes, "*Koffie in die more.*"

MANANA: Didn't he mention *boerewors* and eggs?

SELLO: How can he leave that out?

MANANA: You amuse me when you call him the *boerewors*.

SELLO: He eats so much *boerewors*, I'm sure if you cut him you'll find a piece of *boerewors*.

MANANA: Well, let's celebrate while he's gone.

SELLO: If only he was gone for good.

MANANA: We must find a way of getting rid of him. We must surprise him, just the two of us, tackle him.

SELLO: He carries a gun, you know.

(*Pause.*)

MANANA: I'm so tired.

SELLO: Tired so early in the morning?

MANANA: You overwork me. (*She goes behind Sello and puts both her hands round his neck.*)

SELLO: Well, don't let's start work again.

157

(*They laugh.*)

MANANA: Sello, you must protect us. This is no life.

SELLO: Things will be alright.

MANANA: But you've always said that.

SELLO: What else can I do?

MANANA: Do something Sello, you are the man.

SELLO: Okay. Manana, if you were the man what would you do?

MANANA: I don't know, because I happen not to be the man now. You must know what to do. What is manhood?

SELLO: Okay. Manana, let's not go any further, I know where this is leading. Every little happy moment we have together is always punctuated by John one way or the other.

MANANA: This is your house.

SELLO: I know.

MANANA: Although John has taken it by some screwy means, people know it to be your house, and they are waiting to see what are you doing about it.

SELLO: They tricked my grandfather, they said they were on their way, passing. We were not yet born, my father was still a kid, he had no idea of what was happening. My grandfather had too much faith in these people. He regarded them as some know-all demigods. If only he knew the man was a snake.

MANANA: Sello, you know the man is a snake, kill it!

SELLO (*angrily*): HOW! HOW!

MANANA: I don't care how!

SELLO (*trying to calm himself*): Take it easy.

MANANA: Easy!

SELLO: Easy Manana.

MANANA: Life is not easy Sello. It is not easy for a woman to give birth. It's pain, not easy. I am a woman Sello, ask me. When I was in pain, delivering your son, you were taking it easy with your friends drinking beers and celebrating "I'm going to be a father!" You became a father without even feeling any change. Now Sello, getting John out of here is not like becoming a father. It's like giving birth, it's painful, because you'll be giving birth to a new life.

SELLO: Okay Manana, something must be done.

MANANA: And pretty soon.

SELLO: Okay. Manana.

MANANA: I don't even like the way he looks at me.

SELLO: How?

MANANA: With his eyes fixed around my pelvis.

SELLO: Ah now, just . . .

MANANA: I don't like John, honestly, I hate him. (*Pause.*) I am sorry Sello. I know you are not happy too. But sometimes I just get carried away.

SELLO: I understand Manana. I will do something.

(*He exits. Manana remains tidying up the kitchen. Sello comes back with his trumpet and starts cleaning it.*)

MANANA: Aren't you supposed to be at the pass office?

SELLO: No, I'm okay. I'm going in ten days' time.

MANANA: You must get fixed.

SELLO: With what?

MANANA: You must be allowed to be in this proclaimed kitchen of John Grootboom.

SELLO: And live happily ever after. (*Pause.*) I remember last year. There I was at the pass office. For five years I was not working and not reporting at the pass office.

MANANA (*with an Afrikaans accent*): Looking for trouble, eh?

SELLO: I stood there in the queue with a blank face, armed with a letter on a mental institution's letterhead.

MANANA: And what was your good excuse?

SELLO: Madness.

MANANA: Madness?

SELLO: The letter said I was mad for the past five years and now I was fit to take up employment.

MANANA (*looking at the audience, and in an Afrikaans accent*): Tell me, how do we deal with such people? Tell me.

SELLO: I looked around and there was Thabo with a luminous smile on his face trying to find his way through the crowd towards me. This time I was third in the queue. I was afraid that whatever Thabo would say, the man behind the counter would hear and that would mess up my scheme. So I stared at him as he tried to talk to me. I just stared at him as though I'd never seen him before.

MANANA: And what happened?

SELLO: He gave up and left, puzzled. So then it was my turn at the counter. The man took the pass, examined it, and remarked, "*Ja, waar kom jy vandaan?*"
    "I was sick sir," I replied.
    "Sick for five years?"
    "Yes sir."
    "What was wrong *jong*?"
    "Headache sir."
    "Headache!"
    "Yes sir."
    "Did you see a doctor?"

"Yes sir." I took out the letter from my pocket and gave it to him. "The doctor said I must give you this sir."

MANANA: And so?

SELLO: He read the letter.

MANANA: Were you not scared?

SELLO: Not after sir-ring him so much. It made him feel civilised, and the idiot seemed convinced. He then thought he was being human.

"Are you better now?"

"Yes sir."

He reached out for a rubber stamp. Bang! on my pass. I nearly burst out. He directed me to the backyard. "Go there by the big yard and the big boss will give you work. Okay."

The idiot. Out I went. My friend was waiting for me anxiously outside the yard. I greeted him with laughter. He joined me and we laughed. After that we checked what the stamps were all about.

MANANA: That's what I've been waiting for.

SELLO: One was a workseeker's permit, and the other one said I was a bona fide resident—you know, some string of numbers plus a Ten-One-B. (*They laugh.*) On the way home I wished the police would ask me for my pass. They never did.

MANANA: Didn't you fear that they would get you like that time?

SELLO: Section six? Ah, this was child's play. Section six! of the terrorism act!

MANANA: Hau! Being in prison . . .

SELLO: Section six! of the terrorism act! They don't play marbles. I remember as though it was yesterday. First day. Reception. There was about twelve of them to welcome me.

MANANA: Twelve?

SELLO: Twelve. Boy, they looked very impressive those boys. Man! They looked as though they just came out of a shower. They wore Wranglers, you know, just casual, except the top ones who wore suits and ties, and there was only three of them. Well-fed tall white boys. I was half their height all of them, a typical product of three and a quarter centuries of undernourishment. Those boys! I was surprised why they brought so many of them, because the way they were, one of them could have done the job easily. They were all muscles, not a teaspoon of fat. They stood in a V formation, and I was at the apex of the V. Straight in front of me was their boss sitted on a desk. Everybody was at ease, except me. I was just wondering what was going to happen to me, because being alone with such tall well-fed white boys is not a pleasant experience. Their boss asked me a few questions, casually, and I was answering, biting my lips and my tongue here and there. A-a-h, they didn't mind. After that he told them to take me away. I left with two of them to one of their other offices down the corridor. There I was blindfolded, and boy! The pops began to dance! They asked me so many questions I did not know which one to answer.

MANANA: Were they beating you up?

SELLO: Beating! Claps! Fists! Sjambok! Karate! and all. But the climax came, boy! I was told to lie on my stomach. You see, my hands were tied together behind me, and my feet were also tied together, and then they tied both my hands to my feet, and then one of them sat on my shoulder blades. Then! They put electric wires just behind my ears, held by the material blindfolding me. Man! I thought I was dying.

MANANA: Electric?

SELLO: Electric on my head! Then they started questioning me again, from the start. Jo! I had to invent a lot of lies, and invent a lot of names too, which later added to my troubles. I said Mandla is the one who brought in the TNT, and that Khado is the one who failed to bring down the Carlton Centre, and that Masite was the big brains behind the strikes. They were so happy they were saying, "Now he's talking."

MANANA: And what did you do?

SELLO: What could I do?

MANANA: Bloody sadists!

SELLO: But I realised that I must do something. I knew that they could kill me if I don't cry.

MANANA: What?

SELLO: They are stupid. Their stupid brains tell them that if you do not make a sound you do not feel the pain.

MANANA: And then?

SELLO: I had to try crying.

MANANA: Did you?

SELLO: That's when I got a shock of my life.

MANANA: What?

SELLO: I realised that I could not cry!

MANANA: Why?

SELLO: Because I haven't been crying for a long time and my voice had grown thick. (*He starts making noises with a thick voice and acting as though someone is beating him up. Manana is very moved by this act.*)

MANANA: What happened then?

SELLO: I realised that laughing was the easiest thing we Africans can do. We can make a big sound of it, but when we need that same voice for crying we can't. We just suffer silently, and then they think we are hard and we do not feel it. It makes them fear us.

MANANA: But you did cry, didn't you?

SELLO: What do you mean?

MANANA: They can't recognise a human cry. Those sounds you made were sounds of crying. You too have been made to undermine everything you do. Say you wanted to please them.

SELLO (*angrily*): I don't like that!

MANANA: And then?

SELLO: And then came the million-dollar question.

MANANA: What?

SELLO: What do you know about the ANC?

MANANA: ANC?

SELLO: Yes, the ANC. I was lucky they did not think I was PAC, otherwise I wouldn't be here.

MANANA: And what did you say?

SELLO: For the first time I realised that I knew fuck-all about ANC, but I dared not say, "I don't know," because they never accept such an answer, so I knew I was going to get it. I tried to think, man, I thought hard. I could not come up with anything. At length I said, "All I know is that it's a banned organization." "You talking shit!" That's all I heard and my head started exploding again.

MANANA: Were they not afraid that you could die?

SELLO: Those boys don't care. They think they've got a lot at stake, even with innocent ones like me. After a long process they left me. When the blindfold was removed they were all out, I was left with the original two I was with. I was so tired. My body was not yet aching. I was escorted by an armed police to the toilet. Man! That I loved—although I was thoroughly walloped, I was so dangerous that I had to be escorted at gunpoint to the toilet like they do to the heroes in the movies, who eventually get everything their way. And then I was taken to my cell at about five o'clock in the afternoon.

MANANA: Hm!

SELLO: I tried to drink water and my mouth was all needles, I realised that I had bitten my lips, tongue, and my cheeks inside my mouth, and boy! I tried to sit my buttocks were sore, I tried to sleep my body was sore, I just stood there in the middle of the cell. But what? I could not stand there forever. I went down slowly and eventually I fell asleep, for a good two hours. Then I was rudely awakened by one of the cops: "Are you alright?" I was still waking up trying to remember where I was. Then I remembered that I was not in my mother's house, but by that time he was already gone. Pains again! Then I started sobering up. My head! Oh!

MANANA: They hit you on the head?

SELLO: Never mind that, my head! Then I started getting worried. Who the hell is Khado? Who is Masite? Who is Mandla? What the hell did they do? Man!

MANANA: Hau! Why?

SELLO: I got myself entangled in so many lies I could not even remember who I said did what or who said what. Sheer luck made me remember the names.

MANANA: Oho!

SELLO: I knew that the following day I was going to be in for it if I did not remember what I said the previous day. So I thought. What the hell did I say Mandla did? And what the hell did Khado do? Tsho! Blackout!

MANANA: So?

SELLO: I fell asleep trying to work that one out. The following day they fetched me again for interrogation. Then I thought, man, I must work something out. I told myself that today I must call them boss or something, because I knew the only way to fool a white man is by calling him boss or *baas*. I told myself, "Sello, today you are going to play a fool. But under that fool have all your senses alert." Then we got down to business, this time there was only two of them. "Sello," one of them called me. "*My baas!*" I answered. "*My baas se gat!*"

MANANA: Au!

SELLO: "*My kroon! My kroon se moer!*"

MANANA: You're lying!

SELLO: I wondered too, what now? So quickly I said, "I want to talk, you see, yesterday I was not feeling well." "What made you not feel well *jong*?" Then I went on, "You see, it was Mandla who brought the TNT, and Khado tried to blow Carl . . ." Before I could finish, "*Gots jong!* That's what you said yesterday!" No, I thought I said something different. "*Moenie kak praat!*" Man, the way those boys say it you can even believe that you are talking *kak*. They give it its full value, they really contain it well in their mouths.

MANANA: Sello!

SELLO: Ja, those boys know *kak*. Inwardly I was calling them names too, their mothers and all other censored words.

MANANA: You! And your stories!

SELLO: Hey, how about some grub?

MANANA: Sure, why not. (*She opens the pots.*) Chops are gone.

SELLO: Gone?

MANANA: Or did we have any?

SELLO: Yes, remember you left me some last night.

MANANA: Oh yes, I remember.

SELLO: Now this!

MANANA: The bloody scrounger.

SELLO: The bloody hypocrite. "Let's live together! Let's live together," you'll hear him say.

MANANA: And at night he comes crawling to the pots. He's so secretive. Greedy.

SELLO: The rolls?

MANANA: Yes, the rolls, let me check.

SELLO: It would be a miracle.

MANANA: What?

SELLO: If they are still there, it would be a miracle.

MANANA (*opens the cupboard*): Gone! Only one left.

SELLO: At least he could have left two, because he knows there's two of us.

MANANA: The man is a glutton.

SELLO: You must lock this cupboard.

MANANA: What? I had it locked.

SELLO: You mean . . .

MANANA: He's got a key.

SELLO: It's a scandal. It's a bloody scandal.

MANANA: Greedy. Greed has finished him.

SELLO: Bloody thief.

MANANA: He's got a bad heart. He thinks if he steals we won't realise that he's a cheat.

SELLO: How can we not realise, we do all the dirty work here! If there's any filth we are the first to realise. We work for him, he can't even provide enough food for us. Bloody swine.

MANANA: Oh let's forget that *boerewors* for a while.

SELLO: You're right, let's not allow all this fuck-up to spoil our day. You have me and I have you, that is important.

MANANA (*as Sello unbuttons her overall*): But Sello . . .

SELLO: Wait, wait, wait, he's gone now.

MANANA: How I wish it was for good.

SELLO (*unbuttons all the buttons and pulls her close to him*): We are alone now.

(*The dogs start barking.*)

MANANA (*quickly covers herself*): Oh God!

SELLO: I'll check. (*He goes to the window and looks for some time.*)

MANANA (*busy buttoning up*): It's him?

SELLO: There's no one.

MANANA: These dogs drive me mad. But why?

SELLO: Why what?

MANANA: Why does he keep dogs?

SELLO: Tight security.

MANANA: I mean we have no thieves around here.

SELLO: Well, John is a suspicious man. He suspects everybody. Anyway that's beside the point.

MANANA: So, it means we can't eat until the milkman comes. Then we can have milk with bread.

SELLO: What else? We must wait. In the meantime . . . (*going to his trumpet*). One day, one day, just one day.

MANANA: Two-day, two-day.

SELLO: One day this trumpet is going to make me famous. The world is going to listen to me. They'll say, "He's great."

MANANA: You better make it.

SELLO (*imitating a trumpet*): Twe-e-e, twe-e-e, twi-i-i, twi-i-i.

MANANA: You play too much.

SELLO: You'll see one day, just one day.

MANANA: One day you'll be old, your fingers won't be able to bend. Make it now.

SELLO: Never too late to mend.

MANANA: Only now is not too late. Do it now.

SELLO: I'll be in the newspapers. Pretty girls will be reading about me.

MANANA: Oho!

SELLO (*like he's talking to a girl*): "I'm sorry, I'm married." I'll be signing autographs, and you'll be admiring me and feeling very jealous.

MANANA: Don't let fame go into your head before you even get there. It will make you drunk and nobody will ever know about you.

SELLO: And I'll be playing at nightclubs, playing the blues.

MANANA: Blues!

SELLO: I won't be crying. I'll be ecstatic. I'll be there, in that place, I don't know. I'll be communicating with the black Gods.

MANANA: Oh, I'll be so proud of you.

SELLO: I'll be playing rhythms from the black soil of Africa. I'll be saying things.

MANANA: Sello, the world is waiting for you.

SELLO: Everybody will be on his feet. Those sitted will be nodding to rhythms, and those standing will be hopping.

MANANA: Aroused by your music.

(*Pause.*)

SELLO: Oh, but what's the use. It's discouraging.

MANANA: No Sello, don't lose hope. Don't take heed of what I said. Your fingers can still make it.

SELLO: No, not that.

MANANA: What?

SELLO: You said they'll be aroused by me.

MANANA: Of course.

SELLO: No, no, no Manana.

MANANA: Why?

SELLO: Remember the day you were ill? I went looking for Tshepo, and I was told he was at the nightclub.

MANANA: So you went there, what was wrong with that?

SELLO: Something terribly wrong.

MANANA: Oh Sello, don't be old-fashioned.

SELLO: No Manana, not that.

MANANA: What is it then?

SELLO: Someone was singing, "Too many people are suffering, too many people are sad."

MANANA: So?

SELLO: Somebody sang, "Wake up, everybody." And they were not listening. They were all on their feet. Gesticulat-

ing and gyrating like mating peacocks, shaking their
arses. Boozing, sweating, and giggling. Tall ones, short
ones, thin ones, fat ones—like they were poured into
their jeans—were heaving like worms around a rotten
carcass. "Too many people are suffering." The world is
just a rotten carcass.

MANANA: They do it to ease the tension.

SELLO: What tension?

MANANA: The tension of living like dogs fed on filth.

SELLO: They are the great pretenders.

MANANA: Pretenders.

SELLO: The trouble is that we pretend too much.

MANANA: What pretend?

SELLO: We pretend we are happy when we are not, because
we've got no guts to venture out and look for what we
want. We send our children to white schools: "I want a
better education for my children." Instead of changing
the situation we change ourselves. "I'm no longer John
More, I'm John More" (*pronounced as in English*), and go to
live in Coronationville and get better exploitation because
I'm "Kalad." We spend nights not sleeping, driving
around in Mercedes Benzes, Alfa Romeos, and boozing
and indulging in illicit sex. I'm giving up the whole
damn fuck.

MANANA: Sello, don't be a coward!

SELLO: Don't you ever call me a coward! Hear! I'm not going to
play Jesus Christ to twenty million cowards.

MANANA: Oh Sello, I don't mean to offend you. I did not
mean what I said.

SELLO: Well, I mean what I say.

MANANA: You got the calling, heed it, the people are waiting
to hear from you.

SELLO: Let them wait! They are used to waiting. They've been waiting for three and a quarter centuries. I'm not waiting. I'm getting there. Somehow I'll get there.

MANANA: Sello, take your trumpet, you've got the talent. Talk to the people, give them good music and they'll stand up and do something. Sello, you can make it. Some people have ears, they'll listen.

(*Pause.*)

SELLO: I'm old Manana.

MANANA: Don't give up. Don't give up Sello.

(*Sello takes his trumpet and blows loudly—just disorganised sounds. Manana looks on, frightened. Sello puts his trumpet away.*)

SELLO: That eases my nerves. Just noise. It's too quiet in this damn house because we are afraid. For once we must make noise. Noise! You hear?

MANANA: Oh Sello.

SELLO: Don't try to soften me up!

MANANA: But Sello . . .

SELLO: I must make noise. Play the blues. No, no. I'll invent a new type of music. I'll use the blue note, but the music will be noisy, as noisy as he is—John. When he's drunk. I'll make that noise sober with my trumpet.

MANANA: I really wish you could make that noise when he's here.

SELLO: Don't drive me mad too.

MANANA: Yes, go on, I drive you mad, he doesn't.

SELLO: Stop it Manana.

MANANA: He does not drive you mad because you are afraid of him!

SELLO: I will no more!

(*Dogs start barking. They both look frightened. They go to the window and peep, they come back and sit down. Sello goes to the table and takes a letter.*)

Hey look!

MANANA: What is it?

SELLO: A letter.

MANANA: Hmm . . . by hand, from?

SELLO: John Grootboom. "I had to leave early so I thought . . ."

MANANA (*angrily*): What about "sorry"?

SELLO: What "sorry"?

MANANA: The last time he said, "Sorry I had to leave early."

SELLO: You notice minor things.

MANANA: He said you must always be polite. Every letter you write to him is full of sorry, sorry! What are you so sorry about?

SELLO: Nothing.

MANANA: Then you are going to be sorry.

SELLO: But look Manana . . .

MANANA: I'm not looking anywhere. This is your house. You don't have to be sorry in your house.

SELLO: Not that I'm . . .

MANANA: Made sorry by another man in your house.

SELLO: Okay, I'm sorry.

MANANA: Don't you be sorry! (*Pause. She takes the letter and reads it.*) I told you.

SELLO: Told me what?

MANANA: What is it you are allowed to do in this house? First he said you must be sorry, and now he's giving you instructions left and right, and obstructions day in, day out.

SELLO: If a man gives good advice we must take it.

MANANA: OBSTRUCTIONS and INSTRUCTIONS. No advice. You are not allowed to do this, you are not allowed to do that, fancy! You do everything for him, he should be ashamed! Look at his garden, he's so proud of it. When some of his dump-looking friends come here, the first thing he does is take them around the garden, and he never tells them that you clean up the mess from his dogs. He got the prize for the best garden, not you.

SELLO: You're right Manana.

MANANA: Then you better decide what to do.

SELLO: What?

MANANA: What to do with him.

SELLO: Exactly what do you expect me to do?

MANANA: Get rid of him! (*Pause.*) Get rid of him. Let's live in peace, like human beings.

SELLO (*sighs*): Yeah!

MANANA: He's unpopular with our neighbours. His dogs won't allow anybody inside the yard. We are cut off from everybody.

SELLO: We never even get to know what goes on outside, we are always the last to know. We're actually lagging behind civilisation.

MANANA: It was all a mistake just to have allowed him in here.

SELLO: He took advantage of grandfather's hospitality.

MANANA: He's overstayed his welcome.

SELLO: And now it's time for him to go. He must go!

MANANA: Now you sound like a man.

SELLO: He must go, then we can bring down this *Zonduma-khelwane*.

MANANA: What?

SELLO: This wall around the house, this "hate-thy-neigh-bours" wall.

(*Long pause. Sello takes a magazine on the table and reads, Manana goes on with her household chores.*)

MANANA: Tshepo is completing this year.

SELLO: Yes, we'll soon have a graduate in this house.

MANANA: And I am not going to sleep in the same room with my son anymore.

SELLO: Just for a short while.

MANANA: Not even for a second. One may be careful but never a hundred per cent.

SELLO: What do you mean?

MANANA: I can't have another man seeing me naked, you are enough.

SELLO: What do you mean?

MANANA: You cannot rule out the fact that he's seen me. I know because I have seen him several times, and he's a man. We must cram up in one room while John has got eight rooms to himself.

SELLO: Tshepo said he's not going to tolerate him when he comes from school.

MANANA: Does he know that he carries a gun?

SELLO: He knows, but he does not seem to care. He loves his home more than he fears John.

MANANA: I don't want my boy to get hurt.

SELLO: He's young and agile, he's capable of handling John.

MANANA: How I wish he graduates.

SELLO: He's very intelligent, he'll make it.

MANANA: I know he's intelligent, but there's been so much unrest in the campus.

SELLO: Sometimes I get scared we should not waste our money . . .

MANANA: I don't think it's a waste, things are different now.

SELLO: What's different?

MANANA: Remember, we left school so long ago.

SELLO: You make us seem too old now.

MANANA: No running away from it. Things have changed. Even the books we read have been changed.

SELLO: I know a lot of things have changed.

MANANA: If you've noticed even the weather has changed. It's no longer as we read it in our geography. Last year we had snow in September.

SELLO: Today I don't see the Milky Way. I like gazing at the stars.

MANANA: So do you see how different the world is, and our lives are just static, except that we are nearing our end, wrinkles around our eyes.

SELLO: I'm not wrinkled.

MANANA: Our minds are getting slow and tired, that is why we see things differently from the kids.

SELLO: Well, we educate them hoping that they'll correct the world, but I'm not old.

MANANA: Ho! Ho! I still have my looks, I still get guys whistling when I walk down the street.

SELLO: Oho!

MANANA: A young chap wanted to pat my back at the bus stop. I stopped him just in time.

SELLO: The little bastard.

MANANA: Jealous, eh?

SELLO: I am not jealous. I'm being responsible.

MANANA: I've noticed your hawk's eye when there are other men around.

SELLO: They always seem so happy to see you, but I never met their wives. They don't take their wives out, they are always looking forward to meeting other people's wives.

MANANA: Now you are warming up.

SELLO: It's no joke.

MANANA: Life is a joke, a bloody circus. We sit there and cheer, laugh our lungs out, until the most graceful of artists, the trapeze artist, falls and breaks her neck and dies. A shock for a while, the following day we are there again cheering, heralding the next misfortune.

(*Dogs start barking. Sello goes to the window.*)

Tell me, do you know exactly how did John's people take this house from your people?

(*Sello looks disturbed by this question.*)

SELLO: He says they bought it.

MANANA: How much?

SELLO: I don't know.

MANANA: Does he have any documentary evidence?

SELLO: He's got a piece of paper.

MANANA: A piece of paper?

SELLO: Yes, that's all.

MANANA: What is that piece of paper supposed to mean?

SELLO: Well, it's a sort of a receipt.

MANANA: Receipt?

SELLO: An agreement, I don't know what to call it. It says that my people agreed to give this place to John's people.

MANANA: They just gave it?

SELLO: It's not very clear, but it's something to that effect, and John says it's my grandfather who signed it.

MANANA: Did he sign it?

SELLO: Well, with a cross, yes. John says it's grandfather's cross.

MANANA: A cross?

SELLO: Yes, a cross.

MANANA: And that is your people's cross?

SELLO: Yes, John says it's my people's cross.

MANANA: How does John know, because he was not there?

SELLO: That's what his people told him.

MANANA: That cross was not made by your people. John's people made that cross and they've given it to your people in exchange for the land.

SELLO: That's how I felt.

MANANA: That cross is now your cross. Your heritage gone for a piece of paper.

SELLO: Fraud!

MANANA: That's what it is. A cross. How does one identify one cross from the other?

SELLO (*shrugs*): Well?

MANANA: If your grandfather made that cross it means he couldn't write nor read.

SELLO: Of course he couldn't read and write, so they gave him wrong information and got him to make that cross—that is, if he made it at all.

MANANA: You've got to do something about it Sello.

SELLO: I have tried to argue that out but it was brushed aside.

MANANA: What do you mean, brushed aside?

SELLO: The case was thrown out of court.

MANANA: You took legal action?

SELLO: Yes, but Manana you've got to understand what is law. The law is the will of those who possess power. All our wishes and deeds are illegal as long as they don't tally with the wishes and interests of those who possess power.

MANANA: But this is plain fraud.

SELLO: It is, but we must first seize power, then we can correct things.

MANANA: How do we seize power?

(*Dogs start barking.*)

SELLO: Here he comes.

(*John enters wearing a suit and tie and carrying a briefcase.*)

JOHN: How's everybody? (*Silence.*) Have the dogs been fed? (*Pause.*)

SELLO: I don't care for the dogs.

JOHN: What do you mean you don't care for the dogs?

MANANA: He means he doesn't care whether they eat or die.

JOHN (*emotionally*): These dogs look after this house, they must be fed.

MANANA: They are your responsibility, they look after your property. We've got nothing that needs looking after.

SELLO: Besides that John, we have decided otherwise.

JOHN: How "otherwise"?

SELLO: We have decided that you must go.

JOHN: Go?

SELLO: Yes, go!

JOHN: Can you repeat that?

MANANA: You heard what the man said, you must go, leave us in peace, proceed to wherever you were going when you stopped here.

JOHN: Sello, can I talk to you privately, can you ask your wife to excuse us for a while?

(*Sello signals to Manana to leave.*)

Well, Mr. Modise, let us talk as men. Let me stay a little and you won't regret it. I've got a few plans which will definitely be of great interest to you, and when the time comes for me to leave, you'll be firm on your feet.

SELLO: I'm already used to the life I'm leading.

JOHN: You can lead a better life Sello. This is no life you are leading. The state in which I found your elders here, abominable, and they thought they were living. No Sello let me teach you life.

SELLO: What is life?

JOHN: Life? It's when living becomes worthwhile, when you see yourself progressing towards your goal. It's when you are healthy and feeling human and alive, when you are able to feel the breeze and the sound of the ocean makes sense, when you admire the moon, the stars, the constellations my friend! Ever heard of it? A beautiful word, "constellation." It's all up there my friend, no man can reach for it, but try to reach for it. Life is when you love the changing seasons and love the rain, even if you have no raincoat, when you love the mountains, and most of all, when you fear God.

SELLO: Fear?

JOHN: Fear God my friend. Be a God-fearing person.

SELLO: Why must I fear God?

JOHN: "I am the Lord thy God . . ."

SELLO: Why must I fear the Almighty?

JOHN (*continues*): ". . . who brought you out of Egypt the land of bondage."

SELLO: Why must I fear love?

JOHN (*continues*): "Do not desire another man's house, do not desire his wife."

SELLO: Besides, what has it got to do with your having to go?

JOHN: Don't get me wrong Sello.

SELLO: There's enough fear in this house.

JOHN: What do you fear? What is it you fear?

SELLO: This house is surrounded by vicious dogs.

JOHN: Security Sello.

SELLO: Because you fear us. You feel insecure.

JOHN: ENOUGH!

(*Pause.*)

SELLO: John, you've overstayed your welcome.

JOHN: I SAID ENOUGH! (*Emotionally:*) I asked why have the dogs not been fed?

SELLO: (*shaking*): I told you why.

JOHN: Why question my regulations?

SELLO: You're insane John.

JOHN: Why haven't you paid rent?

SELLO: This is my HOUSE!

JOHN: What makes you think this house is yours?

SELLO: My grandfather built it for me. I, AM, WARNING, YOU, JOHN.

JOHN: Warning me my foot!

SELLO: You told my neighbours that we smell and yet . . .

JOHN: Hey, take it easy chum, and yet what?

SELLO: Why ogle at my wife?

JOHN: Your wife? She is my maid.

SELLO: Answer the question.

JOHN: Who cares for your wife?

SELLO: You care for my wife.

JOHN: Only as a maid.

SELLO: It's good neighbours I've got here.

JOHN: So what?

SELLO: They'll tell me everything you say behind my back.

JOHN: Hey! Take it easy.

SELLO: They are my friends.

JOHN: "Love thy neighbours . . ."

SELLO: They are not your friends.

JOHN: ". . . as you love thyself."

SELLO: They knew me before they knew you—that is, they know you through me.

JOHN: What are you driving at?

SELLO: If you want to befriend them, it's only through me. They are my neighbours, not yours, you can't befriend them by talking bad about me.

JOHN: I've never spoken any ill of you.

SELLO: You're now their enemy, and therefore, my enemy.

JOHN: SELLO!

SELLO: You must go John!

(*Pause. John paces.*)

JOHN: I've decided.

SELLO: What?

JOHN: No. I AM NOT GOING.

SELLO: You must go!

JOHN: Over my dead body! I am not going anywhere. I belong here. You've got the cheek. I'm staying right here, and you're going to dance to my music. You bloody docile thing.

SELLO: Careful John!

(*Manana enters without disturbing the two men. She washes dishes.*)

JOHN: Who the hell are you anyway? I came here on my own and I'll go on my own. I do as I please.

SELLO: In my home?

JOHN: It's our house, not even our house. You've been so damn lazy, I've been doing all the dirty work here, and you tell me to go—bloody ungrateful!

SELLO: You must be grateful for the comfort you've enjoyed all these years. You've even forgotten how your damn home looks like. You've been so bad nobody is waiting to welcome you anywhere in the world. Look here John, you can never belong to this home no matter what you do.

JOHN: This is my home. I belong here, and do what you can.

SELLO (*trying to bring reason to the discussion*): How do you justify your stand that you belong here?

JOHN: I paid my dues.

MANANA: Is that it?

JOHN: You most ungrateful swines.

MANANA: Go on John, if I were you I would go and wash my mouth.

JOHN: One more word from both of you, I blow your bloody heads off.

MANANA: I don't scare that easy John. You've overstayed your welcome. You seem to forget that this place belongs to Sello. Sello is the man of this house.

JOHN: This . . .

MANANA: Whatever your crooked mind tells you, don't try to humiliate us John. Humiliation is dangerous.

JOHN: HUMILIATION?

SELLO: Ever heard of the Middle East?

JOHN: Bloody cheek.

SELLO: Iran?

JOHN: What do you think you are?

SELLO: Angola?

JOHN: A politician?

SELLO: Ever heard of Zimbabwe?

JOHN: What?

SELLO: Do you know what is happening now in Namibia?

JOHN: What the hell . . .

SELLO: Do you know of a thing called war?

JOHN: Bloody Communist, eh?

SELLO: I'll teach you about war.

JOHN: C'mon smart guy, what do you know about war?

SELLO: Wars are fought because of humiliation. They say they fight for freedom, free from humiliation. You want to cause war between you and us. We accepted you as a person, a friend and part of our family, and now you don't seem to respect us any longer. SO YOU MUST GET OUT!

JOHN (*draws a gun*): Enough of this. I said ENOUGH! Hear me?

SELLO: Yes sir.

MANANA (*simultaneously with Sello*): Yes master.

JOHN: I am not going to have any more nonsense, understand?

SELLO: Yes sir.

MANANA: Yes master.

JOHN: Sello!

SELLO: Sir?

JOHN: Go and feed the dogs and clean the yard, water the flowers. I want a good impression when the visitors come here. (*To Manana while Sello exits:*) And you!

MANANA: Yes master.

JOHN: Clean the house, spick-and-span.

MANANA: Yes master.

(*John puts the gun back into the holster. There's a long pause while he paces around uncomfortably. Manana is busy with her work.*)

JOHN: Now Manana . . .

MANANA: Yes master.

JOHN: Okay, call me by my name, I am not a monster, I'm a liberal. I'm quite liberal.

MANANA: Alright . . .

JOHN: Let us get a solution to all this mess. Let us talk, are you with me?

MANANA: I am here.

JOHN: Good. Dialogue, let us have dialogue so that we get to knowing what is bugging who.

MANANA: I thought we know what's bugging us and what's bugging you.

JOHN: Now let us not behave like politicians, right? (*Pause.*) You love your husband, don't you?

MANANA: Very much.

JOHN: We are all human after all.

MANANA: I am glad to hear that.

JOHN: For a moment, we all get to a point where we are reduced to helpless beings, where we are at the mercy of, shall I say, nature, at the mercy of one another. A moment of confession.

MANANA: Then you owe us an apology, you owe Sello my husband an apology.

JOHN: Manana . . .

MANANA: Get to the backyard, get to Sello and apologise.

(*We hear a trumpet offstage.*)

JOHN: I try my best to be reasonable. Look what is happening in the neighbourhood.

MANANA: You stay in this house, and you know that, that man blowing a trumpet is the owner of this house, he inherited it from his grandparents.

JOHN: Now you sound like . . .

MANANA: Don't talk about the neighbourhood. Charity begins at home. Respect Sello, no matter how stupid he

may seem to you. That is how he chose to be, it's not
accidental, it's his heritage, his culture.

JOHN: You people are getting bad influence from your neighbours.

MANANA: What do you mean?

JOHN: They can't put their houses in order, but they want me
to put this house in order. I help them so much that . . .

MANANA: That is where you go wrong, that is what makes
you unpopular.

JOHN: What?

MANANA: What you think is help, they see it differently.

JOHN: How can it be different?

MANANA: You interfere. You interfere in their affairs. Why
waste time helping them when you have so much work
here?

JOHN: People can be very ungrateful. Why do you wish to see
me in trouble, to see me suffer, why?

MANANA: Nobody wishes any bad for you. You have passed
what you think is fair judgement of yourself. You think
you have done so much bad that when we take over we
shall make you suffer. No, we are not bad people, you
know best, you've seen us laughing while we are supposed to be cursing.

JOHN: Yes, what makes you seem so happy?

MANANA: We seem happy because we've got our arms open.
(*She opens her arms.*) We are ready to receive and to give,
ready to help. We seem happy because we love. Hating
for nothing makes you feel insecure, but hating for something makes you feel strong. (*Pause.*) You hate Sello, that
is why you feel insecure.

JOHN: But I don't hate . . .

MANANA (*angry*): I don't care then.

JOHN: I don't know.

MANANA: You'll know.

JOHN: Help me!

MANANA: You can't even sleep a peaceful sleep at night. You've got to keep your gun loaded all the time, you've got to see to it that you don't forget it in the morning. You carry a gun!

JOHN: Stop it Manana.

MANANA: Sello only carries a trumpet. That's all he's got, a trumpet, he's a peaceful man.

JOHN: Manana, stop!

MANANA: He wants to play you music, and you want to kill him for what is his. You are a murderer!

JOHN: That's E N O U G H !

MANANA: You want to kill him in cold blood.

JOHN: ENOUGH!

(*Pause. John goes and sits down. He is watching Manana as she goes about her work. He admires her, he lusts for her. Manana bends to inspect the oven, revealing a good portion of her thighs. John is obviously aroused. He stands up.*)

I am sorry, Manana.

MANANA: That you must tell Sello, he's the man, my husband.

JOHN: He's still blowing his trumpet.

MANANA: You never want him to blow it.

JOHN: Not that I dislike it, but the tunes he plays . . .

MANANA: What's wrong with the tunes he plays?

JOHN: They sound so primitive, they are just irritating. I'm from a musical family, my father and my brother played

Beethoven and Bach. My brother used to excel in Mendelsohn.

MANANA: Sello wants to communicate with his people, with his Gods. He's got no intentions of playing in the Opera House.

JOHN: I don't mean that.

MANANA: He plays our indigenous music.

JOHN: Can't he play something which everybody understands? Sweet music.

MANANA: What is so sweet? Life is not sweet for us John. If you have an ear you'll understand.

JOHN: Well . . . Manana, you know Sello is lucky.

MANANA: Why?

JOHN: To have a woman like you, so intelligent and attractive?

MANANA: Intelligent? Did you say intelligent and attractive?

JOHN: You're irresistible Manana. (*He is advancing towards her and Manana is backing away.*) Please Manana.

MANANA: I am going to scream.

JOHN: I love you Manana.

MANANA (*as John reaches out to hold her*): TAKE YOUR DIRTY HANDS OFF ME! (*She resists as John holds her and starts unbuttoning the overall.*)

JOHN: Come on you dirty bitch!

(*Sello enters with his trumpet still in his hands.*)

SELLO: John, what the hell? MY WIFE! (*John turns and looks at Sello, who is advancing towards him.*) MY WIFE! MY WIFE! IN MY HOUSE! IN MY HOUSE!

JOHN (*sensing trouble and reaching for his gun*): You stay right where you are! (*Sello stops.*)

SELLO (*still full of emotion, still repeating what he is saying, but in a softer tone*): My house! My wife!

JOHN (*signaling to Sello to stand against the wall, then turning to Manana*): And you there!

(*He signals to her to go outside. As Manana exits, John remains at the door. Dogs start barking. John addresses Sello offstage:*)

You think you are smart, eh? You think this is a movie. I'm the Hero, understand? From today you'll know that *your* house, *your* wife . . . (*With emotion:*) I am not going to get this house into irresponsible hands like yours! Understand? You are going to stay in here alone. Nobody is going to see you, I'll be the only one to see you.

SELLO: You're arresting me in my house?

JOHN: I am arresting you in your house, do what you can. (*He collects pots, newspapers, and anything that can be useful to Sello.*)

SELLO (*as John exits*): This will catch up with you John! Bloody bastard!

SCENE TWO

A few years later. Manana and Sello are having a discussion. Things seem to be fairly smooth and quiet.

MANANA: You're right, a lot of things have changed, nothing exciting, just changed.

SELLO: Even this madman seems to be behaving. Since the last time he separated us.

MANANA: Sello?

SELLO: Yes?

MANANA: Do you know that he tried to rape me in the store-room in the backyard. He asked me to go in there to clean up.

SELLO: The bastard, that is why he locked me in.

MANANA: I wouldn't do it Sello. How would I face you? Worst of all, how would I face Tshepo, my son? I would rather die than submit to him. And God gave me extra strength. Now it seems so long ago.

SELLO: Something will erupt soon. Let us hope that this change will take a positive course.

MANANA: It must. We must take control of it. Anyway, let's forget it.

SELLO: There are things that cannot be controlled. Like you said, things have just changed. Take weddings, for instance, they are no longer as enjoyable as before.

MANANA: Wow! Weddings! We were always running to go and see whether the bride was crying. If she wasn't, then everybody thought it was a bad choice.

SELLO: There you are.

MANANA: Maybe it was good, I don't know. Sometimes it seemed so sad.

SELLO: It wasn't. Remember you cried too. Women actually boasted about how they cried.

MANANA: Remember that song *"Dikuku di monate, lenyalo le boima"*?

SELLO: Yes, "Cakes are nice, matrimony is not easy."

MANANA: So you think that was nice.

SELLO: Yes.

MANANA: That people eat your cakes and tell you that they are going and you remain in your house and face the diffi-culties of marriage.

SELLO: That was part of our life, we were proud of that, as you say that when the bride did not cry we always thought it was a bad choice. Those weddings were part of our culture. Remember how men used to compete to see who could dig the deepest hole with his heel when they danced?

MANANA (*sings a wedding song while Sello does the men's dance, stamping hard on the floor*): "*Ukhathaz' umoya wamidali . . .*" Sello!

SELLO (*coming back to Manana*): Yes?

MANANA: There is one promise you never fulfilled, you know?

SELLO: What?

MANANA: Remember when we were still madly in love . . .

SELLO (*suppressing laughter*): Well . . .

MANANA: Remember you said you'd buy me a train and an aeroplane?

SELLO: Well, if such promises were fulfilled, Soweto would be full of trains and aeroplanes. Every housewife would be having a train and an aeroplane. There would be no parking space. (*They both laugh.*) Those were the good old days! When one could buy trousers for three pounds nine and eleven.

MANANA: And a shirt for seven and six.

SELLO: Seven and six—that was a popular price, easy to say and attractive but not easy to pay.

MANANA: Yeah, good old seven and six.

(*Pause.*)

SELLO: Today weddings are not like before. Today weddings are champagne, Scotch, and Teddy Pendergrass. Everybody drinks in the house. Like you said, things have changed, but suffering hasn't changed.

MANANA: The past sounds romantic.

SELLO: There were hard times in the past, only we were kids.

MANANA: Sello, we must live like before, we were so much in love.

SELLO: We were open to each other, we could look each other straight in the face.

MANANA: Why can't we do it now?

SELLO: I don't know. Have you noticed something about yourself?

MANANA: What?

SELLO: You just can't open your hands. I never feel inside of your palm anymore. Your fingers are always drawn, like a fist—even when we are making love. (*Pause.*) Just an open hand can restore our love; an open heart, and say it, "I LOVE YOU."

MANANA: What keeps us together then?

SELLO: Fear.

MANANA: Fear?

SELLO: When people are afraid they stick together. There are many things we fear, I cannot complete the list.

MANANA: Sello, let us love, love like before and not fear.

SELLO: If you can come to me, put your arms around me, with your palms open, look me straight in the face and I do the same, then we shall fall in love again. I love you.

MANANA: I love you too Sello.

(*They stand up, look at each other, and advance towards each other. They hold hands, and just when they are about to kiss, the dogs bark. Sello goes to check at the window.*)

SELLO: Maybe John is in the yard.

MANANA (*still on the same spot*): Sello!

SELLO (*going to Manana*): Yes?

MANANA (*holding his hands again*): Don't ever forget that I am here, that I am a woman, your wife.

SELLO: I won't forget. (*Pause.*) Think of me too. Don't let John come between us.

MANANA (*rushes to the stove*): Oh! my pot! (*She checks the pot and continues with some other work.*)

SELLO: I wonder what happened to Marogo.

MANANA: Your coloured friend?

SELLO: He was no longer coloured.

MANANA: No longer coloured?

SELLO: Yes.

MANANA: How come?

SELLO: It surfaced when his mother died that he wasn't coloured. He was *Majombozi*. His mother stayed with the rest of the family in Mofolo. He had to attend the funeral and be with the rest of the family. After that he disappeared.

MANANA: Probably to go and start afresh somewhere where he is not known.

SELLO: His mother died a tragic death.

MANANA: How?

SELLO: She was queuing for her pension.

MANANA: Hau!

SELLO: As you know, some pensioners queue from as early as three in the morning, even in winter.

MANANA: I know Seipati's mother used to be taken there five o'clock in the morning on a wheelbarrow.

SELLO: See.

MANANA: Marogo, he was some character. How did he get the name?

SELLO: He knew that most coloureds can't pronounce *marogo*, instead they say *marago*. So Marogo, through his good upbringing, couldn't say *marago* because he knew what that means. He knew *marago* was no plaything.

MANANA: Poor Marogo.

SELLO: So that is why he was called Marogo.

(*Slight pause.*)

MANANA: Man, that is sad.

SELLO: Dying in a queue? Yes, queues everywhere. Pension offices, pass offices, superintendent offices, prisons, hospitals, railway stations, bus stops, queues all over, and people dying.

MANANA: Yes, we all grew up in a queue. Many people have died waiting.

SELLO: I'll never forget it.

MANANA: What?

SELLO: As a kid! I'll never forget.

MANANA: What?

SELLO: Queuing at the African Feeding Scheme. A noble scheme to feed the hungry black kids.

MANANA: Sounds good.

SELLO: Good! Did you say good?

MANANA: What was wrong with it?

SELLO: We used to queue.

MANANA: Queue?

SELLO: Queue in the sun. We would queue for what seemed to be eternity, in the heat of the sun, waiting for the good old white man to arrive with milk and brown bread.

MANANA: Milk?

SELLO: And when he arrived it was a celebration. The women in attendance would rearrange us in our queue, get the queue more straight than before. They would hit us and tell us if we are not quiet and our queue not straight the white man would go. Hungry and anxious, we would try our best.

MANANA: Shame.

SELLO: When we were all quiet and the queue was straight, we would be made to sing. (*He sings:*) "Thank you father give us milk."

MANANA: Poor things.

SELLO: And then the queue would start moving slowly forward, slowly, slowly . . . but it would always end up in chaos, when the ones at the back see those in front already with their milk and bread. Hunger and watering mouths made them push forward.

MANANA: Ag, shame.

SELLO: It always ended like those Sunday lunchtime scrums we used to have at home.

MANANA: Scrums?

SELLO: A scrum, I tell you. Sunday was the only day we used to have meat, and a juicy potato, not meshed, the whole potato just peeled, and boy, the main bout was beetroot.

MANANA: Beetroot?

SELLO: Yes, good old beetroot with vinegar and sugar always told us it was Sunday.

MANANA: Beetroot is nice.

SELLO: The rest of the week was unimpressive.

MANANA: What did you have?

SELLO: Porridge mostly. Just clean porridge. Sometimes with sugared water, cold water straight from the tap. When we had a few pennies, then we would buy fish crumbs. My mother used to do washing in town for three white families, one on Monday, one on Tuesday, and one on Thursday. She used to complain about the Tuesday one, Van Jaarsveld. She said his washing was a big dirty pile that caused the blisters on her hands. She said the others were better because they were Jews, and they used to give her bread leftovers. When she was angry with us she used to say we are dirty dogs like Van Jaarsveld.

MANANA: He must have been terrible.

SELLO: He was also always behind with payment. The others were punctual and they gave us a little variety with our food, the bread crumbs. Those made us forget for a while that the white man is bad. Come Tuesday, mother comes empty-handed from Van Jaarsveld, then a revolution. My father was always sick.

MANANA: You better go and roll up the hose-pipe before he comes.

SELLO: So that we have peace and quiet for a change. I'll use the front.

(*He exits through the upstage door leading to the lounge. Manana is left alone. Sello re-enters with a letter in his hand.*)

MANANA: What is it?

SELLO: I found this letter on the lounge table.

MANANA: Hau! But it's opened!

SELLO: That's what surprises me.

MANANA: Who could have done it?

SELLO: Only one man keeps the key to the post-box.

MANANA: But why must he do this?

SELLO: He's afraid Manana. He thinks we could be corresponding with someone who could help us kick him out.

MANANA: This man! My God.

SELLO: He is so scared that he's becoming dangerous.

MANANA: Where is the letter from?

SELLO: It must be from Tshepo. It's stamped Sovenga.

MANANA: From my son! He opens a letter from my son!

SELLO: Anyway let's hear what he says.

MANANA: You must not leave John this time, you must ask him.

SELLO: Okay. I'll do that. Now listen. "Dear Mother and Father. . ."

MANANA: See, he always starts with his mother. His mother first.

SELLO: Okay, you win, okay.

MANANA: Don't be jealous, I've been a good mother, there's no one like mother to a son.

SELLO: Okay, I said you win. Get in touch with the *Sowetan* and the *Rand Daily Mail*. It's great news: SON STARTS WITH MOTHER IN LETTER.

MANANA: Okay, okay, read us the letter, I can see you are jealous.

SELLO: Right. "Dear Mother and Father, I am very glad to get this chance of writing this letter, with only a month to go before exams. I've recovered from flu, and I'm reading like nobody's business, I'm aiming for a distinction. I hope you too are doing fine. One thing that keeps me

disturbed is the presence of John in our home, especially
with his arrogance and uncouth manners, and his
throwing around his weight. It seems he thinks he's the
only man in the house, and he is staying with his little
kids. This disturbs me and keeps coming into my mind
when I'm reading.

"Dad, be bold and tell that man to leave your house,
and make sure that he leaves in peace while the going is
good, because he did not even buy that house, he tricked
grandpa. I grew up with this man pushing you around.
At first I did not understand, and now I am not only
understanding, I've grown to hate that man, I loathe
him! Tell him to go, because I won't have the patience to
talk to him. I'll straightaway break his ass bone if he
continues the way he is. I can cut his throat if it comes to a
push, or even saw it off!

"I know what he thinks of me, and I know he can't hate
me enough because he fears me. Yes, he fears me in spite
of the fact that he carries a gun. He fears me because he
fears the truth. He knows that I will definitely get him
out of that house, even if he could try to stop me with
gangsters, of which he is one. That will only delay, just a
little, the process of getting him out of that house.

"But Dad, do be careful, because that man is insane.
This is quite clear from his goings-on. He is a bloody
insane fanatic. Besides that, he is a moron, he can't dis-
cern between good and bad, but still I am going to get
him out of there. Otherwise, I shall have failed in my
duties as a son in that house! You brought me up and sent
me to school so that I should be able to deal with such
cases, and now I'm fully equipped. We gave John enormous chances to change, and now it is quite clear he
does not want to change.

"Mother, I'm missing you. I'm just looking forward to
the day I arrive home. Very funny, I never feel old
enough. I still wish you could cuddle me, as you always
do when you are excited about my reports. I wonder if

babies feel that way. That is why I feel I must get rid of John, and then we are going to be the happiest trio ever. "Greetings. Your loving son, Tshepo."

(*Pause. Silence as Sello walks around digesting the contents of the letter.*)

Well, what do you think? (*Pause.*) Eh?

MANANA: I'm . . . I don't know what to say. I'm overwhelmed.

SELLO: He's a brave man. He's grown to be a man.

MANANA: I'm so proud of him, my little boy.

SELLO: He's taken after me, you know that.

MANANA: That is news to me.

SELLO: Well, it's a fact.

MANANA: When he does good, he's taken after you. When he's in the wrong: "You're just like your mother!"

SELLO: Anyway, he's a man, he can make his own decisions now.

MANANA: I feel like the curtain has just gone up and we must start acting. I feel like going out to the wind, to the mountaintops, to the ocean shore, and feel nature embracing me. The mighty hand of the black God that rules this land.

SELLO: The soil is black and fertile, the following is over, we must plough and wait for the harvest.

MANANA: The black clouds will soon be rolling and rumbling, heralding the torrents that enhance the harvest.

SELLO: We need a change Manana.

MANANA: A change?

SELLO: Our lives must change.

MANANA: And what about John?

SELLO: He must go. (*Pause.*) I was thinking.

MANANA: What?

SELLO: That when Tshepo graduates we must slaughter for our ancestors. Thank them. Tshepo will be the first graduate in our family.

MANANA: That's an excellent idea.

SELLO: But how do we do it?

MANANA: Sure, we can sacrifice, starting from now.

SELLO: The question is where do we do this, where? We have no place. We no longer have a sacred place where we can talk to our Gods. We must slaughter, shed a bit of blood. Make a sacrifice to our Gods. (*Pause.*) John must go, we need a change.

MANANA: A real change, not the newspaper type. Mr. Harold from the USA here on a fact-finding mission, and he ends up at the Kruger National Park drunk, go swimming at Sea Point, wine and dine at the Sea Point pavilion with the best professional ladies in the country.

SELLO: How? . . . That professional sounds fishy.

MANANA: Smells fishy. A stone's throw from the hustle and bustle of Sea Point with all its glitter, along the mountain slope, there black people live under boulders, in furrows, who spend days without a meal. Mr. Harold, with a hangover from all this, writes a report that we are happy and there is a change, and the man never made contacts with us. We do not need a wind of change, we need a flood of change. Like Noah's flood.

SELLO: Oh! John! John! Everything smells of John.

MANANA: What about the man he killed?

SELLO: Which one?

MANANA: The one he said was coming to rescue you the day he locked you up.

SELLO: He was found not guilty!

MANANA: Not guilty!

SELLO: He is licensed. He's got a license for that gun.

MANANA: If licensed are you licensed to kill innocent people?

SELLO: He said it was self-defence.

MANANA: Self-defence, he's a murderer! Defending with a gun against an unarmed man! Shooting an unarmed man and calling it self-defence?

SELLO (*going towards his trumpet*): Let us wait for him. I'm surely going to tell him to go, and this is final. (*He starts blowing some scales from the trumpet. Each time he blows the dogs start barking.*)

MANANA (*opening the cupboard*): Have you seen the new tea set he bought?

SELLO: No.

MANANA: He said we must not use it.

SELLO: Not use it?

MANANA: You know he thinks he's special.

SELLO: All he's left with is to separate the air, so that we don't breathe the air he breathes. Just keep on making him tea in it but never wash it.

(*Manana laughs.*)

You must never wash it, bloody pig!

MANANA: Oh! Sello, don't kill me.

SELLO: He's so stupid, he reminds me of a certain stupid white guy I used to work with who thought that black men want freedom because they think if they were free they could be great Casanovas.

MANANA: Casanovas?

SELLO: That is how they think.

MANANA: And where is he anyway?

SELLO: Who?

MANANA: Your *boerewors*?

SELLO: He must be in one of their drunken orgies where all their rules are manufactured.

MANANA: And oh God, when he's drunk . . . then he becomes so impossible. Sello, remember the last time he said we must give him six months to change, but now it seems worse.

SELLO: What can an alcoholic do in six months? John is drunk for at least twelve hours out of twenty-four hours. That means in six months he's drunk for three months.

MANANA: Man, you sound like the great mathematician.

SELLO: Compared to John I am. Ja, as I said, drunk for three out of six months. Let's say he sleeps for six hours a day, that means another one and a half months gone. So it means out of six months he has already lost four and a half months not thinking. Right?

MANANA: Au Sello, must you paint him so bad?

SELLO: I am not through yet. When he wakes up, for at least four hours he is trying to rid himself of a hangover. That is equal to one month out of six, and that means five and a half months gone—that is, five and a half months of nonthinking. This means every day there's a loss of twenty hours, for two hours he is busy trying to remember what he did while he was drunk. Now tell me, what change can he undergo in six months?

MANANA: Sello! I fear you.

SELLO: Facts.

MANANA: But you are right, you know.

SELLO: Give me six months, he said, how many years now?

MANANA: Sello, I think, now really, you must plan how to approach him and how to insist that he goes, because change he won't.

SELLO: He won't change.

MANANA: Don't do as you did with your former boss.

SELLO: What did I do?

MANANA: Remember, you were trying to get him fired, but instead you got fired.

SELLO: Well, I learnt a lesson. White people in South Africa will always stick together.

MANANA: You're right, they stick together. Your former boss, he was a character too.

SELLO: You mean Mr. Kromspoor?

MANANA: What a name too! He had silly things to say too.

SELLO: But did I ever tell you about his school and mathematics?

MANANA: No.

SELLO: You see, we used to sell some sheet metal. Most of all customers used to buy either ninety degrees or forty-five degrees, right?

MANANA: Ja.

SELLO: So one day one customer came and he wanted twenty-two and a half degrees. Mr. Kromspoor said there is no such a thing. So I told him that we could bisect the forty-five degrees and make it twenty-two and a half. So I went about the business. Kromspoor was so impressed that I know mathematics. Well, Kromspoor did not want to be outdone by a black man. "You know Sello," he said, "I used to be so good in mathematics, but the trouble is that

I went on leave and when I came back the class was ahead of me, so I left doing mathematics."

MANANA (*laughing*): Going on leave at school while others are schooling!

SELLO: That is what he told me. Kromspoor never went to school. He thought he was being clever and yet he was exposing his ignorance.

MANANA: How did he hold such a position?

SELLO: Stores manager, that was Mr. Kromspoor. He had the right colour. Be white in South Africa, you're made! Going on leave and finding the class ahead of you. How can such a school produce results with every child going on leave at a different time, whenever one's leave is due? All the same I gave him his due respect as a white man in SA.

MANANA: Ja, Kromspoor. I suppose John did the same.

SELLO: Did what?

MANANA: He must have gone on leave when they were teaching manners, and when he came back the class was so advanced that he left. That is why he's got no manners.

SELLO: That is the biggest problem with a moron.

MANANA: What is a moron?

SELLO: It's a person like John who thinks he's a superhuman and the rest are subhumans, and he's so dependent on us. A moron is a man like John, surrounded by dogs and always carrying a gun. That's why he must go. A moron with a gun is dangerous.

MANANA: We must find a way.

SELLO: You're right, we must be tactful.

MANANA: Now let us plan.

SELLO: Right. He'll come in through this door.

MANANA: Drunk.

SELLO: No, let us assume he'll be sober. Let us assume we are dealing with a sober man.

MANANA: Right. He comes in through that door.

SELLO: Gives us his usual look.

MANANA: Right.

SELLO: Then he asks if the dogs are fed.

MANANA: Right, asks if the dogs are fed.

SELLO: We don't answer him. We just look at him.

MANANA: We don't answer him, we just . . . I think we must answer him.

SELLO: What must we say?

MANANA: Say yes, the dogs are fed, and we would like to talk to you.

SELLO: Okay, the dogs are fed, and we would like to talk to you.

MANANA (*acting as John*): What is it you want to talk about?

SELLO (*shouting emotionally*): This is final John, you go!

MANANA (*shocked*): Just like that?

SELLO: It has to be effective if he must go.

MANANA: Then the great moment comes.

SELLO: What?

MANANA: He draws his gun.

SELLO: The gun. How do we take care of his gun?

(*Sello goes to his trumpet, takes it, and blows a few notes. John enters while Sello is blowing. He's got his gun in his right hand and a bottle of whisky in the other hand.*)

JOHN: Stop it! (*Sello and Manana turn to John.*) Go and blow that thing outside, far from here where we cannot hear you. Hear! Out! (*Sello exits with his trumpet. John turns to Manana.*) And you follow him. Out of my sight! (*Manana exits.*)

Bloody bastards. (*He goes and sits on the chair next to the table.*) I'm right after all. Ungrateful bastards. (*Pause.*) Where do they expect me to go? I'm not going anywhere. I'm staying right here. I belong here, whether they like it or not. Go away? Over my dead body! Over my dead body! I'll fight tooth and nail to stay here, even if it means shooting them all plus their neighbours! Me and my wife are here to stay. What do they want with me here? (*Pause.*)

I must just buy another gun, more bullets, then I'll be okay. It's all bloody nice for them to say it's their house. My wife, what do they want to do to my wife! To someone's daughter! Fancy having Sello as a son-in-law! (*He stands up and starts pacing.*)

No, not my wife, don't worry dear, the situation is under control, we are not going anywhere. This has become our house, our home. You must not be tempted by nothing dear. They are not happy. We are happy, we always laugh at suppertime, don't we? Yes, we do laugh. We are happy with our dogs, they give us all the security we want. Don't ever get tempted. Go down on your knees and pray. Shake the devil away, we are God's chosen people. They are not our type, they are inferior. Don't worry dear, you and the dogs will be okay. (*Pause.*)

I must just get more guns. Now they don't even want me to scratch myself. Where must I go to? Their neighbours have got big mouths about me going. What business have they got in this house? We are staying so nicely here, and they just want to cause friction between us. Bloody ungrateful neighbours. I am not interfering in their home affairs, but I try my best to promote harmony in their homes. (*Pause. He takes a sip from the bottle.*)

But God is great. I am just a humble servant of God.
I'll prove to the whole world that I can live peacefully
with these people. I'll show them the way, lead them, like
the children of Israel. Those without faith will rebel
against me. Those who are starving, God will send
manna from heaven. No more high infant mortality rate,
kwashiorkor! I am Moses. As for that little brat at the
university, my dogs will get him. He thinks he can get
me out of here, what a cheek! He must just wait until I
empty the whole barrel on him. (*Pause. He is drunk.*)

What must I do? How can I change? What change,
what change? How can I become something else? I am
myself, good or bad, God wants me this way. Change
over my dead body.

(*Sello and Manana enter quietly. Manana is carrying a pint of milk,
and Sello is carrying a spade and rake. John sees them, composes
himself.*)

Oh, you are back.

MANANA: It's time to prepare for supper, sorry if we disturbed . . .

JOHN: No, not at all, sit down a while, let's talk, talk a while.
Do sit down.

(*Sello and Manana sit down without uttering a word. Pause.*)

I have been doing some thinking, some stock-taking,
and I felt there was a need for me to consult you—that is
about our lives here in the house. Are you with me?

SELLO: We have made so many attempts and all were futile,
because such meetings are meant to come out in your
favour.

JOHN: Explain.

SELLO: We have on several occasions asked you to regard us as
human beings, to let us live normal lives. We are aware
that even if we chased you away, you have nowhere to go,

you have stayed here so long that this has become your home. Our parents lived here, and they have left us in this awkward situation. The most sensible thing for us to do is to resolve the matter. Let this become our home, you and us. Let us have equal powers in this house.

JOHN: Not cutting you short, this is our home, you and I.

SELLO: No, John, at present it's like your home, and we are your servants. It's only our home historically. Now, how would you feel to be a servant in your father's house under a stranger?

JOHN: There, you see, you regard me as a stranger.

SELLO: Because you've made yourself a stranger. We are sitted here because you want so. When we want, you know what happens. We do everything as long as it suits you. We have completely lost ourselves.

JOHN: What do you propose we do?

SELLO: You need to change John, a complete change.

JOHN: But you are free to do as you please. You can do as you please in this kitchen, cook your food, of your choice. You can do as you please in your room.

SELLO: That is not enough John. We want to have a full say in the running of this whole house. We also want to choose which flowers to plant. We also want to show our visitors what we have achieved and be proud of it, like you show your visitors. Now, I'm the one who waters the flowers and keeps the garden clean and green, but I cannot walk freely in that garden.

JOHN: Why?

SELLO: Your dogs.

JOHN: So what must be done?

SELLO: Get rid of your dogs, or teach them that we are respectable people like you, and not thieves or potential thieves. They must change.

JOHN: But Sello, the time is not yet ripe for such changes, they can't be achieved overnight.

SELLO: We feel the time is ripe for us to stop suffering. It has long been ripe. You're right it shouldn't be overnight, that is too long to go on suffering, the night is too long. It must be done now.

JOHN (*angrily*): You're asking for the impossible Sello.

SELLO: What are we talking about?

JOHN: We are talking about nothing. Regulations are regulations. There must be order in this house, and I'll maintain it.

SELLO: I expected such an ending. Our beliefs are too deeply rooted in us. You are firm on what you believe.

JOHN: Can't you accept solutions? Civilised solutions?

SELLO: Accept?

JOHN: Yes, accept.

SELLO: I hate the very word *accept*. We have accepted too much. The black people have accepted a lot of filth. We accepted the pass, we accepted apartheid, we accepted influx control, we accepted bantu education, we accepted bantustans.

JOHN: Be careful of what you say.

SELLO: We accepted Christ, the Bible, Muslims, Rastas, communism, capitalism, the whole heap of rubbish.

JOHN: I said careful . . .

SELLO: All we do is accept, accept, accept. Don't we have brains? Can't we think? Can't we be creative? I am sick and tired of accepting. God gave me brains and I am God's creation too. Don't tell me to accept. I want AFRICA! AFRICA MUST THINK!

JOHN: What do you know of Africa?

SELLO: That is the soil I come from, that is where I belong, and that is where I'll end up.

JOHN: You've been reading that black power poetry, eh?

SELLO: Do you know why the boers in the farms keep the government in power?

JOHN: Who the hell are you? Who's been . . .

SELLO: They keep it because it gives them the land. The government gives them the land so that they can identify with the soil. Those boers know how the soil smells, they know how it smells when it's damp and when it's dry. They know how it feels in the hand. They'll die for that soil.

JOHN: What do you know?

SELLO: The black man is taken away from the soil. They don't even want to call him African, because that is the only link to the soil left. They'll call him nonwhite, kaffir, bantu, plural, or anything as long as it does not link him to the soil. He cannot own land so that he cannot touch the soil. He's taken to the dry bantustans so that he must not know the sweet smell of damp soil. He's given barren soil so that it yields nothing, so that he can come back to the town and be turned into a machine. The only time the black man touches the soil is in Doornkop, in Avalon, when they pass the spade around. We touch the soil to throw it into the grave. The soil is important, and this soil I'm standing on is Africa, and I am an African.

JOHN: Who is not an African?

SELLO: To be an African first respect Africa and the Africans, obey them.

JOHN: You don't scare anybody.

SELLO: I don't want to scare anybody.

JOHN: What the hell . . .

SELLO: I'm not scared too.

JOHN: You think you are getting away with it. Tell me, what is it you trust on your own? People become progressive by accepting modern scientific methods of solving problems . . .

SELLO: Progressive! Ha! Progressive! I have heard that before. I told you that I am past accepting, I am now thinking. It is through an accepted piece of paper that you are clinging on to this place. There is no piece of paper that is going to tell me what to do and what not to do. You are that type of person . . .

JOHN: So you know me, eh, you can analyse me, eh?

SELLO: I know you very well John. It's Manana and I who cook for you, dish for you, we know the amount of food you eat, we know how many blankets you use every season of the year. We know how many trousers you have, how many underpants you have, and we both know which one you are wearing right now. We know you, even every drivel that amuses you and makes you laugh. We know how drunk you become, we know you and your wife do not sleep on one bed.

JOHN: Enough!

SELLO: You do not know us John, you do not know what we eat, you do not know how we sleep. You do not know how often we change our underwear.

JOHN: That is, if you do change at all.

SELLO: You don't even know how we cook your food.

JOHN: I've heard enough of this.

SELLO: There's still a lot more.

JOHN: Shut up! I'll fight you like a mad dog if you push me.

SELLO: You're an ignorant ape!

JOHN: Now you're starting me.

SELLO: Do what you like.

JOHN: Do you hear what you say?

SELLO: Come on! Take out your gun!

JOHN: This is enough. (*Pause.*) The end is too ghastly to contemplate.

SELLO: Come on! What scares you?

JOHN: What are you up to? What do you trust?

SELLO: I trust myself.

JOHN: Do your damndest. Come on! (*He draws his gun.*) Now
you've had it. You asked for it. Both of you, over there!
(*He paces around, keeping his eyes on them. He takes the bottle
of liquor and drinks as he paces around.*) I won't hear any
more from you. All I want is respect. (*He puts his gun back
into the holster. He now looks very drunk and more dangerous.
He takes a few steps towards the door, poised like an army
commander. He steps to and fro with his chest out. He stops and
stands at attention like a soldier and starts shouting commands
to Sello and Manana.*)
    Attention! (*Pause.*) I said attention! (*Sello and Manana
look at each other, confused.*) Attention! (*They quickly
respond. John starts moving around again.*) We need some
discipline here. Discipline. And I'm going to get it.
(*Pause.*)
    People fear the army because the army needs disci-
pline. People fear discipline. (*He marches.*) You get free
food, a holiday allowance, free transport, free entertainment. You can even spend some time with your wife and
have sex. The army is just too good to you. Now I'm
going to have some discipline here, understand? (*Pause.*)
Understand? We support you so that you can obey
orders. Obey orders. Tomorrow or any other day we may
be invaded. A lot of people want to topple us. We are not

going to lose this war. (*Shouts:*) When I say shoot, you shoot! At ease! (*Pause.*)

The army looks after you. You can stay in the army for the rest of your life, and you'll never regret one minute of it. You lose nothing by being in the army. (*He stops pacing and stands at attention.*) Attention! (*Sello and Manana promptly respond.*)

Cleanliness is next to godliness. This place must be kept spick-and-span. We must make a good impression to the visiting officers. I am going to make the best outfit out of you. Start work now, when I come back this place must be spick-and-span, not a speck of dust. Dismiss! (*He exits.*)

MANANA (*clapping her hands*): *Mohlolo!*

SELLO: What a show!

MANANA: What's wrong with him?

SELLO: He looks bad.

MANANA: He went through this alone.

SELLO: All by himself. There's never been anyone with him.

MANANA: Bloody alcoholic!

SELLO: He looks terrible. He's like a caged animal.

MANANA: I heard him cry for mercy at night: "God help me! God forgive me!"

SELLO: Killing people for nothing. You should have seen his eyes, he looked desperate. He was frightening.

MANANA: Drunk! That's all.

SELLO: You think so?

MANANA: Now you see who we are dealing with?

SELLO: A rotten-headed ex-army alcoholic. Now we've got to pay for all the shit he used to carry around in his pants.

(*Pause.*)

MANANA: What about his wife?

SELLO: There must be something wrong with her to love such a brute—that is, if she loves him at all, let alone having sex with him.

(*Pause.*)

MANANA: Sello?

SELLO: Yes.

MANANA: I am leaving.

SELLO: Where to?

MANANA: I am leaving you.

SELLO: Where are you going to?

MANANA: I'm going to look for a man, a man who can protect me.

SELLO (*going towards Manana*): Manana, you can't do this to me.

MANANA: Yes I can. I'm sick and tired of this rotten life.

SELLO: Manana, don't give up when we are about to win.

MANANA: How long Sello? How long must we hope?

SELLO (*trying to hold Manana*): I love you Manana.

MANANA: Don't touch me! I'm leaving you, my mind is made up. You can remain tearing yourself like mad dogs. I am sick Sello. Sick! I'm a nervous wreck! (*She cries.*)

SELLO: Manana, please, don't give up. We are about there, we are winning, we are winning, Manana.

(*Long pause.*)

MANANA: Sello, I'm not feeling well. This is too much for me.

SELLO: Sometimes I also feel like giving it up. We are supposed to be free in our own home, but with John we are as good as in jail. Section six or ten, twelve, twenty-two, or any number, in prison indefinitely. Man just makes life difficult. Man just don't want happiness. The world used to be wide and free, man made it small with restrictions. Your reference book must have the right stamp, and the right stamp is the only one missing at the pass office—Ten-One-B, Ten-One-Z, Twelve-Five-R, who cares! Proclaimed area of shit! Your signature here, your righthand thumb there, your travel document, fences, border gates. Welcome to Bophuthatswana! Sun City! The thirty-million-rand oasis in a desert! You are now leaving the Republic of Vendaland—this is a white area, no blacks allowed. Riot police, sneezing machine, tear gas, Alsatians. The situation—tense or calm or under control—police keep a low profile, watching the mourners from a distance. Railway line bombed. Three terrorists killed at a bank. The leaders welcome the changes. Improve the quality of life in Soweto. Drama in Soweto—the chief slams the bishop, the bishop slams the minister, the minister slams the doctor, the doctor slams the councillor—the grand slam! Immorality Act, the Group Areas Act, mixed marriage—who wants a mixed-up marriage? Love across the colour line—who wants love across any line? School boycotts, student leaders detained, students banned, schools burning. Students leaving the country. Steve Biko dies in detention. They hang themselves in their cells, some slip in the bathroom and die. They jump from the tenth floor and die. The leaders welcome the changes. Our one and only Miriam Makeba makes it in America. Letta Mbulu puts Azania on the map. We are proud of the genius of Hugh Masekela. Millie Jackson was here for the dollars, and she'll be coming back for some more dollars. Ben Satch Masinga, Nick Moyake, Elijah Nkwanyane Mckay Davashe, Cyril Magubane, Kippie Moeketsi . . . Morolong. Great artists, all died penniless. Did you hear that the big American star was drunk on stage?

MANANA: Serves them right. Serves them bloody right.

SELLO: I haven't had a report about the two fat ones!

MANANA: Ho-ho! The two tons of fun. It seems the fat ones had a good time, Azapo gave them a break.

SELLO: They won't forget sunny South Africa and the usual "The people are so friendly."

MANANA: Do you think they left their weight purposely? I mean to make money?

SELLO: They say Americans do things in a big way. They'd do anything for the dollars. Capitalism.

MANANA: Maybe they did it for America.

SELLO: Patriotism.

MANANA: Do you think you'll ever continue with your music?

SELLO: I won't give it up. I'll keep on blowing this trumpet. I am an artist. I will forever struggle for peace and justice to the universe. It's all in the family.

(*Dogs bark continuously throughout this scene. The door is flung open and John runs in. His clothes are soiled. He's got a gun and fires a shot outside. He stops in the middle of the house and looks back towards the door. Manana and Sello are surprised.*)

MANANA: *Bafokeng ke bao!*

JOHN: Don't just stand there, close the door!

(*Manana and Sello are still confused.*)

For God's sake stop staring at me, we're in trouble!

MANANA: Who's in trouble?

JOHN: No time for that.

MANANA: You've been looking for trouble.

JOHN: There's trouble across the road, and from there, it's here.

SELLO: Not here!

JOHN (*panicking*): There's trouble coming.

(*He runs into his room. He comes out a bit calmer, holding a gun in one hand and a bottle of whisky in the other. He takes a swig. He briskly moves towards the door. As he peeps, stones are thrown from outside. They miss him but hit the door. He retreats. He goes to the door again and fires two shots. Sello and Manana are dumbfounded.*)

I said stop staring at me. Guard the door! Guard the door! Get a move on! Get going!

(*Sello moves slowly towards the door.*)

Don't you value this house?

MANANA: Do you value it? Do you respect it?

JOHN: Shut up!

(*Sello is at the door and it's all quiet except for the dogs barking.*)

What do you see? Who is there?

SELLO (*returning to his position next to Manana*): There's nobody here.

(*John goes to the door. Stones are thrown again, continuously. He shoots and retreats into the house. There are screams from children. Sello rushes to the door. He remains staring outside.*)

A child! You killed a child! You killed a child! For nothing.

JOHN (*pointing the gun towards Sello*): Take it easy pal, he asked for it.

SELLO: You killed a defenceless child!

JOHN: 'Twas self-defence.

SELLO: Self-defence? Murderer!

JOHN: What if I was dead? Those stones!

SELLO: Shame on you John. MURDERER!

(*He exits. John is still looking very drunk and as though he's only realising now what is happening. He looks at his gun, at Manana.*)

JOHN: What's wrong? What's happening? Who . . . what? Who fired a shot? (*Lowers his gun.*) This is too much. This is too much for me. Nobody wants to listen to me. Everybody is turning away from me. What have they got to do with us? What have you got to do with them and the rest of the neighbours?

MANANA: We are neighbours.

JOHN: Okay. So what?

MANANA: So-li-da-ri-ty. We share our problems.

JOHN: But you are not in trouble, we live together so peacefully.

MANANA: Not peacefully! You haven't been a nice lodger.

JOHN: What must I do?

MANANA: You've pointed a gun at the owner of this house. You've just killed an innocent child.

JOHN: What must I do? I am trying my best.

(*Sello enters, dejected, and sits next to the table.*)

MANANA: Hand over that gun. Drop it down, because it's going to put you into trouble. Let us live like human beings. If you can't drop that gun, keep it and let us see how far you go.

JOHN: I'll go as far as I please. This is my house, I do as I please! I'm going out. When I come back, you'll tell a different story.

(*He goes into his room. He comes out frantic and busy, trying to put on his jacket and obviously angry. He exits. Manana, realising that John is not carrying the gun, goes to Sello.*)

MANANA: Sello!

SELLO: Yes?

MANANA: The gun!

SELLO: The gun?

MANANA: He's not carrying the gun!

SELLO: The gun!

MANANA: Here's a chance Sello. Go and get it! You've always wanted to do something. Here's a chance Sello.

SELLO: Wait! Now listen carefully. I'll guard the door, just in case he surprises us. I can handle him without a gun. Now you go and get it.

MANANA: Okay, I'll go and get it.

(*Manana goes into John's room. She comes out with her arms folded, concealing the gun in her breast. They hear John's footsteps outside. Manana gets very close to Sello so that she can give him the gun without anyone seeing. John enters, running towards the door of his room. Sello, holding the gun, calls him.*)

SELLO: John!

(*John turns around. He sees Sello with the gun pointing at him. He stares at him in disbelief.*)

JOHN: Don't shoot!

SELLO: Do you feel how it feels to be that side of the gun?

JOHN (*very scared and backing to the wall*): That thing is loaded.

SELLO (*Fires a shot in the air; angrily*): Of course I know!

JOHN: You'll kill me, you are not trained to handle this thing.

SELLO: Of course I'm going to kill you John.

JOHN: Let's talk Sello.

SELLO: I'm tired of talking John. I have exhausted the meaning of all the words I know. You've committed crimes John. You've committed murders, and you must pay for all that John. You've made us live like animals here, in my

father's house! You've made enemies with our neighbours. You despise us. You treat us like kids, you detest
us, you've made us your slaves John! You even wanted to
rape my wife! I'm going to kill you John! I'm going to
shoot you with this gun of yours. You are powerless now
John! Because your only power is this gun, without this
gun you've got no balls. I AM GOING TO SHOOT YOU!
Those well-fed white boys, those well-fed white boys,
you know what they did to me?

JOHN: Please Sello, don't shoot. I'm prepared to talk.

SELLO: Keep quiet! (*He shoots in the air again. Pause as he paces
around.*)

MANANA (*sensing a compromising tone in Sello*): Oh Sello! Do it!
Oh men! Men! You men! What has got hold of you Sello?
Shoot him! He's a killer! Shoot him! For me Sello, for us
Sello. For Tshepo Sello, our son. Your son, from your
loins Sello. Nine months I carried him Sello. Sometimes I
thought I wouldn't make it. I nearly got a miscarriage
because of John. Think of all that Sello. How we struggled for seventeen years, to bring him up to be a man, to
better our lives. Remember the letter he wrote to us from
Varsity? Sello, be a man. Be strong. Where is Tshepo
today? Now? Nobody knows where he is today. We his
parents do not know where is our son. We do not know
whether he still lives or not, and where. Even if he's still
alive, of what good is it when we do not live as a family?
ALL THIS IS BECAUSE OF THIS MAN! How many
innocent little things, children, has he killed? The hopes
of every family? Nobody is at peace with him in the
whole neighbourhood. What makes him think that he's
the only one right in the whole world? Kill him Sello!
You've got every good reason to kill him.

JOHN: Please . . .

SELLO: I said quiet! If I kill you, humanity loses nothing. I'm
going to make a human being out of you. I am not going

to soil my hands with human blood. Besides, if I kill you, you learn nothing. I want to teach you. I'll teach you to be a human being. I'll make a human being out of you, and that will be my contribution to humanity, and then I can sing a new song.

CURTAIN

FOR COLORED GIRLS WHO HAVE CONSIDERED SUICIDE/WHEN THE RAINBOW IS ENUF

A CHOREOPOEM

NTOZAKE SHANGE

for the spirits of my grandma
viola benzena murray owens
and my great aunt
effie owens josey

For colored girls who have considered suicide/when the rainbow is enuf was produced in New York by Joseph Papp and Woodie King, Jr., at the Henry Street Settlement's New Federal Theatre, the New York Shakespeare Festival Public Theatre, and then at the Booth Theatre on Broadway, where it opened on September 15, 1976, with the following cast:

lady in brown	Janet League
lady in yellow	Aku Kadogo
lady in red	Trazana Beverley
lady in green	Paula Moss
lady in purple	Risë Collins
lady in blue	Laurie Carlos
lady in orange	Ntozake Shange

Directed by Oz Scott; scenery by Ming Cho Lee; lighting by Jennifer Tipton; costumes by Judy Dearing; choreography by Paula Moss; music for "I Found God in Myself" by Diana Wharton. Associate Producer, Bernard Gersten. A New York Shakespeare Festival Production in association with the Henry Street Settlement's New Federal Theatre.

AUTHOR'S NOTE

For colored girls who have considered suicide/when the rainbow is enuf was first presented at the Bacchanal, a woman's bar just outside Berkeley, California. With Paula Moss & Elvia Marta who worked with me in Raymond Sawyer's Afro-American Dance Company & Halifu's The Spirit of Dance; Nashira Ntosha, a guitarist & program coordinator at KPOO-FM (one of the few Bay Area stations focusing on women's programming); Jessica Hagedorn, a poet & reading tour companion; & Joanna Griffin, co-founder of the Bacchanal, publisher of Effie's Press, & a poet. We just did it. Working in bars waz a circumstantial aesthetic of poetry in San Francisco from Spec's, an old beat hangout, to 'new' Malvina's, Minnie's Can-Do Club, the Coffee Gallery, & the Rippletad. With as much space as a small studio on the Lower East Side, the five of us, five women, proceeded to dance, make poems, make music, make a woman's theater for about twenty patrons. This was December of 1974. We were a little raw, self-conscious, & eager. Whatever we were discovering in ourselves that nite had been in process among us for almost two years.

I first met Jessica & Nashira thru Third World Communications (The Woman's Collective) when the first anthology of Third World women writers in the U.S.A. was published. With Janice Mirikitani, Avotcja, Carol Lee Sanchez, Janet Campbell Hale, Kitty Tsui, Janic Cobb, Thulani, and a score more, San Francisco waz inundated with women poets, women's readings, & a multilingual woman presence, new to all of us & desperately appreciated. The force of these readings on all our lives waz to become evident as we directed our energies toward clarifying our lives—& the lives of our mothers, daughters, & grandmothers—as women. During the same period, Shameless Hussy Press & The Oakland Women's Press Collective were also reading anywhere & everywhere they could. In a single season, Susan Griffin, Judy Grahn, Barbara Gravelle, & Alta, were promoting the

poetry & presence of women in a legendary male-poet's environment. This is the energy & part of the style that nurtured
for colored girls . . .

More stable as a source of inspiration & historical continuity waz the Women's Studies Program at Sonoma State College, where I worked with J. J. Wilson, Joanna Griffin, &
Wopo Holup over a three-year span. Courses designed to
make women's lives & dynamics familiar to us, such as:
Woman as Artist; Woman as Poet; Androgynous Myths in
Literature; Women's Biography I & II; Third World Women
Writers, are inextricably bound to the development of my
sense of the world, myself, & women's language. Studying
the mythology of women from antiquity to the present
day led directly to the piece *Sechita* in which a dance hall girl
is perceived as deity, as slut, as innocent & knowing.
Unearthing the mislaid, forgotten, &/or misunderstood
women writers, painters, mothers, cowgirls, & union leaders
of our pasts proved to be both a supportive experience & a
challenge not to let them down, not to do less than—at all
costs not to be less woman than—our mothers, from Isis to
Marie Laurencin, Zora Neale Hurston to Käthe Kollwitz,
Anna May Wong to Calamity Jane.

Such joy & excitement I knew in Sonoma, then I would
commute back the sixty miles to San Francisco to study dance
with Raymond Sawyer, Ed Mock, & Halifu. Knowing a
woman's mind & spirit had been allowed me, with dance I
discovered my body more intimately than I had imagined
possible. With the acceptance of the ethnicity of my thighs &
backside, came a clearer understanding of my voice as a
woman & as a poet. The freedom to move in space, to
demand of my own sweat a perfection that could continually
be approached, though never known, waz poem to me, my
body & mind ellipsing, probably for the first time in my life.
Just as Women's Studies had rooted me to an articulated
female heritage & imperative, so dance as explicated by Raymond Sawyer & Ed Mock insisted that everything African,
everything halfway colloquial, a grimace, a strut, an arched

back over a yawn, waz mine. I moved what waz my unconscious knowledge of being in a colored woman's body to my
known everydayness. The depth of my past waz made tangible to me in Sawyer's *Ananse,* a dance exploring the Diaspora to contemporary Senegalese music, pulling ancient
trampled spirits out of present tense Afro-American Dance.
Watching Ed Mock re-create the Step Brothers' or Bert Williams' routines in class or on stage, in black face mimicking
Eddie Cantor or Gloria Swanson, being the rush of irony &
control that are the foundation of jazz dance, was as startling
as humbling. With Raymond Sawyer & Ed Mock, Paula Moss
& I learned the wealth of our bodies, if we worked, if we
opened up, if we made the dance our own.

The first experience of women's theater for me as a per-
former waz the months I spent with Halifu Osumare's The
Spirit of Dance, a troupe of five to six black women who
depicted the history of Black dance from its origins in Western Africa thru to the popular dances seen on our streets.
Without a premeditated or conscious desire to create a
female piece, that's what, in fact, Halifu did. Working in
San Francisco & Berkeley public schools as an adjunct to
Ethnic Studies, I learned the mechanics of self-production &
absorbed some of Halifu's confidence in her work, the legit-
imacy of our visions. After some 73 performances with The
Spirit of Dance, I left the company to begin production of *for
colored girls . . .*

In the summer of 1974 I had begun a series of seven poems,
modeled on Judy Grahn's *The Common Woman,* which were to
explore the realities of seven different kinds of women. They
were numbered pieces: the women were to be nameless &
assume hegemony as dictated by the fullness of their lives.
The first of the series is the poem, 'one' (orange butterflies &
aqua sequins), which prompted the title *& this is for colored
girls who have considered suicide/when the rainbow is enuf.* I waz
smitten by my own language, & called all the performances I
waz to give from then on by that title. In other words, all the
readings & choreopoetry that Paula Moss & I developed after

that summer waz *for colored girls* . . . We started at the Bacchanal & worked through the winter at Ed Mock's Dance Studio
with the assistance of West Coast Dance Works, setting pieces
& cleaning up poems. I found two bands, The Sound Clinic (a
horn trio) & Jean Desarmes & His Raggae Blues Band, who
agreed to work with us if I found space. & I did. The space we
used waz the space I knew: Women's Studies Departments,
bars, cafes, & poetry centers. With the selection of poems
changing, dependent upon our audience & our mood, & the
dance growing to take space of its own, so that Paula inspired
my words to fall from me with her body, & The Sound Clinic
working with new arrangements of Ornette Coleman compo-
sitions & their own, The Raggae Blues Band giving Caribbean
renditions of Jimi Hendrix & Redding, we set dates for Minnie's Can-Do Club in Haight-Ashbury. The poets showed up
for us, the dancers showed up for us, the women's community
showed up, & we were listed as a 'must see' in *The Bay
Guardian*. Eight days after our last weekend at Minnie's, Paula
& I left to drive cross country to New York to do 'the show,' as
we called it, at the Studio Rivbea in New York.

Our work in San Francisco waz over. With the courage of
children, we staged the same sort of informal & improvised
choreopoems at Rivbea during the Summer Music Festival.
Instead of the Standing-Room-Only crowds we were accustomed to in San Francisco, my family & a few friends came to
see our great project. One of these friends, Oz Scott, & my
sister, Ifa Iyaun, who were instrumental in the development
of *for colored girls* . . . saw the show that night. Oz offered to
help me with the staging of the work for a New York audience,
since Paula & I obviously didn't understand some things. We
moved from the Rivbea to the Old Reliable on East 3rd Street
to work through some of the ideas Oz had & the new things
Paula & I were developing. Gylan Kain of the Original Last
Poets waz working there every Monday night. We worked
with him & any other poets & dancers who showed up.
Several members of the original New York show came to us
just this haphazardly. Aku Kadogo & I both had scholarships

at Diane McIntyre's Sounds-in-Motion Dance Studio. I asked her if she felt like improvising on the Lower East Side, she agreed & has been with the show ever since. Laurie Carlos stopped by one evening. She stayed. Somehow word got out & people started coming to the back room of this neighborhood bar. We were moved to a new bar down the street, DeMonte's, after eleven weeks of no-pay hard-work three sets a night—maybe a shot of cognac on the house.

The show at DeMonte's waz prophetic. By this time, December of 1975, we had weaned the piece of extraneous theatricality, enlisted Trazana Beverley, Laurie Carlos, Laurie Hayes, Aku Kadogo, & of course, Paula & I were right there. The most prescient change in the concept of the work waz that I gave up directorial powers to Oz Scott. By doing this, I acknowledged that the poems & the dance worked on their own to do & be what they were. As opposed to viewing the pieces as poems, I came to understand these twenty-odd poems as a single statement, a choreopoem.

We finally hit at DeMonte's. Those institutions I had shunned as a poet—producers, theaters, actresses, & sets—now were essential to us. *for colored girls who have considered suicide/when the rainbow is enuf* waz a theater piece. Woodie King picked up our option to produce us as a Workshop under Equity's Showcase Code at Henry Street. With the assistance of the New York Shakespeare Festival & Joe Papp, we received space & a set, lights & a mailing list, things Paula & I had done without for two years. We opened at Henry Street with two new actress-dancers, Thea Martinez & Judy Dearing. Lines of folks & talk all over the Black & Latin community propelled us to the Public Theatre in June. Then to the Booth Theatre on Broadway in September of 1976.

Every move we've made since the first showing of *for colored girls . . .* in California has demanded changes of text, personnel, & staging. The final production at the Booth is as close to distilled as any of us in all our art forms can make it. With two new actresses, Janet League & Risë Collins, & with the help of Seret Scott, Michelle Shay, & Roxanne Reese, the rest of the cast is enveloping almost 6,000 people a week in the words of a young black girl's growing up, her triumphs & errors, our struggle to become all that is forbidden by our environment, all that is forfeited by our gender, all that we have forgotten.

I had never imagined not doing *for colored girls . . .* It waz just my poems, any poems I happened to have. Now I have left the show on Broadway, to write poems, stories, plays, my dreams. *for colored girls . . .* is either too big for my off-off Broadway taste, or too little for my exaggerated sense of freedom, held over from seven years of improvised poetry readings. Or, perhaps, the series has actually finished itself. Poems come on their own time: I am offering these to you as what I've received from this world so far.

i am on the other side of the rainbow/picking up the pieces of days spent waitin for the poem to be heard/while you listen/i have other work to do/

ntozake shange
new york, 1976

(The stage is in darkness. Harsh music is heard as dim blue lights come up. One after another, seven women run onto the stage from each of the exits. They all freeze in postures of distress. The follow spot picks up the lady in brown. She comes to life and looks around at the other ladies. All of the others are still. She walks over to the lady in red and calls to her. The lady in red makes no response.)

> lady in brown
dark phrases of womanhood
of never havin been a girl
half-notes scattered
without rhythm/no tune
distraught laughter fallin
over a black girl's shoulder
it's funny/it's hysterical
the melody-less-ness of her dance.

don't tell nobody don't tell a soul
she's dancin on beer cans & shingles

this must be the spook house
another song with no singers
lyrics/no voices
& interrupted solos
unseen performances

are we ghouls?
children of horror?
the joke?

don't tell nobody don't tell a soul
are we animals? have we gone crazy?

i can't hear anythin
but maddening screams
& the soft strains of death
& you promised me
you promised me . . .
somebody/anybody
sing a black girl's song
bring her out
to know herself

to know you
but sing her rhythms

carin/struggle/hard times
sing her song of life
she's been dead so long
closed in silence so long
she doesn't know the sound
of her own voice
her infinite beauty
she's half-notes scattered
without rhythm/no tune
sing her sighs
sing the song of her possibilities
sing a righteous gospel
the makin of a melody
let her be born
let her be born
& handled warmly.

    lady in brown
i'm outside chicago

    lady in yellow
i'm outside detroit

    lady in purple
i'm outside houston

    lady in red
i'm outside baltimore

    lady in green
i'm outside san francisco

    lady in blue
i'm outside manhattan

    lady in orange
i'm outside st. louis

lady in brown
& this is for colored girls who have considered suicide
but moved to the ends of their own rainbows.

everyone
mama's little baby likes shortnin, shortnin,
mama's little baby likes shortnin bread
mama's little baby likes shortnin, shortnin,
mama's little baby likes shortnin bread

little sally walker, sittin in a saucer
rise, sally, rise, wipe your weepin eyes
an put your hands on your hips
an let your backbone slip
o, shake it to the east
o, shake it to the west
shake it to the one
that you like the best

lady in purple
you're it

(*As the lady in brown tags each of the other ladies they freeze. When each one has been tagged the lady in brown freezes. Immediately "Dancing in the Streets" by Martha and the Vandellas is heard. All of the ladies start to dance. The lady in green, the lady in blue, and the lady in yellow do the pony, the big boss line, the swim, and the nose dive. The other ladies dance in place.*)

lady in yellow
it waz graduation nite & i waz the only virgin in the
crowd bobby mills martin jerome & sammy yates eddie
jones & randi
all cousins
all the prettiest niggers in this factory town
carried me out wit em
in a deep black buick
smellin of thunderbird & ladies in heat
we rambled from camden to mount holly

laughin at the afternoon's speeches
& danglin our tassles from the rear view mirror
climbin different sorta project stairs
movin toward snappin beer cans &
GET IT GET IT THAT'S THE WAY TO DO IT MAMA
all mercer county graduated the same nite
   cosmetology secretarial pre-college
    autoshop & business
all us movin from mama to what ever waz out there

that nite we raced a big ol truck from the barbeque stand
trying to tell him bout the party at jacqui's
where folks graduated last year waz waitin to hit it wid
us
i got drunk & cdnt figure out
whose hand waz on my thigh/but it didn't matter
cuz these cousins martin eddie sammy jerome & bobby
waz my sweethearts alternately since the seventh grade
& everybody knew i always started cryin if somebody
actually
tried to take advantage of me
   at jacqui's
ulinda mason was stickin her mouth all out
while we tumbled out the buick
eddie jones waz her lickin stick
but i knew how to dance
   it got soo hot
vincent ramos puked all in the punch
& harly jumped all in tico's face
cuz he waz leavin for the navy in the mornin
hadda kick ass so we'd all remember how bad he waz
seems like sheila & marguerite waz fraid
to get their hair turnin back
so they laid up against the wall
lookin almost sexy
didnt wanna sweat
but me & my fellas   we waz dancin

since 1963 i'd won all kinda contests
wid the cousins at the POLICE ATHLETIC LEAGUE
    DANCES
all mercer county knew
any kin to martin yates cd turn somersaults
fore smokey robinson cd get a woman excited

(*The Dells singing "Stay" is heard.*)

we danced   doin nasty ol tricks

(*The lady in yellow sings along with the Dells for a moment. The
lady in orange and the lady in blue jump up and parody the lady in
yellow and the Dells. The lady in yellow stares at them. They sit
down.*)

doin nasty ol tricks i'd been thinkin since may
cuz graduation nite had to be hot
& i waz the only virgin
so i hadda make like my hips waz inta some business
that way everybody thot whoever was gettin it
was a older man cdnt run the streets wit youngsters
martin slipped his leg round my thigh
the dells bumped "stay"
up & down—up & down the new carver homes
WE WAZ GROWN
        WE WAZ FINALLY GROWN

ulinda alla sudden went crazy
went over to eddie cursin & carryin on
tearin his skin wid her nails
the cousins tried to talk sense to her
tried to hold her arms

lissin bitch sammy went on
bobby whispered i shd go wit him
fore they go ta cuttin
fore the police arrived
we teetered silently thru the parkin lot
no un uhuh

we didn't know nothin bout no party
bobby started lookin at me
yeah
he started looking at me real strange
like i waz a woman or somethin/
started talkin real soft
in the backseat of that ol buick
WOW
by daybreak
i just cdnt stop grinnin.

(*The Dells singing "Stay" comes on and all of the ladies except the lady in blue join in and sing along.*)

> *lady in blue*
> you gave it up in a buick?

> *lady in yellow*
> yeh, and honey, it was wonderful.

> *lady in green*
> we used to do it all up in the dark
> in the corners . . .

> *lady in blue*
> some niggah sweating all over you.

> *lady in red*
> it was good!

> *lady in blue*
> i never did like to grind.

> *lady in yellow*
> what other kind of dances are there?

> *lady in blue*
> mambo, bomba, merengue

when i waz sixteen i ran off to the south bronx
cuz i waz gonna meet up wit willie colon

& dance all the time
            mamba bomba merengue

lady in yellow
do you speak spanish?

        lady in blue
olà
my papa thot he was puerto rican & we wda been
cept we waz just reglar niggahs wit hints of spanish
so off i made it to this 36 hour marathon dance
con salsa con ricardo
'suggggggggggar' ray on southern blvd
next door to this fotografi place
jammed wit burial weddin & communion relics
next door to la real ideal genuine spanish barber
            up up up up up stairs & stairs & lotsa hallway
wit my colored new jersey self
didn't know what anybody waz saying
cept if dancin waz proof of origin
            i was jibarita herself that nite
& the next day
i kept smilin & right on steppin
if he cd lead i waz ready to dance
if he cdnt lead
i caught this attitude
            i'd seen rosa do
& wd not be bothered
i waz twirlin hippin givin much quik feet
& bein a mute cute colored puerto rican
til saturday afternoon when the disc-jockey say
'SORRY FOLKS WILLIE COLON AINT GONNA MAKE
            IT TODAY'
& alla my niggah temper came outta control
& i wdnt dance wit nobody
& i talked english loud
& i love you more than i waz mad
uh huh uh huh

more than more than
when i discovered archie shepp & subtle blues
doncha know i wore out the magic of juju
heroically resistin being possessed

oooooooooooooooh the sounds
sneakin in under age to slug's
to stare ata real 'artiste'
& every word outta imamu's mouth waz gospel
& if jesus cdnt play a horn like shepp
waznt no need for colored folks to bear no cross at all

& poem is my thank-you for music
& i love you more than poem
more than aureliano buendia loved macondo
more than hector lavoe loved himself
more than the lady loved gardenias
more than celia loves cuba or graciela loves el son
more than the flamingoes shoo-do-n-doo-wah love
      bein pretty
oyè négro
te amo mas que   te amo mas que
when you play
yr flute

      everyone (very softly)
te amo mas que   te amo mas que

      lady in red
without any assistance or guidance from you
i have loved you assiduously for 8 months 2 wks & a day
i have been stood up four times
i've left 7 packages on yr doorstep
forty poems 2 plants & 3 handmade notecards i left
town so i cd send to you have been no help to me
on my job
you call at 3:00 in the mornin on weekdays
so i cd drive 27½ miles cross the bay before i go to work
charmin charmin

but you are of no assistance
i want you to know
this waz an experiment
to see how selfish i cd be

if i wd really carry on to snare a possible lover
if i waz capable of debasin my self for the love of another
if i cd stand not being wanted
when i wanted to be wanted
& i cannot
so
with no further assistance & no guidance from you
i am endin this affair

this note is attached to a plant
i've been waterin since the day i met you
you may water it
yr damn self

    lady in orange
i dont wanna write
in english or spanish
i wanna sing   make you dance
like the bata   dance   scream
twitch hips wit me cuz
i done forgot all abt words
aint got no definitions
i wanna whirl
      with you

(*Music starts, "Che Che Cole" by Willie Colon. Everyone starts to dance.*)

our whole body
wrapped like a ripe mango
ramblin whippin thru space
on the corner in the park
where the rug useta be
let willie colon take you out
swing your head

push your leg to the moon with me
i'm on the lower east side
in new york city
and i can't   i can't
talk witchu no more

    lady in yellow
we gotta dance to keep from cryin

    lady in brown
we gotta dance to keep from dyin

    lady in red
so come on

    lady in brown
come on

    lady in purple
come on

    lady in orange
hold yr head like it was ruby sapphire
i'm a poet
who writes in english
come to share the worlds witchu

    everyone
come to share our worlds witchu
we come here to be dancin
       to be dancin
      to be dancin
     baya

(There is a sudden light change, all of the ladies react as if they had been struck in the face. The lady in green and the lady in yellow run out up left, the lady in orange runs out the left volm, the lady in brown runs out up right.)

    lady in blue
a friend is hard to press charges against

lady in red
if you know him
you must have wanted it

lady in purple
a misunderstanding

lady in red
you know
these things happen

lady in blue
are you sure
you didnt suggest

lady in purple
had you been drinkin

lady in red
a rapist is always to be a stranger
to be legitimate
someone you never saw
a man wit obvious problems

lady in purple
pin-ups attached to the insides of his lapels

lady in blue
ticket stubs from porno flicks in his pocket

lady in purple
a lil dick

lady in red
or a strong mother

lady in blue
or just a brutal virgin

lady in red
but if you've been seen in public wit him
danced one dance
kissed him good-bye lightly

  lady in purple
wit closed mouth

  lady in blue
pressin charges will be as hard
as keepin yr legs closed
while five fools try to run a train on you

  lady in red
these men friends of ours
who smile nice
stay employed
and take us out to dinner

  lady in purple
lock the door behind you

  lady in blue
wit fist in face
to fuck

  lady in red
who make elaborate mediterranean dinners
& let the art ensemble carry all ethical burdens
while they invite a coupla friends over to have you
are sufferin from latent rapist bravado
& we are left wit the scars

  lady in blue
bein betrayed by men who know us

  lady in purple
& expect
like the stranger
we always thot waz comin

  lady in blue
that we will submit

  lady in purple
we must have known

lady in red
women relinquish all personal rights
in the presence of a man
who apparently cd be considered a rapist

lady in purple
especially if he has been considered a friend

lady in blue
& is no less worthy of bein beat witin an inch of his
     life
bein publicly ridiculed
havin two fists shoved up his ass

lady in red
than the stranger
we always thot it wd be

lady in blue
who never showed up

lady in red
cuz it turns out the nature of rape has changed

lady in blue
we can now meet them in circles we frequent for
companionship

lady in purple
we see them at the coffeehouse

lady in blue
wit someone else we know

lady in red
we cd even have em over for dinner
& get raped in our own houses
by invitation
a friend

(*The lights change, and the ladies are all hit by an imaginary slap,
the lady in red runs off up left.*)

> *lady in blue*
eyes

> *lady in purple*
mice

> *lady in blue*
womb

> *lady in blue & lady in purple*
nobody

(*The lady in purple exits up right.*)

> *lady in blue*
tubes tables white washed windows
grime from age wiped over once
legs spread
anxious
eyes crawling up on me
eyes rollin in my thighs
metal horses gnawin my womb
dead mice fall from my mouth
i really didnt mean to
i really didnt think i cd
just one day off . . .
get offa me alla this blood
bones shattered like soft ice-cream cones

i cdnt have people
lookin at me
pregnant
i cdnt have my friends see this
dyin danglin tween my legs
& i didnt say a thing
not a sigh
or a fast scream
to get
those eyes offa me
get them steel rods outta me

this hurts
this hurts me
& nobody came
cuz nobody knew
once i waz pregnant & shamed of myself.

(*The lady in blue exits stage left volm. Soft deep music is heard, voices calling 'Sechita' come from the wings and volms. The lady in purple enters from up right.*)

    lady in purple
once there were quadroon balls/elegance in st.
    louis/laced
mulattoes/gamblin down the mississippi/to
    memphis/new
orleans n okra crepes near the bayou/where the
    poor white trash
wd sing/moanin/strange/liquid tones/thru the
    swamps

(*The lady in green enters from the right volm; she is Sechita and for the rest of the poem dances out Sechita's life.*)

sechita had heard these things/she moved as if she'd
known them/the silver n high-toned laughin/
the violins n marble floors/sechita pushed the clingin
delta dust wit painted toes/the patch-work tent waz
poka-dotted/stale lights snatched at the shadows/
creole carnival waz playin natchez in ten minutes/
her splendid red garters/gin-stained n itchy on her
thigh/blk-diamond stockings darned wit yellow
threads/an ol starched taffeta can-can fell abundantly
orange/from her waist round the splinterin chair/
sechita/egyptian/goddess of creativity/2nd
millennium/threw her heavy hair in a coil over her
neck/sechita/goddess/the recordin of history/
spread crimson oil on her cheeks/waxed her
eyebrows/n unconsciously slugged the last hard
whiskey in the glass/the broken mirror she used to

decorate her face/made her forehead tilt backwards/
her cheeks appear sunken/her sassy chin only large
enuf/to keep her full lower lip/from growin into her
neck/sechita/had learned to make allowances for
the distortions/but the heavy dust of the delta/left a
tinge of grit n darkness/on every one of her dresses/
on her arms & her shoulders/sechita/waz anxious
to get back to st. louis/the dirt there didnt crawl
from the earth into yr soul/at least/in st. louis/the
grime waz store bought second-hand/here in
natchez/god seemed to be wipin his feet in her face/

one of the wrestlers had finally won tonite/the
mulatto/raul/was sposed to hold the boomin half-
caste/searin eagle/in a bear hug/8 counts/get
thrown unawares/fall out the ring/n then do searin
eagle in for good/sechita/cd hear redneck whoops n
slappin on the back/she gathered her sparsely
sequined skirts/tugged the waist cincher from under
her greyin slips/n made her face immobile/she made
her face like nefertiti/approachin her own tomb/
she suddenly threw/her leg full-force/thru the
canvas curtain/a deceptive glass stone/sparkled/
malignant on her ankle/her calf waz tauntin in the
brazen carnie lights/the full moon/sechita/goddess/
of love/egypt/2nd millennium/performin the rites/
the conjurin of men/conjurin the spirit/in natchez/
the mississippi spewed a heavy fume of barely movin
waters/sechita's legs slashed furiously thru the
cracker nite/& gold pieces hittin the makeshift
stage/her thighs/they were aimin coins tween her
thighs/sechita/egypt/goddess/harmony/kicked
viciously thru the nite/catchin stars tween her toes.

*(The lady in green exits into the stage left volm, the lady in purple
exits into up stage left. The lady in brown enters from up stage
right.)*

lady in brown
de library waz right down from de trolly tracks
cross from de laundry-mat
thru de big shinin floors & granite pillars
ol st. louis is famous for
i found toussaint
but not til after months uv
cajun katie/pippi longstockin
christopher robin/eddie heyward & a pooh bear
in the children's room
only pioneer girls & magic rabbits
& big city white boys
i knew i waznt sposedta
but i ran inta the ADULT READING ROOM
        & came across

       TOUSSAINT

      my first blk man
(i never counted george washington carver
cuz i didnt like peanuts)
      still
TOUSSAINT waz a blk man a negro like my mama say
who refused to be a slave
& he spoke french
& didnt low no white man to tell him nothin
      not napolean
      not maximillien
      not robespierre

TOUSSAINT L'OUVERTURE
waz the beginnin uv reality for me
in the summer contest for
who colored child can read
15 books in three weeks
i won & raved abt TOUSSAINT L'OUVERTURE
at the afternoon ceremony
waz disqualified
      cuz Toussaint

belonged in the ADULT READING ROOM
            & i cried
& carried dead Toussaint home in the book
he waz dead & livin to me
cuz TOUSSAINT & them
they held the citadel gainst the french
wid the spirits of ol dead africans from outta the ground
TOUSSAINT led they army of zombies
walkin cannon ball shootin spirits to free Haiti
& they waznt slaves no more

                    TOUSSAINT L'OUVERTURE
became my secret lover at the age of 8
i entertained him in my bedroom
widda flashlight under my covers
way inta the night/we discussed strategies
how to remove white girls from my hopscotch games
& etc.
TOUSSAINT
waz layin in bed wit me next to raggedy ann
the night i decided to run away from my
                    integrated home
                        integrated street
                            integrated school
1955 waz not a good year for lil blk girls

Toussaint said 'lets go to haiti'
i said 'awright'
& packed some very important things in a brown paper
        bag
so i wdnt haveta come back
then Toussaint & i took the hodiamont streetcar
to the river
last stop
only 15¢
cuz there waznt nobody cd see Toussaint cept me
& we walked all down thru north st. louis
where the french settlers usedta live

in tiny brick houses all huddled together
wit barely missin windows & shingles uneven
wit colored kids playin & women on low porches
    sippin beer

i cd talk to Toussaint down by the river
like this waz where we waz gonna stow away
on a boat for new orleans
& catch a creole fishin-rig for port-au-prince
then we waz just gonna read & talk all the time
& eat fried bananas
            we waz just walkin & skippin past ol
              drunk men
when dis ol young boy jumped out at me sayin
'HEY GIRL YA BETTAH COME OVAH HEAH N
    TALK TO ME'
well
i turned to TOUSSAINT (who waz furious)
& i shouted
'ya silly ol boy
ya bettah leave me alone
or TOUSSAINT'S gonna get yr ass'
de silly ol boy came round de corner laughin all in my
    face
'yellah gal
ya sure must be somebody to know my name so quick'
i waz disgusted
& wanted to get on to haiti
widout some tacky ol boy botherin me
still he kept standin there
kickin milk cartons & bits of brick
tryin to get all in my business
    i mumbled to L'OUVERTURE 'what shd I do'
finally
i asked this silly ol boy
'WELL WHO ARE YOU?'
he say

'MY NAME IS TOUSSAINT JONES'
well
i looked right at him
those skidded out cordoroy pants
a striped teashirt wid holes in both elbows
a new scab over his left eye
& i said
        'what's yr name again'
he say
'i'm toussaint jones'
'wow
i am on my way to see
TOUSSAINT L'OUVERTURE in HAITI
are ya any kin to him
he dont take no stuff from no white folks
& they gotta country all they own
& there aint no slaves'
that silly ol boy squinted his face all up
'looka heah girl
i am TOUSSAINT JONES
& i'm right heah lookin at ya
& i dont take no stuff from no white folks
ya dont see none round heah do ya?'
& he sorta pushed out his chest
then he say
'come on   lets go on down to the docks
& look at the boats'
i waz real puzzled goin down to the docks
wit my paper bag & my books
i felt TOUSSAINT L'OUVERTURE sorta leave me
& i waz sad
til i realized
TOUSSAINT JONES waznt too different
from TOUSSAINT L'OUVERTURE
cept the ol one waz in haiti
& this one wid me speakin english & eatin apples
yeah.

toussaint jones waz awright wit me
no tellin what all spirits we cd move
down by the river
st. louis 1955   hey wait.

(*The lady in brown exits into the stage right volm. The lady in red
enters from the stage left volm.*)

    lady in red
orange butterflies & aqua sequins
ensconsed tween slight bosoms
silk roses dartin from behind her ears
the passion flower of southwest los angeles
meandered down hoover street
past dark shuttered houses where
women from louisiana shelled peas
round 3:00 & sent their sons
whistlin to the store for fatback & black-eyed peas
she glittered in heat
& seemed to be lookin for rides
when she waznt & absolutely
eyed every man who waznt lame white or noddin out
she let her thigh slip from her skirt
crossin the street
she slowed to be examined
& she never looked back to smile
or acknowledge a sincere 'hey mama'
or to meet the eyes of someone
purposely findin sometin to do in
her direction
        she waz sullen
        & the rhinestones etchin the corners of
          her mouth
        suggested tears
        fresh kisses that had done no good
she always wore her stomach out
lined with small iridescent feathers
the hairs round her navel seemed to dance

& she didnt let on
she knew
from behind her waist waz aching to be held
the pastel ivy drawn on her shoulders
to be brushed with lips & fingers
smellin of honey & jack daniels
> she waz hot
> a deliberate coquette
> who never did without
> what she wanted

& she wanted to be unforgettable
she wanted to be a memory
a wound   to every man
arragant enough to want her
> she waz the wrath
> of women in windows
> > fingerin shades/ol lace curtains
> > camoflagin despair &
> > stretch marks

so she glittered honestly
delighted she waz desired
& allowed those especially
schemin/tactful suitors
to experience her body & spirit
tearin/so easily blendin with theirs/
& they were so happy
& lay on her lime sheets full & wet
from her tongue   she kissed
them reverently   even ankles
edges of beards . . .

(*The stage goes to darkness except for a special on the lady in red,
who lies motionless on the floor; as the lights slowly fade up the lady
in red sits up.*)

at 4:30 AM
she rose
movin the arms & legs that trapped her

she sighed affirmin the sculptured man
& made herself a bath
of dark musk oil egyptian crystals
& florida water to remove his smell
to wash away the glitter
to watch the butterflies melt into
suds & the rhinestones fall beneath
her buttocks like smooth pebbles
in a missouri creek
layin in water
she became herself
ordinary
brown braided woman
with big legs & full lips
reglar
seriously intendin to finish her
night's work
she quickly walked to her guest
straddled on her pillows & began
   'you'll have to go now/i've
   a lot of work to do/& i cant
   with a man around/here are yr pants/
   there's coffee on the stove/its been
   very nice/but i cant see you again/
   you got what you came for/didnt you'
& she smiled
he wd either mumble curses bout crazy bitches
or sit dumbfounded
while she repeated
   'i cdnt possibly wake up/with
   a strange man in my bed/why
   dont you go home'
she cda been slapped upside the head
or verbally challenged
but she never waz
& the ones who fell prey to the
dazzle of hips painted with

orange blossoms & magnolia scented wrists
had wanted no more
than to lay between her sparklin thighs
& had planned on leavin before dawn
& she had been so divine
devastatingly bizarre the way
her mouth fit round
& now she stood a
reglar colored girl
fulla the same malice
livid indifference as a sistah
worn from supportin a wd be hornplayer
or waitin by the window
        & they knew
        & left in a hurry
she wd gather her tinsel &
jewels from the tub
& laugh gayly or vengeful
she stored her silk roses by her bed
& when she finished writin
the account of her exploit in a diary
embroidered with lilies & moonstones
she placed the rose behind her ear
& cried herself to sleep.

(*All the lights fade except for a special on the lady in red; the lady in red exits into the stage left volm. The lady in blue enters from up right.*)

      lady in blue
i usedta live in the world
then i moved to HARLEM
& my universe is now six blocks

when i walked in the pacific
i imagined waters ancient from accra/tunis
cleansin me/feedin me
now my ankles are coated in grey filth
from the puddle neath the hydrant

my oceans were life
what waters i have here sit stagnant
circlin ol men's bodies
shit & broken lil whiskey bottles
left to make me bleed

i usedta live in the world
now i live in harlem & my universe is six blocks
a tunnel with a train
i can ride anywhere
remaining a stranger
    NO MAN YA CANT GO WIT ME/I DONT EVEN
    KNOW YOU/NO/I DONT WANNA KISS YOU/
    YOU AINT BUT 12 YRS OLD/NO MAN/PLEASE
    PLEASE PLEASE LEAVE ME ALONE/TOMOR-
    ROW/YEAH/NO/PLEASE/I CANT USE IT
  i cd stay alone
  a woman in the world
  then i moved to
HARLEM
i come in at dusk
stay close to the curb

(*The lady in yellow enters, she's waiting for a bus.*)

round midnite
praying wont no young man
think i'm pretty in a dark mornin

(*The lady in purple enters, she's waiting for a bus.*)

wdnt be good
not good at all
to meet a tall short black brown young man fulla
    his power
in the dark
in my universe of six blocks
straight up brick walls
women hangin outta windows
like ol silk stockings

cats cryin/children gigglin/a tavern wit red curtains
bad smells/kissin ladies smilin & dirt
sidewalks spittin/men cursing/playin

(The lady in orange enters, she is being followed by a man, the lady in blue becomes that man.)

'I SPENT MORE MONEY YESTERDAY
THAN THE DAY BEFORE & ALL THAT'S
MORE N YOU NIGGAH EVER GOTTA
HOLD TO COME OVER HERE BITCH
CANT YA SEE THIS IS $5'

never mind sister
dont play him no mind
go go go go go go sister
do yr thing
never mind

i usedta live in the world
really be in the world
free & sweet talkin
good mornin & thank-you & nice day
uh huh
i cant now
i cant be nice to nobody
nice is such a rip-off
reglar beauty & a smile in the street
is just a set-up

i usedta be in the world
a woman in the world
i hadda right to the world
then i moved to harlem
for the set-up
a universe
six blocks of cruelty
piled up on itself
a tunnel
closin

(*The four ladies on stage freeze, count 4, then the ladies in blue,
purple, yellow, and orange move to their places for the next poem.*)

> *lady in purple*
three of us like a pyramid
three friends
one laugh
one music
one flowered shawl
knotted on each neck
we all saw him at the same time
& he saw us
i felt a quick thump in each one of us
didnt know what to do
we all wanted what waz comin our way
so we split
but he found one
& she loved him

the other two were tickled
& spurned his advances
when the one who loved him waz somewhere else
he wd come to her saying
yr friends love you very much
i have tried
& they keep askin where are you
she smiled
wonderin how long her friends
wd hold out
he waz what they were lookin for
he bided his time
he waited til romance waned
the three of us made up stories
bout usedta & cda been nice
the season waz dry
no men
no quickies

not one dance or eyes unrelentin
one day after another
cept for the one who loved him
he appeared irregularly
expectin graciousness no matter what
she cut fresh strawberries
her friends callt less frequently
went on hunts for passin fancies
she cdnt figure out what waz happenin
then the rose
she left by his pillow
she found on her friends desk
& there waz nothing to say
she said
i wanna tell you
he's been after me
all the time
says he's free & can explain
what's happenin wit you
is nothin to me
& i dont wanna hurt you
but you know i need someone now
& you know
how wonderful he is
her friend cdnt speak or cry
they hugged & went to where he waz
wit another woman
he said good-bye to one
tol the other he wd call
he smiled a lot

she held her head on her lap
the lap of her sisters soakin up tears
each understandin how much love stood between them
how much love between them
love between them
love like sisters

(Sharp music is heard, each lady dances as if catching a disease from the lady next to her, suddenly they all freeze.)

> *lady in orange*
> ever since i realized there waz someone callt
> a colored girl an evil woman a bitch or a nag
> i been tryin not to be that & leave bitterness
> in somebody else's cup/come to somebody to love me
> without deep & nasty smellin scald from lye or bein
> left screamin in a street fulla lunatics/whisperin
> slut bitch bitch niggah/get outta here wit alla that/
> i didnt have any of that for you/i brought you what
> joy i found & i found joy/honest fingers round my
> face/with dead musicians on 78's from cuba/or live
> musicians on five dollar lp's from chicago/where i
> have never been/& i love willie colon & arsenio
> rodriquez/especially cuz i can make the music loud
> enuf/so there is no me but dance/& when i can
> dance like that/there's nothin cd hurt me/but i get
> tired & i haveta come offa the floor & then there's
> that woman who hurt you/who you left/three or
> four times/& just went back/after you put my heart
> in the bottom of yr shoe/you just walked back to
> where you hurt/& i didnt have nothin/so i went to
> where somebody had somethin for me/but he waznt
> you/& i waz on the way back from her house in
> the bottom of yr shoe/so this is not a love poem/
> cuz there are only memorial albums available/& even
> charlie mingus wanted desperately to be a pimp/
> & i wont be able to see eddie palmieri for months/
> so this is a requium for myself/cuz i have died in a
> real way/not wid aqua coffins & du-wop cadillacs/
> i used to joke abt when i waz messin round/but a
> real dead lovin is here for you now/cuz i dont know
> anymore/how to avoid my own face wet wit my
> tears/cuz i had convinced myself colored girls had no
> right to sorrow/& i lived & loved that way & kept

sorrow on the curb/allegedly for you/but i know i did
it for myself/
i cdnt stand it
i cdnt stand bein sorry & colored at the same time
it's so redundant in the modern world

    lady in purple
i lived wit myths & music waz my ol man & i cd
dance a dance outta time/a dance wit no partners/
take my pills & keep right on steppin/linger in
non-english speakin arms so there waz no possibility
of understandin
& you YOU
came sayin i am the niggah/i am the baddest
muthafuckah out there/
i said yes/this is who i am waitin for
& to come wit you/i hadta bring everythin
the dance & the terror
the dead musicians & the hope
& those scars i had hidden wit smiles & good fuckin
lay open
& i dont know i dont know any more tricks
i am really colored & really sad sometimes & you hurt
me more than i ever danced outta/into oblivion isnt far
enuf to get outta this/i am ready to die like a lily in the
desert/& i cdnt let you in on it cuz i didnt know/here
is what i have/poems/big thighs/lil tits/& so much
love/will you take it from me this one time/please
this is for you/arsenio's tres cleared the way & makes
me pure again/please please/this is for you i want
you to love me/let me love you/i dont wanna dance
wit ghosts/snuggle lovers i made up in my
drunkenness/lemme love you just like i am/a colored
girl/i'm finally bein real/no longer symmetrical &
impervious to pain

    lady in blue
we deal wit emotion too much

so why dont we go on ahead & be white then/
& make everythin dry & abstract wit no rhythm & no
reelin for sheer sensual pleasure/yes let's go on & be
white/we're right in the middle of it/no use holdin
out/holdin onto ourselves/lets think our way outta
feelin/lets abstract ourselves some families & maybe
maybe tonite/i'll find a way to make myself come
witout you/no fingers or other objects just thot which
isnt spiritual evolution cuz its empty & godliness is
plenty is ripe & fertile/thinkin wont do me a bit of
good tonite/i need to be loved/& havent the audacity
to say
where are you/& dont know who to say it to

> *lady in yellow*

i've lost it
touch wit reality/i dont know who's doin it
i thot i waz but i waz so stupid i waz able to be hurt
& that's not real/not anymore/i shd be immune/if
i'm still alive & that's what i waz discussin/how i am
still alive & my dependency on other livin beins for
love i survive on intimacy & tomorrow/that's all i've
got goin & the music waz like smack & you knew abt
that & still refused my dance waz not enuf/& it waz
all i had but bein alive & bein a woman & bein
colored is a metaphysical dilemma/i havent conquered
yet/do you see the point my spirit is too ancient to
understand the separation of soul & gender/my love
is too delicate to have thrown back on my face

(*The ladies in red, green, and brown enter quietly; in the background
all of the ladies except the lady in yellow are frozen; the lady in yellow
looks at them, walks by them, touches them; they do not move.*)

> *lady in yellow*

my love is too delicate to have thrown back on my face

(*The lady in yellow starts to exit into the stage right volm. Just as
she gets to the volm, the lady in brown comes to life.*)

lady in brown
my love is too beautiful to have thrown back on my face

lady in purple
my love is too sanctified to have thrown back on my face

lady in blue
my love is too magic to have thrown back on my face

lady in orange
my love is too saturday nite to have thrown back on my
face

lady in red
my love is too complicated to have thrown back on my
face

lady in green
my love is too music to have thrown back on my face

everyone
music
music

(*The lady in green then breaks into a dance, the other ladies follow
her lead and soon they are all dancing and chanting together.*)

lady in green
yank dankka dank dank

everyone
music

lady in green
yank dankka dank dank

everyone
music

lady in green
yank dankka dank dank

everyone (but started by the lady in yellow)
delicate

delicate
delicate

    everyone (but started by the lady in brown)
and beautiful
and beautiful
and beautiful

    everyone (but started by the lady in purple)
oh sanctified
oh sanctified
oh sanctified

    everyone (but started by the lady in blue)
magic
magic
magic

    everyone (but started by the lady in orange)
and saturday nite
and saturday nite
and saturday nite

    everyone (but started by the lady in red)
and complicated
and complicated
and complicated
and complicated
and complicated
and complicated
and complicated
and complicated

(The dance reaches a climax and all of the ladies fall out tired, but full of life and togetherness.)

    lady in green
somebody almost walked off wid alla my stuff
not my poems or a dance i gave up in the street
but somebody almost walked off wid alla my stuff
like a kleptomaniac workin hard & forgettin while

stealin
this is mine/this aint yr stuff/
now why dont you put me back & let me hang out in
my own self
somebody almost walked off wid alla my stuff
& didnt care enuf to send a note home sayin
i waz late for my solo conversation
or two sizes too small for my own tacky skirts
what can anybody do wit somethin of no value on a
open market/did you getta dime for my things/hey
man/where are you goin wid alla my stuff/this is a
woman's trip & i need my stuff/to ohh & ahh abt/
daddy/i gotta mainline number from my own shit/
now wontchu put me back/& let me play this duet/wit
this silver ring in my nose/honest to god/somebody
almost run off wit alla my stuff/& i didnt bring anythin
but the kick & sway of it the perfect ass for my man &
none of it is theirs this is mine/ntozake 'her own
things'/that's my name/now give me my stuff/i see
ya hidin my laugh/& how i sit wif my legs open
sometimes/to give my crotch some sunlight/& there
goes my love my toes my chewed up finger nails/
niggah/wif the curls in yr hair/mr. louisiana hot link/
i want my stuff back/my rhythms & my voice/open
my mouth/& let me talk ya outta/throwin my shit
in the sewar/this is some delicate leg & whimsical
kiss/i gotta have to give to my choice/without you
runnin off wit alla my shit/now you cant have me
less i give me away/& i waz doin all that/til ya run
off on a good thing/who is this you left me wit/
some simple bitch widda bad attitude/i wants my
things/i want my arm wit the hot iron scar/& my
leg wit the flea bite/i want my calloused feet & quik
language back in my mouth/fried plantains/
pineapple pear juice/sun-ra & joseph & jules/i want
my own things/how i lived them/& give me my
memories/how i waz when i waz there/you cant

have them or do nothin wit them/stealin my shit
from me/dont make it yrs/makes it stolen/somebody
almost run off wit alla my stuff/& i waz standin
there/lookin at myself/the whole time & it waznt
a spirit took my stuff/waz a man whose ego walked
round like Rodan's shadow/waz a man faster n my
innocence/waz a lover/i made too much room for/
almost run off wit alla my stuff/& i didnt know i'd
give it up so quik/& the one running wit it/dont
know he got it/& i'm shoutin this is mine/& he dont
know he got it/my stuff is the anonymous ripped off
treasure of the year/did you know somebody almost
got away with me/me in a plastic bag under their
arm/me danglin on a string of personal carelessness/
i'm spattered wit mud & city rain/& no i didnt get
a chance to take a douche/hey man/this is not your
perogative/i gotta have me in my pocket/to get
round like a good woman shd/& make the poem in
the pot or the chicken in the dance/what i got to do/
i gotta have my stuff to do it to/why dont ya find
yr own things/& leave this package of me for my
destiny/what ya got to get from me/i'll give it to ya/
yeh/i'll give it to ya/round 5:00 in the winter/
when the sky is blue-red/& Dew City is gettin
pressed/if it's really my stuff/ya gotta give it to me/
if ya really want it/i'm the only one/can handle it

    lady in blue
that niggah will be back tomorrow, sayin 'i'm sorry'

    lady in yellow
get this, last week my ol man came in sayin, 'i don't
know how she got yr number baby, i'm sorry'

    lady in brown
no this one is it, 'o baby, ya know i waz high, i'm
sorry'

lady in purple
'i'm only human, and inadequacy is what makes us
human, & if we waz perfect we wdnt have nothin to
strive for, so you might as well go on and forgive
me pretty baby, cause i'm sorry'

lady in green
'shut up bitch, i told you i waz sorry'

lady in orange
no this one is it, 'i do ya like i do ya cause i thot
ya could take it, now i'm sorry'

lady in red
'now i know that ya know i love ya, but i aint ever
gonna love ya like ya want me to love ya, i'm sorry'

lady in blue
one thing i dont need
is any more apologies
i got sorry greetin me at my front door
you can keep yrs
i dont know what to do wit em
they dont open doors
or bring the sun back
they dont make me happy
or get a mornin paper
didnt nobody stop usin my tears to wash cars
cuz a sorry

i am simply tired
of collectin
            'i didnt know
            it was so important to you'
i'm gonna haveta throw some away
i cant get to the clothes in my closet
for alla the sorries
i'm gonna tack a sign to my door
leave a message by the phone

'if you called
to say yr sorry
call somebody
else
i dont use em anymore'
i let sorry/didnt meanta/& how cd i know abt that
take a walk down a dark & musty street in brooklyn
i'm gonna do exactly what i want to
& i wont be sorry for none of it
letta sorry soothe yr soul/i'm gonna soothe mine

you were always inconsistent
doin somethin & then bein sorry
beatin my heart to death
talkin bout you sorry
well
i will not call
i'm not goin to be nice
i will raise my voice
& scream & holler
& break things & race the engine
& tell all yr secrets bout yrself to yr face
& i will list in detail everyone of my wonderful lovers
& their ways
i will play oliver lake
loud
& i wont be sorry for none of it

i loved you on purpose
i was open on purpose
i still crave vulnerability & close talk
& i'm not even sorry bout you bein sorry
you can carry all the guilt & grime ya wanna
just dont give it to me
i cant use another sorry
next time
you should admit
you're mean/low-down/triflin/& no count straight out

steada bein sorry alla the time
enjoy bein yrself

    lady in red
there waz no air/the sheets made ripples under his
body like crumpled paper napkins in a summer park/
& lil specks of somethin from tween his toes or the
biscuits from the day before ran in the sweat that
tucked the sheet into his limbs like he waz an ol
frozen bundle of chicken/& he'd get up to make
coffee, drink wine, drink water/he wished one of his
friends who knew where he waz wd come by with
some blow or some shit/anythin/there waz no air/
he'd see the spotlights in the alleyways downstairs
movin in the air/cross his wall over his face/& get
under the covers & wait for an all clear or til he cd
hear traffic again/

there waznt nothin wrong with him/there waznt
nothin wrong with him/he kept tellin crystal/any
niggah wanna kill vietnamese children more n stay
home & raise his own is sicker than a rabid dog/that's
how their thing had been goin since he got back/
crystal just got inta sayin whatta fool niggah beau waz
& always had been/didnt he go all over uptown sayin
the child waznt his/waz some no counts bastard/&
any ol city police cd come & get him if they wanted/
cuz as soon as the blood type & shit waz together/
everybody wd know that crystal waz a no good lyin
whore/and this after she'd been his girl since she waz
thirteen/when he caught her on the stairway/

he came home crazy as hell/he tried to get veterans
benefits to go to school & they kept right on puttin
him in remedial classes/he cdnt read wortha damn/so
beau cused the teachers of holdin him back & got
himself a gypsy cab to drive/but his cab kept breakin
down/& the cops was always messin wit him/plus not
gettin much bread/

& crystal went & got pregnant again/beau most beat
her to death when she tol him/she still gotta scar
under her right tit where he cut her up/still crystal
went right on & had the baby/so now beau willie had
two children/a little girl/naomi kenya & a boy/
kwame beau willie brown/& there waz no air/
how in the hell did he get in this mess anyway/
somebody went & tol crystal that beau waz spendin
alla his money on the bartendin bitch down at the
merry-go-round cafe/beau sat straight up in the bed/
wrapped up in the sheets lookin like john the baptist
or a huge baby wit stubble & nuts/now he hadta get
alla that shit outta crystal's mind/so she wd let him
come home/crystal had gone & got a court order
saying beau willie brown had no access to his
children/if he showed his face he waz subject to
arrest/shit/she'd been in his ass to marry her since
she waz 14 years old & here when she 22/she wanna
throw him out cuz he say he'll marry her/she burst
out laughin/hollerin whatchu wanna marry me for
now/so i can support yr ass/or come sit wit ya when
they lock yr behind up/cause they gonna come for
ya/ya goddamn lunatic/they gonna come/& i'm not
gonna have a thing to do wit it/o no i wdnt marry yr
pitiful black ass for nothin & she went on to bed/

the next day beau willie came in blasted & got ta
swingin chairs at crystal/who cdnt figure out what the
hell he waz doin/til he got ta shoutin bout how she
waz gonna marry him/& get some more veterans
benefits/& he cd stop drivin them crazy spics round/
while they tryin to kill him for $15/beau waz sweatin
terrible/beatin on crystal/& he cdnt do no more with
the table n chairs/so he went to get the high chair/&
lil kwame waz in it/& beau waz beatin crystal with
the high chair & her son/& some notion got inta him
to stop/and he run out/

crystal most died/that's why the police wdnt low
beau near where she lived/& she'd been tellin the kids
their daddy tried to kill her & kwame/& he just
wanted to marry her/that's what/he wanted to marry
her/& have a family/but the bitch waz crazy/beau
willie waz sittin in this hotel in his drawers drinkin
coffee & wine in the heat of the day spillin shit all over
hisself/laughin/bout how he waz gonna get crystal to
take him back/& let him be a man in the house/&
she wdnt even have to go to work no more/he got
dressed all up in his ivory shirt & checkered pants to
go see crystal & get this mess all cleared up/he
knocked on the door to crystal's rooms/& she didnt
answer/he beat on the door & crystal & naomi started
cryin/beau gotta shoutin again how he wanted to
marry her/& waz she always gonna be a whore/or did
she wanna husband/& crystal just kept on screamin
for him to leave us alone/just leave us alone/so beau
broke the door down/crystal held the children in
fronta her/she picked kwame off the floor/in her
arms/& she held naomi by her shoulders/& kept on
sayin/beau willie brown/get outta here/the police is
gonna come for ya/ya fool/get outta here/do you
want the children to see you act the fool again/you
want kwame to brain damage from you throwin him
round/niggah/get outta here/get out & dont show yr
ass again or i'll kill ya/i swear i'll kill ya/he reached
for naomi/crystal grabbed the lil girl & stared at beau
willie like he waz a leper or somethin/dont you touch
my children/muthafucker/or i'll kill you/

beau willie jumped back all humble & apologetic/i'm
sorry/i dont wanna hurt em/i just wanna hold em &
get on my way/i dont wanna cuz you no more
trouble/i wanted to marry you & give ya things
what you gonna give/a broken jaw/niggah get outta
here/he ignored crystal's outburst & sat down motionin

for naomi to come to him/she smiled back at her
daddy/crystal felt naomi givin in & held her tighter/
naomi/pushed away & ran to her daddy/cryin/daddy,
daddy come back daddy/come back/but be nice to
mommy/cause mommy loves you/and ya gotta be
nice/he sat her on his knee/& played with her ribbons
& they counted fingers & toes/every so often he
looked over to crystal holdin kwame/like a statue/&
he'd say/see crystal/i can be a good father/now let
me see my son/& she didnt move/& he coaxed her &
he coaxed her/tol her she waz still a hot lil ol thing &
pretty & strong/didnt she get right up after that lil ol
fight they had & go back to work/beau willie oozed
kindness & crystal who had known so lil/let beau
hold kwame/

as soon as crystal let the baby outta her arms/beau
jumped up a laughin & a gigglin/a hootin & a
hollerin/awright bitch/awright bitch/you gonna
marry me/you gonna marry me . . .
i aint gonna marry ya/i aint ever gonna marry ya/for
nothin/you gonna be in the jail/you gonna be under
the jail for this/now gimme my kids/ya give me
back my kids/

he kicked the screen outta the window/& held the
kids offa the sill/you gonna marry me/yeh, i'll marry
ya/anything/but bring the children back in the
house/he looked from where the kids were hangin
from the fifth story/at alla the people screamin at
him/& he started sweatin again/say to alla the
neighbors/you gonna marry me/

i stood by beau in the window/with naomi reachin for
me/& kwame screamin mommy mommy from the
fifth story/but i cd only whisper/& he dropped em

   lady in red
i waz missin somethin

lady in purple
somethin so important

lady in orange
somethin promised

lady in blue
a layin on of hands

lady in green
fingers near my forehead

lady in yellow
strong

lady in green
cool

lady in orange
movin

lady in purple
makin me whole

lady in orange
sense

lady in green
pure

lady in blue
all the gods comin into me
layin me open to myself

lady in red
i waz missin somethin

lady in green
somethin promised

lady in orange
somethin free

lady in purple
a layin on of hands

lady in blue
i know bout/layin on bodies/layin outta man
bringin him alla my fleshy self & some of my pleasure
bein taken full eager wet like i get sometimes
i waz missin somethin

lady in purple
a layin on of hands

lady in blue
not a man

lady in yellow
layin on

lady in purple
not my mama/holdin me tight/sayin
i'm always gonna be her girl
not a layin on of bosom & womb
a layin on of hands
the holiness of myself released

lady in red
i sat up one nite walkin a boardin house
screamin/cryin/the ghost of another woman
who waz missin what i waz missin
i wanted to jump up outta my bones
& be done wit myself
leave me alone
& go on in the wind
it waz too much
i fell into a numbness
til the only tree i cd see
took me up in her branches
held me in the breeze
made me dawn dew

that chill at daybreak
the sun wrapped me up swingin rose light everywhere
the sky laid over me like a million men

i waz cold/i waz burnin up/a child
& endlessly weavin garments for the moon
wit my tears

i found god in myself
& i loved her/i loved her fiercely

(*All of the ladies repeat to themselves softly the lines 'i found god in myself & i loved her.' It soon becomes a song of joy, started by the lady in blue. The ladies sing first to each other, then gradually to the audience. After the song peaks the ladies enter into a closed tight circle.*)

      lady in brown
& this is for colored girls who have considered
suicide/but are movin to the ends of their own
rainbows

CURTAIN

ZOOMAN AND THE SIGN

CHARLES FULLER

Zooman and the Sign was first presented by the Negro Ensemble Company, Douglas Turner Ward, artistic director, and Gerald S. Krone, managing director. It opened at Theater Four in New York City on December 7, 1980, with the following cast:

ZOOMAN	Giancarlo Esposito
RACHEL TATE	Mary Alice
EMMETT TATE	Carl Gordon
REUBEN TATE	Ray Aranha
VICTOR TATE	Alvin Alexis
RUSSELL ADAMS	Terrance Terry Ellis
DONALD JACKSON	Steven A. Jones
ASH BOSWELL	Frances Foster
GRACE GEORGES	Carol Lynn Maillard

Directed by Douglas Turner Ward; scenery designed by Rodney J. Lucas; lighting by Shirley Prandergast; costumes by Judy Dearing; production stage manager, Clinton Turner Davis.

ACT I

A living-room, middle class and fairly modern, though a bit ornate, occupies much of the stage. In the living-room, the furniture is comfortable. Beyond the living-room is the front door which leads out to a porch. The porch door opens onto a single stoop and the sidewalk, which operates across the entire stage front. Downstage right is a medium-sized raised platform on which an actor should be able to pace. A staircase inside an archway corridor leads to the second floor and to the right of the living-room. Upstage of the archway leads to an unseen dining-room and kitchen offstage. The light rises slowly over the platform. In the spotlight standing on the platform is a young black man. He steps forward, looking at the audience rather contemptuously. He is wearing a mesh and plastic green and white baseball cap tilted to the side. A red T-shirt, with the inscription "Me" on it, hangs outside a pair of slacks or dungarees designed with two large pockets, one on each side of the pants. He is wearing hightop sneaks. There are several thin gold and silver chains around his neck. He is Zooman and is always accompanied when he enters by a low, rather dissonant disco sound. As he stands looking at the audience, his music fades slightly, but lingers in the background. Zooman may carry a radio, but it is not necessary.

(Zooman enters, crosses stage on sidewalk with a stylized dance-walk "bobbing" movement in time to the music, to the platform.)

ZOOMAN: Once upon a time, while the goose was drinkin' wine? Ole' monkey robbed the people on the trolley car line. *(Laughs.)* I carry a gun and a knife. A gun in this pocket—and ole' "Magic" in this one! *(Takes out knife and flicks it open.)* Now you see it— *(makes a stabbing gesture)* Now you don't! *(Smiles.)* I cut a mothafucka' with this baby yesterday. Ole' foreigner walking on the subway platform. *(He waddles, amused.)* Arms swingin' all ova' everywhere—bumpin' into people—glasses, two, three inches thick standin' out from his eyes, can't half see!

And I'm trying to listen to my music too? No-talking mothafucka' needed to get cut. (*Smiles.*) Magic nicked him. Magic is sharp as a razor. He ain't even know he was cut 'til he was halfway down the platform, and the blood started runnin' down the ole' punk's hand. (*Looks at the knife.*) Mothafucka' started screamin'—dropped his newspapa'—jumpin' up and down, pleadin' to everybody waitin' on the subway. Ain' nobody do nothin'— ole' jive West Indian mothafucka' damn near got hit by a train! (*Laughs.*) Fell all down on the ground and shit— peed on hisself! Shiiit, he wasn't hurt that bad! Magic only nicked the scared mothafucka'! (*To himself, after a pause:*) Mothafucka' don't know what scared is! (*Crosses onto the sidewalk area; distinct change of mood.*) They call me, Zoo-man! That's right. Z-O-O-M-A-N! From the Bottom! I'm the runner down thea'. When I knuck with a dude, I fight like a panther. Strike like a cobra! Stomp on mothafuckas' like a whole herd of bi-son! Zooman! (*Irritated.*) That ole' mothafucka' yesterday coulda' put somebody's eye out. Swinging his arms around like he owned the whole fuckin' platform. Lotta' ole' people take advantage of you jes' cause they ole'. Movin' all slow and shit— mumblin' unda' they breath— (*crosses onto his platform*) shufflin' down the street all bent ova and twisted up— skin hangin' off they faces—makes my stomach turn jes' to look at 'em! I got an aunt like that. Me and Kenny useta' stay to that mean bitch's house sometimes. Evil ole' skunk walkin' down the avenue, one mile an hour and shit, useta hit us across the mouth with a fly swatter jes' for talkin' at the mothafuckin' table! I was glad when the junkies would steal her check. We useta' tell her, she was dumb for goin' down there—don't nobody with any sense walk on the Avenue with a social-security check in they hands! (*To himself:*) Lotta' times we'd be to that bitch's house, three—four days, wouldn't eat nothin'. (*Casually crosses onto sidewalk.*) What am I doing here now? I just killed somebody. Little girl, I think. Me and

Stockholm turned the corner of this street?—and there's
Gustav and them jive mothafuckas' from uptown, and
this litte bitch has to be sitting on her front steps playing
jacks—or some ole' kid shit! But I had tol' Gustav if I eva'
saw his ass around the Avenue, I'd blow him away.
(*Shrugs.*) So I started shootin' and she jes' got hit by one
of the strays, that's all. She ain't had no business bein' out
there. That street is a war zone—ain' nobody see her, we
was runnin'—shit! And in that neighborhood you supposed to stay indoors, anyway! (*Pause.*) She was in the
wrong place at the wrong time—how am I supposed to
feel guilty over somethin' like that? Shiiit, I don't know
the little bitch, anyway. (*Zooman exits.*)

(*The lights begin to fade around Zooman as his music comes up
softly in the background. Simultaneously, the light builds in the Tate
living-room as the scrim opens. The Zooman music fades. The mood
is heavy. Action is continuous. On the sofa sits Rachel, an attractive
black woman. Reuben is dressed in a bus driver's uniform, Rachel in
skirt and blouse. Uncle Emmett, a man not much older than Reuben,
is seated in an armchair to left of sofa. Also there is Victor, the Tates'
fifteen-year-old son. He is dressed surprisingly similar to Zooman.
Reuben, standing upstage to the sofa, attempts to comfort Rachel.*)

RACHEL: I keep seeing her, Reuben—feeling her all over the
  room. And I want to say something to her—reach out
  and straighten her hair, touch her dress. And I know
  she's gone—

EMMETT: I say we go out there—me and your Reub, with two
  pistols, hunt the little bastards down, and put a goddamn bullet in each one of 'em's head! Look, these are
  kids that ain't *about* nothin', ain't *goin'* nowhea', and ain't
  no good—and I say let's cut our losses— (*Rises, crosses to
  imaginary window.*) I don't mind tellin' people we've got
  treacherous black kids out there! But let's get rid of 'em,
  Reub!

REUBEN: Come on, Emmett! (*Crosses around the sofa and sits next to Rachel, comforting her. To Rachel:*) Try to relax, baby.

EMMETT (*crosses to sofa*): They just killed your daughter, nephew—on her own front steps! You think anybody's gonna' look too hard for the boys who did it? Where you been? (*He is close to tears.*)

REUBEN: Who do we go out and kill?

EMMETT: All of 'em with their hats tipped to the side, and them goddamn basketball sneaks on, that's who!

VICTOR: I wear sneaks, Uncle Emmett.

EMMETT (*quickly turns to Victor*): Buy you a pair of loafers then, boy!

RACHEL (*immediately*): Emmett, will you please stop it? You're threatening my son. Just stop it!

(*There is a brief silence in the house.*)

EMMETT (*hurt*): I'm sorry—don't pay no attention to me! Tell her, Reuben—he'll tell you, Rachel, I always say too much. (*Crosses above sofa to armchair.*) I ain't gonna' say nothin' else. (*He sits in the armchair.*)

REUBEN: You can talk, Emmett—but just stop that "killin' " business—we just saw Jinny stretched out on a table dead!

EMMETT: Alright— (*slight pause*) I guess y'all the bereaved family, huh? Well, I want you to know, I'm family too!

REUBEN: Nobody said nothin' about you not bein' in the family!

EMMETT: Y'all are not the only people gonna' miss her—I was her godfather too, remember that! I carried her first bassinet down here on the train from New York. (*Rises and crosses above sofa.*) You have any idea what losin' Jinny did to us? There ain't that many of us left! Five—and Ash is

Rachel's kin! (*He points to Victor.*) That's the last Tate sittin' right there—and I'm not supposed to have something to say? (*Crosses to imaginary window.*) I'll tell you what: If they come back through here again with they little gang war—I got something for 'em!

REUBEN: Come on, Emmett—that's enough, now.

EMMETT (*crosses to right of sofa*): What's wrong with you? I can remember the time I'da had to hold him back—nobody messed with the Tates! Thing like this happen, your father and the rest of us would be on the street until we caught the little sons-a'-bitches, and took an eye for an eye!

REUBEN: We're not headhunters. This is not the old days! Emmett—you livin' in the past!

EMMETT: You changed when you got married.

REUBEN: Emmett, the next goddamn thing you say, I'm puttin' your ass back on the train to New York!

EMMETT: I just may go!

REUBEN (*rises*): Then go, dammit!

RACHEL: Will y'all stop it please? Please? All this wild talk is not gonna' bring Jinny back.

(*Emmett crosses above sofa. There is a moment of silence. Reuben crosses toward Emmett and stands by sofa.*)

REUBEN: Why don't you get us both a beer, Emmett? It'll cool us off. Is there still beer in the box, honey?

RACHEL: There's some in there.

REUBEN: Get me a cold one, okay?

EMMETT: I still think I got a right to say something. (*Crosses above sofa. Softer:*) I'm sorry, Rachel. And I didn't mean that about you, Victor. (*Exits to kitchen. Reuben sits on sofa.*)

VICTOR: What was Uncle Emmett talkin' about, Dad?

REUBEN: Aw, mess happened before you was born. I was boxing then. Stuff not worth repeatin'. (*To Rachel:*) You all right?

RACHEL (*nods*): Got a slight headache, though.

REUBEN: Did you take any aspirins?

RACHEL (*nods*): But too many of them, and they work on my stomach. (*Reuben reaches for her.*) I'm all right—but it just happened . . . and it's hard to get over, Reuben!

REUBEN (*gently*): Rachel, come on now—

VICTOR: Can I go out?

RACHEL (*suddenly terrified*): No!

REUBEN: Relax!

RACHEL: Where's he gonna go? Out on the same street, so they can kill him, too? (*To Victor:*) No! You stay in here— we just got back into the house. You just stay in.

VICTOR (*rises, crosses to sofa*): I wanna go out, Mom!

RACHEL: I said, no!

VICTOR: Just on the front steps—I want to be by myself!

RACHEL: We need to be together at a time like this—your father's here—

REUBEN (*firmly; overlapping*): Go out, son. (*Victor rises quickly.*)

RACHEL: I don't want him out there, Reuben.

REUBEN: He's got a right to his own way of handling this thing, Rachel! (*To Victor:*) You heard me, son; go 'head! (*To Rachel:*) Everybody's got their own way— (*Victor crosses hesitantly to front door and opens it.*)

REUBEN: Let him grieve any way he wants to.

RACHEL: Let him grieve in this house and live! (*Victor opens the screen door.*) Victor!

VICTOR (*stopping*): What?

REUBEN: Dammit, leave him alone, Rachel.

RACHEL (*after a pause*): Well, he better not get off those steps then— (*Loud, to Victor:*) You stay around those steps out there, Victor! You hear me? In fact, don't go off the steps!

REUBEN (*shaking his head*): Stay around the steps, son.

VICTOR: All right. (*Closes front door, closes screen door, crosses porch, sits on porch steps.*)

RACHEL: That's right—around those steps. (*She is quiet for a moment, then rises and crosses to bookcase. Looks at picture of Jinny.*) This morning, she got up—took her forever to get her clothes on. She messed around with her food— started an argument with Victor—broke the last of those glasses I got from Ash. I told her I was going to call you if she kept it up. (*Crosses to "window."*) But I made her go outside, Reuben—I made her!

REUBEN: This is not your fault.

RACHEL (*crosses to right window*): She just got on my nerves so bad—she wouldn't listen! I told her three times to clean up that mess she left in her room—three times! (*Quietly:*) You shoulda' been here.

REUBEN: I'm here now—and I was here the weekend—

RACHEL (*interrupting*): Are you going to stay this time—or leave—or what? (*Crosses below sofa to chair.*) Because I really can't take it, Reuben! It's too much to ask me to do by myself right now—

(*Emmett enters with three cans of beer and crosses to sofa. Reuben rises.*)

I can't deal with this and not know what's on your mind!

(*Reuben and Rachel stop abruptly. Reuben crosses to "window." Rachel turns away.*)

EMMETT (*noticing, he crosses to Rachel and gives her a can of beer; Reuben crosses to right window*): I brought you some beer, Rachel—it's cool, in this heat it'll make you feel better— (*Crosses to Reuben and gives him a can of beer.*) Vic didn't leave on account of me, did he?

REUBEN: No.

EMMETT: Good! It's got to be tough on him, too! (*Rachel crosses to sofa, sits.*) You know they startin' to sell Budweiser on the trains now? (*Reuben and Rachel sip.*) They're nice and cold, Reub!

RACHEL: Thank you, Emmett—I'm just— (*Emmett crosses to Rachel, stands above sofa, comforts her. Rachel leans back saddened again*): I just feel so damn empty! (*Emmett crosses to bookcase.*) I keep expecting her to come stomping down the stairs—or hear her disco music playing through that upstairs hall! How do you get used to an empty room? (*Pause.*) Reuben? (*Rachel places beer can beside her on the floor.*) You remember the time she put on all my makeup? You shoulda' seen her that day, Emmett—lipstick from one end of her face to the other—rouge everywhere— powder in her hair—cologne all over her dress— (*Shakes her head.*) She was so much a girl!

REUBEN (*crosses to end table right of sofa*): Don't make yourself upset, baby—

RACHEL: I want to remember! She was born February tenth, weighed eight and a half pounds, and had a star-shaped birthmark on the heel of her right foot— (*To herself:*) I don't know why she had that—I don't have one—and she didn't cry right away when they slapped her—did you know that, Emmett? (*Emmett seems embarrassed; places beer on end table.*) When Reuben first saw her, he said she looked like my side of the family, didn't you, Reuben? And she was easier than Victor. It was almost like she couldn't wait to pull herself out of me.

REUBEN (*crosses around sofa to Rachel*): Rachel.

RACHEL: I'm all right. I was just telling Emmett what I remember, he don't mind.

REUBEN: I think you should lay down.

RACHEL: I can't rest! How can I rest? Or just take aspirins? I keep seeing her crossing the room, Reuben—sitting in that chair—or that one! Or coming through the door.

REUBEN (*gestures to Emmett*): Baby, you hafta' lay down— Emmett, help me.

(*Emmett places his can of beer on floor by armchair, then crosses to Rachel. He takes her left arm, Reuben takes her right arm. They help her stand.*)

RACHEL: She's the baby, Reuben—how could they take the baby? (*Rachel begins to cry as Reuben and Emmett reach for her.*)

REUBEN: Rachel, come on now— (*They cross around the left side of sofa to the hall and stand at the foot of the steps.*) I want you to lay down. Don't argue, you need the rest. You'll feel better.

RACHEL (*nods and begins to climb the stairs*): Yes, I need the rest. (*Reuben guides her up the stairs. She stops and turns to Reuben.*) You call Ash.

REUBEN: Called her when we first got in. She's on her way.

(*Russell, a friend of Victor's, enters, sees Victor, and slowly starts in his direction. Emmett crosses to the armchair and picks up his beer. Sits.*)

RACHEL: She loves Jinny so much. I'm glad you're home, Reuben.

REUBEN: Shhh! You just hold onto me. (*They move up slowly.*)

RUSSELL (*stopping at the steps*): Hey, blood!

VICTOR: Hey, Russ.

RUSSELL: I'm sorry about your sista' man. (*Slight pause. He crosses stage, looks onto porch. Turns to Victor, secretively:*) Word is, it was two dudes from the Bottom.

VICTOR: Who?

RUSSELL (*shrugs*): But a dude named Zooman runs it downtown. They say he's a little crazy. Tommy tol' me Zooman and his brother Kenny beat up they own mom—said they caught her comin' out the bar, and dusted her. That's his own mother!

(*Victor is silent. Stands, pulls Russell to his left.*)

VICTOR (*finally, to Russell*): Can you get me a gun?

RUSSELL (*surprised*): You want a "burner"? (*Victor nods.*) I guess I know how you feel, Vic—but Ward got the bullets.

VICTOR: Can you get the gun now?

RUSSELL (*nods*): It'll take awhile though. I hide it in my mom's room, and she's been in bed sick since they shot—you know, since the shooting. It really shook her up, man.

(*Reuben enters slowly. Crossing down the stairs, he enters living-room, crosses to the end table, and picks up his beer.*)

Everybody around here like Jinny. (*Victor crosses onto porch.*) You goin' in? (*Victor nods.*) I'll see you later—I'll git it though.

(*Russell starts away. Victor enters the living-room, closes the front door, and sits on window seat quietly. Russell exits. As Victor enters, Emmett rises, crosses to right "window." Reuben crosses upstage of sofa to left window. Both look out. A quiet settles over things. Awkwardly Reuben and Emmett try to talk.*)

REUBEN: How was the trip from New York?

EMMETT: Same. How's the bus company?

REUBEN (*shaking his head*): They call theyself upgradin' the system . . . got all new buses.

(*Emmett crosses, sits on sofa, places beer can from floor on end-table.*)

The old ones had that handle—you reached over, threw the handle forward, and the front doors opened. (*Reuben crosses, sits in armchair.*) When the last person got off the bus in the back, the back doors swung back into position, shut, and locked. But these new buses—you got one button to operate the whole system. And the damn thing never works—I have to get out of my seat, walk to the back of the bus, and slam the right side of the back door before the damn thing will close! And they call that progress!

EMMETT: Ain't no different at Bellevue—they hire all these no-readin' niggahs, instead of teachin' 'em somethin'—and the otha' day, this kid been in my section 'bout four-five weeks, takes a bottle of acid off the shelf—how it got there I'll never know—pours it into a bucket, and damn if he don't start moppin' the floor with it! The damn tiles started turnin' brown—couple nurses' shoes start burnin'. I caught it, but you know he told me he couldn't read—imagine that? Couldn't tell the difference between cleanin' compound and acid cause the two bottles look alike.

REUBEN: When do you have to go back to New York?

EMMETT: They told me I might have to be back Wednesday—it's vacation time, and I'm on call—plus most of those brothers I'm workin' with don't know nothin' 'bout cleanin' hospital floors! Average one of 'em ain't neva even picked up a mop! (*Pause.*) What about you?

REUBEN: The union gets us a week for something like this—it's the contract. (*Emmett nods, and Reuben is quiet.*)

EMMETT (*cutting across everything loudly, rises and crosses to Reuben*): I wanna do something, Reuben! Goddamnit!

REUBEN (*shoots back*): What? What, Emmett? Kill somebody? Dammit, let it be! (*Tries to calm.*) There's nothin' to do! Leave it to the police—them boys ran through here in broad daylight! (*Rises and crosses stage.*)

EMMETT: When you ever know the police to catch anybody, when you the victim?

VICTOR (*rises, crosses upstage of sofa*): I'ma go upstairs, Dad.

REUBEN: Alright, go ahead, son.

(*Reuben crosses to Victor, places his arm around Victor's shoulders. They cross to the foot of the stairs. Emmett crosses to window, looks onto porch.*)

Vic, how are you doing?

VICTOR: Alright.

REUBEN: Look in on your mother, okay?

(*Victor nods and starts upstairs, turns.*)

VICTOR: Are you gonna' stay, Dad?

REUBEN: I'll be here.

(*Victor continues up. There is a brief silence. Reuben crosses upstage of sofa.*)

EMMETT: When did you and Rachel start havin' problems?

REUBEN: Four-five months now.

EMMETT: All the times I called you niggahs on the phone, and you ain't neva' said nothin' about it?

REUBEN: Emmett, goddamnit, it's none of your business!

EMMETT: It is my business! (*Crosses above sofa to Reuben.*) I'm in this family—it is my business!

(*Donald Jackson enters and crosses onto the front porch to the front door.*)

REUBEN: This is not the time to talk about it!

EMMETT: Y'all don't need no advice? You know everything?

(*The doorbell rings almost as a reprise. No one moves at first. Reuben and Emmett exchange looks. The strain is beginning to take its toll of Reuben. The doorbell rings again. Reuben holds back his own tears, crosses stage, sits in chair.*)

REUBEN (*gently*): Let me be, Emmett. (*Emmett nods. He is ashamed of himself.*)

EMMETT (*rises and starts to the door*): I'll get it. (*He goes to the door as Reuben sits quietly in his own grief. Emmett glances back at Reuben before opening the door.*) Yes?

JACKSON: Hello, I'm Donald Jackson—I live down the street? I just came by to see if there was anything I could do?

EMMETT (*awkwardly*): Come in— (*Emmett opens the screen door. Jackson enters.*) Reub, Mr. Jackson's here—I'm Emmett Tate, Reuben's uncle. (*The two men shake.*)

REUBEN (*recovering, overlapping*): Hey, Jackson. (*Rises.*) Come on in.

(*Jackson takes a few steps past the door and crosses. Sits on the sofa. Emmett closes front door, sits on window seat.*)

'Xcuse the place.

JACKSON: It's all right, Reub. I been knowin' y'all since you moved 'round here—you don't have to be fancy with me! (*To Emmett:*) I useta' be a fan of his, when he boxed light-heavy—and—I took his missus to the hospital, when the little girl was born. Didn' I, Reub? (*Reuben nods.*) My wife, she come and got me that day—it was cold, I remember that—Reub was workin'— (*There is a slight pause.*) They got me workin' split-shift this week—I go on nights next Thursday—and I tol' my wife I'd just come over for a hot minute, Reub, to see if there was anything I could do.

REUBEN: I appreciate it, Jackson.

JACKSON: My wife, she was in the back hangin' clothes when it happened. By the time she got to the front door, them boys was halfway up the block. She didn't see nothin'— and me, I was at work, Reub—but my wife said there was something y'all might want to know—

REUBEN (*quickly*): What? (*Places beer on floor next to chair.*)

JACKSON: Well—see by us livin' down at the end of the block, they got to us last— (*To Emmett:*) See, my house is actually on Master Street, but we never used that door—we always come out on the Titan Street side—it makes my house seem like the first house at that end of the street. Anyway, he didn't tell me, he told my wife, and she tol' me to tell Reuben. Cop told her he went to every house on the block and not one person claim they saw anything.

REUBEN: What!

JACKSON: That's what the cop said.

REUBEN (*rises and crosses to side of sofa*): There's forty-fifty families around here!

JACKSON: It seemed strange to my wife, too, 'cause she said when she came outside, everybody in the block was on their porch. About half on your side, and most of them on my side.

REUBEN: You sure that's what the cop said? (*Jackson nods.*) And they covered every house?

EMMETT (*rises, looks out window*): They ain't shit, Reub!

REUBEN: That's impossible. Mrs. Smith sits on her porch morning til night. Davis stays at his window—he can't even get upstairs. (*Crosses to left window.*) I don't believe it!

RACHEL (*enters, crossing down the stairs unnoticed*): Believe what?

REUBEN (*answering reflexively*): Nobody on the block says they saw anything.

RACHEL: What! They can't—they're lying!

REUBEN (*realizing it's her*): Rachel, you shouldn't be up—

RACHEL (*crosses to sofa*): I don't care what they say, they're lying! I saw them. They were all out there!

REUBEN (*crosses to Rachel*): Maybe they too shocked to talk yet.

RACHEL (*crosses to right window*): They'll tell me! I saw them. Mrs. Smith, Julius Williams—

REUBEN (*crosses to Rachel*): Rachel—

RACHEL (*crosses to downstage right window*): I saw Mrs. Smith standing by her front door. I looked right at Julius Williams—and Davis, Mr. Cortez, ole' man Washington!

REUBEN: Come on, baby—

(*Crosses to Rachel. She pulls away. Victor enters, crosses down the stairs unnoticed.*)

RACHEL (*crosses to left window*): Dottie Henson was hanging out her window! They're not blind! Let me talk to them—(*Crosses to Reuben. He stops her.*) I'm her mother! They'll talk to me! They'd better tell me! I swear before God they betta tell me!

REUBEN: Stop it, Rachel!

RACHEL: No! They wouldn't dare lie to me! (*Pulls away from Reuben, crosses to left window, shouts:*) I saw you, Dottie!

REUBEN (*crosses to Rachel*): Rachel!

RACHEL (*turns to Reuben. He tries to calm her down*): I saw the bitch, Reuben! How can she say she didn't see it? They've got to tell me! They all saw it. They were all outside when those boys ran through here! They all watched her die!

REUBEN: Rachel . . . Rachel . . .

(*Rachel breaks down crying as Reuben attempts to restrain and comfort her.*)

RACHEL: Goddamnit, I saw them! I saw them! I saw them . . .

(*Reuben continues to hold Rachel as the lights go down in the Tate residence and simultaneously Zooman's music begins to rise. The scrim closes. The light builds over the platform, where Zooman is squatting. He is playing with his gun and almost listening to the music. When it begins to fade, he is almost pleasant.*)

ZOOMAN: When you got nothin' to do, come to the Zoo! (*Quieter:*) First couple hours are the worse. The big blue fools are probably sweeping the neighborhood by now, picking up everybody in sight. So there ain't that many mothafuckin' places to hide—except maybe in a junkie-hole—or out here in the mothafuckin' park— (*Pause.*) I got someplace to go. I just don't wanna' git nobody in trouble, that's all! You stay away from your people as long as you can—besides, my mom neva' could take pressure, no way! She'd just sit there and cry—plus, it's the first damn place the mothafuckin' Man is gonna' look! I ain't that dumb! (*Sudden mood swing.*) I shot the little bitch 'cause I felt like it! Zooman felt like shooting somebody! And that mothafuckin' Gustav is just lucky it ain't him! I got up this morning and felt like killing somebody! So what? (*Beat. He crosses to sidewalk.*) I got picked up twenty-one times last year! Everytime somebody black did somethin' and the cops didn't have a name? They busted me! Fuck y'all! Y'all don't lock up them dirty derelicts on the street—shit smellin' mothafuckas' hair all caked with grease and slime—sleepin' in cardboard boxes, siftin' through trash, talking to theyself—beggin'! I try to set one of them filthy mothafuckas' on fire, every chance I get! (*Pause.*) Jive cunt call herself a teacher and come to school with her titties showin' everyday, in an all-boys school— (*crosses to platform*) then gonna' talk shit when they raped her. I was in Juvenile "D" eighteen months. And I wasn't even in it! Here's a bitch been in the school three years, and ain't neva' looked at nobody! All young niggahs look alike! So me and Stockholm do time because a schoolteacher can't pick out the right boys—from her own fuckin' class in a lineup! (*Crosses to sidewalk.*) And Stockholm's a niggah with straight hair! Bitch neva' taught us nothin'—but she's still there! They shoulda killed the bitch—then theyda' caught the right people. (*Pause.*) Tomorrow's *my* little sista's birthday! Not my sista' here—a half-sista in Birmingham—she'll be ten. She's down there with my fatha's people. I gotta' 'notha half-sista' who's married. I got people everywhere. Detroit. California. I got an uncle in Buffalo—couple cousins in Houston. I got a aunt on my motha's side graduated top of her class at college—plus I got friends in town! PJ—Mooky, Christine—so I got plenty of places to go if I want to! Plenty. (*Pause.*) I just don't want to.

(*The light fades around Zooman simultaneously with the lights building on the Tate household. The scrim closes. It is after midnight, and though dark, the house seems less troubled than before, due mostly to a smallish woman, thin, in her late fifties. Her name is Ash Boswell, and like Rachel, she is dressed in a robe. But there the similarity stops. Ash is stylish and for her age a good-looking woman; her hair is done, her makeup in place despite the hour. Reuben sits on sofa. Rachel sits in armchair. Ash stands upstage of armchair, her hands on Rachel's shoulders. The phone is ringing and Ash picks it up as scene begins.*)

ASH: Hello? Yes—no, this is her cousin—unhuh—it was a shock for everybody—unhuh. I'll tell them. Thanks for calling. (*Hangs up.*) Somebody named Mason—lives down the street. (*Ash hangs phone up, crosses to Rachel.*)

REUBEN: I'm tellin' you, Rachel, it was like they didn't know me! Mr. Davis, and Gibson down the street? They didn't even answer the door! And I could hear Gibson draggin' that bad leg of his across the floor! His screen door was closed but his front door was wide open—the TV was on!

I go down the street to Julius Williams's house, and he acts like he didn't know we *had* a daughter! Not one damn person on the block claims they saw anything! The woman Rachel saw leanin' out her window, Dottie Henson—and that boy Russell's mother claim they didn't even hear the shots!

RACHEL: They're lying!

REUBEN: I know.

ASH: It's a shame how we Negroes have changed through the years, honey—from one extreme to the next, like Jekyll and Hyde! (*Pause.*) How was that uncle of yours when you passed through the dining-room?

REUBEN: He's sleeping.

RACHEL: He drank quite a bit while you were gone.

ASH: Got sassy too, didn't he? (*Winks at Rachel. Crosses above sofa.*) If he wasn't family—a couple of those times he got out of hand, ole' Ash woulda' popped him upside his head! He's younger than I am by seven months, you know, so I can straighten his butt out quick, honey! (*Slight pause.*) But I knew he was taking it pretty bad when I walked in here—he needs his sleep. You Tates get evil when you drink, honey. (*Crosses around sofa, sits right side.*) That's something we don't have on the Boswell side. (*Laughs, but Reuben is distracted. Reuben rises and crosses to right window. Ash notices.*) What's the matter, Reuben?

REUBEN: It's these people. What happens if the police catch the boys they think did it, and nobody comes forward to identify them? They go free?

ASH: Black people don't like to deal with the police, Reuben.

REUBEN: I'm not the police! (*Crosses to sofa.*) Me and Rachel been livin' here fifteen-sixteen years! Jinny was born on this block! And they all act like strangers—what's wrong with them? (*Crosses to right window.*) All I've done for these people—Simpson, Edwards! Loaned Davis my tools—took him to the hospital—and I know he saw it! He sits in front of that goddamn window of his all day! The man's a cripple!—and in the summertime around here, you can't *get* these Negroes off they porches!

ASH: I blame a lot of this on them food stamps, honey.

REUBEN (*crosses upstage of sofa*): Food stamps?

ASH: That's right! When the "Negro" was hungrier, we treated each other better. Nowadays everybody's got their bellies full and we sit up belchin', watching those damn soap operas and game shows all day—hot dog in one hand, the phone in the other, a beer—or a Pepsi on the floor beside us—the baby crawlin' around dirty, the whole house filthy, and honey don't give a damn about nobody! You hear me? (*Slight pause.*) When we knew we might have to borrow a cup of flour—or a pair of pants—or a white shirt from the people across the street, we were a lot more concerned about them, and a lot more conscientious about ourselves.

REUBEN: Now, Ash—

ASH: What else is it, then? There was a time when you didn't see black girls in their teens and early twenties, fat and out of shape, honey! No indeed! Those food stamps got all these children eatin' cookies, candy, and potato chips! A woman reached her forties and fifties, you'd understand the weight, but when I was young, honey, we took care of our figures—humph! Our bustlines and hips were legendary.

RACHEL (*gently*): But Ash, Reuben's—talking about somethin' else.

ASH: It's all the same—if they don't care about themselves, their own health, how they gonna' care about you? Or Jinny or any of it?

REUBEN: It's not food stamps, all right? (*Crosses to window.*) Not one food stamp answered anybody's door on this block, Ash! (*Ash rises, a little hurt.*)

ASH: I'll finish the dishes.

RACHEL: Just leave them, Ash. (*To Reuben:*) You didn't have to holler, Reuben.

REUBEN: I'm sorry, Ash.

ASH: It's all right. (*Crosses to Reuben.*) I know what kind of time this is—besides, I need to do something with my hands—take my mind off things. (*Saddens.*) It's still hard for me to accept it. When your call came, I just sat in a chair beside the window thinking about her. Remember that time she came up to Boston? She went off in those people's hearts like a firecracker. My pastor, Reverend Daniels? He loved her—still talks about what a beautiful child she was. (*Suddenly distracted.*) That reminds me, I'd better call him and ask him to send somebody over to my house. When I got up, I just ran out and jumped in the car—I'm not even sure I closed all the windows. (*Starts away.*) But it's a shame is what it is— (*She exits and the room is quiet for a moment.*)

RACHEL: Did you have any trouble getting away this afternoon?

REUBEN (*shakes head no*): I told Sid the foreman what happened and he let me go right away. How come you didn't go to work?

RACHEL: Inventory. They're bringing in the fall line—changing displays. Sometimes that department store is like a zoo. (*Long pause.*) Are you still seeing Florence?

REUBEN: I was never *seeing* Florence—I was with the woman one time!

RACHEL: I don't want to know about it!

Reuben: You saw me with her—I told you I was sorry about that six months ago! I'm livin' in one room, Rachel, with one bed, one pillow—

Rachel: I don't want my husband to be with other women!

Reuben (*crosses to right of sofa*): I'm not going to say it no more—I'm not with no otha' woman.

Rachel (*to herself*): You better not be! (*Slight pause.*) I don't want my husband to do that—and I'm not saying you're not a good person—or a good father. You do for us—the children love you and I love you, but I'll be damned if I let you live here with me and run around with other women! You are not going to do that to me!

Reuben: I can't keep apologizing for it!

Rachel: And I can't take it—not that and this too! I can't!

Reuben: Then let it be! I feel bad enough, Rachel. I wasn't even here when it happened—I feel bad enough! (*Crosses to foot of stairs. The room is quieter. Rachel softens.*)

Rachel: Jinny asked me yesterday if she could call you.

Reuben: She called—she said you told her it was all right. I was glad you did that.

Rachel: How did she sound?

Reuben: Like Jinny, her mouth going nonstop. (*Crosses to sofa.*) Told me all about this new record she bought by the Commodores—and some book you said she could read that was sexy, but not sexy enough for me to worry about— (*Sits on sofa arm.*) Was she that old?

Rachel: She had her first period a couple of weeks ago—you know what she said? Said she didn't like the blood—it got all over everything, and did I think it would ever happen without all the blood. (*Pause.*) She was laying in it, Reuben—it was all over the steps—and I wanted to save it—bring her back to life!

REUBEN: Try not to think about it.

(*He grabs her and holds her for a moment as she fights back tears and nods, taking several breaths. She is quiet for a moment.*)

RACHEL: She said she wanted us back together again.

REUBEN: She said it to me too—I'm not going anywhere.

RACHEL: Reuben, why don't we move? We could spend more time together—I took the kids out to that shopping-center out on Route 452? It's nice out there! And we're both working—this place is almost paid for, and in a few years if we stay, we won't be able to get our money back!

REUBEN: You know we can't move—the porch isn't paid for— we got a two-hundred-twenty-five-dollar car note—and it's week to week around here!

RACHEL: I don't want to live here anymore! (*Rises, crosses to window. Reuben stands.*) You can't walk the streets—I'm sick of it! And nobody gives a damn! I even had to call the police myself—leave my baby and go to the phone, because I didn't hear a siren! They stood on their porches with their mouths open! What if it had been Grace's little girl, Denise? Or Mr. Davis's granddaughter Phyllis? (*Crosses to Reuben.*) Reuben, I want to move!

REUBEN: We can't go anywhere, until somebody around here says they saw something.

RACHEL (*pulls away from Reuben, crosses to back "window"*): What are you gonna' do, drag them outta' their houses?

REUBEN: Emmett wasn't all wrong, in the old days I'da got them to say something or kicked their damned doors in!

RACHEL: And what would that prove?

REUBEN: I'm her father! I can't just sit here and do nothing!

RACHEL: Reuben, you promised me— (*Crosses to Reuben.*) You're not a fighter anymore, you're a bus driver—

ASH (*enters with apron on, potato and potato peeler in hand*): You all call me?

REUBEN (*quieter*): No, Ash— (*He stares at Rachel, a little frustrated.*)

ASH: I'm making potato salad, Rachel.

RACHEL: Ash, I don't want all that food! (*Crosses to window.*) All the family we have is here, and I don't want these people in this neighborhood in my house, slopping down my food and staggering home drunk! We don't need any potato salad!

ASH: You don't need what?

RACHEL (*crosses to sofa, sits*): You think I want them in my living-room, sitting on my furniture—

ASH (*crosses to sofa*): I never heard of a black family in mourning in my life that didn't have potato salad for people who come by to pay their respects. Never in my life! It's bad manners! What are people supposed to eat?

REUBEN (*turns to Ash*): Make the potato salad, Ash.

ASH (*nods*): Where's the relish?

REUBEN: I think it's in the refrigerator—in those shelves on the door.

ASH (*starts out, shaking her head; to herself*): I never heard of that in my life! (*Exits.*)

(*There is a long pause. Reuben and Rachel stare at one another for awhile, but Rachel breaks their silence with a sudden painful outburst.*)

RACHEL (*on the verge of tears*): Reuben, tell me it's not so. Please tell me it's not so. I think I'm just gonna' explode and die in a minute! And keep exploding—and dying, and dying—over, and over, and over— (*Reuben crosses to Rachel, sits left of her on the sofa, attempts to comfort her.*) My stomach's sour, Reuben! Where she was in my stomach is empty! And I'm sick! God, I'm so sick! I'm so sick!

(*The lights begin to fade around the Tate household as the scrim closes, and rise slowly over the platform along with Zooman's music. Zooman steps slowly on to the platform, smiling.*)

ZOOMAN: You know, I damn near got caught? I go snatch this ole' bitch's pocketbook, and she started yellin'—wig came off, and shit! I had to knock her down! Then this hero mothafucka' chases my ass five blocks before I could duck into an all-night movie. (*Shakes head.*) And sure enough, the Big Blues comes walking down the aisle shinin' a flashlight in everybody's face—and all these nasty mothafuckas' with their flies open started jumpin' up coverin' their faces, cause the Big Blues came in while this bitch on the screen is screwing four dudes, and half the scum in the movie has their fucky ass dicks out! (*Disgusted:*) Sick mothafuckas'! I acted like I had dropped somethin' but the Man stood *right* there, 'til I straightened up— (*Crosses onto sidewalk.*) But just then this crazy Brother down front leaps up, starts shoutin' at the screen—"The day of judgment is coming! The day of judgment is coming!" Ran all up on the stage, waving a gun—callin' everybody filth—and the Big Blues took off after him. (*To himself:*) I'm glad I got rid of that gun. Magic is all I need anyway. (*Opens switchblade.*) You shoulda' seen that bitch when I stuck it in her face—she was lucky her pocketbook was all I took. You ain't expect me to eat out of no garbage can, did you? (*Chuckles.*) Bitch screamed her fuckin' head off! Help! Thief! (*Crosses to platform. Pause.*) But they ain't caught Zooman yet. And they may never catch me.

(*Lights fade slowly around Zooman along with his music as he exits and comes up on the sidewalk area. Reuben enters, crosses to sidewalk. He is dressed in his uniform and cap and is carrying a sign rolled up and tied. It is cloth.*)

REUBEN: Some promises are hard to keep. Losing Jinny was like waking up and discovering the sun had a hole in it. She had the softest black skin I'd ever seen, came out of her mother like an explosion, and a way of smiling at you, made you feel somebody had given you a gift. She was an extension of me! I wanted to see her grown—bring a boy around here for me to meet—do something—be something! Twelve years old ain't nothin'! It took me fifteen years to get seniority on my job—twenty-thirty— years to grow up! Twelve years ain't nothin'! (*Confused.*) I promised her life! We all did—or at least a chance! And right here! Not out on Route 452! Here, where her memory is. (*Slight pause.*) But I made Rachel a promise, too. I couldn't break it—and God knows I wanna' beat somebody up! (*Slight pause.*) So instead, I went downtown this morning and had this sign made to hang over our porch. Get these folks off their asses. It sure can't hurt nobody. Not the way I could. But maybe it'll make somebody come forward.

(*Reuben crosses sidewalk onto the porch. He enters the house as the lights begin to fade. A sign is projected on the screen:* THE KILLERS OF OUR DAUGHTER JINNY ARE FREE ON THE STREETS BECAUSE OUR NEIGHBORS WILL NOT IDENTIFY THEM. *Light bathes the sign for one bright moment. Then slowly the sign fades. A larger sign is then projected, an enlargement of the first sign. The stage goes to black as the sign remains projected through the intermission.*)

ACT II

As before. A window in the Tate home is broken, and has been covered over with a piece of cardboard. There is a wreath on the front door. Lights build around the sidewalk. Rachel enters. She looks tired, drawn, but she has changed into another blouse, skirt, and shoes. She is now carrying a bag of groceries. She looks at the sign for a moment, then faces the audience.

RACHEL: What is it about men, that won't let them leave well-enough alone? No one buried in a graveyard can read the inscription on their headstone! And this neighborhood is dead! (*She is quiet, remembering.*) Reuben had quit prizefighting a year, before they hired him at the bus company. I was three months pregnant with Victor, and we went to Emmett and borrowed seven hundred dollars to make settlement on that house. Place only cost us seven five, but in those days that was a lot of money! (*Smiles.*) We didn't have a stick of furniture—Reuben never made no money in the ring. Reuben's mother—God rest her soul, gave us all she could, in a card table and two of those fold-up chairs. We ate off that until we bought our first kitchen set—and had to use an old single bed for a couch. (*Slight pause.*) This neighborhood was already black then and we never turned on ourselves—we kept the block clean, swept the sidewalks, gave our little block parties, and watched out for each otha's kids. I could run to the store and leave my front door open. (*Pause.*) But I can remember the day, and the hour, that fool down at the end of the street, Julius Williams, began fixing used cars in the middle of the damn sidewalk, and the oil stains and dirt tracked their way through the entire block. And outside of Reuben and Mr. Neal up at the corner nobody around here said or did anything! Couple months later they shot Scherr in the

302

grocery store—the Armstead family across the street staged a gun battle with the cops, then the riots closed all the stores on the Avenue, and gave the nighttime to the thieves! It's been like livin' on a burning fuse! (*Quietly:*) Reuben can hang up all the signs he wants to—you can't bring the dead back to life. Not them—not Jinny. I just want to move. (*Crosses onto the porch as the music from the stereo rises and the scrim and dovatien open.*)

(*Victor and Russell are in the living-room. They are listening to music and watching a portable TV with the sound turned off. Victor is sitting in the armchair, which has been turned to face the TV. Russell sprawls on the sofa.*)

RUSSELL: I wouldn't do it, Vic. You got your whole life ahead of you, Cutty! How you gonna' make it to the pros if the cops lock you in the slams? (*Rachel enters the living-room. Russell sits up straight on the sofa.*) Hello, Mrs. Tate.

RACHEL: Hello, Russell. (*Closes front door.*) Victor, turn that music down, please! (*She passes through the room and exits on the right as Victor turns the music down grumbling.*)

VICTOR: I can't even hear it! (*Once he feels she is out of earshot, he turns the music up a trifle and sits back down.*)

RUSSELL: Homicide is a deep offense, Vic. And you know if you go to jail, they hafta' send you to Trayburg, and I heard they like to make girls outta' young guys like us. (*Victor waves disdainfully.*) What could you do, if two-three old heads—say, dudes in their twenties and thirties—jumped your ass and take it?

VICTOR: I'd kill somebody—or kill myself.

RUSSELL: Let the cops catch Zoo and those guys, man! Besides, you don't know that it's Zoo anyway—the rumor is that it was just some *guys* from the Bottom.

VICTOR: If he's the runner, I want him to know I'm after him too—maybe he'll give up the dudes that did it.

RUSSELL (*amused*): Paint a sign like your old man did! (*Stands, crosses around sofa.*) Hang it at the bottom of that one. (*Across the air in front of him:*) "Zooman! I'm comin' to get you and your boys!" (*Laughs. Crosses upstage left of sofa.*) I'm sorry, Vic, but I never heard of anybody hanging up a sign like that before—the whole neighborhood is laughing—I saw a guy walk by it and fall out on the street, he was laughing so hard! (*Teasing. Crosses to Victor, spars a few punches to him.*) Did all those fights shake your ole' man's thing loose?

VICTOR: It ain't funny, man—my father has his way—I have mine!

RUSSELL: What if Zoo and them kill you?

VICTOR: They'll just have to kill me, then, okay?

RUSSELL: (*annoyed*): Don't play no martyr, Vic—you gettin' like your fatha'! My mom said half these niggahs 'round here can't even read that sign, and those that can, it just pisses them off, 'cause it brings the whole neighborhood down—'n somebody's always claimin' our people ain't no good. (*Crosses to downstage left of sofa.*) And even if you saw what happened, don't nobody like to deal with the cops. So she don't see why your father put it up in the first place, unless he's just trying to call attention to himself, like you tryin' to do.

VICTOR (*rises, crosses to Russell*): You better stop making fun of my father, Russell—unless you want to fight. (*He turns the TV off.*)

RUSSELL: I didn't say nothin' 'bout your ole' man—I told you what my mom said. Mr. Williams said it too! (*Pause.*) Hey, I'm trying to save your life, Cutty! Because I'm not gonna' help you kill nobody— (*sits on the sofa*) Zooman or anybody else!

VICTOR (*surprised, crosses to Russell*): You're not getting the bullets from Ward?

RUSSELL: Nope! They sell bullets in the hardware store, my man—Sears! In fact, I'm sorry I gave you the gun!

VICTOR: You're not getting it back.

RUSSELL: It's not worth a fight, Vic—just leave me out of it.

VICTOR: You're out of it.

RACHEL (*offstage; at once*): Victor?

VICTOR: Huh?

RACHEL: Is your father upstairs?

ASH (*emerging at the head of the stair; overlapping to Victor*): Is that your mother?

(*A woman Rachel's age, Grace Georges, enters and crosses to the porch. She will look at the sign, read it for a moment, then shake her head before crossing the porch to the door.*)

VICTOR (*to Ash*): She's looking for my father. (*Loud; crosses to foot of stairs.*) He went to Buster's Bar—him and Uncle Emmett! Said he'd be right back.

RACHEL (*still offstage*): Where'd this potato salad come from?

ASH (*starting down*): That man Jackson—said his wife made some more—just in case. It's the second batch he's brought over here. He came while you were at the store. He acts funny to me! (*Grace rings the doorbell; Ash looks toward the door.*) Who is this?

RACHEL (*offstage*): You're too suspicious, Ash.

ASH (*moving toward door*): I think that Jackson knows something about the shooting. (*Doorbell rings again.*)

GRACE (*outside; at once*): Rachel. It's me honey, Grace!

RACHEL (*offstage*): Let her in!

(*Ash crosses to front door and opens it. Victor crosses to stereo.*)

ASH (*simultaneously with Rachel above*): Hello!

RUSSELL (*rises and crosses to Victor*): I gotta' go, Cutty—my mom wants to know when the wake is.

(*Grace steps inside smiling at Ash.*)

GRACE (*overlapping*): I'm Grace Georges, a friend of Rachel's from down the street?

(*Ash gestures for Grace to enter. They cross to sofa.*)

VICTOR: Tuesday—Lincoln Funeral Home.

RUSSELL (*starting out*): You're wrong, Vic.

VICTOR: She wasn't your sista'.

GRACE: Hi, Russell.

RUSSELL: Hello, Mrs. Georges. (*Russell and Victor move toward the door.*) See you later, Vic. (*Russell goes out front door, crosses off porch, and exits.*)

ASH: Have a seat, hon, she'll be out in a minute—I'm her cousin, Ash Boswell. (*Ash and Grace shake hands.*)

GRACE: Pleased to meet you. Hi, Victor.

VICTOR (*closes door and starts to dining-room*): Hello.

GRACE: I'm sorry about your sister.

(*Rachel enters as Victor smiles faintly at Grace, passing his mother on his way offstage. Rachel seems a little tired.*)

VICTOR: I'ma get something to eat. (*Exits.*)

RACHEL (*nods*): Hi, Grace.

GRACE: How you feelin', girl? (*Rachel crosses to Grace, who takes her hand comfortingly.*) I just dropped by to pay my respects. Denise started to come over, but she's feeling a bit under the weather—asthma's bothering her in this heat, chile. (*Grace sits on sofa.*) Mike said he'd see Reuben at the layout—he's got to work. (*Rachel goes to the stereo and turns it off.*)

ASH (*to Grace*): Can I get you a little plate of something? We've got plenty of potato salad, and I'm fixing some greens—and chicken—and cornbread.

GRACE: Nawww—nope, I'd better not. Mike'll be home soon and if I eat over here, I sure won't feel like standin' in front of no hot stove cooking his dinner—no, thank you. Girl, the way that man loves to eat, he'd have a shit fit! I'm not going to stay that long. (*Ash shrugs.*) Girl, I guess you've just about run outta' line, huh? (*Rachel nods.*) It's a shame, Rachel. I think I woulda' went out of my mind if it hada' been Denise—I don't know how you can stand it. Theyda' had to carry me to the hospital—somethin'! My only child? Theyda' had to strap me down! (*Pause.*) I am really sorry it happened, Rachel. If you need anything, just send Victor—or anybody!

RACHEL: Thanks, Grace—Ash came to help me out.

GRACE (*to Ash*): My little girl, Denise, and Jinny useta' play together. Rachel is strong—if it hada' been Denise—and the way Mike loves that child? They mighta' had to strap us both down! Men always love their little girls the most. (*There is an awkward moment of silence.*) Well, I didn't intend to stay long. (*Grace starts to rise.*)

RACHEL: You don't have to rush, Grace. (*Grace sits.*)

GRACE: I didn't lock my front door, girl—but I did want to ask you one thing. (*Lower.*) Why did you let Reuben hang that sign up, Rachel? He's got these people around here climbing the walls! Don't none of them appreciate it—in fact, Cortez and Williams told Mike they were planning to hold a block meeting about it. (*Pause.*) And the truth is, I kinda' think it makes the whole street look bad myself. You know what I mean? Like, what if you didn't see it? Thing like that lumps the good with the bad—and every-time you turn around black folks are saying something terrible about each other! "We can't get together—our men ain't no good—we're triflin', everywhere we live is a slum!" I get tired of it myself—and Reuben's sign makes this look like the worse place in the world.

ASH (*crosses, sits on window seat*): But then you didn't lose your little Denise, did you, honey?

GRACE: If we had, I wouldn't have let Mike advertise about it! That's y'all's private business!

ASH: Seems like a killing on the block would be everybody's business . . .

GRACE: The Tates ain't no better than nobody else! Rachel and Reuben didn't come to Myrtle Coleman's layout—or to Mr. Stewart's funeral either! I didn't see the Tates get excited when those hoodlums raped Lou Jefferson's little girl—or robbed my place! Why should anybody go out of their way for them? I didn't hang up no sign!

RACHEL: Did you see it, Grace?

GRACE (*stiffens defensively*): What? No! Don't you accuse me!

(*Two bricks crash against the screen door, break, and splatter. A bottle breaks beside them. Grace screams at the crash. At once, Victor enters suddenly and crosses the room quickly to the front door. Ash stands and crosses upstage center of sofa. Grace stands and crosses left of sofa. Rachel stands and crosses downstage left.*)

VICTOR (*incredulous*): They trying to knock the door down! (*Moves to the door. Ash follows him.*)

ASH: Stay in here, boy!

(*Victor is outside, where he pulls the gun. Ash sees him, Rachel cannot.*)

GRACE (*interjecting*): I knew this would happen!

ASH: What are you doing with that, Victor? (*Ash crosses onto porch.*) He's got a gun.

(*Victor crosses off porch to sidewalk.*)

RACHEL: What gun? (*Crosses below sofa to front door.*) Victor?

ASH (*overlapping*): Git in here! (*Tosses bricks and kicks glass off porch.*)

VICTOR: No.

RACHEL (*reaches door*): Give me that thing!

VICTOR: Suppose they come through here again? What do we do then? We need protection, Mom! The Tates just don't let people mess with them!

RACHEL (*steps onto the porch and crosses to Victor*): You give me that damn gun right now! (*She snatches at it.*) You give it to me! You hear me? (*She swings at him and snatches it.*) Damn you, Victor! Are we supposed to lose you, too? (*Victor is immediately sorry, as Rachel looks at the gun with a mixture of horror and rage.*)

ASH (*quickly*): Boy, get in here and get a broom and clean this mess up off the porch!

RACHEL (*lashing out as Victor starts past her, and hitting him, in tears*): Don't you eva'! (*Victor moves past her quickly.*) I'll knock the living hell outta' you! You hear me, Victor?

VICTOR: Yes.

(*Victor exits offstage, as Ash holds the door for Rachel as she enters. She hands the gun to Ash.*)

RACHEL: Throw this thing in the trash.

ASH: Where in the name of hell did he get it?

GRACE: It's goin' to get worse, Rachel. People don't like being accused when they haven't done anything!

RACHEL: Get the hell out of here, Grace—Get out!

(*Grace, angry, starts out without a word. She goes to the door, stops for a moment to look at Ash and Rachel, then exits. In the house, there is a moment of quiet. Rachel paces.*)

Glass all over the porch! Did you hear him—the Tates! Will somebody please tell me what good that sign is accomplishing? Are we supposed to take turns sitting guard on the front steps? We're supposed to be in mourning for our daughter—there's a wreath on the door, and where the hell is he? Comes back three days, disrupts everything—turns things inside out. Putting up signs, it's—it's disrespectful! (*To herself:*) I almost wish I had let him beat up a few of them.

ASH: No you don't.

RACHEL: I don't want this! (*Victor reenters with a broom and dustpan and crosses to the front door. Ash crosses to front door.*) I'm sick of you, Victor—give me that broom and go someplace outta' my sight! (*She snatches the broom and starts outside. Victor starts back in and heads upstairs.*)

ASH: Are you all right?

RACHEL (*outside sweeping*): I'm fine! Just fine! (*Ash starts toward the dining-room looking at the gun and shaking her head. Rachel sweeps glass on porch; to herself:*) I didn't go to Mr. Stewart's funeral because Reuben wasn't here! And he wasn't here when the Jefferson girl got raped—and I get tired of walking around by myself or with my kids, Reuben! Florence wasn't the first one! (*She bends over and picks up the debris.*) What kinda people would do something like this? (*She starts in, leaving the broom behind.*)

(*Reuben and Emmett emerge. It is clear they have been in a fight. They both seem in pain, Emmett holding his arm, Reuben's hand is wrapped in a handkerchief. They cross on sidewalk to porch. . . . They both have trouble making it up to the porch. However, once Reuben sees the debris his own pain is unimportant. Carrying the broom, he reaches for the door and enters, leaving Emmett behind him.*)

REUBEN: Rachel? What the hell happened?

RACHEL (*reenters, carrying dustpan, sees him and is shocked*): Oh, my God! (*Crosses left of armchair. Emmett enters.*)

REUBEN (*quickly*): I'm all right. We got into a fight at Buster's—
what happened?

ASH (*reentering; takes broom from Reuben*): Some fools threw a
couple bricks at the door— (*Rachel leads Reuben to the sofa.*)
Probably some nasty kids— (*Ash sees Emmett.*) What
happened to you two?

RACHEL: A fight at Buster's! (*Ash exits with broom.*)

EMMETT: We turned that bar OUT! (*Staggers in and flops into
window seat.*) Didn't we, Reub? (*Ash reenters and crosses to
Emmett.*)

RACHEL: Did you have to get into a fight? (*Places dustpan on
floor near armchair.*)

REUBEN (*crosses downstage of sofa*): What choice did I have?

EMMETT (*overlapping*): We didn't have no choice, Rachel!
(*Aside:*) Pure case of survival.

ASH (*closing window; quickly*): You half drunk! (*Emmett makes a
face at her.*)

REUBEN: We were drinking two beers—and this fella' from
Croskey Street—I've seen him before. He walks up in *my*
face, and tells *me*, he didn't want us in there—unless I
took my sign down! (*Mimics:*) "You givin' the black community a bad name!" Here's a man, in my face, for no
reason, and I'm givin' the community a bad name? (*Quieter:*) I tol' him, I wasn't takin' nothin' down, until it got
some results! (*Sits on sofa.*)

EMMETT: Then the other guy punched me—and Reub
punched him, and it was on!

(*Victor emerges, crosses down steps, stands upstage center.*)

ASH (*crosses to Emmett, examines his arm*): Hold still and let me
look at this arm, fool!

REUBEN (*overlapping*): Help me get this jacket off, honey?

(*Rachel crosses to Reuben, helps him take off jacket reluctantly; lays jacket over back of sofa.*)

VICTOR: What's going on? (*Crosses upstage right of sofa.*)

EMMETT: Hey, nephew—me and your fatha' was in a fight! You shoulda' seen him . . . He's still got a mean left hook!

RACHEL: You know how crazy you sound? (*Crosses left of sofa.*) Two grown men bragging?

REUBEN: Who's bragging? We didn't start it!

RACHEL: Is that where Victor got it—

REUBEN: What'd you expect me to do, Rachel?!

RACHEL: —pointing a gun all over the porch.

REUBEN: What?!—A gun! (*Rises.*)

RACHEL: A gun, that's what!

REUBEN (*crosses around sofa to Victor, who backs to foot of stairs*): What were you doing with a gun, Victor—where'd you get it?!

RACHEL (*crosses to upstage right of sofa*): Why weren't you here to find out?!

VICTOR: I found it.

REUBEN: Where?!

VICTOR: It wasn't loaded!

RACHEL (*crosses downstage left*): You had no business with it!

REUBEN: You want me to let loose on you, boy?

(*The phone interrupts as Ash also chimes in.*)

ASH: This arm feels broken to me.

EMMETT: I been workin' in hospitals all my life! If it was broken, I'd know if it was broke!—

ASH (*exploiting the occasion to rescue Victor; to Emmett*): Come on you ole' fool and let me see if I can do anything with this. (*Helps Emmett stand. They cross upstage center.*) You ain't got the sense you was born with. Like I said, you Tates is one evil bunch when you drink. (*To Victor:*) Come on and help me, boy!

(*Victor rushes to obey. They exit as Reuben goes to answer the insistent phone.*)

REUBEN: Hello? Yes, this is Reuben Tate . . . Say that to my face, punk! Come around here and say that to my face! (*He slams the phone down.*)

RACHEL: So now you're inviting them! (*Crosses and sits in chair.*)

REUBEN: Rachel, I'm not going to stand around while people beat us the hell up! (*The phone interrupts again. This time, Reuben rushes to grab it.*) Listen here, you—?? What? Channel 22? Yes, this is the Tates' residence. You're talking to him. Channel 22? Well, I hung it the other day. But I've never been on TV before, what would I say? Unhuh—just talk about the sign? Guess so—can't hurt. Unhuh. Well, I'd have to think about it—give me a day— I'll let you know. Sure, thanks for calling. (*Hangs up and crosses to left of sofa.*) They heard about the sign and want to interview me.

RACHEL: I'm sick of that sign!

REUBEN: What's wrong with the sign?

RACHEL: We're supposed to be in mourning—We lost Jinny three days ago—why are you doing this now?

REUBEN (*crosses to Rachel*): Rachel, that sign hasn't hurt anybody unless they feel guilty—it doesn't fire bullets— punch out people—

RACHEL: It is making people hate us, Reuben!

REUBEN (*angrily*): That's because there's not *enough* signs! I'ma put up more of 'em— (*crosses right*) saturate the whole neighborhood! Telephone poles—store windows—buses—let everybody know! They want to be nasty?

RACHEL: You're making this a sideshow! You know that?

REUBEN: The sideshow was the day they ran through here, shot up the street, killed our daughter, and nobody on this block did anything about it! (*Crosses right of sofa.*) I'm not gonna' let them forget Jinny's life!

RACHEL: Jinny? Who the hell is that? Guns, fights, signs on telephone poles— (*rises, crosses to sofa*) TV interviews, and all in the name of Jinny? Hallelujah! Well *Jinny* was gentle, Reuben—did you forget that? A shy child—and this is her time! The last little bit of her time we have left, and someone in this family better pay her some attention, you know that? Somebody better pay some attention to her!

(*Reuben turns and faces Rachel. He starts to reply but is interrupted by the reappearance of Ash, Emmett, and Victor. They enter urgently, Emmett obviously in deep pain, bent over holding his bruised arm, which has been wrapped in an improvised sling bandage. Ash crosses above sofa. Emmett, assisted by Victor, crosses to front door, crosses onto porch, and exits.*)

ASH: Come on, Reuben, we gotta' drive him to the hospital. He's getting worse. I know his arm is broken.

(*Ash picks up Reuben's jacket, Reuben takes jacket and crosses to front door. Exits, following Victor and Emmett. Ash crosses to front door, exits closing front door, crosses off porch and exits. Rachel is left alone.*)

RACHEL (*quietly, to no one in particular*): Somebody needs to pay more attention to Jinny.

(*Lights fade out and rise up on Zooman once more at the platform.*)

ZOOMAN: It kin be fun being on the run. One time me an' Stockholm dodged the Big Blue fools for ten days. We holed up in a junkie-hole right 'round the corner from

where we robbed the dude! Nighttime, we useta' go out,
ride the bus crosstown, break into a store or somethin',
then get on the same bus and come back. Like Robin
Hood! Sometime we just laid dead and got high—
Christine would sneak in with chicken and shit from
Kentucky-fried. (*Pause.*) I been goin' with Christine
almost two years—she ain't got no kids of mine yet, but
she says she wants one—But Christine can't half take
care of the kid Arnold gave her—little mothafucka' be
dirty all the time, smellin' like pee, and Christine be
layin' up on the bed watchin' television—besides, she
ain't got as much education as I got! (*Slight pause. Crosses
to sidewalk.*) I ain't really worried yet. And I happen to
know, if a black kills a black, and they don't catch you
right away, they liable to forget about it— But that niggah
with them signs? Ain't nobody ever pulled that kinda
shit before! Killings, rapes, drugs—all kinds of shit be
goin' on everyday and nobody says nothin'! That section
was always rundown and dangerous—vacant junkie-
holes everywhea', trash on the streets— (*Shakes head.*)
Always some mothafucka' wanna' be a hero! (*Crosses to
platform.*) Wasn' neva' no stores on the Avenue! You have
to go halfway around the world to get to the Chinese
laundry—get your clothes cleaned, or your shoes fixed!
Ain' nothin' in there but barbershops and junky corner
groceries—and every now and then a drugstore where
the man sells you your pills and cough syrup behind a
bulletproof glass! Shiiittt! The first junkie I ever met was
a mothafucka' lived 'cross the street—and I know every
mothafucka' that's stealin', muggin', hustlin', and pro-
curin'—grew up with all of 'em! (*Crosses to sidewalk.*)
Everybody I know buys hot clothes! Curtis' mother?
Walkin' around passin' out all that, Let-Jesus-Save-You
shit? Buys truckloads of hot dresses and be sellin' them
to her Holy-Moly congregation. And I've seen Greenie's
fatha' stealin' cookies out the supermarket—puttin' tuna
fish and shit under his coat. (*Crosses to platform.*) Now he's

gonna make that zoo a neighborhood puttin' everybody on me? The little bitch was in the way, that's all! Who the fuck he think he is? Sendin' people afta' me, like I'm some animal! If he wants to blame somebody—you don't leave no little girl sittin' on her steps by herself nowadays! I don't let my sista' go out by herself. He shoulda' known better—what kinda' fatha' is he? (*Slight pause.*) But I'll tell you what—if somebody don't git his ass straight soon, I'ma show him just what a killer is— Niggahs can't be heroes, don't he know nothin'?

(*Zooman's music comes up for a moment, then begins to fade as the light around him goes to black. Simultaneously the light builds around the Tate household. Emmett's arm is in a sling and cast. They are all dressed in black. It is evening.*)

ASH: How was the service?

REUBEN: Not much you can say about a wake, Ash. They said the prayers, blessed the casket—one little girl got up and read a little poem from her school, but there's not that much to say about a wake.

EMMETT: What was that preacher's name, Reub?

REUBEN: Walker—Reverend Walker.

EMMETT (*to Ash*): He gave a good eulogy. It made me feel better—he didn' have the whole place cryin'! (*Rachel sobs.*)

VICTOR (*at once*): You all right, Mom? (*She nods.*)

EMMETT: Like the way he talked about kids—and heaven, you didn't feel weighted down.

RACHEL (*overlapping*): I'm just numb, son. (*Slight pause.*)

EMMETT: At least it felt that way to me.

REUBEN (*to Ash*): Your old girlfriend Mrs. Rheinhard was there. She asked about you.

ASH: Really? That was nice of her—how'd she look? The last time I talked to her, she was complaining about her arthritis.

REUBEN: She looked all right to me.

EMMETT (*out of nowhere, as Victor opens window*): Children must be spared hell's fire, 'cause they're innocent. You hear that, Reub?

REUBEN (*nods*): A couple of the drivers I work with were there—and Lefty Cohen my old trainer—did you see him? (*Rachel slams register closed.*) Rachel? Honey, you want an aspirin? (*Rachel shakes her head no.*)

ASH: Did they sing? (*Crosses around sofa, sits.*)

EMMETT: "Nearer My God to Thee"—all the standard stuff. (*To Reuben:*) What was that one Jinny liked so much?

REUBEN and ASH: "Amazing Grace."

EMMETT: They sung that. It was a nice service, I thought. (*Looks around.*) Jinny looked peaceful.

REUBEN: I was just thinking about her—she'd be sleeping by now—only child I ever saw slept with a smile on her face.

VICTOR: Didn't look nothin' like her to me. Why'd they put all that powder on her face?

REUBEN: That's just how they do it, son.

RACHEL: Other undertakers don't make people look like that, and you know it! I've been to enough wakes— (*almost crying*) and the people didn't look like that!

REUBEN: What can we do about it now—take her someplace else?

RACHEL: That's not funny!

REUBEN (*gentle*): I didn't like it anymore than you did.

RACHEL: The whole thing was just so ugly! (*Reuben puts his arm around her.*)

ASH: Y'all got to forgive me for not going—I started to after you left, but I couldn't. I didn't want to see her like that. I sat here trying to find something to do—I even laid down to rest, and was surprised when the doorbell woke me up that I had fallen asleep. I dreamed about her. She was standing there, by the window, smiling. It startled me, it seemed so real.

EMMETT: We understand. (*To Reuben:*) Who sent that big wreath? The one with twelve carnations on it?

REUBEN: I think her class took up a collection—I was surprised to see a bouquet from the block committee. Ash? Who came to the door—you said somebody woke you up?

ASH: That man who's been bringing all that potato salad over here—Jackson. This time he brought a pot of greens— said he wanted to talk to you and Rachel. He acts funny to me.

REUBEN: What did he do?

ASH: Nothin'—I don't know—he just acts funny—like he wants to say something and never says it! He's been back and forth over here everyday—he acts like he's got things botherin' him. When I asked him to come in, he almost ran off the porch.

EMMETT: Maybe he saw something, Reub.

REUBEN: Jackson was at work.

EMMETT: Maybe his wife saw something—she's the one makin' all the food—and he keeps comin' by to see if anybody else came forward. You know we don't like to stick our necks out—and he acted strange to me the first time he came by.

REUBEN: She does have a clear view of the street from her yard—maybe she did see it. She could be scared. They both might be.

EMMETT: They probably trying to get out of it!

ASH: He said he'd be by later.

REUBEN (*to Emmett*): Everybody ain't like that! A whole lot of them came to the wake.

RACHEL: Well, which ones raised all the hell, Reuben?

REUBEN: Those people were ignorant—Smith, Williams, and Judson wasn' never worth a damn!

EMMETT: (*overlapping*): Anybody want a beer? (*Rises.*) Reub?

RACHEL (*as Emmett rises*): They whispered about his sign all through the whole damn service.

ASH (*at once*): You don't need no more to drink, mistah.

(*Emmett waves at her disdainfully as he exits.*)

RACHEL (*to Ash*): They wrote threats—and, and filth in the register! (*She holds up the book.*) The only thing we got left! The layout register! You ever in your life hear of anything as rotten and lowdown as that? (*She throws it down.*)

REUBEN: You know some kids wrote that—look at the hand-writing! (*Rises, crosses around sofa.*) A lot of people came over to me and said they were glad about the sign—

RACHEL: Is Davis a kid? (*To Victor:*) Tell your father what he told you—

VICTOR: He just said he was sorry about Jinny, and he thought the sign would bring us trouble.

REUBEN: I didn't hear him say that.

(*Emmett enters with beer, crosses above of sofa.*)

VICTOR: He was in line—he leaned over and whispered it to me. Uncle Emmett heard it.

EMMETT (*hands Reuben a beer*): Yeah, I heard it. (*Crosses to Victor.*) I tried to tap him with this cast a couple times, too!

RACHEL: Did you hear Julius Williams shouting all over the sidewalk?

REUBEN (*crosses upstage of armchair*): Julius Williams ain't gonna' do a damn thing—he is nothin' but mouth. If he ever lights a cigarette in front of this house, I'll have him locked up!

RACHEL: And if someone else decides to set fire to it?

ASH: Fire?

RACHEL: They were threatening to burn the damn place down!

REUBEN: Then let 'em! I'm not taking down that sign because some drunken bum like Williams got loud!

(*Jackson enters with two loaves of bread; crosses onto porch, stopping to look at the sign.*)

EMMETT: Reub, I think I know how you feel, but people ain't like they used to be, they do vicious things nowadays, Reub. You got this to protect.

(*The doorbell rings. Ash rises and crosses to front door. Rachel rises and places register on chair, crosses to stereo, tosses glove, and exits.*)

REUBEN: That sign doesn't come down until someone comes forward.

ASH (*opens the door*): Mr. Jackson!

(*Everyone turns around. Reuben rises and goes to the door. Emmett crosses and sits on sofa.*)

REUBEN: Jackson, come on in! (*Jackson crosses through the doorway.*)

JACKSON: No thanks, I'm on my way to work. I just came by to bring this bread my wife made. (*He hands it to Ash as Reuben approaches. Ash exits with bread.*) She said she knew y'all would be havin' company and we both—me and my wife—figured Rachel would have enough to do.

REUBEN: Thanks.

JACKSON (*as Ash reenters and crosses above sofa*): I came by earlier—how's your missus?

REUBEN: Okay. (*There's a slight awkward silence; Jackson is uneasy.*) Jackson—your wife? She saw the whole thing, didn't she?

JACKSON (*surprised and hurt*): No, Reuben!

ASH (*crosses left of armchair*): Ask him why he's been comin' over here so much then?

JACKSON (*to Ash and Reuben*): My wife and me thought y'all needed a little help—I—my wife's been after me to tell y'all how we felt about you and the little girl. I came and took Rachel to the hospital when she was born. I—but I just couldn't say it. I tol' my wife, I said, "Sayin' something like that to people can embarrass a man!" But I figured if I brought something ova'—a little gift or something, I wouldn't have to say it, 'cause y'all would know. But she kept pesterin' me—"You ain't said it!" She said that everyday—and it was on me, 'cause I took her to the hospital.

REUBEN: Jackson, I—

JACKSON: Let me say it, all right? We like y'all! You and Rachel raised nice kids, and y'all ain't loud and don't raise a whole lotta' hell around here! And I'm glad you put up that sign, but we didn't see nothin'—my wife or me. (*Indignant.*) We ain't them kinda' people, Reuben! (*Slight pause. Rachel reenters and stands in hall unseen by Jackson.*) They come by my house this evenin' to ask me if me and my wife would join some march they plannin'. A group of 'em intend to pull that sign down, or set it on fire. I don't want no part of it! But we— (*Pause. Crosses to door.*) It's getting kinda' late, and I gotta' go to work. Tell your missus that bread's an easy recipe. My wife said, if she wants it, she'll give it to her. (*Turns away and starts out.*)

Goodnight. (*He exits through front door, crosses off porch, and exits.*)

REUBEN (*crosses onto porch*): I'm sorry, Jackson.

(*Jackson doesn't hear. Reuben reenters. Rachel crosses to foot of stairs. The family is quiet for awhile. Reuben closes the door and crosses to window.*)

EMMETT: Everybody makes mistakes.

RACHEL: That sign is making us crazy!

REUBEN: (*irritated*): The sign stays up. (*Crosses right of sofa.*)

ASH: I think it's too dangerous to keep up now, Reuben. Why not take it down just for tonight? After all, you can always put it back up.

EMMETT: After the funeral wouldn't hurt.

(*Reuben shakes his head no. The phone rings almost like a reprise. Victor rises to get it.*)

REUBEN: Once she's in the ground, they'll forget it.

VICTOR: Hello? Who? (*To Reuben:*) It's for you. (*Reuben crosses to Victor, takes receiver. Victor crosses and picks up and reads the register.*)

REUBEN: And if they ever catch the boys, these people won't even remember her name! Besides, it's the principle of the thing. (*Ash sits in the armchair. Reuben puts receiver to ear.*) Hello? Who? Sergeant Harrison? No, I'm all right, we're not long back from the layout, so we are a little tired. Unhuh—you caught one of them. (*Rachel crosses and sits on sofa.*)

ASH: Thank God!

REUBEN: Unhuh—well, that's a start. I hope so— (*Smiles suddenly.*) You saw the picture in the paper? Yeah, I useta' box light-heavy, I was ranked number three for a while. Well, they're supposed to send some people out to interview me. (*Chuckles.*) Listen, you open up us bus drivers anything's liable to come out. Unhuh. (*Serious.*) There is one thing, though. Could you have a patrol car pass through this street from time to time tonight? No—nothing serious—fine. Thanks, sarge. You too! (*Hangs up. Crosses right of sofa.*) A patrol car will swing through here tonight, are y'all satisfied?

EMMETT: When you ever known the police to be where they're supposed to be, when they're supposed to be there? Man, you crazy! I know what I'ma do, and it ain't gonna' wait on no cops eitha'!

ASH (*giving Emmett a nasty look*): What did he say about the boys?

REUBEN (*sitting*): They caught one of 'em. He's fifteen.

ASH: They get younger and weaker in every generation.

REUBEN (*disturbed*): There were two of 'em. They picked up some kid named Stockholm and he told on the other one—boy they call Zooman. (*To himself:*) I never thought of them as that young. They felt like men.

RACHEL: I'm glad they caught him. (*Rises, crosses to window.*)

EMMETT (*overlapping*): They got 'em out here sellin' dope at ten and eleven—where have you been, Reub?

REUBEN (*crosses toward Victor*): You ever heard of them, Victor?

RACHEL: How would Victor know somebody named Zooman?

VICTOR: I've heard of him—I don't know him.

RACHEL: You better not know him!

REUBEN: Is that the one you wanted to get? (*Victor nods.*) Did you know he had done it?

VICTOR: Naw—it was the rumor that it came from down the Bottom and he's the runner down there—(*shrugs*) so—

RACHEL (*crosses to right of sofa*): What? What kinda crazy—are you in some gang?

VICTOR: No! That was just the rumor on the street—I'm not in no gang! (*A long pause.*) Can I sit outside on the steps?

REUBEN: Go 'head.

(*Victor places register on chair and crosses to front door, crosses onto porch, and sits on steps. Rachel crosses to window, looks out. Reuben crosses above sofa.*)

The kids know who's on the street and who isn't.

RACHEL (*calmly*): Will you please take that sign down?

REUBEN: Nope. The cop just said (*crosses to right window*) he thought it was a good idea to leave it up. They got a lotta' phone calls today after my picture was in the paper— said a lot of people are behind it. (*Rachel shakes her head.*)

ASH: Rachel, you want an aspirin?

RACHEL (*crosses to Reuben*): I want this man to take down that damn sign!

REUBEN: Rachel, why can't you back me up! When I was hanging those telephone pole signs? (*Crosses to left window.*) The Democratic committeeman over on Shelby Street? Man ain't never spoke to me since we moved here—came up to me and told me I was right! Right! Morgan the barber put one in his shop, and it made him feel proud. Cobb at the corner grocery—Baker at the shoeshine parlor, they all said they were for it!

RACHEL (*crosses to Reuben*): You put up a few signs, get your name in the paper, and you're Martin Luther King?

REUBEN (*turns to face Rachel*): Nobody's trying to be King—if somebody comes forward maybe—those boys won't run through here no more!

RACHEL: I thought you put it up for Jinny?

REUBEN: I did!

RACHEL: The people around here want to do something to you, Reuben.

EMMETT (*rises*): I got to agree with her, Reuben—all that stuff you talkin' (*Crosses above sofa.*) Listen, we got to be on guard right here!

REUBEN: Goddamn—don't y'all understand? You can't live across the street from me, see my daughter get killed, and not do nothin'! I don't have to be in no newspapers— or TV either! You can't do that shit to me!

RACHEL (*crosses to chair and picks up register*): You know what they wrote in this book? (*Crosses to left of armchair and shows Ash the register.*) They want to kill you, Reuben— and I love you!

REUBEN: Then they gonna hafta' do it. I'm not scared of them.

RACHEL: You're not scared, but the rest of us are scared to death.

REUBEN: I can't take the sign down until somebody comes forward—and I don't want anybody in this family to mess with it, eitha'! (*Crosses to window.*)

RACHEL (*crosses to Reuben*): We just got through sitting in front of Jinny—and Reuben, I don't want to wind up sitting in front of you. (*Hesitant.*) If you don't take it down—I want you to leave!

(*Rachel exits up the stairs. There is silence. Ash rises, crosses, and exits up the stairs. The silence continues. Emmett picks up jacket and exits with a can of beer.*)

REUBEN: Rachel? I ain't goin' nowhere! (*Exits as the lights fade and the scrim closes. Victor rises and crosses on the sidewalk. He is a little sad. Lights rise on the sidewalk.*)

VICTOR: They always tell me that I've got a better education than they had—that I know more—should do great things, but they never let me say anything. I don't have a voice in nothin'—no opinions, no pros—cons—and most of the time they talk over me like I'm not even there. And I know a whole lot more than they know. (*Pause.*) I'm the one misses Jinny the most—I was around her the most! We useta' have arguments sometimes, but she was all I had—you can't talk to them—not like you can with someone you're close to—grow up with. Me and Jinny had secrets—things they never even knew we talked about. They weren't big secrets, but sometimes she would tell me things—like how she wanted them to get back together. And how angry she would get with my mom, when she wouldn't let my father stay here. She told me once that sometimes, when she missed him a lot, she would show off just to get on my mom's nerves so bad, she would have to call my father over, just to punish her. At least she would see him. (*Slight pause.*) That's what she was doin' the other day—and they don't know that. I know it, but I'll never tell them!

(*Zooman enters and crosses to sidewalk. He glances at the sign; he notices Victor, who notices him. They both straighten. Zooman reaches into his pocket, the one away from the audience, and removes his knife. We hear it click. He holds it down at his side, out of sight. Victor registers an immediate sense of caution. Both boys are tense as they start toward each other at the same time. They will reach each other and pass by in silence, aware and prepared for one another. Victor goes directly to the porch and looks back at Zooman. Zooman exits; he reenters and crosses on the sidewalk to the platform. When he reaches it, he looks at his knife, closes it, and puts it back into his pocket. He smiles as Victor exits through the house. Victor crosses and exits up the stairs as the lights fade in the house and rise on the sidewalk and platform. Through all of this Zooman's music has played.*)

ZOOMAN: They got me a little scared. If they got Stockholm's ass in the slams, it's just a matter of time, 'cause the Big Blues put a lotta' pressure on you once they pick you up. Anybody can snap under that. I'm not even sure what *I* would do! 'Specially since I got a previous record—the Big Blues can be a bitch! At the Seventh? They hit my little brother Kenny 'cross the mouth with a blackjack! (*To himself:*) Stockholm probably screamed his guts out. Y'all won't have to wait too long—Stock probably gave the Man a complete description by now. I'm not mad with him, though—his mom probably got him some wise-ass lawyer and that mothafucka' will make Stockholm swear he wasn' even there! "Zooman had the gun!" "Zooman fired the shots" "Zooman told me to do it!" (*Smiles.*) It's all right, 'cause I'd put the whole thing on him if I got the chance. Don't *nobody* want to go to jail for murder. My aunt—she'll be down there cryin' all ova' the place. My mom won't come—and my fatha' probably won't even know about it, unless they put it in the Chicago papers. (*Shakes head.*) That dude—if I had a nickel for every time I laid eyes on that mothafucka', I wouldn' have fifty cents! (*Tired.*) Last night, I slept squattin' over the toilet seat in the train station with a faggot! Mothafucka' had the nerve to proposition me, while I was peein'! I kicked his ass, and when the mothafucka' started pleadin' I jes *cut* the mothafucka'—shiiitt! And y 'all got the nerve to hunt me? Y'all let anything walk the streets—and you mothafuckas' never showed me no mercy! (*Pause.*) I'll be off your streets soon, don't worry—I just got one more thing to do.

(*Zooman steps from the platform and starts across the stage boldly toward the Tate house. Before he reaches the steps he is hollering, his knife in his hand.*)

Hey, mothafucka'! This is Zooman out here! (*He reaches up and begins to rip and tear at the sign.*) Don't nobody do this shit! You don't send people after me! You hear that, mothafucka'!? This is Zooman you fuckin' with!

(*Lights come on inside the house and Emmett, half frightened, half asleep, comes down the stairs with a gun in his hand.*)

EMMETT: Reuben? Reuben?

(*Emmett crosses above sofa. He fires immediately through the window. The shot hits Zooman and knocks him down, and he pulls the sign down with him. He is in surprised agony for a few moments. He staggers and crawls off the porch to the sidewalk.)*

　　Reuben! They're outside! Reuben!

REUBEN: Emmett—what the hell are you doin'? (*He starts down, crosses to Emmett.*)

EMMETT: They're outside! They were pulling on the sign! I heard 'em—it woke me up! They were trying to come in!

(Reuben starts toward the front door and crosses onto the porch.)

REUBEN: That sounded like some kid—

EMMETT: That wasn' no kid I heard!

(Reuben crosses on sidewalk to Zooman.)

　　Them people were coming in! I heard 'em on the porch! I heard 'em!

REUBEN (*bends over the body*): Be still.

ZOOMAN: Fuck you! I'm Zooman!

(Rachel, Ash, and Victor ad-lib offstage: Victor, is your father in the room with you? No, Mom, I thought he was with you. Rachel, I think I heard shots downstairs. Where's Reuben? Emmett? Etc.)

ASH (*enters and crosses down the stairs to Emmett*): What happened, Emmett?

EMMETT: I heard 'em tryin' to get in—they were outside the window, screamin' and yellin'.

(Rachel enters, crosses down the stairs, crosses to the front door. Victor enters, crosses down the stairs.)

RACHEL: Reuben? Reuben! (*She opens the door, crosses onto the porch, crosses down steps to sidewalk.*)

EMMETT (*dazed; overlapping*): It sounded like they were comin' in—

(Ash crosses to the front door, stands on porch in doorway.)

It did to me! (*He drops the pistol.*)

REUBEN (*rises, crosses to porch*): Call the police—

(*Victor goes to the phone as Rachel steps toward Reuben. Reuben crosses to Zooman, stands upstage of him.*)

RACHEL: Who is it, Reuben?

REUBEN: Zooman—I heard him yell it.

RACHEL: Zooman? (*She moves forward menacingly.*) This is the one killed my baby? (*To the body:*) Get up! (*She is enraged, but Reuben stops her.*) I'ma kill him! Get up goddamnit!

REUBEN: He's dead, Rachel! (*She struggles to get loose.*)

RACHEL: Let him get up!

REUBEN: He's dead!

RACHEL: Oh, Reuben—oh, my God, Reuben—

REUBEN (*puts his arm around her and holds her as she cries*): I know, baby. I know.

(*Slowly Reuben starts Rachel back toward the house. Reuben and Rachel enter the house followed by Ash as the lights fade out slowly and another sign is projected on the scrim. It reads:* HERE, LESTER JOHNSON WAS KILLED. HE WILL BE MISSED BY FAMILY AND FRIENDS. HE WAS KNOWN AS ZOOMAN. *A spotlight builds to brilliance on this new sign, then slowly fades out. The stage goes to black, but Zooman's music lingers in the air, mixed with the sound of a distant siren.*)

CURTAIN

MA RAINEY'S
BLACK BOTTOM

AUGUST WILSON

Ma Rainey's Black Bottom opened at the Yale Repertory Theatre on April 6, 1984, with the following cast:

STURDYVANT	Richard M. Davidson
IRVIN	Lou Criscuolo
CUTLER	Joe Seneca
TOLEDO	Robert Judd
SLOW DRAG	Leonard Jackson
LEVEE	Charles S. Dutton
MA RAINEY	Theresa Merritt
POLICEMAN	David Wayne Nelson
DUSSIE MAE	Aleta Mitchell
SYLVESTER	Steven R. Blye

Directed by Lloyd Richards; settings designed by Charles Henry McClennahan; costumes designed by Daphne Pascucci; lighting designed by Peter Maradudin; musical direction by Dwight Andrews; stage managed by Mortimer Halpern.

Ma Rainey's Black Bottom opened at the Cort Theatre on October 11, 1984, with the following cast:

STURDYVANT	John Carpenter
IRVIN	Lou Criscuolo
CUTLER	Joe Seneca
TOLEDO	Robert Judd
SLOW DRAG	Leonard Jackson
LEVEE	Charles S. Dutton
MA RAINEY	Theresa Merritt
DUSSIE MAE	Aleta Mitchell
SYLVESTER	Scott Davenport-Richards
POLICEMAN	Christopher Loomis

Directed by Lloyd Richards; settings designed by Charles Henry McClennahan; costumes designed by Daphne Pascucci; lighting designed by Peter Maradudin; musical direction by Dwight Andrews; stage managed by K. White.

ACT I

A female vocal rendition of "C.C. Rider" is heard. The lights fade to black, then after a moment a warm glow fades up in the front hall from the overhead fixture spilling in through the double door windows, creating a dim glow in the studio, and cool daylight fades up, streaming through the dirty casement window in the bandroom. The song ends.

Sturdyvant enters down the front hall carrying a small bundle, followed by Irvin. Sturdyvant flips a light switch left of the double door. The overhead practicals go on, generally illuminating the studio. Sturdyvant quickly surveys the studio, moves toward the spiral staircase and finds his path blocked by the wooden stool. He moves the stool toward the right wall and starts to climb the staircase as Irvin crosses to the radiator. Irvin shivers, touches the radiator, and turns the valve. Sturdyvant reaches the top of the staircase, opens the control booth door, and flips a switch just inside the door.

The lamps come on in the control booth and the stairwell of the spiral staircase. Sturdyvant unwraps the bundle revealing recording discs, which he begins to examine as Irvin crosses to the singer's platform, picks up the music stand, moves the cane chair off the platform to the right and crosses to the left door. Irvin opens the door, exits into the back hall, and disappears into a closet to the right.

The closet light comes up, dimly illuminating the back hall and a descending step to the left. Irvin returns carrying a microphone with a coiled cable on a tall stand. He places it in the center of the singer's platform, uncoils the mic cable, plugs it into the jack box, then returns to the mic. Irvin cranes his neck to blow into mic, taps it a few times, glances up to the control booth, shrugs his shoulders, then crosses to the piano as Sturdyvant looks up and puts on his headphones. Irvin reaches for the piano keys.

STURDYVANT (*speaks into the control booth microphone and is heard over speaker horn in the studio*): Irv . . . let's check that mic, huh? (*Irvin steps away from the piano, points at the mic, and nods his head. Into the booth mic:*) Let's do a check on it.

IRVIN (*sighs, crosses to the mic, and speaks into it*): Testing . . . one
. . . two . . . three. . . . (*There is a piercing squeal of feedback
over the horn speaker. Irvin covers his ears in pain and glares at
Sturdyvant. Sturdyvant turns and adjusts the dials on the
mixer. Irvin speaks into the mic again. Cautiously:*) Testing
. . . one . . . two . . . three . . . Testing. . . . (*Sturdyvant
takes off his headphones and examines the recording discs.*)
How's that, Mel? (*Irvin pauses, then continues loudly.*) Testing . . . one . . . two. . . .

STURDYVANT (*looks at Irvin, hastily, into the booth mic*): Okay . . .
that checks. We got a good reading. (*Irvin crosses to the
music stand. Into the booth mic:*) You got that list, Irv?

IRVIN (*picks up the music stand and crosses toward the door*): Yeah
. . . yeah I got it. Don't worry about nothing. (*Exits
through the doorway and into the closet.*)

STURDYVANT (*into the booth mic*): Listen, Irv . . . you keep her in
line, okay? (*Irvin returns and looks at Sturdyvant. Into the
booth mic:*) I'm holding you responsible for her . . . if she
starts any of her . . .

IRVIN: Mel . . . what's with the goddamn horn? You wanna
talk to me . . . okay! I can't talk to you over the goddamn
horn . . . Christ!

STURDYVANT (*into the booth mic*): I'm not putting up with any of
her shenanigans. You hear? Irv? (*Irvin crosses to the piano
and bangs on the keys. Sturdyvant tries to yell over the cacophony, into the booth mic:*) I'm just not gonna stand for it. I
want you to keep her in line. Irv? (*Sturdyvant leaves the
control booth and bounds down the spiral staircase. Irvin stops
pounding the piano keys.*) Listen, Irv . . . you're her manager . . . she's your responsibility. . . .

IRVIN (*crosses to the double door*): Okay, okay, Mel . . . let me
handle it.

STURDYVANT (*fuming*): She's your responsibility. I'm not putting up with any of this Royal Highness . . . Queen of the Blues bullshit!

IRVIN (*humorously*): Mother of the Blues, Mel. Mother of the Blues. (*He opens the double door and goes into the front hall.*)

STURDYVANT (*crosses to the double door, grabs it, and holds it open; Irvin hangs his hat and coat on the wall hooks*): I don't care what she calls herself. I'm not putting up with it. I just want to get her in here . . . record those songs on that list . . . and get her out. Just like clockwork, huh?

IRVIN (*crosses through the open door to Sturdyvant*): Like clockwork, Mel. You just stay out of the way and let me handle it.

STURDYVANT (*lets the door swing shut, crosses to the radiator, and turns the valve, as Irvin picks up two of the wooden folding chairs and crosses toward the singer's platform*): Yeah . . . yeah . . . you handled it last time. (*Irvin unfolds one chair.*) Remember? She marches in here like she owns the damn place . . . doesn't like the songs we picked out . . . says her throat is sore . . . doesn't want to do more than one take. . . .

IRVIN (*unfolds the other chair and sets it over the mic cable*): Okay . . . okay . . . I was here! I know all about it.

STURDYVANT (*crosses to the microphone as Irvin counters to the radiator; arranges the mic stand and cable*): Complains about the building being cold . . . and then . . . trips over the mic wire and threatens to sue me. That's taking care of it?

IRVIN (*touches the radiator and turns the valve*): I've got it all worked out this time. I talked with her last night. Her throat is fine . . . we went over the songs together . . . I got everything straight, Mel. (*Crosses to Sturdyvant.*)

STURDYVANT: Irv, that horn player . . . the one who gave me those songs . . . is he going to be here?

IRVIN: Yeah.

STURDYVANT: Good. I want to hear more of that sound. Times are changing. This is a tricky business now. We've got to jazz it up . . . put in something different. You know, something wild . . . with a lot of rhythm. (*Irvin looks at him blankly.*) You know what we put out last time, Irv? We put out garbage last time. (*Irvin crosses to the door and exits into closet as Sturdyvant straightens the folding chairs.*) It was garbage. I don't even know why I bother with this anymore.

IRVIN (*returns from the closet carrying a crate of empty Coke bottles and crosses toward the double door*): You did alright last time, Mel. Not as good as before, but you did alright.

STURDYVANT: You know how many records we sold in New York? You wanna see the sheet? And you know what's in New York, Irv? Harlem. (*Irvin opens the double door, crosses into the front hall, and the doors swing shut. Sturdyvant shouts:*) Harlem's in New York, Irv. (*Irvin props the crate against the wall.*)

IRVIN (*crosses through the double door to Sturdyvant*): Okay, so they didn't sell in New York. But look at Memphis . . . Birmingham . . . Atlanta . . . Christ . . . you made a bundle.

STURDYVANT: It's not the money, Irv. You know I couldn't sleep last night? This business is bad for my nerves. My wife is after me to slow down and take a vacation. Two more years and I'm gonna get out . . . get into something respectable. Textiles. That's a respectable business. You know what you could do with a shipload of textiles from Ireland?

(*A door buzzer is heard. Irvin and Sturdyvant look at one another, relieved.*)

IRVIN: Why don't you go upstairs and let me handle it, Mel?

STURDYVANT: Remember . . . you're responsible for her.

(*Irvin exits up the front hall as Sturdyvant climbs the spiral staircase, goes into the control booth, and closes the door behind him.*)

IRVIN (*from off right*): How you boys doing, Cutler? Come on in.

(*Toledo enters down the front hall, carrying a book and a newspaper, goes through the double door, and holds it open as Cutler enters, carrying a trombone case and a guitar case, followed by Slow Drag, struggling with a string bass in a soft case. Cutler crosses and puts the cases on the floor. Slow Drag lays down his bass. Irvin enters down the front hall and crosses into the studio.*)

Where's Ma? Is she with you?

CUTLER: I don't know, Mr. Irvin. She told us to be here at one o'clock. That's all I know.

(*Toledo releases the door, crosses to the piano, takes off his gloves, and stuffs them into his coat pocket.*)

IRVIN: Where's . . . uh . . . the horn player . . . is he coming with Ma?

CUTLER: Levee's supposed to be here same as we is. I reckon he'll be here in a minute. I can't rightly say.

IRVIN: Well, come on . . . I'll show you to the bandroom, let you get set up and rehearsed. (*Irvin flips the light switch above the piano, illuminating the back hall. He crosses to Cutler as Slow Drag picks up his bass.*) You boys hungry? I'll call over to the deli and get some sandwiches. Get you fed and ready to make some music.

(*Toledo exits followed by Slow Drag. Cutler picks up a case in each hand and starts to follow. Irvin takes a piece of paper from his vest pocket and holds it up. Loudly:*)

Cutler . . . here's the list of songs we're gonna record. (*Irvin glances up at the control booth, tucks the paper into one of Cutler's full hands, and Cutler exits. Irvin starts to follow.*)

STURDYVANT (*over the speaker*): Irvin . . . what's happening? Where's Ma?

IRVIN (*turns back into the studio*): Everything's under control, Mel. I got it under control.

STURDYVANT (*grows more animated*): Where's Ma? How come she isn't with the band?

IRVIN: She'll be here in a minute, Mel. Let me get these boys down to the bandroom, huh?

(*Irvin exits. Toledo opens the bandroom door and enters, followed by Slow Drag. Toledo crosses to the piano and drops the book and newspaper on top of it. Slow Drag carries his bass to behind the piano and lays it down on its side. Cutler enters the bandroom as Irvin appears in the doorway and flips the light switch, illuminating the bandroom. The studio slowly dims.*)

You boys go ahead and rehearse. I'll let you know when Ma comes.

(*Irvin crosses into the back hall and closes the bandroom door. Cutler leans his guitar case against the wall by the lockers and puts the trombone case under a bench as Toledo takes off his hat and coat, drops them on the end of the piano, and sits on the piano chair. Slow Drag crosses to another bench and sits.*)

CUTLER (*crosses to Toledo and holds out the piece of paper*): What we got here, Toledo?

(*Irvin appears in the doorway and crosses into the closet. The closet light goes out.*)

TOLEDO (*takes the paper and reads it*): We got . . . "Prove It on Me" . . . "Hear Me Talking to You" . . . "Ma Rainey's Black Bottom" . . . and "Moonshine Blues."

(*Irvin enters the studio. Sturdyvant looks down from the control booth as Irvin opens the double door and exits up the front hall. Sturdyvant leaves the control booth, climbs down the spiral staircase, and follows Irvin up the front hall.*)

CUTLER (*takes the paper, crosses to the bandroom door, and opens it*): Where Mr. Irvin go? Them ain't the songs Ma told me. (*Steps into the back hall and looks up the stairway.*)

SLOW DRAG: I wouldn't worry about it if I were you, Cutler. They'll get it straightened out. Ma will get it straightened out.

CUTLER (*turns to Slow Drag*): I just don't want no trouble about these songs, that's all. Ma ain't told me them songs. She told me something else. (*Cutler steps back into the bandroom, closes the door, and crosses to the piano.*)

SLOW DRAG: What she tell you?

CUTLER: This "Moonshine Blues" wasn't in it. That's one of Bessie's songs.

TOLEDO: Slow Drag's right. . . . I wouldn't worry about it. Let them straighten it up.

CUTLER: Levee know what time he's supposed to be here?

SLOW DRAG: Levee gone out to spend your four dollars. He left the hotel this morning talking about he was gonna go buy some shoes. Say it's the first time he ever beat you shooting craps.

CUTLER (*opens a locker, takes off his coat, hangs it in the locker, and closes it*): Do he know what time he's supposed to be here? That's what I wanna know. I ain't thinking about no four dollars.

SLOW DRAG: Levee sure was thinking about it. That four dollars like to burn a hole in his pocket.

CUTLER (*crosses to Slow Drag*): Well, he's supposed to be here at one o'clock. That's what time Ma said. That nigger get out in the streets with that four dollars and ain't no telling when he's liable to show. (*Crosses to Toledo, as Slow Drag rises, crosses around the bench, takes off his hat and coat, and hangs them in an open locker.*) You ought to have seen him at the club last night, Toledo. Trying to talk to some gal Ma had with her.

TOLEDO: You ain't got to tell me. I know how Levee do.

(*The door buzzer is heard.*)

SLOW DRAG (*reaches into the locker and takes a half-pint bottle of bourbon from his coat pocket*): Levee tried to talk to that gal and got his feelings hurt. She didn't want no part of him. She told Levee he'd have to turn his money green before he could talk with her.

(*Irvin enters down the front hall, followed by Levee, carrying a horn case and a shoebox. Levee enters the studio and exits into the back hall. Irvin exits up the front hall.*)

CUTLER: She out for what she can get. Anybody could see that.

SLOW DRAG: That's why Levee run out to buy some shoes. He's looking to make an impression on that gal. (*Opens the bottle and takes a drink.*)

CUTLER (*crosses to chair, sits, and lifts the trombone case onto the bench*): What the hell she gonna do with his shoes? She can't do nothing with the nigger's shoes.

TOLEDO: Let me hit that, Slow Drag.

SLOW DRAG (*hands the bottle to Toledo*): This some of that good Chicago bourbon!

(*Levee opens the bandroom door abruptly and slams it shut behind him. He crosses to the piano and drops the horn case on top of it.*)

CUTLER: Levee . . . where Mr. Irvin go?

LEVEE: Hell, I ain't none of his keeper. He gone on down the hall.

SLOW DRAG: What you got there, Levee?

LEVEE (*takes a pair of shiny new shoes from the shoebox and holds them up; mockingly*): Look here, Cutler . . . I got me some shoes!

CUTLER: Nigger, I ain't studying you.

(*Levee drops the empty shoebox on top of the lockers, then crosses to bench and sits.*)

TOLEDO: How much you pay for something like that, Levee?

LEVEE (*taking off his old shoes*): Eleven dollars. Four dollars of it belong to Cutler. (*Puts on his new shoes.*)

SLOW DRAG: Levee say if it wasn't for Cutler . . . he would have no new shoes!

CUTLER: I ain't thinking about Levee or his shoes. Come on . . . let's get ready to rehearse.

SLOW DRAG (*crosses to behind the piano, picks up the bass, and begins to remove the casing*): I'm with you on that score, Cutler. I wanna get out of here. I don't want to be around here all night. When it comes time to go up there and record them songs . . . I just wanna go up there and do it. Last time it took us all day and half the night.

TOLEDO: Ain't but four songs on the list. Last time we recorded six songs.

SLOW DRAG: It felt like it was sixteen!

LEVEE (*rises and struts around, admiring the new shoes*): Yeah! Now I'm ready! I can play me some good music now! (*Glances up from the shoes, stops, and looks around the room.*) Damn! They done changed things around. Don't never leave well enough alone. (*Picks up the old shoes, crosses around the bench, and puts the old shoes in the shoebox on the lockers. Cutler opens the trombone case.*)

TOLEDO: Everything changing all the time. Even the air you breathing change. You got monoxide, hydrogen . . . changing all the time. Skin changing . . . different molecules and everything.

LEVEE (*opens a locker, takes off his coat and scarf, hangs them in the locker, and closes it*): Nigger, what is you talking about? I'm talking about the room. I ain't talking about no skin and air. I'm talking about something I can see! Last time the bandroom was upstairs. This time it's downstairs. Next time it be over there. I'm talking about what I can see. I ain't talking about no molecules or nothing.

(*Cutler begins to assemble his trombone.*)

TOLEDO: Hell, I know what you talking about. I just said everything changing. I know what you talking about, but you don't know what I'm talking about.

LEVEE (*crosses around the bench and faces Toledo; points at the bandroom door*): That door! Nigger, you see that door? That's what I'm talking about. That door wasn't there before.

(*Slow Drag drops the bass case in the corner and carries the bass to the piano.*)

CUTLER: Levee, you wouldn't know your right from your left. This is where they used to keep the recording horns and things . . . and damn if that door wasn't there. How in hell else you gonna get in here? Now if you talking about they done switched rooms, you right. But don't go telling me that damn door wasn't there!

SLOW DRAG (*takes Levee's horn case off the piano and drops it on the bench with a bang*): Damn the door and let's get set up. I wanna get out of here.

LEVEE: Toledo started all that about the door. I'm just saying that things change.

TOLEDO: What the hell you think I was saying? Things change. The air and everything. Now you gonna say you was saying it. You gonna fit two propositions on the same track . . . run them into each other, and because they crash you gonna say it's the same train.

LEVEE: Now this nigger talking about trains! We done went from the air to the skin to the door . . . and now trains. (*Crosses toward Toledo.*) Toledo, I'd like to be inside your head for five minutes. Just to see how you think. You done got more shit piled up and mixed up in there than the devil got sinners. You been reading too many goddamn books. (*Crosses to the corner and looks at himself in the mirror.*)

TOLEDO: What you care about how much I read? I'm gonna ignore you 'cause you ignorant.

SLOW DRAG: Come on, let's rehearse the music.

LEVEE: You ain't got to rehearse that . . . ain't nothing but old jug band music. (*Steps up onto the crates and admires his shoes in the mirror.*) They need one of them jug bands for this.

SLOW DRAG: Don't make me no difference. Long as we get paid.

LEVEE: That ain't what I'm talking about, nigger. I'm talking about art!

SLOW DRAG: What's drawing got to do with it?

LEVEE (*points at Slow Drag*): Where you get this nigger from, Cutler? He sound like one of them Alabama niggers.

CUTLER: Slow Drag's alright. It's you talking all the weird shit about art. Just play the piece, nigger. You wanna be one of them . . . what you call . . . virtuoso or something, you in the wrong place. You ain't no Buddy Bolden or King Oliver . . . you just an old trumpet player come a dime a dozen. Talking about art.

LEVEE (*jumps down from the crates, crosses to bench, and sits*): What is you? I don't see your name in lights.

CUTLER: I just plays the piece. Whatever they want. I don't go talking about art and criticizing other people's music.

LEVEE (*moves his horn case to the end of the bench, opens it, and takes out a silver-plated cornet*): I ain't like you, Cutler. I got talent! Me and this horn . . . we's tight! If my daddy knowed I was gonna turn out like this he would've named me Gabriel. (*Slow Drag smiles derisively at Levee and plucks a single low note on his bass.*) I'm gonna get me a band and make me some records. I done give Mr. Sturdy-vant some of my songs I wrote and he say he's gonna let me record them when I get my band together. (*Levee replaces the horn in the case, takes out some sheet music, and waves it at Cutler.*) I just gotta finish the last part of this song. Mr. Sturdyvant want me to write another part to this song.

SLOW DRAG (*looks over Levee's shoulder at the sheet music*): How you learn to write music, Levee?

LEVEE: I just picked it up . . . like you pick up anything. Miss Eula used to play the piano . . . she learned me a lot. I knows how to play real music . . . not this old jug band shit. (*Crosses his legs; conceitedly:*) I got style!

TOLEDO: Everybody got style. (*Slow Drag crosses to the piano.*) Style ain't nothing but keeping the same idea from beginning to end. Everybody got it.

LEVEE: But everybody can't play like I do. Everybody can't have their own band.

CUTLER: Well, until you get your own band where you can play what you want, you just play the piece and stop complaining. I told you when you came on here, this ain't none of them hot bands. This is an accompaniment band. You play Ma's music when you here. (*Takes a rag from the trombone case and polishes the trombone.*)

LEVEE (*drops the sheet music into the cornet case*): I got sense enough to know that. Hell, I can look at you all and see what kind of band it is. I can look at Toledo and see what kind of band it is.

TOLEDO: Toledo ain't said nothing to you now. Don't let Toledo get started. You can't even spell music, much less play it.

LEVEE: What you talking about? I can spell music. (*Leaps up, pulls out a roll of bills, and peels off a single dollar bill.*) I got a dollar say I can spell it! Put your dollar up. Where your dollar? (*Slaps the dollar bill on the floor in front of Toledo.*) Now, come on. Put your dollar up. Talking about I can't spell music.

TOLEDO: Alright, I'm gonna show you. (*Slowly rises, pulls a dollar bill from his pocket, and places it on top of Levee's bill.*) Cutler. Slow Drag. You hear this? The nigger betting me a dollar he can spell music. I don't want no shit now! (*Sits; confidently:*) Alright. Go ahead. Spell it.

LEVEE: It's a bet then. Talking about I can't spell music.

TOLEDO: Go ahead then. Spell it. Music. Spell it.

LEVEE: I can spell it, nigger! M-U-S-I-K. There! (*Leaps toward the dollar bills.*)

TOLEDO (*steps on the bills and blocks Levee with his arm*): Naw! Naw! Leave that money alone! You ain't spelled it.

LEVEE: What you mean I ain't spelled it? I said M-U-S-I-K!

TOLEDO: That ain't how you spell it! That ain't how you spell it! It's M-U-S-I-C! C, nigger! Not K! C! M-U-S-I-C! (*Scoops up the bills and slips the money into his coat pocket.*)

LEVEE: What you mean, C? Who say it's C?

TOLEDO: Cutler! Slow Drag. Tell this fool. (*Picks up his newspaper and begins to read. Cutler and Slow Drag look away sheepishly and play a few notes on their instruments. Levee looks at Toledo, expectantly. Toledo looks at Levee, then at Slow Drag and Cutler.*) Well, I'll be a monkey's uncle! (*Drops the newspaper on the piano, pulls the dollars out of his pocket, and hands one to Levee.*) Here's your dollar back, Levee. I done won it, you understand. I done won the dollar. But if don't nobody know but me, how am I gonna prove it to you?

LEVEE (*stuffs the bill into his pants pocket*): You just mad 'cause I spelled it.

TOLEDO: Spelled what! M-U-S-I-K don't spell nothing. I just wish there was some way I could show you the right and wrong of it. How you gonna know something if the other fellow don't know if you're right or not? Now I can't even be sure that I'm spelling it right. (*Picks up the newspaper.*)

LEVEE: That's what I'm talking about. You don't know it. Talking about C. You ought to give me that dollar I won from you. (*Sits on bench.*)

TOLEDO: Alright. Alright. (*Drops his newspaper on the piano and turns toward Levee.*) I'm gonna show you how ridiculous you sound. You know the Lord's Prayer?

LEVEE (*slides down the bench toward Toledo; eagerly*): Why? You wanna bet a dollar on that?

TOLEDO: Just answer the question. Do you know the Lord's Prayer or don't you?

LEVEE: Yeah, I know it. What of it?

TOLEDO: Cutler?

CUTLER: What you Cutlering me for? I ain't got nothing to do with it. (*Leans the trombone against the bench and takes a tobacco pouch and a package of cigarette papers from the trombone case, then closes the case and puts it under the bench.*)

TOLEDO: I just want to show the man how ridiculous he is.

CUTLER: Both of you all sound like damn fools. Arguing about something silly. Yeah, I know the Lord's Prayer. My daddy was a deacon in the church. Come asking me if I know the Lord's Prayer. Yeah, I know it.

TOLEDO: Slow Drag?

SLOW DRAG (*uncertainly*): Yeah.

TOLEDO: Alright. Now I'm gonna tell you a story to show just how ridiculous he sound. There was these two fellows, see. So, the one of them go up to this church and commence to taking up the church learning. The other fellow see him out on the road and he say . . . I done heard you taking up the church learning. Say . . . is you learning anything up there? The other one say . . . Yeah, I done taken up the church learning and I's learning all kinds of things about the Bible and what it say and all. Why you be asking? The other one say . . . Well, do you know the Lord's Prayer? And he say . . . Why sure I know the Lord's Prayer, I'm taking up learning at the church ain't I? I know the Lord's Prayer backwards and forwards. And the other fellow say . . . I bet you five dollars you don't know the Lord's Prayer, 'cause I don't think you knows it. I think you be going up to the church 'cause the widow Jenkins be going up there and you just wanna be sitting in the same room with her when she cross them big, fine, pretty legs she got. And the other one say . . . Well, I'm gonna prove you wrong and I'm gonna bet you that five dollars. So he say . . . Well, go on and say it then. So he commenced to saying the Lord's Prayer. He say . . . Now I lay me down to sleep, I pray the Lord my soul to keep. . . . The other one say . . . Here's your five dollars. I didn't think you knew it. (*Toledo, Cutler, and Slow Drag all laugh; Levee looks at them, confused.*) Now that's just how ridiculous Levee sound. Only 'cause I knowed how to spell music, I still got my dollar.

LEVEE: That don't prove nothing. What's that supposed to prove?

TOLEDO: I'm through with it. (*Turns away from Levee and picks up his paper, as Cutler opens his tobacco pouch, takes out a rolling paper, and begins to roll a cigarette.*)

SLOW DRAG: Is you all gonna rehearse this music or ain't you?

LEVEE: How many times you done played them songs? What you gotta rehearse for?

SLOW DRAG: This is a recording session. I wanna get it right the first time and get on out of here.

CUTLER: Slow Drag's right. Let's go on and rehearse and get it over with.

LEVEE (*picks up the sheet music, takes a pencil from his case, and straddles the bench*): You all go and rehearse then. I got to finish this song for Mr. Sturdyvant.

CUTLER: Come on, Levee . . . I don't want no shit now. You rehearse like everybody else. You in the band like everybody else. Mr. Sturdyvant just gonna have to wait. You got to do that on your own time. This is the band's time.

LEVEE: Well, what is you doing? You sitting there rolling a reefer talking about let's rehearse. Toledo reading a newspaper. Hell, I'm ready if you wanna rehearse. I just say there ain't no point in it. Ma ain't here. What's the point in it?

CUTLER: Nigger, why you gotta complain all the time?

TOLEDO: Levee would complain if a gal ain't laid across his bed just right.

CUTLER: That's what I know. That's why I try to tell him just play the music and forget about it. It ain't no big thing. (*Takes a box of matches from his coat pocket and lights the cigarette.*)

TOLEDO: Levee ain't got an eye for that. He wants to tie on to some abstract component and sit down on the elemental.

(*Exasperated, Slow Drag lays down his bass behind the piano as Cutler puts the tobacco pouch, papers, and matches in his coat pocket.*)

LEVEE: This is get on Levee time, huh? Levee ain't said nothing except this some old jug band music.

TOLEDO: Under the right circumstances you'd play anything. If you know music then you play it. Straight on or off to the side. Ain't nothing abstract about it.

LEVEE: Toledo, you sound like you got a mouth full of marbles. You is the only cracker-talking nigger I know.

TOLEDO: You ought to have learned yourself to read . . . then you'd understand the basic understanding of everything.

SLOW DRAG: Both of you all gonna drive me crazy with that philosophy bullshit. (*Crosses to Cutler.*) Cutler, give me a reefer.

CUTLER: Ain't you got some reefer? Where's your reefer? Why you all the time asking me?

SLOW DRAG: Cutler, how long I done known you? How long we been together? Twenty-two years. (*Cutler turns away from Slow Drag and continues to smoke the reefer.*) We been doing this together for twenty-two years. All up and down the back roads, the side roads, the front roads . . . we done played in the juke-joints, the whorehouses, the barn dances, and city sit-downs. . . . I done lied for you and lied with you . . . we done laughed together, fought together, slept in the same bed together, done sucked on the same titty . . . and now you don't wanna give me no reefer.

CUTLER: You see this nigger trying to talk me out of my reefer, Toledo? Running all that about how long he done knowed me and how we done sucked on the same titty. (*Turns to Slow Drag, laughing.*) Nigger, you still ain't getting none of my reefer!

TOLEDO: That's African.

SLOW DRAG (*suspiciously*): What? What you talking about? What's African?

LEVEE (*defensively*): I know he ain't talking about me. You don't see me running around in no jungle with no bone between my nose.

TOLEDO: Levee, you worse than ignorant. You ignorant without a premise. (*Turns to Cutler and Slow Drag.*) Now, what I was saying is what Slow Drag was doing is African. That's what you call an African conceptualization. That's when you name the gods or call on the ancestors to achieve whatever your desires are.

SLOW DRAG: Nigger, I ain't no African! I ain't doing no African nothing!

TOLEDO: Naming all those things you and Cutler done together is like trying to solicit some reefer based on a bond of kinship. That's African. An ancestral retention. Only you forgot the name of the gods.

SLOW DRAG: I ain't forgot nothing. I was telling the nigger how cheap he is. Don't come talking that African nonsense to me.

TOLEDO: You just like Levee. No eye for taking an abstract and fixing it to a specific. There's so much that goes on around you and you can't even see it.

CUTLER: Wait a minute . . . wait a minute. Toledo, now when this nigger . . . when an African do all them things you say and name all the gods and whatnot . . . then what happens?

TOLEDO: Depends on if the gods is sympathetic with the cause for which he is calling them with the right names. Then his success comes with the right proportion of his naming. That's the way that go. (*Returns to his newspaper.*)

CUTLER (*hands an unlit reefer to Slow Drag*): Here, Slow Drag. Here's a reefer. You done talked yourself up on that one.

SLOW DRAG (*takes the reefer and pulls a box of matches from his vest pocket*): Thank you. You ought to have done that in the first place and saved me all the aggravation.

CUTLER: What I wants to know is . . . what the same titty we done sucked on? That's what I want to know.

SLOW DRAG: Oh, I just threw that in there to make it sound good. (*Sits on bench and lights a match.*)

CUTLER: Nigger, you ain't right.

SLOW DRAG: I knows it. (*Lights the reefer and starts to take a drag.*)

CUTLER: Well, come on . . . let's get rehearsed. Time's wasting.

(*He picks up the trombone, rises, and plays a few notes as he crosses to chair. Levee picks up his cornet, rises, and plays. Slow Drag picks up his bass and crosses to the piano.*)

Let's do it. "Ma Rainey's Black Bottom." A-one. A-two. You know what to do.

(*Toledo plays a short piano introduction to "Ma Rainey's Black Bottom" as Levee plays a louder and faster introduction. Cutler and Slow Drag join in at a leisurely tempo. Levee stops playing.*)

LEVEE: Naw! Naw! We ain't doing it that way. (*The band stops playing.*) We doing my version. It say so right there on that piece of paper you got. Ask Toledo. That's what Mr. Irvin told me . . . say it's on the list he gave you.

CUTLER: Let me worry about what's on the list and what ain't on the list. How you gonna tell me what's on the list?

LEVEE: 'Cause I know what Mr. Irvin told me! Ask Toledo!

CUTLER (*irritated*): Let me worry about what's on the list. You just play the song I say.

LEVEE: What kind of sense it make to rehearse the wrong version of the song? That's what I wanna know. Why you wanna rehearse that version?

SLOW DRAG (*with forced patience*): You supposed to rehearse what you gonna play. That's the way they taught me. Now, whatever version we gonna play . . . let's go on and rehearse it.

LEVEE: That's what I'm trying to tell the man.

CUTLER: You trying to tell me what we is and ain't gonna play. And that ain't none of your business. Your business is to play what I say.

LEVEE (*crowing*): Oh, I see now. You done got jealous 'cause Mr. Irvin using my version. You done got jealous 'cause I proved I know something about music.

CUTLER: Nigger, you talk like a fool! What the hell I got to be jealous of you about? The day I get jealous of you I may as well lay down and die.

TOLEDO: Levee started all that 'cause he too lazy to rehearse. (*Turns to Levee.*) You ought to just go on and play the song . . . what difference does it make?

LEVEE (*steps toward Cutler*): Where's the paper? Look at the paper! Get the paper and look at it! See what it say. (*Turns away, disgusted.*) Gonna tell me I'm too lazy to rehearse.

CUTLER: We ain't talking about the paper. We talking about you understanding where you fit in when you around here. You just play what I say.

LEVEE (*turns to Cutler; curtly*): Look . . . I don't care what you play! Alright? It don't matter to me. Mr. Irvin gonna straighten it up! I don't care what you play. (*Crosses right a few steps.*)

CUTLER: Thank you. (*Turns to Toledo.*) Let's play this "Hear Me Talking to You" till we find out what's happening with the "Black Bottom." (*Levee and Toledo glance at one another, laugh conspiratorially, and look at Slow Drag. They look at Cutler. He chuckles.*) Slow Drag, you sing Ma's part. (*Slow Drag feigns insult, then minces and lays his bass down on the floor.*)

"Hear Me Talking to You." Let's do it. A-one. A-two. You know what to do.

(*Toledo plays a short introduction to "Hear Me Talking to You." Levee and Cutler join in. Slow Drag mimes opening a bottle and drinking, then sets the imaginary bottle on the piano, picks up Toledo's newspaper, and fans himself.*)

SLOW DRAG (*singing*):
RAMBLIN' MAN MAKES NO CHANGE IN ME.
I'M GONNA RAMBLE BACK TO MY USED-TO-BE, AH—

HEAR ME TALKING TO YOU, I DON'T BITE MY TONGUE.
YOU WANT TO BE MY MAN, YOU GOT TO FETCH IT WITH YOU
   WHEN YOU COME.

EVE AND ADAM IN THE GARDEN TAKING A CHANCE.
ADAM DIDN'T TAKE TIME TO GET HIS PANTS, AH—
HEAR ME TALKING TO YOU, I DON'T BITE MY TONGUE.
YOU WANT TO BE MY MAN, YOU GOT TO FETCH IT WITH YOU
   WHEN YOU COME.

(*Irvin enters down the front hall into the studio. He crosses and exits into the back hall.*)

OUR OLD CAT SWALLOWED A BALL OF YARN.
WHEN THE KITTENS WAS BORN THEY HAD
   SWEATERS ON.

(*Irvin opens the bandroom door, crosses to behind the piano, leans on it, and listens.*)

HEAR ME TALKING TO YOU, I DON'T BITE MY TONGUE.
YOU WANT TO BE MY MAN, YOU GOT TO FETCH IT WITH YOU
   WHEN YOU COME.

(*Slow Drag turns toward the piano, sees Irvin, and stops. The band stops. All laugh. Slow Drag returns the newspaper to the piano and crosses to the bass.*)

IRVIN (*seriously*): Any of you boys know what's keeping Ma?

CUTLER: Can't say, Mr. Irvin. She'll be along directly, I reckon. I talked to her this morning, she say she'll be here in time to rehearse.

IRVIN: Well, you boys go ahead. (*Starts toward the bandroom door.*)

CUTLER: Mr. Irvin, about these songs . . . Levee say . . .

IRVIN (*turns to Cutler*): Whatever's on the list, Cutler. You got that list I gave you?

CUTLER (*pats his coat pocket*): Yessir, I got it right here.

IRVIN: Whatever's on there. Whatever that says. (*Turns toward the bandroom door again.*)

CUTLER: I'm asking about this "Black Bottom" piece . . . Levee say . . .

IRVIN (*crosses to Cutler*): Oh, it's on the list. "Ma Rainey's Black Bottom" is on the list.

CUTLER: I know it's on the list. I wanna know what version. We got two versions of that song.

IRVIN: Oh. Levee's arrangement. (*Turns to Levee; he grins.*) We're using Levee's arrangement.

CUTLER: Okay. I got that straight. Now, this "Moonshine Blues" . . .

IRVIN: We'll work it out with Ma, Cutler. Just rehearse whatever's on the list and use Levee's arrangement on that "Black Bottom" piece.

(*He exits. Slow Drag picks up the bass and crosses to the piano.*)

LEVEE (*crosses toward Cutler a step; triumphantly*): See, I told you! It don't mean nothing when I say it. You got to wait for Mr. Irvin to say it. Well, I told you the way it is.

CUTLER: Levee, the sooner you understand it ain't what you say, or what Mr. Irvin say . . . it's what Ma say that counts.

SLOW DRAG: Don't nobody say when it comes to Ma. She's gonna do what she wants to do. Ma says what happens to her.

LEVEE: Hell, the man's the one putting out the record! He's gonna put out what he wanna put out!

SLOW DRAG (*crosses to Levee*): He's gonna put out what Ma want him to put out.

LEVEE (*raises his hand threateningly toward Slow Drag*): You heard what the man told you . . . "Ma Rainey's Black

Bottom," Levee's arrangement. There you go! (*Pokes Slow Drag on the nose.*) That's what he told you.

SLOW DRAG (*crosses to the piano*): What you gonna do, Cutler?

CUTLER: Ma ain't told me what version. Let's go on and play it Levee's way.

TOLEDO (*pedantically*): See, now . . . I'll tell you something. As long as the colored man look to white folks to put the crown on what he say . . . as long as he looks to white folks for approval . . . then he ain't never gonna find out who he is and what he's about. He's just gonna be about what white folks want him to be about. That's one sure thing.

LEVEE: I'm just trying to show Cutler where he's wrong.

CUTLER: Cutler don't need you to show him nothing.

SLOW DRAG: Come on, let's get this shit rehearsed! You all can bicker afterward!

CUTLER: Levee's confused about who the boss is. He don't know Ma's the boss.

LEVEE: Ma's the boss on the road! We at a recording session. Mr. Sturdyvant and Mr. Irvin say what's gonna be here! We's in Chicago, we ain't in Memphis. I don't know why you all wanna pick me about it, shit! I'm with Slow Drag . . . let's go on and get it rehearsed.

CUTLER: Alright. Alright. I know how to solve this. "Ma Rainey's Black Bottom," Levee's version. Let's do it. Come on. A-one. A-two. . . .

TOLEDO: How that first part go again, Levee?

LEVEE: It go like this. (*Plays a short staccato introduction to his version of the "Black Bottom."*) That's to get the people's attention to the song. That's when you and Slow Drag come in with the rhythm part. Me and Cutler play on the breaks. (*Paces in circles; animatedly:*) Now we gonna dance it . . . but we ain't gonna countrify it. This ain't no barn dance. This a city dance. We gonna play it like . . .

CUTLER (*impatiently*): The man asked you how the first part go. He don't wanna hear all that. Just tell him how the piece go.

TOLEDO: I got it. I got it. Let's go. I know how to do it.

CUTLER: "Ma Rainey's Black Bottom." Levee's version. One. Two. You know what to do.

(*Levee plays his introduction to the "Black Bottom," then the band joins in at a slower tempo. Levee stops playing. He glares at the band, infuriated.*)

LEVEE: You all got to keep up now. You playing in the wrong time. (*The band stops playing.*) Ma come in over the top. She got to find her own way in.

CUTLER: Nigger, will you let us play this song. When you get your own band . . . then you tell them that nonsense. We know how to play the piece. I was playing music before you was born. Gonna tell me how to play. (*Slow Drag examines the strings of the bass.*) Alright. Let's try it again. A-one. A-two. . . .

SLOW DRAG: Cutler, wait till I fix this. This string started to unravel. And you know I want to play Levee's music right.

LEVEE (*crosses to Slow Drag*): If you was any kind of a musician you'd take care of your instrument. Keep it in tip-top order. If you was any kind of a musician . . . I'd let you be in my band.

SLOW DRAG: Shhheeeeet! (*Turns and inadvertently steps on Levee's shoe.*)

LEVEE: Damn, Slow Drag! Watch them big-ass shoes you got.

SLOW DRAG (*crosses and sits on the crates, holding his bass*): Boy, ain't nobody done nothing to you.

LEVEE (*crosses to bench, takes a rag out of his horn case, and wipes his shoe*): You done stepped on my shoes.

SLOW DRAG: Move them the hell out the way then. You was in my way . . . I wasn't in your way. (*Stretches one foot out toward Levee; mockingly:*) You can shine these when you get done, Levee. (*All laugh except Levee.*)

CUTLER (*leans his trombone against the piano, takes another reefer and a box of matches out of his pocket, and lights the reefer*): If I had them shoes Levee got, I could buy me a whole suit of clothes.

LEVEE (*tosses the rag back into the horn case and sits on the bench*): What kind of difference it make what kind of shoes I got? Ain't nothing wrong with having nice shoes. I ain't said nothing about your shoes. Why you wanna talk about me and my Florsheims?

CUTLER (*puts the matchbox in his pocket*): Any man . . . who takes a whole week's pay . . . and puts it on some shoes— you understand what I mean, what you walk around on the ground with—is a fool! And I don't mind telling him.

LEVEE: What difference it make to you, Cutler!

SLOW DRAG: The man ain't said nothing about your shoes. Ain't nothing wrong with having nice shoes. Look at Toledo.

TOLEDO: What about Toledo?

SLOW DRAG: I said ain't nothing wrong with having nice shoes.

LEVEE: Nigger got them clodhoppers! Old brogans! He ain't nothing but a sharecropper. (*Levee and Slow Drag laugh.*)

TOLEDO: You can make all the fun you want. It don't mean nothing. I'm satisfied with them and that's what counts.

LEVEE: Nigger, why don't you get some decent shoes? Got nerve to put on a suit and tie with them farming boots.

CUTLER: What you just tell me? It don't make no difference about the man's shoes. That's what you told me.

LEVEE: Aw, hell, I don't care what the nigger wear. I'll be honest with you. I don't care if he went barefoot. (*Looks at Slow Drag, puts the cornet in the case, and rises.*) Play something for me, Slow Drag. (*Slow Drag plays a fast vamp on his bass. Levee does an easy shuffling dance.*) A man got to have some shoes to dance like this! You can't dance like this with them clodhoppers Toledo got.

SLOW DRAG (*plays "Dr. Jazz"; singing*):
HELLO CENTRAL, GIVE ME DOCTOR JAZZ.
HE'S GOT JUST WHAT I NEED, I'LL SAY HE HAS.
WHEN THE WORLD GOES WRONG AND I HAVE GOT THE BLUES,
HE'S THE MAN WHO MAKES ME GET ON MY DANCING SHOES.

(*He continues vamping as Levee dances.*)

TOLEDO: That's the trouble with colored folks . . . always wanna have a good time. Good times done got more niggers killed than God got ways to count. What the hell having a good time mean? That's what I wanna know.

LEVEE: Hell, nigger . . . it don't need explaining. Ain't you never had no good time before?

TOLEDO: The more niggers get killed having a good time . . . the more good times niggers wanna have.

(*Slow Drag stops playing, rises, and puts his bass on the floor. Levee groans disgruntledly.*)

There's more to life than having a good time. If there ain't . . . then this is a piss-poor life we're having . . . if that's all there is to be got out of it.

SLOW DRAG (*turns to Toledo; Levee crosses to behind the piano and leans on it*): Toledo, just 'cause you like to read them books and study and whatnot . . . that's your good time. People got other things they likes to do to have a good time. Ain't no need you picking them about it. (*Crosses to chair, sits, and puts his feet up on a bench.*)

CUTLER: Niggers been having a good time before you was born, and they gonna keep having a good time after you gone.

TOLEDO: Yeah, but what else they gonna do? Ain't nobody talking about making the lot of the colored man better for him here in America.

LEVEE: Now you gonna be Booker T. Washington.

TOLEDO: Everybody worried about having a good time. Ain't nobody thinking about what kind of world they gonna leave their youngens. "Just give me a good time, that's all I want." It just makes me sick.

SLOW DRAG: Well, the colored man's gonna be alright. He got through slavery and he'll get through whatever else the white man put on him. I ain't worried about that. Good times is what makes life worth living. Now, you take the white man . . . the white man don't know how to have a good time. That's why he's troubled all the time. He don't know how to have a good time. He don't know how to laugh at life.

LEVEE (*crosses to Slow Drag*): That's what the problem is with Toledo . . . reading all them books and things. He done got to the point where he forgot how to laugh and have a good time. Just like the white man.

TOLEDO: I know how to have a good time as well as the next man. I said, there's got to be more to life than having a good time. I said the colored man ought to be doing more than just trying to have a good time all the time.

LEVEE: Well, what is you doing, nigger? Talking all them highfaluting ideas about making a better world for the colored man. What is you doing to make it better? You playing the music and looking for your next piece of pussy same as we is. What is you doing? That's what I wanna know. Tell him, Cutler.

CUTLER: You all leave Cutler out of this. Cutler ain't got nothing to do with it.

TOLEDO: Levee, you just about the most ignorant nigger I know. Sometimes I wonder why I even bother to try and talk with you.

LEVEE: Well, what is you doing? Talking that shit to me about I'm ignorant! What is you doing! You just a whole lot of mouth. A great big windbag. Thinking you smarter than everybody else. What is you doing, huh?

TOLEDO: It ain't just me, fool! It's everybody! What you think . . . I'm gonna solve the colored man's problems by myself? I said, we. You understand that? We. That's every living colored man in the world got to do his share. Got to do his part. I ain't talking about what I'm gonna do . . . or what you or Cutler or Slow Drag or anybody else. I'm talking about all of us together. What all of us is gonna do. That's what I'm talking about, nigger. (*Turns away from Levee and picks up his newspaper.*)

LEVEE (*looks at Toledo for a moment, then crosses to him and puts a hand on his shoulder, subdued*): Well, why didn't you say that then? (*Toledo shakes off Levee's hand.*)

CUTLER: Toledo, I don't know why you waste your time on this fool.

TOLEDO: That's what I'm trying to figure out.

LEVEE: Now there go Cutler with his shit. Calling me a fool. You wasn't even in the conversation. Now you gonna take sides and call me a fool.

CUTLER: Hell, I was listening to the man. I got sense enough to know what he saying. I could tell it straight back to you.

LEVEE: Well, you go on with it. But I'll tell you this . . . I ain't gonna be too many more of your fools. I'll tell you that. Now you can put that in your pipe and smoke it.

CUTLER: Boy, ain't nobody studying you. Telling me what to put in my pipe. Who's you to tell me what to do?

LEVEE (*crosses toward the crates*): Alright, I ain't nobody. Don't pay me no mind. I ain't nobody.

TOLEDO: Levee, you ain't nothing but the devil.

LEVEE: There you go! That's who I am. I'm the devil. I ain't nothing but the devil.

CUTLER: I can see that. That's something you know about. You know all about the devil.

LEVEE (*crosses toward Cutler*): I ain't saying what I know. I know plenty. What you know about the devil? Telling me what I know. What you know?

SLOW DRAG: I know a man sold his soul to the devil.

LEVEE (*crosses to bench and sits, facing Slow Drag*): There you go! That's the only thing I ask about the devil . . . to see him coming so I can sell him this one I got. 'Cause if there's a God up there . . . he done went to sleep. (*Takes his cornet and a rag from the case and polishes the cornet.*)

SLOW DRAG: Sold his soul to the devil himself. Name of Eliza Cotter. Lived in Tuscaloosa County, Alabama. The devil came by and he done upped and sold him his soul.

CUTLER: How you know the man done sold his soul to the devil, nigger? You talking that old woman foolishness.

SLOW DRAG: Everybody know. It wasn't no secret. He went around working for the devil and everybody knowed it. Carried him a bag . . . one of them carpet bags. Folks say he carried the devil's papers and whatnot where he put your fingerprint on the paper with blood.

LEVEE: Where he at now? That's what I want to know. He can put my whole handprint if he want to!

CUTLER: That's the damnedest thing I ever heard! Folks kill me with that talk.

TOLEDO (*puts the newspaper on the piano and turns to Cutler*): Oh, that's real enough, alright. Some folks go arm in arm with the devil, shoulder to shoulder and talk to him all the time. That's real, ain't nothing wrong in believing that.

SLOW DRAG: That's what I'm saying. Eliza Cotter is one of them. Alright. The man living up there in an old shack on Ben Foster's place, shoeing mules and horses, making them charms and things in secret. He hooked up with the devil. Showed one day all fancied out with just the finest clothes you ever seen on a colored man . . . dressed just like one of them crackers . . . and carrying this bag with them papers and things in. Alright. Had a pocketful of money, just living the life of a rich man. Ain't done no more work or nothing. Just had him a string of women he run around with and throw his money away on. Bought him a big fine house . . . well, it wasn't that big, but it did have one of them white picket fences around it. Used to hire a man once a week just to paint that fence. Messed around there and one of the fellows of them gals he was messing with got fixed on him wrong and Eliza killed him. And he laughed about it. Sheriff come and arrest him, and then let him go. And he went around in that town laughing about killing this fellow. Trial come up, and the judge cut him loose. He must have been in converse with the devil, too . . . 'cause he cut him loose and give him a bottle of whiskey! Folks ask what done happened to make him change, and he'd tell them straight out he done sold his soul to the devil and asked them if they wanted to sell theirs 'cause he could arrange it for them. Preacher see him coming, used to cross on the other side of the road. He'd just stand there and laugh at the preacher and call him a fool to his face.

CUTLER: Well, whatever happened to this fellow? What come of him? A man who, as you say, done sold his soul to the devil is bound to come to a bad end.

TOLEDO: I don't know about that. The devil's strong. The devil ain't no pushover.

SLOW DRAG: Oh, the devil had him under his wing alright. Took good care of him. He ain't wanted for nothing.

CUTLER: What happened to him? That's what I want to know.

SLOW DRAG: Last I heard, he headed up north with that bag of his handing out hundred dollar bills on the spot to whoever wanted to sign on with the devil. That's what I hear tell of him.

CUTLER: That's a bunch of fool talk. I don't know how you fix your mouth to tell that story. I don't believe you.

SLOW DRAG: I ain't asking you to believe it. I'm just telling you the facts of it.

LEVEE: I sure wish I knew where he went. He wouldn't have to convince me long. Hell, I'd even help him sign people up.

CUTLER: Nigger, God's gonna strike you down with that blasphemy you talking.

LEVEE: Oh, shit! God don't mean nothing to me. Let him strike me! (*Stands and looks upward; mockingly:*) Here I am, standing right here. What you talking about he's gonna strike me? Here I am! Let him strike me! I ain't scared of him. (*Looks at Cutler disdainfully.*) Talking that stuff to me.

CUTLER: Alright. You gonna be sorry. You gonna fix yourself to have bad luck. Ain't nothing gonna work for you.

(*The door buzzer is heard.*)

LEVEE: Bad luck? What I care about bad luck? You talking simple. I ain't had nothing but bad luck all my life. Couldn't get no worse. What the hell I care about some bad luck? Hell, I eat it everyday for breakfast! You dumber than I thought you was . . . talking about bad luck. (*Turns away from Cutler and sits on bench.*)

CUTLER: Alright, nigger, you'll see! Can't tell a fool nothing. You'll see.

IRVIN (*enters the studio, then crosses and shouts down the back hall*): Cutler . . . you boys' sandwiches are up here . . . Cutler?

CUTLER: Yessir, Mr. Irvin . . . be right there. (*Starts to rise.*)

TOLEDO (*rises and crosses to the bandroom door*): I'll walk up there and get them.

(*He crosses into the back hall and closes the door. Simultaneously, Irvin crosses back into the studio and moves to below the piano as Sturdyvant enters down the front hall and crosses to Irvin.*)

STURDYVANT (*anxiously*): Irv . . . what's happening? Is she here yet? Was that her?

IRVIN: It's the sandwiches, Mel. I told you . . . I'll let you know when she comes, huh?

(*Toledo opens the door a few inches, glances at Sturdyvant, and quietly backs into the back hall, closing the door behind him.*)

STURDYVANT: What's keeping her? Do you know what time it is? Have you looked at the clock? You told me she'd be here. You told me you'd take care of it.

IRVIN (*crosses to a folding chair and sits; exasperated*): Mel, for Chrissakes! What do you want from me? What do you want me to do?

STURDYVANT (*points at the clock above the piano*): Look what time it is, Irv. You told me she'd be here.

IRVIN: She'll be here, okay? I don't know what's keeping her. You know they're always late, Mel.

STURDYVANT: You should have went by the hotel and made sure she was on time. You should have taken care of this. That's what you told me, huh? "I'll take care of it."

IRVIN: Okay! So I didn't go by the hotel! What do you want me to do? She'll be here, okay? The band's here . . . she'll be here.

(*Toledo quietly opens the door and steps into the studio.*)

STURDYVANT: Okay, Irv. I'll take your word. But if she doesn't come . . . (*Turns and crosses to the spiral staircase.*) . . . If she doesn't come . . .

(*He climbs the staircase, goes into the control booth, and closes the door. Toledo steps toward Irvin, hesitantly.*)

TOLEDO: Mr. Irvin . . . I come up for the sandwiches.

IRVIN (*rises and crosses to Toledo*): Say . . . uh . . . look . . . one o'clock, right? She said one o'clock.

TOLEDO: That's what time she told us. Say be here at one o'clock.

IRVIN: Do you know what's keeping her? Do you know why she ain't here?

TOLEDO: I can't say, Mr. Irvin. Told us one o'clock.

(*The door buzzer begins to ring incessantly. Irvin goes quickly through the double door and exits up the front hall. The door buzzer stops ringing. Shouting and scuffling is heard.*)

MA RAINEY (*enters down the front hall, rushes furiously through the double door, and crosses to above the platform, followed by Irvin, Dussie Mae carrying a small purse, Sylvester carrying a large loop-handled bag, and a Policeman carrying a night-stick*): Irvin . . . you better tell this man who I am! You better get him straight!

IRVIN: Ma, do you know what time it is? Do you have any idea? We've been waiting . . .

DUSSIE MAE (*to Sylvester*): If you was watching where you was going . . .

SYLVESTER: I was watching . . . what you mean?

IRVIN (*turns away and notices the Policeman for the first time*): What's going on here? Officer . . . what's the matter?

MA RAINEY: Tell the man who he's messing with!

POLICEMAN: Do you know this lady?

MA RAINEY: Just tell the man who I am. That's all you got to do!

POLICEMAN (*angrily*): Lady, will you let me talk, huh?

MA RAINEY: Tell the man who I am!

IRVIN (*turns to Ma*): Wait a minute . . . wait a minute! Let me handle it. Ma, will you let me handle it?

MA RAINEY: Tell him who he's messing with!

IRVIN: Okay! Okay! Just give me a chance! (*Turns to the Policeman.*) Officer . . . this is one of our recording artists . . . Ma Rainey.

MA RAINEY: Madame Rainey! Get it straight! Madame Rainey! Talking about taking me to jail.

IRVIN (*steps toward Ma*): Look, Ma . . . give me a chance, okay? Here . . . sit down. I'll take care of it. (*Turns back to the Policeman.*) Officer . . . what's the problem?

DUSSIE MAE: It's all your fault!

SYLVESTER: I ain't done nothing . . . ask Ma.

POLICEMAN: Well . . . when I walked up on the incident . . .

DUSSIE MAE (*scornfully*): Sylvester wrecked Ma's car.

SYLVESTER: I d-d-did not! (*To the Policeman:*) The m-m-man ran into me!

POLICEMAN (*to Irvin*): Look, buddy . . . if you want it in a nutshell . . . we got her charged with assault and battery.

MA RAINEY (*astounded*): Assault and what for what!

DUSSIE MAE: See . . . we was trying to get a cab . . . and so Ma . . .

MA RAINEY: Wait a minute! I'll tell you if you want to know what happened. (*Dussie Mae crosses indignantly to the piano. Ma turns to Irvin and points at Sylvester.*) Now, that's Sylvester. That's my nephew. He was driving my car. . . .

POLICEMAN: Lady, we don't know whose car he was driving.

MA RAINEY: That's my car!

DUSSIE MAE and SYLVESTER (*simultaneously*): That's Ma's car!

MA RAINEY: What you mean you don't know whose car it is? I bought and paid for that car. Registered to me, Gertrude "Ma" Rainey!

POLICEMAN: That's what you say, lady . . . we still gotta check. (*To Irvin*): They hit a car on Market Street. The guy said the kid ran a stoplight.

SYLVESTER (*indignantly*): What you mean? The man c-c-come around the corner and hit m-m-me!

POLICEMAN: While I was calling a paddy wagon to haul them to the station . . . they try to hop into a parked cab. The cabbie said he was waiting on a fare. . . .

MA RAINEY: The man was just sitting there. Wasn't waiting for nobody. I don't know why he wanna tell that lie. (*Dussie Mae crosses to Ma.*)

POLICEMAN (*wearily*): Look, lady . . . will you let me tell the story?

MA RAINEY: Go ahead and tell it then. But tell it right!

POLICEMAN: Like I say . . . she tries to get in this cab. The cabbie's waiting on a fare. She starts creating a disturbance. The cabbie gets out to try to explain the situation to her . . . and she knocks him down.

DUSSIE MAE: She ain't hit him! He just fell!

SYLVESTER: He j-j-j-just slipped!

POLICEMAN: He claims she knocked him down. We got her charged with assault and battery.

MA RAINEY: If that don't beat all to hell! I ain't touched the man! The man was trying to reach around me to keep his car door closed. I opened the door and it hit him and he fell down. I ain't touched the man!

IRVIN (*turns to Ma; placatingly*): Okay. Okay . . . I got it straight now, Ma. You didn't touch him. Alright? (*Takes the Policeman by the arm and starts toward the double door.*) Officer . . . can I see you for a moment?

DUSSIE MAE (*to Irvin; insistently*): Ma was just trying to open the door. (*Irvin stops, annoyed.*)

SYLVESTER: He j-j-just got in t-t-the way!

MA RAINEY: Said he wasn't gonna haul no colored folks . . . if you want to know the truth of it.

IRVIN (*to Ma*): Okay, Ma . . . I got it straight now. (*Turns back to the Policeman.*) Officer?

(*He leads the Policeman through the double door and into the front hall; they talk quietly. Sylvester crosses to the double door and peers through the windows. Ma crosses to Toledo; Dussie Mae follows Ma.*)

MA RAINEY: Toledo, Cutler, and everybody here?

TOLEDO: Yeah, they down in the bandroom. What happened to your car?

STURDYVANT (*leaves the control booth and bounds down the spiral staircase*): Irv . . . what's the problem? (*Stops and looks around the room.*) What's going on? (*Opens the double door and looks into the front hall.*)

IRVIN (*crosses through the open double door*): Mel, let me take care of it. I can handle it.

STURDYVANT: What's happening? What the hell's going on?

IRVIN: Let me handle it, Mel, huh?

STURDYVANT (*releases the door and turns to Ma; suspiciously*): What's going on, Ma? What'd you do?

MA RAINEY: Sturdyvant, get on away from me! That's the last thing I need . . . to go through some of your shit!

IRVIN (*moves toward Sturdyvant; appeasingly*): Mel, I'll take care of it. I'll explain it all to you. Let me handle it, huh?

(*Sturdyvant looks dubiously at Irvin, then crosses to the spiral staircase, climbs up to the control booth, enters, and closes the door. The Policeman opens the double door and steps into the studio. The door swings shut.*)

POLICEMAN (*impatiently*): Look, buddy, like I say . . . we got her charged with assault and battery . . . and the kid with threatening the cabbie.

SYLVESTER (*clutches the bag to his chest; stubbornly*): I ain't done n-n-nothing!

MA RAINEY: You leave the boy out of it. He ain't done nothing. What's he supposed to have done?

POLICEMAN: He threatened the cabbie, lady! You just can't go around threatening people.

SYLVESTER (*crosses to Irvin*): I ain't done nothing to him! He's the one talking about he g-g-gonna get a b-b-baseball bat on me! I just told him what I'd do with it. But I ain't done nothing cause he didn't get the b-b-bat!

IRVIN (*takes the Policeman by the arm*): Officer . . . look here. . . .

POLICEMAN: We was on our way down to the precinct . . . but I figured I'd do you a favor and bring her by here. I mean, if she's as important as she says she is . . .

IRVIN (*reaches into his pants pocket, pulls out a roll of bills, and peels off three dollar bills*): Look, Officer . . . I'm Madame Rainey's manager . . . it's good to meet you. (*Shakes the Policeman's hand and slips the dollar bills into his palm. The Policeman looks at the money in his hand, then glances at Irvin quizzically. Irvin quickly peels off another bill and slips it into the Policeman's hand. Reassuringly:*) As soon as we're finished with the recording session . . . I'll personally stop by the precinct house and straighten up this misunderstanding.

POLICEMAN (*looks at the money in his hand, then at Irvin*): Well . . . I guess that's alright. As long as someone is responsible for them. (*Puts the money in his pocket.*) No need to come down . . . I'll take care of it myself. (*Glares at Ma and Sylvester.*) Of course, we wouldn't want nothing like this to happen again.

IRVIN: Don't worry, Officer . . . I'll take care of everything. Thanks for your help. (*He escorts the Policeman through the double door. The Policeman exits up the front hall as Irvin crosses back through the double door to Ma.*) Here, Ma . . . let me take your coat. (*Takes Ma's coat and turns to Dussie Mae; solicitously:*) I don't believe I know you.

MA RAINEY: That's my nephew, Sylvester.

IRVIN (*stares at Dussie Mae, puzzled, then, after a moment, quickly turns and crosses to Sylvester*): I'm very pleased to meet you. Here . . . you can give me your coat. (*Takes Sylvester's coat and hangs it on his arm.*)

MA RAINEY: That there is Dussie Mae.

IRVIN (*crosses to Dussie Mae, takes her coat, and smiles broadly*): Hello . . . listen Ma, just sit there and relax. The boys are in the bandroom rehearsing. You just sit and relax a minute.

MA RAINEY (*obstinately*): I ain't for no sitting. I ain't never heard of such. Talking about taking me to jail. Irvin, call down there and see about my car.

IRVIN: Okay, Ma . . . I'll take care of it. You just relax. (*Crosses through the double door and hangs the coats in the front hall peevishly.*)

MA RAINEY: Why you all keep it so cold in here?

IRVIN (*from hall*): Huh?

MA RAINEY: Sturdyvant try and pinch every penny he can. (*Irvin crosses back into the studio to the radiator.*) You all wanna make some records you better put some heat on in here or give me back my coat.

IRVIN (*cautiously touches the radiator*): We got the heat turned up, Ma. It's warming up. It'll be warm in a minute.

DUSSIE MAE (*whispers to Ma*): Where's the bathroom?

MA RAINEY: It's in the back, down the hall next to Sturdyvant's office. Come on, I'll show you where it is. Irvin, call down there and see about my car. I want my car fixed today.

IRVIN: I'll take care of everything, Ma. (*Ma and Dussie Mae exit up the front hall. Irvin turns to Toledo.*) Say . . . uh . . . uh . . . (*Snaps his fingers.*)

TOLEDO: Toledo.

IRVIN: Yeah, Toledo. I got the sandwiches you can take down to the rest of the boys. We'll be ready to go in a minute. (*Crosses to the double door, followed by Toledo.*) Give you boys a chance to eat and then we'll be ready to go.

(*He exits up the front hall, followed by Toledo. Sylvester watches them leave, then looks up at Sturdyvant in the control booth, looks around the empty room, crosses to the piano stool, and sits. The studio slowly dims as lights fade up in the bandroom. Slow Drag is playing solitaire. Levee polishes his cornet. Cutler is sitting, drowsily, in a chair.*)

LEVEE: Slow Drag, you ever been to New Orleans?

SLOW DRAG: What's in New Orleans that I want?

LEVEE: How you call yourself a musician and ain't never been to New Orleans?

SLOW DRAG: You ever been to Fat Back, Arkansas? (*Levee shakes his head.*) Alright, then. Ain't never been nothing in New Orleans that I couldn't get in Fat Back.

LEVEE: That's why you backwards. You just an old country boy talking about Fat Back, Arkansas, and New Orleans in the same breath.

CUTLER: I been to New Orleans. What about it?

LEVEE: You ever been to Lula White's?

CUTLER: Lula White's? I ain't never heard of it. (*Slow Drag gathers the playing cards and puts them in his vest pocket.*)

LEVEE: Man, they got some gals in there just won't wait! I seen a man get killed in there once. Got drunk and grabbed one of the gals wrong . . . I don't know what the matter of it was. (*Rises and crosses toward Cutler.*) But he grabbed her and she stuck a knife in him all the way up to the hilt. He ain't even fell. He just stood there and choked on his own blood. (*Picks up the piano chair, carries it up to Slow Drag, and sits on it.*) I was just asking Slow Drag 'cause I was gonna take him to Lula White's when we get down to New Orleans and show him a good time. Introduce him to one of them gals I know down there. (*Slow Drag snorts.*)

CUTLER: Slow Drag don't need you to find him no pussy. He can take care of his ownself. (*Humorously:*) Fact is . . . you better watch your gal when Slow Drag's around. They don't call him Slow Drag for nothing. (*Rises and crosses to Levee.*) Tell him how you got your name, Slow Drag.

SLOW DRAG: I ain't thinking about Levee.

CUTLER: Slow Drag break a woman's back when he dance. (*Mimes Slow Drag dancing with an imaginary partner.*) They had this contest one time in this little town called Bolingbroke about a hundred miles outside Macon. We was playing for this dance and they was giving twenty dollars to the best slow draggers. (*Mimes Slow Drag's dance again.*) Slow Drag looked over the competition, got down off the bandstand, grabbed hold of one of them gals, and stuck to her like a fly to jelly. Like wood to glue. Man had the gal whooping and hollering so . . . everybody stopped to watch. This fellow come in . . . this gal's fellow . . . and pulled a knife a foot long on Slow Drag.

(*Mimes the fellow pulling an imaginary knife and glaring at Slow Drag.*) 'Member that, Slow Drag?

SLOW DRAG (*chuckles*): Boy, that mama was hot! The front of her dress was wet as a dishrag!

LEVEE (*excitedly*): So what happened? What the man do?

CUTLER: Slow Drag ain't missed a stroke. (*Dances with the imaginary partner.*) The gal, she just look at her man with that sweet dizzy look in her eye. She ain't about to stop! Folks was clearing out, ducking, and hiding under tables, figuring there's gonna be a fight. (*Ducks behind Levee, then steps right and resumes his dance.*) Slow Drag just looked over the gal's shoulder at the man and said . . . "Mister, if you'd quit hollering and wait a minute . . . you'll see I'm doing you a favor. I'm helping this gal win ten dollars so she can buy you a gold watch." (*Stops and mimes the fellow stroking a long imaginary knife.*) The man just stood there and looked at him, all the while stroking that knife. Told Slow Drag, say "Alright then, nigger. You just better make damn sure you win." (*All laugh as Cutler crosses to Slow Drag and sits on bench.*) That's when folks started calling him Slow Drag. The women got to hanging around him so bad after that, them fellows in that town ran us out of there.

(*Toledo opens the bandroom door, enters, carrying a small cardboard box, and closes the door.*)

LEVEE: Yeah . . . well, them gals in Lula White's will put a harness on his ass.

TOLEDO (*drops the box on top of the piano and crosses to Levee*): Ma's up there. Some kind of commotion with the police.

CUTLER (*starts*): Police? What the police up there for?

TOLEDO: I couldn't get it straight. Something about her car. They gone now . . . she's alright. Mr. Irvin sent some sandwiches. (*Gestures toward the piano as Levee leaps up, crosses to the piano, and grabs the box.*)

LEVEE: Yeah, alright. What we got here? (*Crosses to bench, sits, and greedily takes two sandwiches wrapped in wax paper from the box.*)

TOLEDO (*indignantly*): What you doing grabbing two? There ain't but five in there . . . how you figure you get two?

LEVEE: 'Cause I grabbed them first. (*Toledo takes the box out of Levee's hand and crosses to Cutler.*) There's enough for everybody . . . what you talking about? It ain't like I'm taking food out of nobody's mouth. (*Toledo offers the box to Cutler.*)

CUTLER: That's alright. He can have mine too. I don't want none.

TOLEDO (*crosses to Slow Drag; Levee leaps toward the box; Toledo shoves Levee away as Slow Drag takes a sandwich from the box*): Nigger, you better get out of here. (*Offers the box to Slow Drag again.*) Slow Drag, you want this?

SLOW DRAG: Naw, you can have it. (*Unwraps his sandwich.*)

TOLEDO (*picks up the piano chair and places it at the piano as Levee unwraps a sandwich*): With Levee around, you don't have to worry about no leftovers. I can see that. (*Takes a sandwich, drops the box in a chair, and sits at the piano.*)

LEVEE: What's the matter with you? Ain't you eating two sandwiches? (*Toledo unwraps his sandwich; Slow Drag starts to eat.*) Then why you wanna talk about me? Talking about there won't be no leftovers with Levee around. Look at your ownself before you look at me.

TOLEDO: That's what you is. That's what we all is. A leftover from history. You see now, I'll show you. . . . (*Puts his sandwich on the piano and turns toward Cutler and Slow Drag.*)

LEVEE: Aw, shit . . . I done got the nigger started now. (*Turns away from Toledo and begins to devour his sandwich.*)

TOLEDO: Now I'm gonna show you how this goes . . . where you just a leftover from history. Everybody come from different places in Africa, right? Come from different tribes and things. Soonawhile they began to make one big stew. You had the carrots, the peas, and potatoes, and whatnot over here. And over there, you had the meat, the nuts, the okra, corn . . . and then you mix it up and let it cook right through to get the flavors flowing together . . . then you got one thing. You got a stew.

Now you take and eat the stew. You take and make your history with that stew. Alright. Now it's over. Your history's over and you done ate the stew. But you look around and you see some carrots over here, some potatoes over there. That stew's still there. You done made your history and it's still there. You can't eat it all. So what you got? You got some leftovers. That's what it is. You got some leftovers and you can't do nothing with it. You already making you another history . . . cooking you another meal, and you don't need them leftovers no more. What to do?

See, we's the leftovers. The colored man is the leftovers. Now what's the colored man gonna do with himself? That's what we waiting to find out. But first we gotta know we the leftovers.

Now, who knows that? You find me a nigger that knows that and I'll turn any which-a-way you want me to. I'll bend over for you. You ain't gonna find that. And that's what the problem is. The problem ain't with the white man. The white man know you just a leftover. 'Cause he the one who done the eating and he know what he done ate. But we don't know that we been took and made history out of. Done went and filled the white man's belly and now he's full and tired and wants you to get out the way and let him be by himself. Now, I know what I'm talking about. And if you wanna find out, you just ask Mr. Irvin what he had yesterday for supper. And if he's an honest white man . . . which is asking for a whole heap of a lot . . . he'll tell you he done ate your black ass and if you please, I'm full up with you . . . so go on and get off the plate and let me eat something else. (*Turns to the piano and picks up his sandwich.*)

SLOW DRAG (*bewildered*): What that mean? What's eating got to do with how the white man treat you? He don't treat you no different according to what he ate.

TOLEDO: I ain't said it had nothing to do with how he treat you. (*Begins eating his sandwich.*)

CUTLER: The man's trying to tell you something, fool!

SLOW DRAG: What he trying to tell me? Ain't you here? Why you say he was trying to tell me something? Wasn't he trying to tell you, too?

LEVEE: He was trying, alright. He was trying a whole heap. I'll say that for him. But trying ain't worth a damn. I got lost right there trying to figure out who puts nuts in their stew. (*Finishes his sandwich and tosses away the wax paper.*)

SLOW DRAG: I knowed that before. My grandpappy used to put nuts in his stew. He and my grandma both. That ain't nothing new.

TOLEDO: They put nuts in their stew all over Africa. But the stew they eat, and the stew your grandpappy made, and all the stew that you and me eat, and the stew Mr. Irvin eats . . . ain't in noway the same stew. That's the way that go. I'm through with it. That's the last you know me to ever try and explain something to you.

CUTLER (*rises, sighs*): Well, time's getting along . . . come on, let's finish rehearsing.

(*Toledo picks up the sandwich box and puts it on top of the piano. Cutler sits down. Slow Drag crumples his wax paper, puts it in his pocket, crosses to the crates, and picks up his bass.*)

LEVEE (*puts his cornet and the second sandwich in the case under the bench and stretches out on his back, lazily*): I don't feel like rehearsing. I ain't nothing but a leftover. You go and rehearse with Toledo . . . he's gonna teach you how to make a stew.

SLOW DRAG: Cutler, what you gonna do? I don't want to be around here all day.

LEVEE: I know my part. You all go on and rehearse your part. You all need some rehearsal.

CUTLER: Come on, Levee, get up off your ass and rehearse the songs.

LEVEE: I already know them songs . . . what I wanna rehearse them for?

SLOW DRAG: You in the band ain't you? You supposed to rehearse when the band rehearse.

TOLEDO (*playfully*): Levee think he the King of the Barnyard. He thinks he's the only rooster know how to crow.

LEVEE: Alright! Alright! (*Toledo grins at Cutler as Levee jumps up and grabs his cornet.*) Come on. I'm gonna show you I know them songs. Come on, let's rehearse. I bet you the first one mess up be Toledo. Come on . . . I wanna see if he know how to crow.

CUTLER: "Ma Rainey's Black Bottom," Levee's version. Let's do it. A-one. A-two. You know what to do.

(*The band mimes playing as the bandroom dims and lights fade up in the studio. Sylvester is sitting at the piano and Sturdyvant is arranging his files in the control booth.*)

MA RAINEY (*singing a cappella, from off right*):
OH LORD, THESE DOGS OF MINE
THEY SURE DO WORRY ME ALL THE TIME.

(*She enters the front hall carrying one shoe and wearing the other as Dussie Mae follows languidly behind her. Ma opens the double door and crosses into the studio.*)

THEY REASON WHY, I DON'T KNOW
LORD, I BEG TO BE EXCUSED
I CAN'T WEAR ME NO SHARP-TOED SHOES

(*Ma crosses to a folding chair, sits, and drops her purse on the other chair. Dussie Mae crosses and rests a hand on Ma's shoulder.*)

I WENT FOR A WALK
I STOPPED TO TALK
OH, HOW MY CORNS DID BARK.

(*Ma laughs loudly and rubs her foot as Dussie Mae looks around the studio. Sylvester plunks a few high notes on the piano.*)

DUSSIE MAE: It feels kinda spooky in here. I ain't never been in no recording studio before. (*Sylvester plunks a few lower notes.*) Where's the band at?

MA RAINEY: They off somewhere rehearsing. I don't know where Irvin went to. (*Sylvester hits a few notes further down the keyboard as Ma takes off the other shoe and puts both shoes under her chair.*) All this hurry up and he goes off back there with Sturdyvant. (*Sylvester hits a few low keys.*) I know he better come on 'cause Ma ain't gonna be waiting. (*Sylvester pounds a few notes at the bottom of the keyboard as Ma turns to look at Dussie Mae.*) Come here . . . let me see that dress. (*Dussie Mae crosses to Ma and turns, showing off the dress. Ma touches the dress, approvingly.*) That dress looks nice. I'm gonna take you tomorrow and get you some more things before I take you down to Memphis. They got clothes up here you can't get in Memphis. I want you to look nice for me. If you gonna travel with the show, you got to look nice.

DUSSIE MAE (*crosses to the cane chair, sits, puts her purse under the chair, and rubs her foot*): I need me some more shoes. These hurt my feet.

MA RAINEY: You get you some shoes that fit your feet. Don't you be messing around with no shoes that pinch your feet. Ma know something about bad feet. (*Gestures toward Sylvester.*) Hand me my slippers out my bag over yonder. (*Dussie Mae rises and starts toward Sylvester as he jumps up, takes a pair of slippers out of the bag, crosses to Ma, and kneels.*)

DUSSIE MAE (*crosses back to the cane chair, sits, and glares at Sylvester, who tucks the bag under one arm and puts Ma's slippers on her feet*): I just want to get a pair of them yellow shoes. About a half-size bigger.

MA RAINEY: We'll get you whatever you need. (*Sylvester rises and stands attentively, his shirttail hanging out of his pants.*) Sylvester, too . . . I'm gonna get him some more clothes. (*Looks at Sylvester's shirttail.*) Sylvester . . . tuck your clothes in. Straighten them up and look nice. Look like a gentleman. (*Sylvester looks at his clothes, hurriedly tucks in the shirt, and straightens his coat.*)

DUSSIE MAE (*scornfully*): Look at Sylvester with that hat on.

MA RAINEY: Sylvester, take your hat off inside. Act like your mama taught you something. (*Sylvester glares at Dussie Mae, takes his hat off, crosses to the piano.*) I know she taught you better than that. (*Sylvester sits at the piano.*) Come on over here and leave that piano alone.

SYLVESTER: I ain't d-d-doing nothing to the p-p-piano. I'm just l-l-looking at it.

MA RAINEY: Well. Come on over here and sit down. (*Sylvester rises obediently, crosses, and sits, holding the bag and his hat on his lap.*) As soon as Mr. Irvin comes back, I'll have him take you down and introduce you to the band.

(*Dussie Mae stretches out one leg, lifts her skirt, and adjusts her stocking garters. Irvin enters the studio, stops, and stares silently at Dussie Mae's leg.*)

He's gonna take you down there and introduce you in a minute . . . have Cutler show you how your part go. And when you get your money you gonna send some of it

home to your mama. Let her know you doing alright.
Make her feel good to know you doing alright in the
world.

(*Dussie Mae turns and glances at Irvin. She picks up her purse,
rises, and straightens her skirt.*)

IRVIN (*crosses a step toward Ma*): Ma, I called down to the
garage and checked on your car. It's just a scratch. They'll
have it ready for you this afternoon. They're gonna send
it over with one of their fellows.

MA RAINEY: They better have my car fixed right, too. I ain't
going for that.

(*Dussie Mae looks down the back hall as the band lifts their instruments and plays Levee's version of the "Black Bottom," quietly.*)

Brand new car . . . they better fix it like new.

IRVIN: It was just a scratch on the fender, Ma. . . .

(*Ma cocks her ear towards the door, listening to the faint sound of the
band, then turns to Dussie Mae. Dussie Mae swings her hips and
snaps her fingers to the music.*)

They'll take care of it . . . don't worry . . . they'll have it
like new.

(*Ma looks disapprovingly at Dussie Mae. Dussie Mae glances at
Ma, then crosses to the piano stool.*)

MA RAINEY: Irvin . . . what is that I hear? What is that the
band's rehearsing? I know they ain't rehearsing Levee's
"Black Bottom." I know I ain't hearing that.

IRVIN: Ma, listen. . . . (*Turns the cane chair backwards and sits
facing Ma; casually:*) That's what I wanted to talk to you
about . . . Levee's version of that song . . . it's got a nice
arrangement . . . a nice horn intro . . . it really picks it
up. . . .

MA RAINEY (*crossly*): I ain't studying Levee nothing. I know
what he done to that song and I don't like to sing it that

way. I'm doing it the old way. That's why I brought my nephew to do the voice intro.

IRVIN: Ma . . . that's what the people want now. (*Rises and crosses toward the radiator; persuasively:*) They want something they can dance to. Times are changing. Levee's arrangement gives the people what they want. It gets them excited . . . makes them forget about their troubles.

MA RAINEY: I don't care what you say, Irvin. Levee ain't messing up my song. If he got what the people want . . . let him take it somewhere else. I'm singing Ma Rainey's song. I ain't singing Levee's song. Now that's all there is to it. Carry my nephew on down there and introduce him to the band. (*Sylvester rises, hopefully.*) I promised my sister I'd look out for him and he's gonna do the voice intro on the song my way.

IRVIN (*crosses to the cane chair and sits*): Ma . . . we just figured that . . .

MA RAINEY (*irritated*): Who's this "we"? What you mean "we"? You and Sturdyvant? You and Levee? Who's "we"? I ain't studying Levee nothing. Come talking this "we" stuff. Who's "we"?

IRVIN: Me and Sturdyvant. We decided that it would . . .

MA RAINEY: You decided, huh? I'm just a bump on the log. I'm gonna go whichever way the river drift. Is that it? You and Sturdyvant decided.

IRVIN: Ma. It was just that we thought it would be better.

MA RAINEY (*ironically*): I ain't got good sense. I don't know nothing about music. I don't know what's a good song and what ain't. You know more about my fans than I do.

IRVIN (*pleadingly*): It's not that, Ma. It would just be easier to go. It's more what the people want.

MA RAINEY (*exasperated*): I'm gonna tell you something, Irvin . . . and you go on up there and tell Sturdyvant. What you all say don't count with me. You understand? Ma listens to her heart. Ma listens to the voice inside her. That's what counts with Ma. Now, you carry my nephew on down there . . . tell Cutler he's gonna do the voice intro on that "Black Bottom" song . . . and that Levee ain't messing up my song with none of his music shit. Now, if that don't set right with you and Sturdyvant . . . then I can carry my black bottom on back down south to my tour, 'cause I don't like it up here no ways.

IRVIN: Okay, Ma . . . I don't care. I just thought . . .

MA RAINEY (*angrily*): Damn what you thought! What you look like telling me how to sing my song? This Levee and Sturdyvant nonsense . . . I ain't going for it! (*Turns to Sylvester.*) Sylvester, go on down there and introduce yourself. I'm through playing with Irvin.

SYLVESTER (*runs out the door, turns into the closet, then crosses back, flustered*): Which way you go? Where they at?

MA RAINEY (*rises*): Here . . . I'll carry you down there myself.

DUSSIE MAE (*rises; expectantly*): Can I go? I wanna see the band.

MA RAINEY (*curtly*): You stay your behind up here. Ain't no cause in you being down there. (*Starts toward the back hall. Dussie Mae sits on the piano stool.*) Come on, Sylvester.

IRVIN (*rises, resigned*): Okay, Ma. Have it your way. We'll be ready to go in fifteen minutes.

MA RAINEY (*turns back into the studio; haughtily*): We'll be ready to go when Madame says we're ready. That's the way it goes around here.

(*Ma crosses into the back hall followed by Sylvester. He closes the door. Simultaneously the studio dims as the lights fade up in the bandroom; the band plays louder as Irvin goes through the double door and exits up the front hall; Sturdyvant comes down the staircase and follows Irvin out. Dussie Mae watches Irvin and Sturdy-*

vant exit, then follows after them. Levee crosses to downstage center as he plays. Ma opens the bandroom door and crosses slowly toward Levee. Sylvester follows Ma into the bandroom and crosses to above the piano. Cutler glances at Ma, and drops out, followed by Toledo, then rises and looks at Ma sheepishly. Slow Drag glances toward Ma, drops out, and tries to get Levee's attention. Levee continues to play. Ma crosses to Levee and glares at him disparagingly. Levee glances toward Ma, stops playing, and crosses upstage right. Ma turns to Cutler; dryly:)

> Cutler . . . this here is my nephew, Sylvester. He's gonna do that voice intro on the "Black Bottom" song using the old version.

LEVEE (*crosses to Ma; angrily*): What you talking about? Mr. Irvin said he's using my version. What you talking about?

MA RAINEY (*coldly*): Levee, I ain't studying you or Mr. Irvin. (*Levee crosses upstage right.*) Cutler . . . get him straightened out on how to do his part. I ain't thinking about Levee. These folks done messed with the wrong person this day. Sylvester, Cutler gonna teach you your part. (*To Sylvester, patiently:*) You go ahead and get it straight. Don't worry about what nobody else say. (*She crosses into the back hall and closes the door. Everyone is silent for a moment. Sylvester looks around the room.*)

CUTLER (*resigned*): Well, come on in, boy. (*Sylvester enters hesitantly. Cutler picks up his trombone.*) I'm Cutler. You got Slow Drag . . . (*Slow Drag smiles and waves.*) Levee . . . (*Levee growls, crosses to chair, and sits. Cutler turns and gestures toward Toledo.*) And that's Toledo over there. (*Toledo nods at Sylvester.*) Sylvester, huh?

SYLVESTER: Sylvester Brown.

LEVEE (*snarls to himself*): I done wrote a version of that song what picks it up and sets it down in the people's lap! Now she come talking this! You don't need that old circus bullshit! I know what I'm talking about. You gonna mess up that song, Cutler, and you know it.

CUTLER: I ain't gonna mess up nothing. Ma say . . .

LEVEE (*turns to Cutler; abruptly*): I don't care what Ma say! I'm talking about what the intro gonna do to the song. The peoples in the North ain't gonna buy all that tent-show nonsense. They wanna hear some music!

CUTLER: Nigger, I done told you time and again . . . you just in the band. You plays the piece . . . whatever they want! Ma says what to play! Not you! You ain't here to be doing no creating. Your job is to play whatever Ma says.

LEVEE: I might not play nothing! I might quit!

CUTLER: Nigger, don't nobody care if you quit. Who's heart you gonna break?

TOLEDO: Levee ain't gonna quit. He got to make some money to keep him in shoe polish. (*All laugh except Levee and Sylvester.*)

LEVEE: I done told you all . . . you all don't know me. You don't know what I'll do.

CUTLER: I don't think nobody too much give a damn! (*Turns to Sylvester.*) Sylvester . . . here's the way your part go. The band plays the intro . . . I'll tell you where to come in. The band plays the intro and then you say . . . Alright boys, you done seen the rest . . . Now I'm gonna show you the best . . . Ma Rainey's gonna show you her black bottom. You got that? (*Crosses to chair and sits.*) Let me hear you say it one time.

SYLVESTER (*breathes deeply*): Alright boys, you d-d-done seen the rest, n-n-now I'm gonna show you the best. M-M-M-M-M-M-Ma Rainey's gonna s-s-show you her black b-b-bottom. (*Looks at Cutler expectantly. Cutler nods and smiles.*)

LEVEE (*dumbfounded, turns slowly to Sylvester, then explodes*): What kind of . . . Alright, Cutler! Let me see you fix that! You straighten that out! You hear that shit, Slow Drag?

How in the hell the boy gonna do the part and he can't even talk!

SYLVESTER (*crosses a step toward Levee, boldly*): W-W-W-Who's you tell me what to do, nigger! This ain't you band. Ma tell me to d-d-d-do it and I'm gonna do it. You can go to hell, n-n-n-nigger!

LEVEE (*slowly rises, facing Sylvester*): B-B-B-Boy, ain't nobody studying you. You go on and fix that one, Cutler. (*Crosses to the crates disgustedly.*) You fix that one and I'll . . . I'll shine your shoes for you! You go on and fix that one!

TOLEDO: You say you Ma's nephew, huh?

SYLVESTER (*defensively*): Yeah. So w-w-w-what that mean?

TOLEDO: Oh, I ain't meant nothing . . . I was just asking.

SLOW DRAG (*turns his face away from Sylvester and tries to stifle a laugh*): Well, come on and let's rehearse so the boy can get it right.

LEVEE: I ain't rehearsing nothing! (*Crosses to chair and sits.*) You just wait till I get my band. I'm gonna record that song and show you how it supposed to go!

CUTLER: We can do it without Levee. Let him sit on over there. Sylvester, you remember your part?

SYLVESTER: I remember it pretty g-g-good.

CUTLER: Well, come on, let's do it then. One. Two. You know what to do.

(*Levee sulks as Toledo plays a brief piano introduction, then Cutler and Slow Drag join in on "Ma Rainey's Black Bottom." Sturdyvant opens the bandroom door and crosses to the piano, smiling broadly.*)

STURDYVANT: Good . . . you boys are rehearsing, I see. (*The band stops playing as Levee jumps up and crosses to Sturdyvant.*)

LEVEE (*enthusiastically*): Yessir! We rehearsing. We know them songs real good.

STURDYVANT: Good! Say . . . Levee . . . did you finish that song?

LEVEE: Yessir, Mr. Sturdyvant. (*Takes two sheets of music from the horn case under the bench; confidently:*) I got it right here. I wrote that other part just like you say. It go like:

> You can shake it, you can break it
> You can dance at any hall
> You can slide across the floor
> You'll never have to stall
> My jelly, my roll, sweet mama don't you let it fall.

(*Turns to the second sheet of music.*) Then I put that part in there for the people to dance, like you say, for them to forget about their troubles.

STURDYVANT: Good! Good! I'll just take this. (*Takes both sheets of music from Levee's hand and smiles.*) I wanna see you about your songs as soon as I get the chance. (*Crosses to the bandroom door.*)

LEVEE: Yessir! As soon as you get the chance, Mr. Sturdyvant. (*Sturdyvant exits and closes the door. Levee paces excitedly as the men stare at him.*)

CUTLER: You hear Levee? You hear this nigger? "Yessuh, we's rehearsing boss."

SLOW DRAG (*mockingly*): I heard him. Seen him, too. Shuffling them feet.

TOLEDO: Aw, Levee can't help it none. He's like all of us. Spooked up with the white man.

LEVEE (*stops and glares*): I'm spooked up with him alright. You let one of them crackers fix on me wrong. I'll show you how spooked up I am with him.

TOLEDO: That's the trouble of it. You wouldn't know if he was fixed on you wrong or not. You so spooked up by him, you ain't had the time to study him.

LEVEE (*resentfully*): I studies the white man. I got him studied good. The first time one fixes on me wrong, I'm gonna let him know just how much I studied him. Come telling me I'm spooked up by the white man. You let one mess with me . . . I'll show you how spooked up I am.

CUTLER: You talking out your hat. The man come in here, call you a boy, tell you to get up off your ass and rehearse . . . and you ain't had nothing to say to him, 'cepting "Yessir!"

LEVEE (*crosses a step toward Cutler*): I can say "yessir" to whoever I please. What you got to do with it? I know how to handle white folks. I been handling them for thirty-two years, and now you're gonna tell me how to do it. Just 'cause I say "yessir" don't mean I'm spooked up by him. I know what I'm doing. Let me handle him my way.

CUTLER: Well, go on and handle it then.

LEVEE: Toledo, you always messing with somebody! Always agitating somebody with that old philosophy bullshit you be talking. You stay out of my way about what I do and say. I'm my own person. Just let me alone.

TOLEDO: You right, Levee. I apologize. It ain't none of my business . . . (*turns to Cutler and smirks*) that you spooked up by the white man. (*Cutler and Slow Drag laugh.*)

LEVEE (*warningly*): Alright! See! That's the shit I'm talking about. You all back up and leave Levee alone.

SLOW DRAG: Aw, Levee, we was all just having fun. Toledo ain't said nothing about you he ain't said about me. You just taking it all wrong.

TOLEDO (*appeasingly*): I ain't meant nothing by it, Levee. (*Turns to Cutler.*) Cutler, you ready to rehearse?

LEVEE (*paces angrily*): Levee got to be Levee! And he don't need nobody messing with him about the white man— 'cause you don't know nothing about me. You don't know Levee. You don't know nothing about what kind of blood I got! What kind of heart I got beating here! I was eight years old when I watched a gang of white mens come into my daddy's house and have to do with my mama anyway they wanted. Never will forget it.

We was living in Jefferson County, about eighty miles outside of Natchez. My daddy's name was Memphis . . . Memphis Lee Green . . . had him near fifty acres of good farming land. I'm talking good land! Grow anything you want! He done gone off of shares and bought this land from Mr. Hallie's widow-woman after he done passed on. Folks called him an uppity nigger 'cause he done saved and borrowed to where he could buy this land and be independent.

It was coming on planting time and my daddy went into Natchez to get him some seed and fertilizer. Called me, say, Levee, you the man of the house now. Take care of your mama while I'm gone. I wasn't but a little boy, eight years old.

My mama was frying up some chicken when them mens come in that house. Must have been eight or nine of them. She was standing there frying that chicken and them mens come and took hold of her just like you take hold of a mule and make him do what you want.

There was my mama with a gang of white mens. She tried to fight them off, but I could see where it wasn't gonna do her any good. I didn't know what they were doing to her . . . but I figured whatever it was they may as well do to me, too. My daddy had a knife that he kept around there for hunting and working and whatnot. I knew where he kept it and I went and got it. (*Crosses to bench and puts his cornet on it.*) I'm gonna show you how spooked up I was by the white man. I tried my damnedest to cut one of them's throat! I hit him on the shoulder with it. (*Crosses to other bench.*) He reached back and grabbed hold of that knife and whacked me across the chest with it. (*Pulls up his shirt and exposes a long, ugly scar on his chest.*) That's what made them stop. They was scared I was gonna bleed to death. My mama wrapped a sheet around me and carried me two miles down to the Furlow place and they drove me up to Doc Albans. He was waiting on a calf to be born and said he ain't had time to see me. They carried me up to Miss Etta, the midwife, and she fixed me up.

My daddy came back and acted like he done accepted the facts of what happened. But he got the names of them white men from my mama. He found out who they was and then we announced we was moving out of the county. Said good-bye to everybody . . . all the neighbors. My daddy went and smiled in the face of one of them crackers who had been with my mama. Smiled in his face and sold him our land. We moved over with relations in Caldwell. He got us settled in and then he took off one day. I ain't never seen him since. He sneaked back hiding up in the woods, laying to get them eight or nine men.

He got four of them before they got him. They tracked him down in the woods. Caught up with him, hung him, and set him afire. (*Turns to the silver cornet on the bench.*) My daddy wasn't spooked up by the white man. Nosir! And that taught me how to handle them. (*Slowly crosses to the cornet, lifts it, and clutches it tightly to his chest, grief-stricken.*) I seen my daddy go up and grin in this cracker's face . . . smile in his face, and sell him his land. All the while he's planning how he's gonna get him and what he's gonna do to him. That taught me how to handle them. So you all just back up and leave Levee alone about the white man. I can smile and say "yessir" to whoever I please. (*Crosses to the other bench, subdued.*) I got my time coming to me. You all just leave Levee alone about the white man. (*Sits on the bench, facing upstage.*)

SLOW DRAG (*starts a slow, rhythmic beat on the body of the bass; singing*):

IF I HAD MY WAY
IF I HAD MY WAY
IF I HAD MY WAY

(*He stops the rhythmic beat.*)

I WOULD TEAR THIS OLD BUILDING DOWN.

(*The stage fades quickly to black. After a moment, a dim glow warms the front hall, the studio, and the bandroom. After a few moments, Intermission music begins: female vocalist renditions of blues songs.*)

ACT II

A female vocal rendition of "Trust No Man." The stage fades to black. The song ends. A single note is heard repeatedly on a piano. The bandroom lights fade up to a dim glow as the studio lights fade up brightly revealing Ma at the studio piano singing quietly and playing a single note; and Dussie Mae seated in a folding chair, holding her purse. Sturdyvant enters, followed by Cutler carrying his guitar case and trombone, Toledo, Slow Drag carrying his bass, Levee carrying his cornet, and Sylvester carrying his hat and Ma's bag. Sturdyvant crosses to the microphone, moves it a few inches, then crosses up the spiral staircase to the control booth as Ma crosses to the mic. Cutler places his guitar case behind the door and crosses to downstage right. Toledo crosses to the piano and sits on the stool. Slow Drag crosses and stands right of the piano. Sylvester crosses and sits. Levee crosses to the other folding chair, eyeing Dussie Mae. Ma nods approvingly at the placement of her microphone, crosses through the double doors into the front hall as Irvin enters down the front hall and crosses into the studio. Ma sings softly in the front hall. Levee sits on the folding chair. Cutler motions to Irvin, then Irvin crosses to Cutler.

CUTLER (*quietly*): Mr. Irvin, I don't know what you gonna do. I ain't got nothing to do with it, but the boy can't do the part. He stutters. He can't get it right. He stutters right through it everytime. . . .

IRVIN: Christ! Okay. We'll . . . shit! We'll just do it like we planned. We'll do Levee's version. I'll handle it, Cutler. Come on, let's go. I'll think of something.

(*Irvin crosses to the double doors and knocks on the window. He crosses to the spiral staircase, climbs to the top of the stairs, pulls the drape across the stairwell, then enters the control booth and closes the door. Cutler starts to cross toward Toledo as Ma comes through the double doors and steps into the studio. She looks at Levee; he is staring at Dussie Mae's leg.*)

393

MA RAINEY: Cutler, Levee's got his eyes in the wrong place. You better school him, Cutler.

CUTLER (*crosses toward Levee*): Come on, Levee . . . let's get ready to play! (*Levee rises. Cutler glares at him. Emphatically:*) Get your mind on your work!

(*Levee crosses to Slow Drag. Ma picks up a stool and moves it to the radiator. She taps the stool and stares at Dussie Mae. Dussie Mae rises obediently, crosses to the stool, and sits.*)

IRVIN (*into the booth mic*): Okay, boys . . . we're gonna do "Moonshine Blues" first. "Moonshine Blues," Ma.

MA RAINEY (*crosses to the platform, muttering loudly*): I ain't doing no Moonshine nothing. I'm doing the "Black Bottom" first. Come on, Sylvester. (*Sylvester rushes to Ma's microphone. Ma turns to the control booth.*) Where's Sylvester's mic? You need a mic for Sylvester. (*Takes Sylvester by the arm and pushes him toward Dussie Mae.*) Irvin . . . get him a mic.

IRVIN (*into the booth mic*): Uh . . . Ma . . . the boys say he can't do it.

MA RAINEY (*crosses to her mic and speaks into it, testily*): Who say he can't do it? What boys say he can't do it?

IRVIN (*into the booth mic*): The band, Ma . . . the boys in the band.

MA RAINEY (*into her mic*): What band? The band work for me! I say what goes! (*Turns to Cutler.*) Cutler, what's he talking about? (*Turns to Levee suspiciously.*) Levee, this some of your shit?

IRVIN (*into the booth mic*): He stutters, Ma. They say he stutters.

MA RAINEY (*turns back to her mic*): I don't care if he do. I promised the boy he could do the part . . . and he's gonna do it! That's all there is to it. He don't stutter all the time. Get a microphone down here for him.

IRVIN (*into the booth mic*): Ma . . . we don't have time. We can't. . . .

MA RAINEY (*into her mic*): If you wanna make a record you gonna find time. I ain't playing with you, Irvin. I can walk out of here and go back to my tour. I got plenty fans. I don't need to go through all of this. Just go and get the boy a microphone.

(*Sturdyvant and Irvin confer quietly in the control booth for a moment, then Irvin opens the door and climbs down the spiral staircase.*)

STURDYVANT (*into the booth mic*): Alright, Ma . . . we'll get him a microphone. But if he messes up . . . he's only getting one chance . . . the cost . . .

(*Irvin crosses and disappears into the closet.*)

MA RAINEY (*into her mic*): Damn the cost. You always talking about the cost. I make more money for this outfit than anybody else you got put together. If he messes up he'll just do it till he gets it right.

(*Irvin reappears, carrying a microphone on a stand with a coiled cable, and crosses toward Sylvester. Ma turns to Levee.*)

Levee . . . I know you had something to do with this. You better watch yourself.

(*Irvin places the microphone below Sylvester, uncoils the cable, crosses to the jackbox, and plugs it in.*)

LEVEE: It was Cutler!

SYLVESTER (*turns on Levee*): It was you! You the only one m-m-mad about it.

LEVEE (*crosses a step toward Ma*): The boy stutter. He can't do the part. Everybody see that. I don't know why you want the boy to do the part noways.

(*Irvin crosses to the spiral staircase, climbs up to the control booth, enters, and closes the door.*)

MA RAINEY: Well, can or can't . . . he's gonna do it! You ain't got nothing to do with it!

LEVEE (*disgusted*): I don't care what you do! He can sing the whole goddamned song for all I care! (*Crosses to Slow Drag.*)

MA RAINEY: Well, alright. Thank you. (*Crosses to Sylvester.*) Come on, Sylvester. (*She takes the hat and bag out of Sylvester's hands and places them on the cane chair. Sylvester steps hesitantly toward the mic. Encouragingly:*) You just stand here and hold your hands like I told you. (*Sylvester assumes an opera singer's posture. Reassuringly:*) Just remember the words and say them . . . that's all there is to it. Don't worry about messing up. If you mess up we'll do it again. Now, let me hear you say it. (*Turns to Cutler.*) Play it for him, Cutler.

CUTLER: One. Two. You know what to do.

(*Toledo plays a short piano intro, then the band begins to play "Ma Rainey's Black Bottom." Sylvester rocks back and forth in front of the mic. Ma smiles.*)

SYLVESTER: Alright, boys, you d-d-d-done s-s-s-seen the best . . . now I'm gonna show you the rest. . . . (*Slow Drag drops out, followed by Levee.*) Ma Rainey's gonna show you . . . (*Cutler drops out, followed by Toledo.*) . . . her b-b-black b-b-bottom. (*Everyone is silent as Sylvester looks hopefully at Ma.*)

MA RAINEY (*smiles broadly and crosses to Sylvester*): That's alright. That's real good. You take your time, you'll get it right.

STURDYVANT (*into the booth mic*): Listen Ma . . . now when you come in . . . don't wait so long to come in. Don't take so long on the intro, huh?

MA RAINEY (*tips Sylvester's mic toward her and speaks into it*): Sturdyvant, don't you go trying to tell me how to sing.

You just take care of that up there and let me take care of this down here. (*Crosses to the platform and looks around the room; absently:*) Where's my Coke?

IRVIN (*into the booth mic*): Okay, Ma. We're all set up to go up here. "Ma Rainey's Black Bottom," boys.

MA RAINEY: Where's my Coke? I need a Coke. You ain't got no Coke down here? Where's my Coke?

IRVIN (*into the booth mic*): What's the matter, Ma? What's . . .

MA RAINEY: Where's my Coke? I need a Coca-Cola.

IRVIN (*into the booth mic, cajolingly*): Uh . . . Ma . . . look . . . I forgot the Coke, huh? Let's do it without it, huh? Just this one song. What say, boys?

MA RAINEY (*turns to the control booth and shouts*): Damn what the band say! You know I don't sing nothing without my Coca-Cola!

(*Sturdyvant leaves the control booth, bounds down the spiral case, and crosses to Ma. Irvin follows, patiently.*)

STURDYVANT (*outraged*): Now, just a minute here, Ma. You come in an hour late . . . we're way behind schedule as it is . . . the band is set up and ready to go . . . I'm burning my lights . . . I've turned up the heat . . . we're ready to make a record, and what? You decide you want a Coca-Cola?

MA RAINEY (*coldly*): Sturdyvant, get out of my face. (*Turns to Irvin.*) Irvin . . . I told you keep him away from me.

IRVIN: Mel, I'll handle it.

STURDYVANT (*turns to Irvin*): I'm tired of her nonsense, Irv. I'm not gonna put up with this!

IRVIN: Let me handle it, Mel. I know how to handle her. (*Crosses to Ma. Slow Drag puts his bass on top of the piano.*) Look, Ma . . . I'll call down to the deli and get you a

Coke. But let's get started, huh? Sylvester's standing there ready to go . . . the band's set up . . . let's do this one song, huh?

(*Sturdyvant, exasperated, crosses through the double door and exits up the front hall.*)

MA RAINEY (*obstinately*): If you too cheap to buy me a Coke . . . I'll buy my own. (*Turns to Slow Drag.*) Slow Drag! Sylvester, go with Slow Drag and get me a Coca-Cola. (*Picks up her purse from the folding chair, takes out a dollar bill, and hands it to Slow Drag.*) Slow Drag, walk down to that store on the corner and get me three bottles of Coca-Cola. (*Slow Drag crosses, exits up the front hall, followed by Sylvester. Ma turns to Irvin.*) Get out of my face, Irvin. You all just wait until I get my Coke. It ain't gonna kill you.

IRVIN (*grudgingly*): Okay, Ma. Get your Coke, for Chrissakes! Get your Coke!

(*He throws up his hands and exits up the front hall. Levee exits into the back hall. Toledo crosses to the back hall. Cutler leans his trombone against the piano and starts toward the door.*)

MA RAINEY (*crosses to the cane chair*): Cutler, come here a minute. I want to talk to you.

(*Toledo exits into the back hall, closing the door behind him. Ma turns the cane chair and sits with her feet on the platform as Cutler crosses reluctantly and sits.*)

What's all this about "the boys in the band say"? I tells you what to do. I says what the matter is with the band. I say who can and can't do what.

(*Levee opens the bandroom door, enters, crosses to bench, and sits. Toledo follows Levee into the bandroom, crosses to the piano, and sits.*)

CUTLER: We just say 'cause the boy stutter . . .

MA RAINEY: I know he stutters. Don't you think I know he stutters. This is what's gonna help him.

CUTLER: Well, how can he do the part if he stutters? You want him to stutter through it? We just thought it be easier to go on and let Levee do it like we planned.

(*Dussie Mae rises, carrying her purse. She picks up Ma's purse, sits, and puts both purses under the chair.*)

MA RAINEY: I don't care if he stutters or not! He's doing the part and I don't wanna hear anymore of this shit about what the band says. And I want you to find somebody to replace Levee when we get to Memphis. Levee ain't nothing but trouble.

CUTLER: Levee's alright. He plays good music when he puts his mind to it. He knows how to write music, too.

(*Dussie Mae rises and crosses to Ma's mic.*)

MA RAINEY: I don't care what he know. He ain't nothing but bad news. Find somebody else. I know it was his idea about who to say who can do what.

(*Dussie Mae fondles the mic, swings her hips, and snaps her fingers rhythmically. Cutler glances surreptitiously at Dussie Mae. Ma looks at Cutler. Curtly:*)

Dussie Mae, go sit your behind down somewhere and quit flaunting yourself around.

DUSSIE MAE (*resentfully*): I ain't doing nothing.

MA RAINEY (*softens*): Well, just go on somewhere and stay out the way.

(*Dussie Mae crosses sulkily to the chair.*)

CUTLER: I been meaning to ask you, Ma . . . about these songs. This "Moonshine Blues" . . .

(*Dussie Mae bends over and picks up the purses. Cutler glances uneasily at Dussie Mae's "behind" as it swings inches from his face. Ma glares at Cutler.*)

. . . that's one of them songs Bessie Smith sang, I believes.

(*Dussie Mae puts Ma's purse on the chair and crosses to the piano.*)

MA RAINEY (*indignantly*): Bessie what? Ain't nobody thinking about Bessie. I taught Bessie. She ain't doing nothing but imitating me. What I care about Bessie? I don't care if she sell a million records. She got her people and I got mine. I don't care what nobody else do. Ma was the first and don't you forget it!

(*Dussie Mae sits on the piano stool and looks around the room.*)

CUTLER: Ain't nobody said nothing about that. I just said that's the same song she sang.

MA RAINEY: I been doing this a long time. Ever since I was a little girl. I don't care what nobody else do. That's what gets me so mad with Irvin. White folks try to be put out with you all the time. Too cheap to buy me a Coca-Cola. I lets them know it, though. Ma don't stand for no shit. Wanna take my voice and trap it in them fancy boxes with all them buttons and dials . . . and then too cheap to buy me a Coca-Cola. And it don't cost but a nickel a bottle.

CUTLER: I knows what you mean about that.

(*Dussie Mae takes a nail file out of her purse and files her nails.*)

MA RAINEY: They don't care nothing about me. All they want is my voice. Well, I done learned that and they gonna treat me like I want to be treated no matter how much it hurt them. They back there now calling me all kinds of names . . . calling me everything but a child of God. But they can't do nothing else. They ain't got what they wanted yet. As soon as they get my voice down on them recording machines, then it's just like if I'd be some whore and they roll over and put their pants on. Ain't got no use for me then. I know what I'm talking about. You watch. Irvin right there with the rest of them. He don't care nothing about me either. He been my manager for six years and the only time he had me in his house was to sing for some of his white friends.

CUTLER: I know how they do.

(*Dussie Mae slides off the piano stool, crosses quietly toward the door, and opens it.*)

MA RAINEY: If you colored and can make them some money, then you alright with them. Otherwise you just a dog in the alley.

(*Dussie Mae exits through the left door and shuts it.*)

I done made this company more money from my records than all the other recording artists they got put together. And they wanna balk about how much this session is costing them.

CUTLER: I don't see where it's costing them all what they say.

MA RAINEY: It ain't! I don't pay that kind of talk no mind.

(*The studio dims as the bandroom lights fade up. Levee is straddling the bench and working on a sheet of music. Toledo, seated at the piano, reads a newspaper. Dussie Mae opens the bandroom door a crack.*)

LEVEE (*singing*):
YOU CAN SHAKE IT, YOU CAN BREAK IT
YOU CAN DANCE AT ANY HALL
YOU CAN SLIDE ACROSS THE FLOOR
YOU'LL NEVER HAVE TO STALL
MY JELLY, MY ROLL, SWEET MAMA DON'T YOU LET IT FALL

(*Dussie Mae opens the door a bit further.*) Wait till Mr. Sturdyvant hear me play that! I'm talking about some real music here, Toledo! I'm talking about real music! (*Glances at the bandroom door.*) Hey, mama! Come on in. (*Takes a rag out of his case, puts his foot on the bench, and polishes his shoe.*)

DUSSIE MAE: Oh, hi . . . I just wanna see what it looks like down here.

LEVEE (*drops the rag into his case and rises*): Well, come on in . . . I don't bite.

DUSSIE MAE (*crosses to the piano*): I didn't know you could really write music. I thought you was just jiving me at the club last night.

LEVEE: Naw, baby . . . I knows how to write music. (*Picks up the cornet.*) I done give Mr. Sturdyvant some of my songs and he say he's gonna let me record them. Ask Toledo. I'm gonna have my own band! Toledo . . . ain't I give Mr. Sturdyvant some of my songs I wrote!

TOLEDO (*rises, drops the newspaper on the piano, and starts toward the bandroom door*): Don't get Toledo mixed up in nothing.

(*Dussie Mae steps into Toledo's path, smiles at him, and after a moment, steps to the left. Toledo crosses quickly to the bandroom door, exits, and closes the door.*)

DUSSIE MAE (*crosses to the piano and drops her purse on the piano chair*): You gonna get your own band, sure enough?

LEVEE (*crosses tentatively toward Dussie Mae and puts his cornet on the piano*): That's right! Levee Green and His Foot-stompers.

(*Toledo enters the studio. He crosses to the piano and sits.*)

DUSSIE MAE: That's real nice.

LEVEE: That's what I was trying to tell you last night. A man whats gonna get his own band need to have a woman like you.

DUSSIE MAE: A woman like me wants somebody to bring it and put it in my hand. I don't need nobody wanna get something for nothing and leave me standing in my door.

LEVEE: That ain't Levee's style, sugar. I got more style than that. I knows how to treat a woman. Buy her presents and things . . . treat her like she want to be treated.

DUSSIE MAE: That's what they all say . . . till it come time to be buying the presents.

LEVEE: When we get down to Memphis, I'm gonna show you what I'm talking about. I'm gonna take you out and show you a good time. Show you Levee know how to treat a woman.

DUSSIE MAE (*crosses to left of bench*): When you getting your own band?

LEVEE (*follows Dussie Mae to bench*): Soon as Mr. Sturdyvant say. I done got my fellows already picked out. Getting me some good fellows know how to play real sweet music. (*Starts to put his arm around her waist.*)

DUSSIE MAE (*pushes his arm away and moves away*): Go on now, I don't go for all that pawing and stuff. When you get your own band, maybe we can see about this stuff you talking.

LEVEE (*crosses to left of bench*): I just want to show you I know what the women like. (*He crosses above the bench to Dussie Mae. She slowly backs away.*) They don't call me Sweet Lemonade for nothing. (*Levee pursues her.*)

DUSSIE MAE: Stop it now! Somebody's gonna come in here.

LEVEE (*catches her, puts his arms around her waist, and holds her tightly*): Naw, they ain't. Look here, sugar . . . what I wanna know is . . . can I introduce my red rooster to your brown hen?

DUSSIE MAE: You get your band, then we'll see if your rooster know how to crow.

LEVEE (*grins and pulls her in more tightly*): Damn, baby! Now I know why my grandpappy sat on the back porch with his straight razor when my grandma hung out the wash.

DUSSIE MAE: Nigger, you crazy!

LEVEE: I bet you sound like the midnight train from Alabama when it crosses the Mason Dixon line.

DUSSIE MAE: How'd you get so crazy?

LEVEE: It's women like you . . . drives me that way.

(*He pulls her tighter to him and kisses her. Dussie Mae jerks away. Levee grabs her wrist and stops her. He slowly sits on the bench, staring at her, then releases her wrist. She crosses hesitantly toward him. The bandroom dims as the studio lights come up. Dussie Mae kisses Levee and sinks onto his lap as Ma, in the studio, looks around and sighs.*)

MA RAINEY: It sure done got quiet in here. I never could stand no silence. I always got to have some music going on in my head somewhere. It keeps things balanced. Music will do that. It fills things up. The more music you got in the world, the fuller it is.

CUTLER: I can agree with that. I got to have my music, too.

MA RAINEY: White folks don't understand about the blues. They hear it come out but they don't know how it got there. They don't understand that's life's way of talking. You don't sing to feel better. You sing 'cause that's a way of understanding life.

CUTLER: That's right. You get that understanding and you done got a grip on life to where you can hold your head up and go on to see what else life got to offer.

MA RAINEY: The blues help you get out of bed in the morning. You get up knowing you ain't alone. (*Crosses left a step.*) There's something else in the world. Something's been added by that song. This be an empty world without the blues. I take that emptiness and try to fill it up with something.

TOLEDO (*rises and crosses to the folding chair*): You fill it up with something the people can't be without, Ma. That's why they call you the Mother of the Blues. (*Picks up Ma's purse and sits.*) You fill up that emptiness in a way ain't nobody ever thought of doing before. And now they can't be without it.

MA RAINEY: I ain't started the blues way of singing. The blues always been here.

CUTLER: In the church sometimes you find that way of singing. They got blues in the church.

MA RAINEY: They say I started it . . . but I didn't. I just helped it out. Filled up that empty space a little bit. That's all. But if they wanna call me the Mother of the Blues, that's alright with me. It don't hurt none.

(*Slow Drag enters down the front hall and bursts through the double door, followed by Sylvester. Slow Drag, shivering, carries a paper bag. Sylvester, his collar turned up and his hat on his head, still carries Ma's bag.*)

It sure took you long enough. That store ain't but on the corner.

SLOW DRAG (*crosses to Ma and kneels; takes a Coke and a bottle opener out of the paper bag, opens the bottle, and hands it to Ma*): That one was closed. We had to find another one.

(*He drops the opener and the bottle cap in the bag and shoves the bag under Cutler's chair, rises, and exits into the back hall. Ma takes a long drink of the Coke.*)

MA RAINEY (*over her shoulder, to Sylvester*): Sylvester, go and find Mr. Irvin and tell him we ready to go.

(*Sylvester exits up the front hall. The studio dims slightly as the bandroom lights fade up. Slow Drag opens the bandroom door, surprising Levee and Dussie Mae. She springs off Levee's lap and turns to Slow Drag.*)

SLOW DRAG: Cold out. (*Dussie Mae relaxes and crosses to the piano.*) I just wanted to warm up with a little sip. (*He crosses to the open locker, takes out the bourbon bottle, opens it, and drinks. Levee stares hungrily at Dussie Mae.*) Ma got her Coke, Levee. We about ready to start. (*Slow Drag crosses to the bandroom door, pushes it wide open, looks back into the room for a moment, and exits into the back hall. Levee, still staring at Dussie Mae, rises and starts toward her.*)

DUSSIE MAE (*picks up her purse*): No . . . Come on! I got to go. You gonna get me in trouble.

(*She exits swiftly into the back hall. Levee starts to follow her, stops in the doorway, and stares after her. Slow Drag enters the studio, crosses to the piano, and takes down his bass.*)

LEVEE (*crosses to the piano and picks up his cornet*): Good God! Happy Birthday to the lady with the cakes.

(*The bandroom dims as the studio lights fade up. Levee exits into the back hall. Sturdyvant enters down the front hall into the studio, closely followed by Irvin and Sylvester. Irvin and Sturdyvant cross to the spiral staircase and climb up to the control booth. Sylvester stands just inside the double door. Dussie Mae enters the studio, then crosses to Ma. She kisses Ma lightly on the cheek, crosses to stool, and sits.*)

IRVIN (*into the booth mic*): We're all set up here, Ma. We're all set to go. You ready down there?

MA RAINEY (*rises and turns to Sylvester, who puts his hat and bag on the cane chair and crosses to his mic*): Sylvester, you just remember your part and you say it. That's all there is to it. (*Sylvester looks anxiously at the mic and pulls at his tie as Ma crosses calmly over to the platform and speaks into her mic.*) Yeah, we ready.

(*Levee enters and crosses hurriedly to Slow Drag. Ma glares at Levee. He glances at Dussie Mae.*)

IRVIN (*flips a switch and the red "recording" light comes on over the double door; into the booth mic*): Okay, boys. "Ma Rainey's Black Bottom." Take one.

CUTLER: A-one. A-two. You know what to do.

(*Toledo plays a brief piano introduction, then the band plays "Ma Rainey's Black Bottom."*)

SYLVESTER (*lurches toward the mic and pulls at his tie*): Alright boys, you d-d-done seen . . . (*The band quickly drops out.*)

IRVIN (*shouts into the booth mic*): Hold it! (*Sturdyvant takes a disc off the recording machine and replaces it with a new disc. He nods at Irvin. Into the booth mic:*) Take two.

CUTLER: A-one. A-two. You know what to do.

(*Toledo plays the introduction, then the band plays "Ma Rainey's Black Bottom."*)

SYLVESTER (*lurches again toward the mic and pulls at his tie*): Alright boys, you done seen the rest . . . now I'm gonna show you the best. Ma Rainey's g-g-g-gonna . . . (*rushing*) . . . show you her black bottom!

IRVIN (*into the booth mic*): Hold it! Hold it! (*The band drops out reluctantly. Sturdyvant takes the disc off the recording machine and replaces it with another one. Irvin sighs. Into the booth mic:*) Take three. Ma . . . let's do it without the intro, huh? No voice intro . . . just come in singing.

MA RAINEY: Irvin, I done told you . . . the boy's gonna do the part. He don't stutter all the time . . . just give him a chance. (*Crosses to Sylvester and takes his tie out of his hands.*) Sylvester . . . hold your hands like I told you and just relax. Just relax and concentrate. (*Crosses back to the platform and nods at Irvin. Sylvester assumes the opera singer's posture.*)

IRVIN (*into the booth mic*): Alright. Take three.

CUTLER: A-one. A-two. You know what to do.

(*Toledo plays the introduction, then the band plays "Ma Rainey's Black Bottom." Sylvester stands stiffly in front of his mic. Irvin and Sturdyvant cross their fingers.*)

SYLVESTER: Alright boys, you done seen the rest . . . now, I'm gonna show you the best. Ma Rainey's gonna show you her black bottom.

(*Sylvester looks at Ma, amazed. Irvin and Sturdyvant cheer silently in the control booth. Ma smiles broadly, then steps up to her mic.*)

MA RAINEY (*singing*):

> WAY DOWN SOUTH IN ALABAMY
> I GOT A FRIEND THEY CALL DANCING SAMMY
> WHO'S CRAZY ABOUT ALL THE LATEST DANCES
> BLACK BOTTOM STOMPING, TWO BABIES PRANCING
>
> THE OTHER NIGHT AT A SWELL AFFAIR
> AS SOON AS THE BOYS FOUND OUT THAT I WAS THERE
> THEY SAID, COME ON MA, LET'S GO TO THE CABARET
> WHEN I GOT THERE YOU OUGHT TO HEAR THEM SAY
>
> I WANT TO SEE THE DANCE YOU CALL THE BLACK BOTTOM
> I WANT TO LEARN THAT DANCE
> I WANT TO SEE THE DANCE YOU CALL YOUR BIG BLACK BOTTOM
> IT'LL PUT YOU IN A TRANCE
>
> ALL THE BOYS IN THE NEIGHBORHOOD
> THEY SAY YOU BLACK BOTTOM IS REALLY GOOD
> COME ON AND SHOW ME YOUR BLACK BOTTOM
> I WANT TO LEARN THAT DANCE
>
> I WANT TO SEE THE DANCE YOU CALL THE BLACK BOTTOM
> I WANT TO LEARN THAT DANCE
> COME ON AND SHOW THE DANCE YOU CALL YOUR BIG BLACK
>   BOTTOM
> IT PUTS YOU IN A TRANCE
>
> EARLY LAST MORNING ABOUT THE BREAK OF DAY
> GRANDPA TOLD MY GRANDMA, I HEARD HIM SAY
> GET UP AND SHOW YOUR OLD MAN YOUR BLACK BOTTOM
> I WANT TO LEARN THAT DANCE

(*Ma slaps her hips as the band plays a short instrumental break.*)

> I DONE SHOWED Y'ALL MY BLACK BOTTOM
> YOU OUGHT TO LEARN THAT DANCE.

(*Everyone is silent for a moment. Sturdyvant lifts the needle from the recording disc.*)

IRVIN (*into the booth mic*): Okay, that's good, Ma. That sounded great. Good job, boys.

(*He flips the recording light switch off, opens the control booth door, and climbs down the spiral staircase. Everyone bursts into congratulations and cheers.*)

MA RAINEY (*crosses to Cutler*): See! I told you. I knew you could do it. (*Turns to Sylvester.*) You just have to put your mind to it. Didn't he do good, Cutler? Sound real good. I told him he could do it. (*Crosses to Sylvester.*)

CUTLER: He sure did. He did better than I thought he was gonna do. (*Sylvester smiles broadly.*)

IRVIN (*picks up Sylvester's mic, moves it a few feet, and starts toward the spiral staircase as Ma smiles happily and crosses back to her mic*): Okay, boys . . . Ma . . . let's do "Moonshine Blues" next, huh? "Moonshine Blues," boys.

STURDYVANT (*into the booth mic*): Irv! Something's wrong down there. We don't have it right.

IRVIN (*crosses to Ma and speaks into her mic*): What? What's the matter? Mel . . .

STURDYVANT (*shouts into the booth mic*): We don't have it right. Something happened. We don't have the goddamn song recorded!

IRVIN (*patiently*): What's the matter? Mel, what happened? You sure you don't have nothing?

STURDYVANT (*into the booth mic*): Check that mic, huh, Irv. (*Irvin reaches for Ma's mic. Sharply, into the booth mic:*) No. It's the kid's mic. Something's wrong with the mic. We've got everything all screwed up here.

IRVIN (*throws up his hands*): Christ almighty! (*Turns to Ma; quietly:*) Ma . . . we got to do it again. We don't have it. We didn't record the song. (*Crosses to Sylvester's mic and traces the mic cable to the jack box.*)

MA RAINEY: What you mean you didn't record it? What was you and Sturdyvant doing up there?

IRVIN (*holds up the jack*): Here . . . Levee must have kicked the plug out. (*Coils the cable.*)

LEVEE: I ain't done nothing! I ain't kicked nothing!

SLOW DRAG: If Levee had his mind on what he's doing . . .

MA RAINEY: Levee, if it ain't one thing it's another. You better straighten yourself up!

LEVEE (*crosses toward Ma a step*): Hell . . . it ain't my fault. I ain't done nothing!

STURDYVANT (*into the booth mic*): What's the matter with that mic? Irv? What's the problem?

IRVIN (*waves the jack at the control booth*): It's the cord, Mel. The cord's all chewed up. We need another cord. (*Picks up the mic, and exits into the closet.*)

MA RAINEY (*explodes*): This is the most disorganized . . . Irvin, I'm going home! Come on, Dussie.

(*She crosses through the double door into the front hall, gets her coat and Dussie Mae's coat. Sturdyvant leaves the control booth and rushes down the staircase. Irvin enters.*)

STURDYVANT (*crosses to Irvin; furiously*): Where's she going?

IRVIN (*smiles faintly*): She said she's going home.

STURDYVANT: Irvin . . . you get her! If she walks out of here . . .

MA RAINEY (*comes through the double door, drops Dussie Mae's coat onto her lap, then starts to put on her own coat*): Come on, Sylvester.

IRVIN: Ma . . . Ma . . . listen. (*Crosses to Ma and helps her with her coat.*) Fifteen minutes. All I ask is fifteen minutes!

MA RAINEY: Come on, Sylvester . . . get your coat.

STURDYVANT (*threateningly*): Ma . . . if you walk out of this studio . . .

IRVIN: Fifteen minutes, Ma!

STURDYVANT: You'll be through . . . washed up! If you walk out on me . . .

IRVIN (*turns to Sturdyvant, loudly*): Mel, for Chrissakes, shut up and let me handle it! (*Turns to Ma; calmly:*) Ma, listen. These records are gonna be hits! They're gonna sell like crazy! Hell, even Sylvester will be a star. Fifteen minutes. That's all I'm asking! Fifteen minutes.

MA RAINEY (*looks at Irvin, then at Sturdyvant; sternly*): Fifteen minutes! You hear me, Irvin? Fifteen minutes . . . and then I'm gonna take my black bottom on back down to Georgia. Fifteen minutes. Then Madame Rainey is leaving!

IRVIN (*kisses Ma on the cheek; she stares at him in astonishment; jubilantly*): Alright, Ma . . . fifteen minutes. I promise. (*Turns to the band.*) You boys go ahead and take a break. Fifteen minutes and we'll be ready to go.

(*He exits up the front hall, followed by Sturdyvant. Toledo exits into the back hall, followed by Levee. Ma takes off her coat, hands it to Dussie Mae, crosses to Sylvester, and takes a large feather fan from his bag. She crosses to a folding chair and sits. Slow Drag puts his bass on top of the piano.*)

CUTLER (*leans his trombone on the piano*): Slow Drag, you got any of that bourbon left?

SLOW DRAG: Yeah, there's some down there.

(*Cutler exits into the back hall, followed by Slow Drag. The studio dims and the bandroom lights fade up. Dussie Mae crosses into the front hall and hangs up the coats. Sylvester crosses to the piano stool and sits. Ma gently fans herself. Toledo opens the bandroom door, crosses to the piano chair, and sits. Levee enters the bandroom, crosses to bench, and stretches out on his back with his cornet resting on his chest. Dussie Mae crosses back into the studio and sits on a stool. Cutler enters the bandroom, followed by Slow Drag. Cutler crosses to Slow Drag's locker and takes out the bourbon bottle.*)

CUTLER: I could use a little nip. (*Opens the bottle, takes a drink, closes it, and returns it to the locker.*)

SLOW DRAG (*sits*): Don't make me no difference if she leave or not. I was kinda hoping she would leave.

CUTLER (*sits*): I'm like Mr. Irvin . . . after all this time we done put in here, it's best to go ahead and get something out of it.

TOLEDO: Ma gonna do what she want to do, that's for sure. If I was Mr. Irvin, I'd best go on and get them cords and things hooked up right. And I wouldn't take no longer than fifteen minutes doing it.

CUTLER (*reprovingly*): If Levee had his mind on his work we wouldn't be in this fix. We'd be up there finishing up. Now we got to go back and see if that boy get that part right. Ain't no telling if he ever get that right again in his life.

LEVEE: Hey, Levee ain't done nothing!

SLOW DRAG: Levee up there got one eye on the gal and the other on his trumpet.

CUTLER (*rises and crosses to Levee*): Nigger, don't you know that's Ma's gal?

LEVEE: I don't care whose gal it is. I ain't done nothing to her. I just talk to her like I talk to anybody else.

CUTLER (*crosses to above Levee*): Well, that being Ma's gal and that being that boy's gal is one and two different things. The boy is liable to kill you, but your ass gonna be out here scraping the concrete looking for a job if you messing with Ma's gal.

LEVEE: How am I messing with her? I ain't done nothing to the gal. I just asked her her name. Now, if you telling me I can't do that . . . then Ma will just have to go to hell.

CUTLER: All I can do is warn you.

SLOW DRAG: Let him hang himself, Cutler. Let him string his neck out.

LEVEE: I ain't done nothing to the gal! You all talk like I done went and done something to her. Leave me go with my business.

CUTLER (*crosses to right of Levee*): I'm through with it. Try and talk to a fool . . . (*Crosses back to chair and sits.*)

TOLEDO (*turns to Slow Drag*): Some mens got it worse than others . . . this foolishness I'm talking about. Some mens is excited to be fools. That excitement is something else. I knows about it. I done experienced it. It makes you feel good to be a fool. But it don't last long. It's over in a minute. Then you got to tend with the consequences. You got to tend with what comes after. That's when you wish you had learned something about it.

LEVEE (*cranes his neck and grins at Toledo*): That's the best sense you made all day. Talking about being a fool. That's the only sensible thing you said today. Admitting you was a fool.

TOLEDO: I admit it, alright. Ain't nothing wrong with it. I done been a little bit of everything.

LEVEE: Now you're talking. You as big a fool as they make.

TOLEDO: Gonna be a bit more things before I'm finished with it. Gonna be foolish again. But I ain't never been the same fool twice. I might be a different kind of fool, but I ain't gonna be the same fool twice. That's where we part ways.

SLOW DRAG: Toledo, you done been a fool about a woman?

TOLEDO: Sure. Sure I have. Same as everybody.

SLOW DRAG: Hell, I ain't never seen you mess with no woman. I thought them books was your woman.

TOLEDO: Sure I messed with them. Done messed with a whole heap of them. And gonna mess with some more. But I ain't gonna be no fool about them. What you think? I done come in the world full-grown with my head in a book? I done been young. Married. Got kids. I done been around and I done loved women to where you shake in your shoes just at the sight of them. Feel it all up and down you spine.

SLOW DRAG: I didn't know you was married.

TOLEDO: Sure. Legally. I been married legally. Got the papers and all. I done been through life. Made my marks. Followed some signs on the road. Ignored some others. I done been all through it. I touched and been touched by it. But I ain't never been the same fool twice. That's what I can say.

LEVEE: But you been a fool. That's what counts. Talking about I'm a fool for asking the gal her name and here you is one yourself.

TOLEDO: Now, I married a woman. A good woman. To this day I can't say she wasn't a good woman. I can't say nothing bad about her. I married that woman with all the good graces and intentions of being hooked up and bound to her for the rest of my life. I was looking for her to put me in my grave.

But you see . . . it ain't all the time what your intentions and wishes are. She went out and joined the church. Alright. There ain't nothing wrong with that. A good Christian woman going to church and wanna do right by her God. There ain't nothing wrong with that. But she got up there, got to seeing them good Christian mens and wondering why I ain't like that. Soon she figure she got a heathen on her hands. She figured she couldn't live like that. The church was more important than I was. So she left. Packed up one day and moved out. To this day I ain't never said another word to her. Come home one day and my house was empty! And I sat down and figured out that I was a fool not to see that she needed something that I wasn't giving her. Else she wouldn't have been up there at the church in the first place. I ain't blaming her. I just said it wasn't gonna happen to me again. So yeah, Toledo been a fool about a woman. That's part of making life.

CUTLER: Well, yeah, I been a fool, too. (*Levee sits up and chuckles. He takes a rag out of his case and polishes his cornet.*) Everybody done been a fool once or twice. But you see, Toledo, what you call a fool, and what I call a fool, is two different things. I can't see where you was being a fool for that. You ain't done nothing foolish. You can't help what happened, and I wouldn't call you a fool for it. (*Levee holds the cornet up and looks into the bell.*) A fool is responsible for what happens to him. A fool cause it to happen. Like Levee . . . (*Levee looks away from the cornet and scowls at Cutler.*) . . . If he keep messing with Ma's gal and his feet be out there scraping the ground. That's a fool.

LEVEE: Ain't nothing gonna happen to Levee. Levee ain't gonna let nothing happen to him. Now, I'm gonna say it again. I asked the gal her name. That's all I done. And if that's being a fool . . . then you are looking at the biggest fool in the world . . . cause I sure as hell asked her.

SLOW DRAG: You just better not let Ma see you ask her. That's what the man's trying to tell you.

LEVEE: I don't need nobody to tell me nothing.

CUTLER: Well, Toledo, all I gots to say is that from the looks of it, from your story . . . I don't think life did you fair.

TOLEDO: Oh, life is fair. It's just in the taking what it gives you.

LEVEE: Life ain't shit. You can put it in a paper bag and carry it around with you. It ain't got no balls. Now, death . . . death got some style! Death will kick your ass and make you wish you never been born! That's how bad death is!

But you can rule over life. Life ain't nothing. (*Slow Drag looks right and puts his feet on bench.*)

TOLEDO (*turns to Cutler*): Cutler, how's your brother doing?

CUTLER: Who, Nevada? Oh, he's doing alright. Staying in St. Louis. Got a bunch of kids last I heard.

TOLEDO: Me and him was alright with each other. Done a lot of farming together down in Plattsville.

CUTLER: Yeah, I know you all was tight. He in St. Louis now. Running an elevator last I hear about it.

SLOW DRAG (*turns to Cutler*): That's better than stepping in muleshit.

TOLEDO: Oh, I don't know now. I liked farming. Get out there in the sun . . . smell that dirt. Be out there by yourself . . . nice and peaceful. Yeah, farming was alright by me. Sometimes I think I'd like to get me a little old place . . . but I done got too old to be following behind one of them balky mules now.

LEVEE: Nigger talking about life is fair. And ain't got a pot to piss in.

TOLEDO: See, now, I'm gonna tell you something. A nigger gonna be dissatisfied no matter what. Give a nigger some bread and butter . . . and he'll cry cause he ain't got no jelly. Give him some jelly and he'll cry cause he ain't got no knife to put it on with. If there's one thing I done learned in this life . . . it's that you can't satisfy a nigger no matter what you do. A nigger's gonna make his own dissatisfaction.

LEVEE: Niggers got a right to be dissatisfied. Is you gonna be satisfied with a bone somebody done throwed you when you see them eating the whole hog?

TOLEDO: You lucky they let you be an entertainer. They ain't got to accept your way of entertaining. You lucky and don't even know it. You's entertaining and the rest of the people is hauling wood. That's the only kind of job for the colored man.

SLOW DRAG: Ain't nothing wrong with hauling wood. I done hauled plenty wood. My daddy used to haul wood. Ain't nothing wrong with that. That's honest work.

LEVEE (*puts his cornet in the case under the bench*): That ain't what I'm talking about. I ain't talking about hauling no wood. I'm talking about being satisfied with a bone somebody done throwed you. That's what's the matter with you all. You satisfied . . . sitting in one place. You got to move on down the road from where you sitting . . . and all the time you got to keep an eye out for the devil who's looking to buy up souls. And hope you get lucky and find him!

CUTLER: I done told about that blasphemy. Talking about selling your soul to the devil.

TOLEDO: We done the same thing, Cutler. There ain't no difference. We done sold Africa for the price of tomatoes. We done sold ourselves to the white man in order to be like him. Look at the way you dressed . . . that ain't African. That's the white man. We trying to be just like him. We done sold who we are in order to become someone else. We's imitation white men.

CUTLER: What else we gonna be living over here?

LEVEE: I'm Levee. Just me. I ain't no imitation nothing!

SLOW DRAG: You can't change who you are by how you dress. That's what I got to say.

TOLEDO: It ain't how you dress. It's how you act, how you see the world. It's how you follow life.

LEVEE: It don't matter what you talking about. I ain't no imitation white man. And I don't want to be no white man. (*Rises; arrogantly:*) As soon as I got my band together and make them records like Mr. Sturdyvant done told me I can make, I'm gonna be like Ma and tell the white man just what he can do. Ma tell Mr. Irvin she leavin' . . . and Mr. Irvin get down on his knees and beg her to stay! That's the way I'm gonna be! Make the white man respect me! (*Sits on bench.*)

CUTLER: The white man don't care nothing about Ma. The colored folks made Ma a star. White folks don't care nothing about who she is . . . what kind of music she make.

SLOW DRAG: That's the truth about that. You let her go down to one of them white folks' hotels and see how big she is.

CUTLER: Hell, she ain't got to do that. She can't even get a cab up here in the North. I'm gonna tell you something. (*Rises and crosses to Levee.*) Reverend Gates . . . you know Reverend Gates? Slow Drag know who I'm talking about. Reverend Gates . . . now, I'm gonna show you how this go where the white man don't care a thing about who you is. Reverend Gates was coming from Tallahassee to Atlanta, going to see his sister who was sick at that time with the consumption. The train come up through Thomasville, then past Moultrie, and stopped in this little town called Sigsbee . . .

LEVEE (*emphatically*): You can stop telling that right there! That train don't stop in Sigsbee. I know what train you talking about. That train got four stops before it reach Macon to go on to Atlanta. One in Thomasville, one in Moultrie, one in Cordele . . . and it stop in Centerville.

CUTLER: Nigger, I know what I'm talking about. You gonna tell me where the train stop?

LEVEE: Hell, yeah, if you talking about it stop in Sigsbee. I'm gonna tell you the truth.

CUTLER (*increasingly agitated*): I'm talking about this train! I don't know what train you been riding. I'm talking about this train!

LEVEE: Ain't but one train. Ain't but one train come out of Tallahassee heading north to Atlanta and it don't stop at Sigsbee. Tell him, Toledo . . . that train don't stop at Sigsbee. The only train that stops at Sigsbee is the Santa Fe, and you have to transfer at Moultrie to get it!

CUTLER: Well, hell, maybe that's what he done! I don't know! I'm just telling you the man got off the train at Sigsbee!

LEVEE: Alright . . . you telling it. Tell it your way. Just make up anything.

SLOW DRAG (*rises, crosses to chair, and sits*): Levee, leave the man alone and let him finish.

CUTLER: I ain't paying Levee no never mind.

LEVEE: Go on, tell it your way.

CUTLER: Anyway . . . Reverend Gates got off this train in Sigsbee. (*Glances testily at Levee, then crosses to Toledo.*) The train done stopped there and he figured he'd get off and check the schedule to be sure he arrive in time for somebody to pick him up. Alright. While he's there checking the schedule, it come upon him that he had to go to the bathroom. Now, they ain't had no colored restrooms at the station. The only colored restroom is an outhouse they got sitting way back two hundred yards or so from the station. Alright. He in the outhouse and the train go off and leave him there. He don't know nothing about this town. Ain't never been there before—in fact, ain't never even heard of it before.

LEVEE (*jumps up, impatiently*): I heard of it! I know just where it's at . . . and he ain't got off no train coming out of Tallahassee in Sigsbee! (*Crosses to chair and sits.*)

CUTLER: The man standing there trying to figure out what he's gonna do . . . where this train done left him in this strange town. It started getting dark. He see where the sun's getting low in the sky, and he's trying to figure out what he's gonna do, when he noticed a couple of white fellows standing across the street from this station. Just standing there watching him. And then two or three more come up and joined the other ones. He look around, ain't seen no colored folks nowhere. He didn't know what was gettin in these here fellows minds, so he started walkin. (*Walks in place.*) He ain't knowed where he was going. He just walking down the railroad tracks when he hear them call him, "Hey, nigger!" See, just like that, "Hey, nigger!" He kept on walking. They call him some more and he just keep walking. Just going on down the tracks. And then he heard a gunshot where somebody done fired a gun in the air. (*Makes a loud explosive noise.*) He stopped then, you know.

TOLEDO: You don't even have to tell me no more. I know the facts of it. I done heard the same story a hundred times. It happened to me, too. Same thing.

CUTLER: Naw, I'm gonna show you how the white folks don't care nothing about who or what you is. They crowded around him. These gang of mens made a circle around him. Now, he's standing there, you understand . . . got his cross around his neck like them preachers wear. Had his little Bible with him what he carry all the time. So they crowd on around him and one of them ask who he is. He told them he was Reverend Gates and that he was going to see his sister who was sick and the train left without him. And they said, "Yeah, nigger . . . but can you dance?" He looked at them and commenced to dancing. (*Hesitates a moment, then does a slow shuffle.*) One of them reached up and tore his cross off his neck. Said he was committing a heresy by dancing with a cross and Bible. Took his Bible and tore it up and had him dancing till they got tired of watching him.

SLOW DRAG: White folks ain't never had no respect for the colored minister.

CUTLER: That's the only way he got out of there alive . . . was to dance. Ain't even had no respect for a man of God! Wanna make him into a clown. Reverend Gates sat right in my house and told me that story from his own mouth. (*Crosses to Levee; emphatically:*) So . . . the white folks don't care nothing about Ma Rainey. She's just another nigger who they can use to make some money. (*Glares at Levee a moment, then crosses to bench and sits.*)

LEVEE: What I wants to know is . . . if he's a man of God . . . then where the hell was God when all of this was going on? Why wasn't God looking out for him? Why didn't God strike down them crackers with some of this lightning you talking about to me?

CUTLER: Levee, you gonna burn in hell.

LEVEE: What I care about burning in hell? You talking like a fool . . . burning in hell. Why didn't God strike some of them crackers down? Tell me that! That's the question! Don't come telling me this burning in hell shit! He a man of God . . . why didn't God strike some of them crackers down? I'll tell you why! I'll tell you the truth! It's sitting out there as plain as day! 'Cause he a white man's God. That's why! God ain't never listened to no nigger's prayers. (*Rises and crosses to Cutler.*) God take a nigger's prayers and throw them in the garbage. God don't pay niggers no mind. In fact, God hate niggers! Hate them with all the fury in his heart. Jesus don't love you. Jesus hate your black ass! (*Turns and crosses back to bench.*) Come talking that shit to me. Talking about burning in hell! (*Turns to Cutler; tauntingly:*) God can kiss my ass.

CUTLER (*leaps toward Levee and punches him on the jaw; Levee reels backwards and falls*): You worthless . . . that's my God! That's my God! That's my God! You wanna blaspheme my God!

(*Cutler starts toward Levee as Levee sprawls on the floor. Toledo and Slow Drag grab Cutler and hold him back.*)

SLOW DRAG: Come on, Cutler . . . let it go! It don't mean nothing!

CUTLER: Wanna blaspheme my God! You worthless . . . talking about my God!

LEVEE (*scrambles to his feet, reaches into his pocket, pulls out a large pocketknife, opens it, and flashes it at Cutler*): Naw, let him go! Let him go! (*Toledo and Slow Drag release Cutler and step away.*) That's your God, huh? That's your God, huh? Is that right? Your God, huh? Alright. (*Levee waves the knife at Cutler.*) I'm gonna give your God a chance. I'm gonna give your God a chance. I'm gonna give him a chance to save your black ass. (*Levee chases Cutler. Slow Drag picks up chair and crosses to behind the piano.*)

TOLEDO: Come on, Levee . . . put that knife up!

LEVEE (*swings the knife towards Toledo, who steps quickly away*): Stay out of this, Toledo!

TOLEDO: That ain't no way to solve nothing.

LEVEE (*turns to Cutler as Cutler crosses to the piano and picks up the piano chair*): I'm calling Cutler's God! I'm talking to Cutler's God! You hear me? Cutler's God! I'm calling Cutler's God. Come on and save this nigger! (*Levee crosses toward Cutler and swings the knife as Cutler holds the chair out defensively and backs away.*) Strike me down before I cut his throat! (*Levee chases Cutler.*)

SLOW DRAG: Watch him, Cutler! Put that knife up, Levee!

LEVEE (*follows Cutler as Cutler backs down toward the piano*): I'm calling your God! I'm gonna give him a chance to save you! I'm calling your God! We gonna find out whose God he is!

CUTLER (*backs into the corner and holds the chair out toward Levee*): You gonna burn in hell, nigger!

LEVEE (*looks upward*): Cutler's God! Come on and save this nigger! Come on and save him like you did my mama! Save him like you did my mama! I heard her when she called you! I heard her when she said, "Lord have mercy! Jesus help me! Please God have mercy on me, Lord! Jesus help me!" And did you turn your back? Did you turn your back, motherfucker? Did you turn your back? (*Stabs at the air above his head; frantically:*) Come on! Come on and turn your back on me! Turn your back on me! Come on! Where is you? Come on and turn your back on me! Turn your back on me, motherfucker! I'll cut your heart out! Come on, turn your back on me! Come on! What's the matter? Where is you? Come on and turn your back on me! Come on, what you scared of? Turn your back on me! Come on! Coward, motherfucker! (*Lowers the knife and looks around the room, closes the knife, slips it into his pants pocket and turns to Cutler, grins sardonically.*) Your God ain't shit, Cutler.

(*Both rooms plunge into darkness. Solo trumpet wails a long phrase, then the band plays "Hear Me Talking to You."*)

MA RAINEY (*singing*):
HEAR ME TALKING TO YOU,
I DON'T BITE MY TONGUE.

(*Studio lights come up brightly. The recording light is on. Ma, standing on the platform with a bottle of Coke in one hand and the feather fan in the other, sings into her mic. Toledo is sitting on the piano stool, playing the studio piano. Cutler is playing the guitar. Slow Drag is playing the bass. Levee is playing the cornet. Dussie Mae and Sylvester are sitting on stools. Sturdyvant and Irvin watch from the control booth. Sylvester's mic is in the corner. Ma waves the feather fan.*)

YOU WANT TO BE MY MAN,
YOU GOT TO FETCH IT WITH YOU WHEN YOU COME.

(*The song ends. Everyone is silent as Sturdyvant lifts the recording needle.*)

IRVIN (*enthusiastically*): Good! Wonderful! We have that, boys. Good session. That's great, Ma. We've got ourselves some winners.

(*He flips the recording light switch off. Cutler turns to the guitar case, opens it, puts the guitar in it, and closes the case.*)

TOLEDO (*relieved*): Well, I'm glad that's over.

MA RAINEY (*crosses to Toledo*): Slow Drag, where you learn to play the bass at? You had it singing! I heard you! Had that bass jumping all over the place.

SLOW DRAG (*steps toward Ma*): I was following Toledo. Nigger got them long fingers . . . striding all over the piano. I was trying to keep up with him.

TOLEDO: That's what you supposed to do, ain't it? Play the music. Ain't nothing abstract about it.

MA RAINEY (*turns to Cutler*): Cutler, you hear Slow Drag on that bass? He make it do what he want it to do! Spank it just like you spank a baby.

CUTLER: Don't be telling him that. Nigger's head get so big his hat won't fit him.

SLOW DRAG: If Cutler tune that guitar up . . . we would really have something!

CUTLER: You wouldn't know what a tuned-up guitar sounded like if you heard one.

TOLEDO: Cutler was talking. I heard him moaning. He was all up in it. (*Levee looks expectantly at Ma.*)

MA RAINEY: Levee . . . what is that you was doing? (*Levee steps toward Ma.*) Why you playing all them notes? You play ten notes for every one you supposed to play. It don't call for that.

LEVEE: You supposed to improvise on the theme. That's what I was doing.

MA RAINEY (*sternly*): You supposed to play the song the way I sing it. The way everybody else play it. You ain't supposed to go off by yourself and play what you want.

LEVEE: I was playing the song. I was playing it the way I felt it.

MA RAINEY: I couldn't keep up with what was going on. I'm trying to sing the song and you up there messing up my ear. That's what you was doing. Call yourself playing music.

LEVEE (*turns his back to Ma*): Hey . . . I know what I'm doing. I know what I'm doing, alright. I know how to play music. You all back up and leave me alone about my music.

CUTLER: I done told you . . . it ain't about your music. It's about Ma's music.

MA RAINEY: That's alright, Cutler. (*Crosses to folding chair and sits.*) I done told you what to do. (*Takes off her slippers.*)

LEVEE: I don't care what you do. You supposed to improvise on the theme. Not play note for note, the same thing over and over again. (*Cutler picks up Ma's shoes and hands them to her.*)

MA RAINEY (*putting on her shoes*): You just better watch yourself. You hear me?

LEVEE (*turns to Ma*): What I care what you or Cutler do? Come telling me to watch myself. What's that supposed to mean?

MA RAINEY (*warning*): Alright . . . you gonna find out what it means.

LEVEE (*insolently*): Go ahead and fire me. I don't care. I'm gonna get my own band anyway.

MA RAINEY: You keep messing with me.

LEVEE: Ain't nobody studying you. You ain't gonna do nothing to me. Ain't nobody gonna do nothing to Levee.

MA RAINEY (*sharply*): Alright, nigger . . . you fired!

LEVEE (*looks at Dussie Mae; she looks at the floor; he turns back to Ma*): You think I care about being fired? I don't care nothing about that. You doing me a favor.

MA RAINEY: Cutler, Levee's out! He don't play in my band no more!

LEVEE: I'm fired . . . good! Best thing that ever happened to me. (*Crosses to the door.*) I don't need this shit! (*Exits into the back hall. The bandroom lights fade up.*)

MA RAINEY (*picks up her purse, rises, and crosses to the double door*): Cutler, I'll see you back at the hotel.

(*She goes through the double door and gets her coat and Dussie Mae's coat. Levee opens the bandroom door, enters, and sits. Irvin and Sturdyvant leave the control booth. Irvin opens the drape and crosses down the spiral stairs, followed by Sturdyvant.*)

IRVIN (*crosses to the piano as Sturdyvant exits up the front hall*): Okay, boys . . . you can pack up. I'll get your money for you.

CUTLER (*crosses to Irvin*): That's cash money, Mr. Irvin. I don't want no check.

(*Toledo crosses into the back hall, followed by Slow Drag carrying his bass.*)

IRVIN: I'll see what I can do. I can't promise you nothing.

CUTLER (*doggedly*): As long as it ain't no check. I ain't got no use for a check.

IRVIN: I'll see what I can do, Cutler.

(*He turns away from Cutler as Ma comes through the double door. She drops Dussie Mae's coat onto her lap. Irvin crosses to Ma. Cutler picks up the guitar case and the trombone and exits into the back hall. Toledo opens the bandroom door and enters, followed by Slow Drag. Toledo crosses to the piano, sits, picks up his newspaper, and reads.*)

Slow Drag crosses to behind the piano, puts down his bass, then crosses to the lockers. Irvin helps Ma on with her coat.)

Oh, Ma, listen, I talked to Sturdyvant, and he said . . . now, I tried to talk him out of it . . . he said the best he can do is take twenty-five dollars of your money and give it to Sylvester.

MA RAINEY (*turns to Irvin, incredulous*): Take what and do what?

(Sylvester rises. Cutler enters the bandroom, puts his guitar case down, and sits.)

Irvin, you better go and talk to him! If I wanted the boy to have twenty-five dollars of my money, I'd give it to him! He supposed to get his own money. He's supposed to get paid like everybody else. And you go on up there and tell Sturdyvant he better pay the boy his own money.

IRVIN: Ma . . . I talked to him . . . he said . . .

MA RAINEY: Go talk to him again! Tell him if he don't pay that boy . . . he'll never make another record of mine again. Tell him that! You supposed to be my manager. Always talking about sticking together. Start sticking! Go on up there and get that boy his money!

IRVIN (*crosses to the double door*): Okay, Ma . . . I'll talk to him again. I'll see what I can do.

(He exits up the front hall. The studio dims slightly as the bandroom brightens.)

SLOW DRAG (*takes a deck of cards out of his pocket and crosses to Levee*): Come on, Levee, let me show you a card trick.

LEVEE: I don't want to see no card trick. What you wanna show me for? Why you wanna bother me with that?

SLOW DRAG: I was just trying to be nice.

LEVEE (*sulks*): I don't need you to be nice to me. What I need you to be nice to me for? I ain't gonna be nice to you. I ain't even gonna let you be in my band no more.

SLOW DRAG (*crosses to behind the piano*): Toledo . . . let me show you a card trick.

CUTLER: I just hope Mr. Irvin don't bring no check down here. What the hell I'm gonna do with a check?

SLOW DRAG (*fans the cards and holds them out toward Toledo*): Alright, now . . . pick a card. Any card . . . go on . . . take any of them. I'm gonna show you something.

TOLEDO (*takes a card from the deck*): I agrees with you, Cutler. I don't want no check either.

CUTLER: It don't make no sense to give a nigger a check.

SLOW DRAG: Okay, now. Remember your card. Remember which one you got. Now . . . put it back in the deck. Anywhere you want. I'm gonna show you something. (*Toledo glances at his card and slips it back into the deck.*) You remember your card? Alright. Now. I'm gonna shuffle the deck. (*Shuffles the deck a few times.*) Now . . . I'm gonna show you what card you picked. Don't say nothing, now. I'm gonna tell you what card you picked.

CUTLER: Slow Drag, that trick is as old as my mama.

SLOW DRAG (*turns to Cutler*): Naw . . . naw . . . wait a minute! I'm gonna show him his card. . . . (*Turns to Toledo, takes a card off the top of the deck, and holds it up, triumphantly.*) There it go! The six of diamonds. Ain't that your card? Ain't that it?

TOLEDO: Yeah, that's it . . . the six of diamonds.

SLOW DRAG: Told you! Told you I'd show him what it was!

(*He slips the card back into the deck, looks proudly around the room as Toledo returns to his newspaper and Levee and Cutler stare at the floor. Slow Drag turns dejectedly to the locker and puts the cards in his coat pocket.*)

STURDYVANT (*enters down the front hall, followed by Irvin, carrying a pen and two forms*): Ma, is there something wrong? Is there a problem?

MA RAINEY: Sturdyvant, I want you to pay that boy his money.

(*Slow Drag crosses to behind the bandroom piano and puts the cover on the bass.*)

STURDYVANT: Sure, Ma. I got it right here. (*Takes a large roll of money from his pants pocket, counts several bills into Irvin's hand, and puts the rest of the roll in his pocket.*) Two hundred for you and twenty-five for the kid, right? (*Turns to Ma.*) Irvin misunderstood me. It was all a mistake. Irv made a mistake.

MA RAINEY: A mistake, huh?

IRVIN (*crosses to Sylvester and hands him twenty-five dollars*): Sure, Ma. I made a mistake. He's paid, right? I straightened it out.

(*He crosses to Ma and hands her two hundred dollars. Sylvester stares at the money in his hands, then puts it in his pocket.*)

MA RAINEY: The only mistake was when you found out I hadn't signed the release forms. That was the mistake! Come on, Dussie Mae. (*Rises, puts the money in her purse, and crosses to the double door.*)

STURDYVANT: Hey, Ma . . . come on, sign the forms, huh?

IRVIN: Ma . . . come on now.

MA RAINEY: Get your coat, Sylvester. (*Turns to Irvin.*) Irvin, where's my car?

(*Sylvester rises, picks up Ma's slippers, puts them in the bag, crosses through the double door, and gets his coat. Dussie Mae rises and puts on her coat.*)

IRVIN: It's right out front, Ma. Here . . . I got the keys right here. (*Takes the keys out of his pocket, crosses to Ma, and holds out the forms.*) Come on, sign the forms, huh?

(*Sylvester puts on his coat.*)

MA RAINEY: Irvin, give me my car keys!

IRVIN (*hands the keys to Ma*): Sure, Ma . . . just sign the forms, huh?

MA RAINEY: Send them to my address and I'll get around to them. (*Turns to the double door.*)

IRVIN: Come on, Ma . . . I took care of everything, right? I straightened everything out.

MA RAINEY (*turns back to Irvin*): Give me the pen, Irvin. (*Signs the papers in Irvin's hand, gives Irvin the pen.*) You tell Sturdyvant . . . one more mistake like that and I can make my records someplace else. (*Turns toward the double door and sees Sylvester in the doorway.*) Sylvester, straighten up your clothes. (*Sharply:*) Come on, Dussie!

(*She crosses through the open double door and exits up the front hall, followed reluctantly by Dussie Mae. Sylvester plants his hat firmly on his head, nods at the men, and follows Dussie Mae. The door swings shut as Irvin turns to Sturdyvant. He taps the forms irritatedly and shoves the papers and the pen into Sturdyvant's hand. Irvin crosses through the double door into the front hall. He takes his hat and coat off the wall hooks and puts them on. Sturdyvant crosses to the piano, places the forms on the piano stool, and signs them. Slow Drag crosses to the open locker.*)

CUTLER (*picks up the trombone case, puts it on the bench, and opens it*): I know what's keeping him so long. He up there writing out checks. You watch. I ain't gonna stand for it. He ain't gonna bring me no check down here. If he do, he's gonna take it right back upstairs and get some cash. (*Disassembles the trombone and puts it in the case.*)

TOLEDO: Don't get yourself all worked up about it. Wait and see. Think positive.

CUTLER: I am thinking positive. He positively gonna give me some cash. Man give me a check last time . . . you remember . . . we went all over Chicago trying to get it cashed. See a nigger with a check, the first thing they think is he done stole it someplace.

LEVEE: I ain't had no trouble cashing mine.

CUTLER: I don't visit no whorehouses.

(*Irvin comes into the studio and exits into the back hall. Sturdyvant follows after. The studio slowly dims.*)

LEVEE (*rises and steps threateningly toward Cutler*): You don't know about my business. So don't start nothing. I'm tired of you as it is. I ain't but two seconds off your ass noway.

TOLEDO: Don't you all start nothing now.

CUTLER: What the hell I care what you tired of. I wasn't even talking to you. I was talking to this man right here.

(*Irvin opens the bandroom door and crosses to behind the piano. Sturdyvant enters and crosses to right of Toledo.*)

IRVIN: Okay, boys. Mr. Sturdyvant has your pay.

CUTLER: As long as it's cash money, Mr. Sturdyvant. 'Cause I have too much trouble trying to cash a check.

STURDYVANT: Oh, yes . . . I'm aware of that. Mr. Irvin told me you boys prefer cash, and that's what I have for you. (*Takes the roll of money out of his pocket and crosses to Cutler.*) That was a good session you boys put in . . . that's twenty-five for you. (*Counts out twenty-five dollars and hands it to Cutler; he puts it in his pocket.*) Yessir, you boys really know your business and we are going to . . . twenty-five for you . . . (*Turns to Slow Drag, counts out twenty-five dollars, and hands it to him. Slow Drag puts it in his pocket and crosses to the open locker.*) We are going to get you back in here real soon . . . twenty-five . . . (*Turns to Levee, counts out twenty-five dollars, and hands it to him. Levee stuffs the money into his pants pocket. Slow Drag takes his coat out of the locker and puts it on.*) And have another session so you can make some more money . . . and twenty-five for you. (*Crosses to Toledo, counts out twenty-five dollars, and hands it to him. Toledo puts the money in his jacket pocket. Sturdyvant turns toward Cutler and puts the rest of the roll in his pants pocket.*) Okay, thank you, boys. You can get your things together and Mr. Irvin will make sure you find your way out.

IRVIN: I'll be out front when you get your things together, Cutler. (*Crosses to the bandroom doorway. Sturdyvant starts to follow.*)

LEVEE: Mr. Sturdyvant, sir. About them songs I give you?

STURDYVANT (*stops and turns to Levee*): Oh, yes . . . uh . . . Levee. About them songs you gave me. I've thought about it and I just don't think the people will buy them . . . they're not the type of songs we're looking for. (*Starts toward the bandroom door as Irvin exits into the back hall.*)

LEVEE: Mr. Sturdyvant, sir. . . . (*Sturdyvant stops again and turns back to Levee.*) I done got my band picked out and they're real good fellows. They knows how to play real good. I know if the peoples hear the music, they'll buy it.

STURDYVANT: Well, Levee . . . I'll be fair with you . . . but they're just not the right songs.

(*Irvin passes through the studio, goes through the double door, and exits up the front hall.*)

LEVEE: Mr. Sturdyvant, you got to understand about the music. That music is what the peoples is looking for. They're tired of jug band music. They want something that excites them. Something with some fire to it.

STURDYVANT (*crosses to Levee*): Okay, Levee. I'll tell you what I'll do. I'll give you five dollars a piece for them. Now, that's the best I can do.

LEVEE (*querulously*): I don't want no five dollars, Mr. Sturdyvant. I wants to record them songs like you say.

STURDYVANT: Well, Levee, like I say . . . they just aren't the kind of songs we're looking for.

LEVEE (*restrained*): Mr. Sturdyvant, you asked me to write them songs. Now, why didn't you tell me that before when I first give them to you? You told me you was gonna let me record them. What's the difference between then and now?

STURDYVANT: Well, look . . . I'll pay you for your trouble. . . .

LEVEE (*insistently*): What's the difference, Mr. Sturdyvant? That's what I wanna know.

STURDYVANT (*crosses to the piano*): I had my fellows play your songs . . . and when I heard them . . . They just didn't sound like the kind of songs I'm looking for right now.

LEVEE (*crosses to Sturdyvant*): You got to hear me play them, Mr. Sturdyvant! You ain't heard me play them. That's what's gonna make them sound right.

STURDYVANT (*crosses to Cutler*): Well, Levee, I don't doubt that really. It's just that . . . well, I don't think they'd sell like Ma's records. But I'll take them off your hands for you.

LEVEE (*crosses to Toledo*): Mr. Sturdyvant, sir. I don't know what fellows you had playing them songs . . . but if I could play them! I'd set them down in the peoples lap! Now, you told me I could record them songs!

STURDYVANT (*dismissively*): Well, there's nothing I can do about that. (*Takes a roll of money from his pants pocket.*) Like I say, it's five dollars a piece. That's what I'll give you. (*Counts out three five-dollar bills and puts the rest of the money in his pocket.*) I'm doing you a favor. Now, if you write any more, I'll help you out and take them off your hands. The price is five dollars a piece. Just like now.

(*He holds out the money and waits for Levee to take it. Levee stares blankly as Sturdyvant crosses and stuffs the money in Levee's breast pocket. Sturdyvant exits as Levee springs toward the door and puts his hand on his back pocket. Levee leans against the closed door for a moment, then crosses to Toledo. Cutler closes his trombone case, rises, and carries it to below the lockers. Slow Drag puts on his hat and crosses to behind the piano. Cutler sets down the trombone case, opens his locker, takes out his coat, and puts it on. Toledo rises, takes his coat off the piano, and puts it on. Levee takes the money out of his breast pocket, stares at it, and turns toward the bandroom door. Toledo reaches for his hat, puts it on, and turns as Levee curses silently, whirls, and collides with Toledo.*)

LEVEE: Hey! Watch it . . . shit! You stepped on my shoe! (*Crumples the money in his hand, throws it away, and looks down at his shoe.*)

TOLEDO: Excuse me there, Levee.

LEVEE (*points at his shoe; angrily*): Look at that! Look at that! Nigger, you stepped on my shoe. What you do that for?

TOLEDO: I said I'm sorry.

LEVEE (*enraged*): Nigger gonna step on my goddamn shoe! You done fucked up my shoe! Look at that! Look at what you done to my shoe, nigger! I ain't stepped on your shoe! What you wanna step on my shoe for?

CUTLER (*crosses to Toledo*): The man said he's sorry.

LEVEE (*puts his foot on bench and unties his shoe*): Sorry! How the hell he gonna be sorry after he done ruint my shoe? Come talking about sorry! (*Takes off his shoe and crosses to Toledo.*) Nigger, you stepped on my shoe! You know that! (*Waves the shoe in Toledo's face.*) See what you done?

TOLEDO (*earnestly*): What you want me to do about it? It's done now. I said excuse me.

LEVEE: Wanna go and fuck up my shoe like that. I ain't done nothing to your shoe. Look at this! (*Toledo turns toward the bandroom door. Levee grabs Toledo by the arm and turns him back.*) Naw . . . naw . . . look what you done! Look at that! That's my shoe! Look at that! You did it! (*Throws the shoe; furiously:*) You did it! You fucked up my shoe! You stepped on my shoe with them raggedy-ass clodhoppers!

TOLEDO (*exasperated*): Nigger, ain't nobody studying you and your shoe! I said excuse me. If you can't accept that . . . then the hell with it. What you want me to do? (*Turns to the piano and picks up the book and newspaper.*)

LEVEE (*reaches into his back pocket, takes out the pocketknife, opens it, lunges toward Toledo, and stabs him in the back*): Nigger, you stepped on my shoe!!

(*Toledo groans and falls backwards into Levee's arms. Levee quickly lowers Toledo's body to the floor, crosses upstage center and drops the knife. The bandroom slowly dims. Cutler crosses to above Toledo, kneels, and touches Toledo's neck. Levee turns to Cutler, shocked.*)

He . . . he stepped on my shoe. He did. Honest. Cutler, he stepped on my shoe. What he do that for? (*Cutler rises and crosses to upstage left, shaking his head. Levee turns to Toledo. Remorsefully:*) Toledo, what you do that for? (*Crosses to Toledo's body, kneels, and pulls at Toledo's arm, turns to Cutler.*) Cutler . . . help me. He stepped on my shoe, Cutler. (*Turns back to Toledo.*) Toledo! Toledo, get up! (*Tries to lift Toledo.*) It's okay, Toledo. Come on, stand up now. Levee'll help you. (*Toledo's body slips out of Levee's hands and falls heavily to the floor. Levee lifts the limp body by the shoulders and looks into Toledo's open eyes.*) Don't look at me like that! Toledo! (*Drops Toledo, stands, and glares down at the body.*) Nigger, don't look at me like that! I'm warning you, nigger! (*Backs away.*) Close your eyes! Don't you look at me like that! (*Turns to Cutler; whimpering:*) Tell him to close his eyes, Cutler. Tell him don't look at me like that.

CUTLER: Slow Drag . . . get Mr. Irvin down here.

(*Slow Drag crosses to the bandroom door, opens it, and exits into the back hall. A trumpet begins to play a low, wailing solo. The stage begins to fade slowly. Cutler looks at Levee, shakes his head sadly, and sits. The trumpet builds in intensity and pitch and hits a high final note as the stage fades to black.*)

CURTAIN

AMERI/CAIN GOTHIC

A MYSTERY PLAY
IN TWO ACTS

PAUL CARTER HARRISON

Ameri/Cain Gothic, presented by Henry Street Settlements, New Federal Theatre, Woodie King, Jr., producer, premiered at the New Federal Theatre in New York City on March 16, 1985, with the following cast:

CASS (Casandra) PRUITT	Sylvia Miles
I. W. HARPER	Moses Gunn

Directed by Woodie King, Jr.; set design by Richard Harmon; light design by William H. Grant III; costume design by Judy Dearing; sound design by Regge Life; stage manager, Malik.

CHARACTERS

CASS (CASANDRA) PRUITT   a middle-aged white woman
I. W. HARPER   a middle-aged black man

AUTHOR'S NOTE

The assassination of Dr. Martin Luther King is the culminating event of the play. However, the play does not presume to be a factual account or documentary of the circumstances surrounding the tragedy of Dr. Martin Luther King. *Ameri/Cain Gothic* uses the context of the assassination to focus the manifest violence of race and sex in American society.

Stylistically, the play is conceived as a ritual wherein myth and reality are fused in a common field of experience. Allusions to the past should not be treated as linear flashbacks but should rather be manipulated as mythic elements—bigger than life—that amplify present reality. The event is urged forward magically by galvanic, transitional shifts of time; in such transitional moments, transformation of character becomes essential in the process of illuminating the physical and metaphysical forces that precipitate sexual and racial violence.

ACT I

Open Curtain: Memphis, Tennessee, 1968. The interior of a sparsely furnished, rundown rooming house. The decaying grandeur of the room is redolent of a faded old Southern gentility, with its pride peeling unbenevolently from the unattended wallpaper. A claustrophobic if not otherwise ominous atmosphere pervades the dark, musty room as in a dungeon. The offstage sound of a piano can be heard playing stride and boogie tunes such as "Flat Foot Floogie," "Just a Gigolo," "Sweet Lorraine," and a traditional "Boogie Blues," ending with "After Hours" just before curtain.

It is spring. Late afternoon. Frayed velvet drapes cover the window at stage left. All the furnishings, with the exception of the fourposter bed at stage right, are draped with white sheets.

Upstage left is an old, completely draped chest of drawers, upon which is a double picture frame that displays the images of Jesus and a robust frontiersman. On both sides of the frame are two large black candles. Against the wall is a crudely formed cross of meshed wire. A Bible rests in front of the picture frame. The area, slightly elevated, suggests a sort of altar. Down left, just past the window, is a completely draped dress form.

Upstage right, and slightly elevated, is a small refrigerator, upon which rests a hotplate. Against the wall above the refrigerator is a large, draped, ornate oval picture frame. Just right of the refrigerator are a wash sink and towel rack, both clearly exposed. Down right of the sink is a four-poster bed draped with gauze. Left of the bed is an undraped nightstand upon which rests a lamp. At the foot of the bed is an old travel trunk, which is clearly exposed. Further down right is a completely draped one-armed bandit.

Down center is a low, completely draped, oblong marble-topped table standing in front of two medium-sized, completely draped wicker chairs. An exposed white antiqued telephone rests upon the table. Above, suspended from the ceiling, is a large four-bladed fan.

Elevated upstage center is the room door, which is sealed with an assortment of bolts and locks. At least three locks use conventional keys, while a combination master lock is secured to a main hinge.

Left of the door is an umbrella stand, with the handle of a parasol exposed.

Opening: The lights go to dark as the final bars of the somber "After Hours" come to an end. Darkness. The syncopated, thus animated, sound of "Flat Foot Floogie" is heard once more emanating from a jukebox offstage. A piercing, horrific scream. Lights up on a petrified Cass (Casandra) Pruitt sitting up in her draped bed with one hand on the lamp switch, the other clutching her throat.

She scans the room with her eyes for a beat, then quickly throws back the sheets, and parts the drapes to come to her feet. She examines her appearance curiously. She is wearing a slip, and a chain of three keys hangs around her neck. She discovers the keys, then quickly goes to the door to check the locks. Satisfied that the door is secured, she slowly advances toward the window. Trepidly, she pulls back the velvet drapes. Discovering nothing more than the light that comes through, she separates the drapes and ties them to the wall.

She groggily crosses over to the sink, wets her face briskly, and turns downstage while wiping her face with a towel. Wearily, she discovers that the fan is not on. She puts down the towel, moves toward the door, and turns on the wall switch, which sets the fan in motion while adding another light from a globe at the center of the fan. She moves downstage to just behind the draped chairs with her head angled upward, her hands pulling her hair away from her face to catch the ventilating breeze of the fan. She suddenly becomes aware of the loud music, and her head begins to angle down toward the floor to locate the sound. Contemptuously, she stomps her foot against the floor three times. The music stops.

She inspects, momentarily, the bottom of her foot, which she has both hurt and soiled by the effort. She crosses to the chest of drawers, raises the sheet, and opens a drawer, producing the clamorous sound of dishes and silverware. She closes the drawer and opens another, where she locates a pumice stone. She crosses quickly to the bed, still somewhat unnerved, sits facing upstage, and begins to pumice her feet with great urgency, then continues up along her leg. Her action has the appearance of a cleansing ritual.

The telephone rings, intruding upon the ritual. Cass stops abruptly and gazes apprehensively at the persistently ringing tele-

phone. She places the pumice stone under the pillow and slowly advances to the telephone. Indignantly, and without giving the caller a chance for introductions, she responds.

CASS: How many times have I got to tell you, lover, I'm not at home! And I won't be home to you in the future, either. Not as long as you, whoever you are, don't have the guts to show your mealy face. In the meantime, Jack Mormon, go haul your ashes in the Mississippi River! (*She hangs up the telephone forcefully.*) Creep!

(*She gazes curiously at the hand that held the telephone, moves briskly to the bed, recovers the pumice stone, and begins to pumice her hand. Preoccupied with the effort, she is inattentive to the sound of footsteps climbing the squeaky stairs outside the door and slowly advancing down the hallway. Cass is suddenly aware of the footsteps. She places the pumice stone under the pillow and alertly runs up to the door to listen apprehensively. The footsteps stop outside the door.*

A silent pause. Quizzically, Cass places her ear against the door. Satisfied that nobody is there, she turns away and moves toward the bed, only to be startled by a knock at the door.)

CASS (*apprehensively*): Who is it? . . .

VOICE: Me! . . .

CASS: Me, who? . . .

VOICE: Me, ma'am! . . .

CASS (*opens a peephole in the door and peers out quizzically*): Wha'cha doin' here today? Did I send for you?

VOICE: No, ma'am! . . .

CASS: The manager sent you up here, huh? . . .

VOICE: Yes, ma'am! . . .

CASS: But, this is not your regular day, is it?

VOICE: No, ma'am! . . .

CASS: Then come back on your regular day! (*She closes peephole and turns away.*)

VOICE: No, ma'am!!!

CASS (*turns back toward the door*): Wha'cha mean, no? . . .

VOICE: Last day, ma'am! . . . Bye! . . . Bye, now! . . . Bye! . . .

(*Cass looks around the room nervously. She quickly turns to the door and begins to unlatch the bolts.*)

CASS: Wait! . . . I might need you in here.

VOICE: Gotta go, ma'am! . . .

CASS: You just hold your horses! . . . And don't give me no sass!!! (*She quickly unlocks the lock with keys suspended on chain around her neck. She then dials the combination on the master lock.*) You still there? . . .

VOICE: Yes, ma'am! . . .

CASS: You people are always in a hurry. (*She removes the lock from the main hinge and opens the door.*) C'mon, c'mon, now, hurry! . . .

(*Entering briskly is I. W. Harper, disguised as a maid. He is wearing a one-piece housedress and a netted work cap. His socks are rolled down below his ankles, his pants legs rolled up above the hemline of the dress. He is carrying an oversized black totebag and smoking a cigar. He passes Cass briskly, looks around the room, discovers the window, and heads for it.*

Cass glances at Harper curiously, takes a quick, guarded peek out the door, then closes the door and begins securing the locks.)

HARPER: Be outta your way in a jiffy, ma'am.

CASS: Take your time. You gals are always in a hurry.

(*She is unaware of Harper, who removes a pair of binoculars from the totebag and begins to peer out the window.*)

And when you get to the refrigerator, don't just poke a broom behind there. Pull it away from the wall. I think I'm being invaded by God's anathema . . . mice! And before you go . . . (*The locks secured, Cass turns to gaze at Harper with great astonishment.*) What on earth do you think you're doin', missee? . . .

HARPER: Just lookin', ma'am.

CASS: Lookin' for what? . . . Hold it . . . you just hold it right there! You're not the regular girl!

HARPER (*turns away from the window and smiles at her with a sheepish grin; normal voice*): No, I'm not!

CASS (*suspiciously*): Then, what the hell are you doin' in my room?

HARPER: Just lookin'!

(*Cass moves briskly toward the telephone. Harper cuts her off alertly and holds down the receiver. Cass, surprised, backs off.*)

I can explain this, ma'am.

CASS (*indignantly*): Stand outta my way so I can call the manager!

HARPER: No need in all that, ma'am. I already spoke to the manager. Nice lady, too. I gave her twenty bucks to inspect these rooms. Just doin' my job. She called you a short while ago to say I was comin'.

CASS (*backs away apprehensively*): Who are you, anyway? . . .

(*Harper releases a billow of smoke from his cigar, smiles, and raises the hem of his dress to search his left pants pocket and then his right pocket, taking his eyes off Cass, who stealthily attempts to cross over to window.*)

HARPER: I guess you gotta have a special knack to pass for a woman. I knew it wouldn't work. I told the manager so. I just ain't got that kinda knack.

(*He removes his identification card from his right hip pocket and flashes it in Cass's face just as she is about to slip past him. She is startled.*)

I. W. Harper! . . . (*He removes the netted work cap from his head.*) Private dick!

(*Cass, alarmed, races toward the door, only to be cut off once again by Harper. She retreats downstage to the edge of the bed and stares at him with great anxiety.*)

Now, there ain't no cause to be alarmed, ma'am. Just take it easy!

CASS (*vituperatively*): You just get yo'self outta here!

HARPER: Ain't gonna be here no longer than I have to, ma'am. Soon as I finish this little job I gotta do, I'm through.

CASS: I'm gonna scream!

HARPER: Ain't no need in all that. Now, I know you don't like men in your room . . . the manager told me. That's why I got into this cover, so you wouldn't get upset.

CASS: She had no right to send you up here!

HARPER: I paid her twenty bucks. You get a lotta cooperation in my business when you float a couple of tens. You see, I've gotta inspect these rooms for my client.

CASS: Didn't she tell you this room is already occupied?

HARPER (*crosses downstage to retrieve his binoculars, which had been left on the table*): Don't worry about a thing, ma'am. My client doesn't want your room. He's gonna stay in the motel across the street.

(*He looks around the room as he casually strolls toward the window. Cass scurries around, searching under the bed and behind the trunk in search of her wedge-soled slip-on slippers.*)

I guess you've been living here a long time.

CASS: Too long!

HARPER: You live here alone?

CASS: That's none of your business! (*She slips into her slippers.*) You've got one helluva nerve poking your nose around in my private affairs.

HARPER (*casually peers out the window with his binoculars*): Just part of the job, ma'am.

(*Cass crosses quickly to the telephone and dials. Harper ignores her.*)

CASS: Well, I won't stand for it another minute! The police will know what to do with you. (*The sound of a busy tone. She hangs up receiver with a despondent expression.*)

HARPER: Busy, huh? . . . I could've told you that much. Not much chance of gettin' a cop on a day like this. My client's got the whole Memphis department jumpin', and he ain't even in town yet. He's got me hoppin' around pretty good, too.

(*As Harper peers out the window, Cass furtively moves upstage to the door and quietly begins to dial the combination master lock.*)

But it's a good thing I landed on this spot. Only a stone's throw from his motel across the street. Hell, I can look right into his room from this window. That's his room with the balcony! . . . (*He turns away from the window and offers the binoculars to Cass, who reacts with a startled expression.*) You wanna have a look?

CASS (*apprehensively*): Look, mister . . .

HARPER: Harper! . . . I. W. Harper! (*He puts the binoculars down and removes the dress, which he folds and places into the totebag.*)

CASS: Yeah, sure, whatever you wanna call yo'self! . . . But I just don't want no trouble outta you. Now, I ain't a bit narrow-minded or nothing, but what's really your game? You some kind of peep freak? . . . I mean, don't get me wrong. It takes all kinds of people to live in this world, and I ain't a bit prejudiced. If that's how you get your kicks, be my guest! But this ain't the best time for me to be havin' company, I've got too many problems of my own today. So I want you outta here in ten minutes, you understand? Get a good eyeful, but in ten minutes, you've gotta go!

(Harper adjusts his socks, pants legs, and shirt sleeves. His entire outfit—shirt, trousers, socks, and shoes—is black.)

HARPER: Do I look queer to you, ma'am? . . .

CASS: I told you, I ain't prejudiced!

HARPER: I thought maybe you never saw a black dick before!

CASS: Don't play games with me, mister!!!

HARPER: I showed you my credentials. All I'm tryin' to do is make a livin' by keepin' an eye on folks. Honest to God, I'm official!

CASS *(circumspectly)*: You some kinda cop? . . .

HARPER: Not exactly, ma'am. I'm self-employed. I'm what you call an undercover specialist. I don't surface much. I kinda cover my beat like a shadow, if you get my meaning.

CASS: Then, would you mind turning around while I put on something decent. You suddenly make me feel naked.

HARPER: Don't mind me! . . . Pretend I'm not even here.

(Harper picks up his binoculars and turns to peer out the window as Cass crosses briskly to the trunk, opens it, and removes a green mesh housecoat, which she puts on, barely concealing her skin-toned slip.)

CASS: So, you're a spook! Didn't know Memphis had any spooks on the force.

HARPER: I couldn't swear to it, ma'am. I'm from the District of Columbia myself.

CASS: Wha'cha doin' in Memphis? . . . You're a long way off your beat, aren't you?

HARPER: Just following the action. And you've got plenty of action right here in Memphis. Just last week, my client was here in town to lead a garbage collector's demonstration. You must have read about how the good Reverend . . .

(*Cass crosses to the chest of drawers, raises the drape, opens a drawer clamorously, and locates a mirror, powder puff, and powder. She begins to tidy up her features.*)

CASS: Don't mention that man's name in my house!

HARPER: I thought you said you weren't prejudiced, ma'am.

CASS: And I'm not! But that preacher came in town and caused a big stink out there, and I've got to live with it. He had those garbage pickers raisin' all kinds of Cain!

HARPER: You can't blame that on the Reverend. He was just tryin' to help those fellers win some dignity for their work.

CASS: And all that garbage piled up on the street still stinks! Wasn't worth having that li'l colored boy killed over all that crap!

HARPER (*soberly*): It was an accident. The kid got caught in the crunch. Somebody always gets caught in the crunch when a mob builds up a full head of steam. The Reverend couldn't turn down the dampers on those hot tempers. But he's a dreamer, so he's coming back to try again.

(*Cass places the mirror, powder, and powder puff back into the drawer, pulls down the drape, and crosses behind Harper.*)

CASS (*reciting with mock reverence*): "And they said to another, Behold, this dreamer cometh. Come now, therefore, and let us slay him . . . and we shall see what will become of his dreams . . ." Genesis!

HARPER (*turns around to face her quizzically; firmly*): Ain't gonna be no trouble this time, ma'am!

CASS: Does God follow your Reverend?

HARPER: I couldn't swear on it, ma'am.

CASS: Then we're in for plenty of trouble. (*She crosses over to the bed and begins spreading the sheets tidily, pulling back the gauze drape.*)

HARPER (*quizzically*): You know something I don't know?

CASS: You wouldn't be here if you weren't expecting trouble.

HARPER (*insistently*): Ain't gonna be no trouble, ma'am.

CASS: Is that a professional opinion?

HARPER: I can stake my reputation on it.

CASS: Then you can't be much of a spook.

HARPER (*quizzically*): Ma'am? . . .

CASS (*turning toward him sharply*): If you were half the spook you say you are, you'd know you're standin' in the thick of trouble.

HARPER (*guardedly*): What's the trouble, ma'am?

CASS: Can't you see I'm alone?

HARPER: Oh, that ain't no trouble, ma'am.

CASS: Well, you know what happens to women who live alone.

HARPER: Yeah! . . . They get lonely! (*He turns away from her and peers out the window with binoculars.*)

CASS: Listen, mister! . . . My life is in danger.

HARPER (*turns away from the window and stares at her for a beat before crossing toward the telephone*): Maybe you'd better call the police.

CASS: The line is busy! (*She picks up the telephone and places it on the night table near bed.*)

HARPER (*cryptically*): Funny how you can never find a cop when you need one.

CASS (*solicitously*): Look, I don't want to interfere with your work, but I've got a serious problem.

HARPER: Ain't no problem, ma'am! . . .

CASS: I need your help! . . .

HARPER: Sorry, ma'am, can't afford to do no moonlightin'!

CASS (*insistently*): It's an emergency!!!

HARPER: So is my job! And a good job ain't easy to find out here. Not after all I've been through. So I don't moonlight when I'm doin' a major assignment.

CASS (*insistently*): Look, some creep got into my room this afternoon and tried to take advantage of me in my sleep. I screamed. And he disappeared.

HARPER (*stares at her for a beat, then moves upstage toward the locked door*): I suggest you keep your door secured and don't let anybody in.

CASS: I didn't let anybody in!

HARPER: You let me in, didn't you? Nothing unusual about a lonely woman bein' taken by surprise. You read about it all the time. A woman entertains a familiar acquaintance and ends up . . . a victim. I . . . er . . . I knew such a woman once.

CASS: Did you try to help her, even offer a little prayer?

HARPER: It was too late for prayers, ma'am.

CASS: Uh-huh, you're a phony, mister. A big fake, and I knew it. You thought you could come in here and pull the wool over my eyes, pollutin' my room with your cigar, dumpin' your ashes wherever you please. Well, the garbage is out on the street, mister, so get out there and haul yo'self on the heap!

HARPER: Listen, ma'am! . . .

CASS: And stop callin' me ma'am. You can't win me over with that mamby-pamby stuff. I would never trust anybody who couldn't call me Casandra Pruitt.

HARPER: Well, let me tell you somethin', Miss Pruitt . . .

CASS: Cass! . . . Friends and relations call me Cass!

HARPER: Makes no difference, 'cause I know we ain't related, and you sure ain't been too friendly. But I didn't mean you no disrespect, so don't you disrespect me. Now, I'm sorry if I got you all upset, but I don't have to accept no abuse from you. So, if you'll kindly open up, Miss Pruitt, I will never darken your door again.

CASS: Not till I get your name. I might have to report this entire incident to the authorities.

(*Harper impatiently removes his identification card once more from his hip pocket and hands it to Cass, who inspects it carefully under the lamp.*)

HARPER: Harper! . . . I. W. Harper! . . . Private investigator! Certified in the District of Columbia!

CASS: Your name . . . in full . . . please!

HARPER (*impatiently*): Iroquois . . . Iroquois Washington Harper!

CASS (*circumspectly*): You don't look much like no Indian to me!

HARPER: I'm not! . . . I'm just a true-blooded spook. But my momma named me so that nobody would mistake me for anything but American. You see, Iroquois is for the Native Son, Washington, the Great White Father, and Harper, well, he was just one of the common caretakers, you know, a guardian of the Great Estate. So I guess that makes me a born-again American!

CASS (*hands Harper his I.D. card*): Is that God's honest truth?

HARPER: Would you kindly open the door, Miss Pruitt?

(*Cass turns away from Harper and begins to remove the sheet draping one of the chairs. Harper turns to the master lock and begins an attempt to work the combination as Cass folds the sheet and places it in the trunk.*)

CASS (*buoyantly*): You must be what the Mormon prophets would call a Lamanite. My Daddy told me all about one of them Lamanites who was a thick-set man of God named Zelf. He was a noble chief under the great prophet Onandagus, and known from the Eastern Sea to the Rocky Mountains. Ever heard of him, Harper?

(*Both are distracted from what they are doing by the sound of static and a voice which is transmitted through a two-way transistor radio.*)

TRANSISTOR VOICE: Home to Harper! . . . Home to Harper! . . . Come on in, Harper! This is Home callin' Harper! . . . Come on in, Harper!

(*Harper quickly reaches into his totebag, removes the transistor radio, adjusts the antenna, and responds as Cass begins to fold the sheet of the second chair and gazes toward him curiously.*)

HARPER: Harper, speaking! . . . Come in, Home! . . .

TRANSISTOR VOICE: Pheeoouuu! We picked a helluva day to go lookin' for trouble.

HARPER: It's the humidity, Home. It's got that garbage reekin'!

TRANSISTOR VOICE: You check those clouds, Harper? . . .

HARPER (*crosses alertly to the window*): Yeah . . . sure! . . .

TRANSISTOR VOICE: I think it's gonna rain.

HARPER: Yeah! . . . But still no sign of trouble.

TRANSISTOR VOICE: Are you kiddin'? . . . The Reverend got delayed by a bomb scare at the Atlanta airport.

HARPER: Really? . . . I couldn't figure out what was keepin' him.

TRANSISTOR VOICE: Where you hidin' out, baby?

HARPER: Reconnoitering South Main Street. Got a good view of the motel on Mulberry Street. How 'bout you?

TRANSISTOR VOICE: I'm staked out down here on the banks of the Mississippi. The river ain't no rose blossom either, but it beats all that garbage on Front Street.

HARPER: By the way, Home, I wouldn't go near that new City Hall down on Adams Street if I were you. That area used to be a slave market and I wouldn't want you callin' up no ghosts.

TRANSISTOR VOICE: Don't you worry 'bout it, bruh! . . . You just keep your cover.

HARPER: Like the shadow do!!!

TRANSISTOR VOICE: I'll be in touch. Over and out!

(*Cass, having placed the second sheet in the trunk, sits on the trunk and observes curiously as Harper adjusts the antenna, crosses to the door, and puts the transistor in the totebag.*)

CASS: Now, that's what I call real spooky!

HARPER (*moves toward her forcefully*): Are you gonna give me those keys or do I have to knock that damn hinge off the door?

CASS (*stands and backs away*): Are you tryin' to frighten me, Harper?

HARPER: I'm tryin' to get outta here!

CASS: You're frightening me, Harper!

HARPER: Listen, miss . . . er . . . Cass! . . . The sooner I get outta here, the better you're gonna feel.

CASS (*tearfully*): You know nothin' about how I'm gonna feel. Nothin'! (*She crosses and sits in one of the chairs.*) You ever try livin' alone? . . . Wakin' up to shadows on the wall that materialize to pull your pants down around your ankles before some wreckage is forced deep up inside your pelvis? . . . You know, givin' it to yah! . . . Givin' it to yah till your navel bleeds. You think it's easy, mister?

When was the last time some creep took advantage of you? (*She weeps lightly; Harper remains ambivalent.*)

HARPER: Sorry, Cass! . . . I've got a job to do.

CASS (*irately*): Then . . . go! (*She removes chain of keys from around her neck and throws them at the door.*) Take the damn keys, and beat it!

HARPER (*picks up the keys and begins to unlock the locks with an apologetic attitude*): You know, if you knew how hard it is for a fella like me to get a job, a decent job, I mean, one he could be proud of, you'd understand why I've gotta go. Before I became self-employed, I was unemployed for a real long time because I couldn't find work in what I was trained to do. Carpentry! (*Harper unlocks the locks but does not remove them from the latch. He crosses toward Cass and hands her the chain of keys.*) I apprenticed as a carpenter for thirteen years, for which I received a Longine Wittnauer watch and a membership in the Masons, who told me that the chisel insignia stood for the advantages of education, the gavel, the power of conscience, and the twenty-four-inch gauge was supposed to represent the twenty-four hours of a day divided into prayer, work, refreshment, and helping friends. Well, I believed all that bunk, but I still couldn't get into the union. I prayed, but my journeyman's card never came. I prayed, and a watermelon seed stuck in my throat. I prayed, but how was I gonna help others if I couldn't even help myself. I'm not bitter or nothin'. But the union ignored my prayers, so I stopped prayin' and went into business for myself. (*He turns to examine combination lock on the door.*)

CASS (*reflectively*): Prayer is our only salvation.

HARPER: Yeah, well, if you give up the combination, salvation will ride on outta here.

CASS: What combination?

HARPER: To the master lock. I could probably figure it out, but it would take too much time. So, would you kindly give up the numbers.

CASS: I can't remember them.

HARPER: What do you mean, you can't remember? Don't you live here?

CASS: There's so much goin' through my head.

HARPER: Okay! . . . Maybe a couple of tens can jog your memory?

CASS: My memory is clear. I simply can't fix my mind on the numbers.

HARPER: You've got a block, okay? A little lapse of memory. It could happen to anybody. All you've got to do is concentrate on that block. Just concentrate real hard.

CASS: I'm concentrating! . . .

HARPER: And what do you see?

CASS (*despondently*): Assault with a deadly weapon!

(*Harper turns away from her and begins manipulating the master-lock combination as Cass stares toward the window despondently.*)

You'll read about it in the mornin' paper!

HARPER (*turns away from his futile effort and gazes quizzically toward Cass*): Look, you really oughtn't play that kind of game on yourself. It's a rotten game. A lotta women do it. Lonely women in particular. They always go 'round thinkin' they're up for grabs. You really oughtn't play that! You can get folks in trouble.

(*Cass gazes toward the window without responding. Harper comes down slowly.*)

You ain't so sure about this thing, anyway!

(*Cass does not respond. Harper moves behind her and acquiesces slightly.*)

When did it happen?

CASS: I woke up this mornin'. A jackdaw was perched on my windowsill. I covered the windows and went back to sleep. When I woke this afternoon, I discovered the shadow of a man over my bed. He clutched me by the throat. I screamed. He ran away.

HARPER: Did you get a good look at him?

CASS: It was too dark to see anything.

HARPER (*glances toward the bolted door as he crosses toward chest of drawers*): How did he get in?

CASS: I dunno.

HARPER: I see! . . . (*He looks around the room curiously.*)

CASS: Are you gonna take the case?

HARPER: As far as I can see, you don't have a case. Perhaps grounds for a complaint, but not a bona fide case! Your story kinda got the wheel turnin' in my head, but no real professional can go into action with such premature information. We need facts. And there's not much to go on here, is there?

CASS: You don't believe me, do you?

HARPER: Never mind what I believe. You're gonna have to convince the police that something more than a routine break 'n entry occurred here.

CASS (*stands to confront him*): There's nothin' routine about a man entering a woman's private quarters uninvited!

HARPER: Did he take anything?

CASS: What do you think? (*She turns downstage toward the bed as Harper inspects the room for clues, ending up at the umbrella stand to inspect the parasol curiously.*)

HARPER: Maybe he left something behind, you know, like a hat or a glove . . . an umbrella?

CASS: They usually take something, don't they?

(*Harper replaces the parasol in umbrella stand and gazes at Cass, who is staring at the bed.*)

HARPER: What did he take?

CASS: I hate to think about it.

HARPER: C'mon, now, women always know when they've been taken.

CASS (*turns to him vituperatively*): I was violated! And I've lost more than a little sleep over it.

HARPER: Can you be more specific?

CASS (*turns away from him, crosses to the door, and relocks the unlocked locks*): The very thought of it makes me feel just a trifle tawdry.

HARPER: I wouldn't be concerned over a little bruised vanity, if I were you. The fella might've killed you.

CASS: Do I have to be a corpse before you take me seriously? I woke up with a man's ugly hand around my throat. And I consider that damn serious!

(*The muted sound of "After Hours" can be heard coming from jukebox as Cass sits in chair disgruntledly and Harper crosses down to inspect bed.*)

HARPER: I'd say you were lucky. I knew this woman, you know, the one I told you about, she wasn't so lucky. She never woke up. A good woman, too. At least I thought so. She treated me with a lotta respect when I used to do odd jobs at a horse stable. Diana . . . her name was Diana . . . had a big thing for horses. She sure could ride those ponies. But her vanity got the best of her. Kept too much company. So whoever did it got away without a trace. Not much of a trace here either, is there? I mean, you can't go 'round chasin' shadows.

CASS (*reflectively*): I've got a good idea who did it.

HARPER: It would help if you did. (*He crosses over to the chest of drawers, examines the photos in the picture frame, and handles the Bible.*)

CASS: One of them colored boys downstairs in the amusement parlor. You must have seen them when you came in. Those idlers are always hanging around down there playing that disgusting race music. You can hear them now, can't you?

HARPER: Can you identify any one of them?

CASS (*confrontationally*): Are you tryin' to protect those boys, Harper?

HARPER (*holds up the Bible*): Can you swear on a stack of Bibles it was one of them?

CASS: It's only a guess, but I got a good mind it was one of those idlers that tried to assault me . . . whether you like it or not.

HARPER: Listen, I am a professional. And accordin' to my trainin' manual, an investigator should always avoid guesswork and confine himself to the accumulation and systematic interpretation of factual evidence. And I go by the book!

CASS: For God sakes, Harper, how do you expect me to trust you if I've gotta go up against your book?

(*Jukebox music ends. Harper crosses over to the window and peers out.*)

I sure as hell can't afford to pay for that kind of trust.

HARPER: I didn't say I was for hire.

CASS (*crosses over to the trunk, opens it, and searches around*): Oh, I'm willing to pay you, Harper. I don't have much cash, though. Not like I used to before I came to Memphis. I live on a little gift from the county which I receive on the first and fifteenth of the month. Just barely enough to get me over the hump, don't you know!

HARPER: I haven't asked you for a single dime, have I?

CASS: No, but trust always has a price tag on it, I know. (*She locates a jewel-box replica of the trunk and searches inside it.*)

HARPER: I deliberately didn't quote you a fee, because I haven't decided to moonlight, you understand? I'm just killin' some time till the Reverend gets in town.

CASS: What time is it, Harper?

(*Reflexively, Harper raises his wrist, but there is no watch. He lowers his arm.*)

HARPER (*self-consciously*): I can't say for sure. I lost my watch a while back. Good watch, too. Longine Wittnauer.

(*Cass removes a watch from the jewel box, which she closes and puts back inside the trunk. She closes the lid, crosses to Harper, and offers him the watch.*)

CASS: A busy man like you oughta keep up with the time, Harper. Take this little token for your trouble.

HARPER (*gazes at the watch suspiciously*): I told you! . . . They always leave something behind.

CASS: It belonged to my father.

(*Harper removes a handkerchief from his hip pocket to receive the watch gingerly. He then removes a jeweler's eyepiece from his side pocket to examine the watch.*)

HARPER: Looks expensive.

CASS: My Daddy's only possession. And he was very proud of it.

(*The muted sound of "Just a Gigolo" comes from the jukebox as Cass turns away from Harper and sits in one of the chairs.*)

HARPER: I dunno, Cass. I'm not the kinda fella that takes gifts from a lady.

CASS: Truly? . . . You must be an endangered species, Harper.

HARPER (*places the watch on his wrist and examines it*): Hell, I've got a good reputation, you know. I don't like to see people pay for services they can't get. The little advice you're gettin' from me is strictly off the cuff, and it might not be worth it. But when you give advice, you've gotta accept the responsibility for it. And that always leads to unforeseen involvement. That's why my clients trust me. I always get involved in my work. But they only get exactly what they pay for, nothin' more, and nothin' less.

CASS: Fair enough! . . . So let's see what a little moonlight can do.

(*Harper goes upstage to fetch his totebag and brings it over to the window, where he removes his binoculars.*)

HARPER: Sure, as long as you understand that I've got priorities. One of the first things you learn in this business is
not to overload your priorities. When the Reverend hits
town, I'm gonna be ready for action. So I can't get too
deeply involved in this mess. But I'm simply not the kind
of fella that hides behind the mornin' newspaper when a
neighbor is in trouble.

CASS: Good Lord, Harper, you're a saint. I knew it when I first
laid eyes on you.

HARPER (*glances at her for a beat, then peers out the window with
the binoculars*): I don't know about all that, but I once
heard the Reverend quote an old slave who said . . . "We
ain't what we ought to be, we ain't what we want to be,
and we ain't what we're gonna be, but thank de Lawd,
we ain't what we was!"

CASS (*ruminating*): You know what just occurred to me, Harper? . . .

HARPER (*inattentively*): Helluva lotta fuss over a heap of dead
garbage! . . .

CASS: Those colored boys probably had nothin' to do with it! . . . I've got a funny notion it might've just been my lover.

(*Harper turns away from the window to gaze at her for a beat, then places binoculars in totebag as the jukebox music ends.*)

HARPER: You've got a lover?

CASS: Does that surprise you?

HARPER (*crosses and sits in chair*): Why would your lover want to hurt you?

CASS: Maybe he wasn't tryin' to hurt me. He might've just been tryin' to caress my neck.

HARPER: How often does he come around?

CASS: Oh, I ain't seen him in a coon's age!

HARPER: Don't see how he can qualify as a lover if ain't around to keep the furnace warm.

CASS: I'd appreciate it if you'd keep your mind outta my bed!

HARPER: I'm tryin' to establish a motive.

CASS: I didn't have no papers on him, if that's what you mean.

HARPER: I just figured if he's been gone so long, what would he want with you now?

CASS: Ain't no moss growin' on me, Harper.

HARPER: You didn't get my point! . . .

CASS (*indignantly*): I most certainly did! (*She stands abruptly and crosses over to the trunk, opens it, and searches out a fancy garter. Sitting on the trunk, she puts the garter around her leg up to the knee.*) You sat down there and insinuated that I could not be wanted . . . like I was some worn-out old shoe ready to be tossed in the trash.

HARPER: The point I'm tryin' to make . . .

CASS (*interrupting*): Your point is clear, pal! . . . But if my Daddy has told me once, he's told me a hundred times, all you need to get ahead in this world is one good leg to stand on! (*She crosses down in front of Harper and places the gartered leg forcefully on the table.*) Take a look at that leg! Go on, take a good look. It's alright, you can handle it. Go on, take a good grip!

(*Harper reluctantly touches her ankle, then runs his hand along her calf reflectively.*)

These legs have had to support a lotta mileage, but I can still cover more road than any red pony you ever rode!

(*As Harper strokes her calf, Cass's agitation begins to subside, her demeanor suggesting an ambivalence about the subtle petting.*)

HARPER (*reflectively*): I dunno, Diana—you remember, the woman I told you about—she had a pretty mean leg. She was built like a Clydesdale, you know, fully packed on top, tight and firm on the bottom. When that woman fit her legs in her jodhpurs and climbed up on her cobalt colt, she looked like a white goddess. There was nothin' like bein' in the saddle with Diana. But it's hard to keep up with a woman like that.

(*Cass, responding to his Diana reverie, withdraws her leg from his grip abruptly.*)

CASS: She turned you on, huh? . . .

(*She crosses to the trunk, removes the garter, and puts it in the trunk. Harper, in an effort to conceal the awkwardness of his revelations, takes a cigar from his pocket and lights up.*)

HARPER: What? . . .

CASS: That bitch goddess, Diana, she turned you on! . . .

HARPER (*defensively*): The lady had class!

CASS: I used to kick up a pretty good heel not so long ago. And I've never met a horny man that cared a good damn about class.

HARPER: What do you know about class? Runnin' around on the fast track the way you do, it's a wonder you have any heels left. You can always tell a woman who has class by her feet. If her heels curl over the edge of her open-back shoes, you know right then and there, she has no class. But if her feet fits snug, you know, like a nut in a shell . . . Now, when I look at your feet . . .

CASS (*steps out of her slippers to expose her feet to Harper; interrupting*): My feet are clean, Harper. I scrub them every day with pumice stone. That's how we Mormons were brought up . . . clean and pure of heart. And that should be enough class for any horny lover! (*She puts her feet in the slippers, crosses to the chest, picks up the Bible, and thumbs through it urgently as she advances toward Harper.*)

HARPER: So, where is your lover now?

CASS: For your information, I was raised to be the wife and mother of prophets! It's all here in the Golden Book. I may have slipped a little, turning the bend to find love, but I do know my way back to Zion. I know love as well as I know God, Harper. I'm bound to marry a prophet! (*She places the open Bible down on the table in front of Harper, who picks it up to peruse the pages as she returns to the chest of drawers to cradle the picture frame.*)

HARPER: Maybe there's something to the story I heard about a Christian who died and went to heaven. When he got there, St. Peter escorted him around to meet the other heavenly guests. The good Christian was surprised to find some Chinese, a bunch of coloreds, and a few Indians, too. But he really became curious when he saw a group of white folks sittin' off by themselves. St. Peter said, "Shhhhhh, those are the Mormons. They think they're the only ones up here!"

(*Cass turns the frame toward him downstage, revealing the images of Jesus and an aging frontiersman, her father.*)

CASS: Which one of these two men do you think is my lover? The one on the right or the left?

HARPER (*perplexed*): I'd probably be lyin' if I told you the truth!

(*Cass cradles the picture frame, examines the photos for a brief beat, then puts the frame back on top of the chest as she lights the candles.*)

CASS: The one on the left is my Daddy, you know the other one. My Daddy never had much in this world, but he gave me more love than any little girl could ever hope for. He was a sharecropper in Arkansas before we settled down in the Nevada desert to open a roadside motel in Lovelock. It wasn't much more than a dusty truckstop, but we were blessed with a snack bar and a one-armed bandit which stopped a lotta truckers.

(*Harper crosses over to the window with the Bible, removes a raccoon hat from his totebag, and stands facing upstage with a sanctimonious demeanor.*)

Daddy wouldn't let the truckers get too close to me, though. I was much too precious. He just loved me to pieces. Every night, he would bathe the road dust off my body with oil and witch hazel. Then he would take me to bed, and pray to God that someday I would be found by a righteous husband.

(*Lights shift for Cass's private moment as Harper crosses upstage to her to assume the attitude of her father.*)

HARPER: As men as God once was, my precious, as God as men may become. I place my hand upon your head to give you my fatherly blessing. You're a blessing to your family, precious, and not long away from matrimonial devotion.

(*He blows out the candles as Cass rises from her kneeling posture. They cross downstage, his arm embracing her shoulders, leading her to the table, where she stretches out.*)

The Lord will give you power over disease, and his angels will lay around you to warn against seen and

unseen dangers of the night. And now I lay you down to
sleep! . . . I pray the Lord your soul will keep.

CASS (*with emotional fervor*): May Jesus come! . . . May Jesus
come! . . .

(*Harper leans forward to kiss her brow, her cheeks, then kisses her
firmly on the mouth. Cass responds passionately, hugging him with
conjugal fervor.*
   *The lights return to normal as the roaring sound of motorcycles
and an urgent call from the transistor radio interrupt them. Harper
quickly responds, removing the raccoon hat, which he places in the
totebag, and taking out the transistor radio as Cass slowly recovers
from her reverie, places the Bible on the chest, and sits languidly.*)

TRANSISTOR VOICE (*urgently*): Home to Harper! . . . Home to
Harper! . . . Come on in, Harper, wherever you are! . . .
Home to Harper! . . . Come on in! . . .

HARPER: Harper, speakin'! . . .

TRANSISTOR VOICE: Damn, man, where in hell are you?

HARPER: On the case, Home!

TRANSISTOR VOICE: Then, why didn't you blow my whistle
when the Reverend came in?

HARPER: What? . . . (*He anxiously removes binoculars from the
totebag and peers out the window.*)

TRANSISTOR VOICE: You sure you on the case, bruh? . . .

HARPER: Yeah . . . sure! . . . I just didn't wanna blow my
cover.

TRANSISTOR VOICE: The Reverend is on the move again.

HARPER: I can see that! Must be headed for the rally over at the
Mason Street Temple.

TRANSISTOR VOICE: Better get yo' butt in gear, bruh! . . .

(*The sound of thunder and lightning.*)

HARPER: Looks like we got rain! . . .

TRANSISTOR VOICE: Don't let wet feet stop you. You supposed to keep my back covered, baby!

HARPER: Don't worry, Home, I've got you covered!

TRANSISTOR VOICE: Over and out!!!

(*Harper places the transistor and binoculars in the totebag. He looks up at Cass, who sits dejectedly in a chair.*)

CASS: I guess you've gotta go.

HARPER: It's raining outside.

CASS: I know! . . . And you have your priorities.

HARPER (*crosses with cigar and stands near the chair with a confident demeanor*): I don't figure the Reverend will draw much of a crowd in this rain. So, I'll wait here until he gets back.

CASS: Gold-brickin'! . . .

HARPER: Who's gold-brickin'? . . . I'm on the case! I just analyzed the situation.

CASS: Look, when you're sniffin' around for trouble, you've gotta put your nose right into the armpits of the problem.

HARPER: I don't have to get that personal. All I need to do is make an accurate assessment of the facts.

CASS: That's your problem, Harper. You have no feelings.

HARPER: Don't talk to me about feelings! I have very deep feelings. But not on the job. You get sentimental, the facts get all bent outta shape. You can't afford to get personal in this business.

CASS: Just another payday, huh? . . .

HARPER: I work hard for every penny I earn.

CASS: I dunno, Harper, I don't think I can trust an impersonal spook!

HARPER: Trust only depends on whose side you're on. Like, I had a case in Chicago not long ago . . .

CASS: How long ago? . . .

HARPER: Recently! . . . A three-year-old girl was missin' on Lake Michigan . . .

CASS: What was she doin' out there alone?

HARPER: She wasn't alone, she was just out there! . . . Everybody thought she had drowned, but her body never turned up.

CASS: She was buried in the sand!! . . .

HARPER: No, turned out she was snatched by a wealthy industrialist from Lake Forest.

CASS: Bastard!

HARPER: See, you're gettin' sentimental! . . . There was nothin' criminal about that man. He simply got tired of livin' alone with his money.

CASS (*outraged*): There's nothin' worse than a rich scumbag take advantage of a young girl's body!!!

HARPER: He never touch her. He loved that little girl like she was his very own.

CASS: How'd you get involved?

HARPER: The local authorities called me in to investigate. The old man never even blinked an eye when I turned up to work as a custodian, you know, tightening up the bolts and screws of the estate.

CASS: He just trusted you on face value? . . .

HARPER: Paid me good, too. He was a pretty nice old fella, and I even got to like him. He never once suspected I was a spook. It took me three months to come outta the closet. I said, "Hey, boss, you know who I am?" He said, "Sure, you're my boy." I said, "No, I'm the Man!" He was shocked. He cried like a baby, even offered me ten thousand dollars to keep my mouth shut. My reputation was at stake. I turned him in!

CASS: You disappoint me, Harper. I mean, professionally, you really disappoint me.

HARPER (*defensively*): I take a lotta pride in my work!

CASS: You should've taken the money and run. Otherwise, you should've blown the pervert's head off!

HARPER: Neither option was necessary. Besides, I don't carry a weapon.

CASS: A spook without a gun?

HARPER: Look, if you carry a weapon, you've gotta use it, right? There's too much violence in my business anyway.

CASS: How do you expect to make a killing, Harper?

HARPER: You just don't understand the business. Few women do!

(*Cass stands and crosses to the trunk, where she removes a print-laced shawl and ties it around her hips seductively.*)

CASS: Oh, I know plenty about business, Harper. I guess I should've told you I was once a lady of the night trade. Hell, I could knock off a dozen clients a night before the sun could wink its eye. Then I'd give the rest of my day over to self-devotion. (*She crosses upstage to the umbrella stand, removes the parasol, and strikes a demure yet provocative pose.*)

HARPER: Sounds like a pretty quick buck to me.

CASS: It was quick, alright. But lifting your rump over some John is not exactly light work.

(*Harper turns upstage to observe her pose quizzically. The jukebox music plays "Sweet Lorraine" as she strolls alluringly downstage and sits on the edge of the table.*)

HARPER: What exactly were you tradin'?

CASS: I worked one of the best good-time houses in New Orleans. It wasn't just some crummy dive. It was a first-class house where the Johns came to cabaret and listen to colored musicians play that dreadful race music. Those fellas played like they'd never quit, which is probably why they never got to cabaret with the ladies. (*She angles the parasol like a rifle, mimicking the Johns, closing it shut forcefully.*) Not like the Johns who came in for the kill like big-game hunters, taking pop shots at the ladies with their toy pistols.

HARPER (*disdainfully*): A prostitute!

CASS: I was never a prostitute, Harper. I was a whore! A whore, but never a tramp.

HARPER (*stands and crosses to the window*): That's the dirtiest business that ever turned a buck!

CASS: It was steady! And I made a killing! . . . (*She stands, centers the parasol between her spread legs, and illustrates action.*) This ole gal just opened up her legs without batting an eye, reared back on her haunches with a stiff upper lip, then tilted her rump at just the right angle! . . . If you didn't give those jokers a target, for heaven sakes, they'd miss the mark!

HARPER: And what have you got to show for it?

CASS (*sits disconsolately on the edge of table*): Nothing! I used to think havin' someone that close to you regularly was a godsend. But those Johns were so disappointing. You wrap one good leg around those jokers, all that phony cologne evaporates in the smell of sweat, and it's all over. Wham-bam, and they were suckin' wind. Spent! All that high spirit would abandon their bodies. Dead to the world! And I was left alone with the stale aroma of tobacco and the foul taste of beer in my mouth.

HARPER: It's a lousy business!

CASS: Are you judging me, Harper? (*She stands and crosses to the umbrella stand to return the parasol.*)

HARPER: You've got nothin' to be proud of!

CASS: I dunno, I once slept with a real European prince. Who have you ever slept with, pal? (*She crosses to the trunk, puts the shawl inside, removes a green gingham apron, and puts it on.*)

HARPER: That's a personal matter. I'm only dealin' with the fact that sleepin' around the way you do makes you a sittin' duck for an assault. You're lucky to be alive today!

(*Cass crosses downstage to the one-armed bandit and pulls the sheet-drape off with one clean sweeping action. Harper looks on quizzically.*)

CASS: Luck had nothing to do with it. It was a matter of fate. Luck is a poor man's weapon against chaos, a substitute for fate. I was fated to seek love.

(*Harper moves over to the totebag and removes a MacArthur soldier's hat, which he places on his head as lights shift to focus Cass's private moment. He then crosses to the one-armed bandit and pumps the handle.*)

I was fourteen years old when a large colored G.I. struck me dumb. He was playing the one-armed bandit at my Daddy's motel. Now, I had seen a lotta truckers come through, some cowboys, and a few Indians too. Even met a logger from Eureka! But I'd never really been so close to a real black man before.

He had just finished doing time in the South Pacific, and stopped off at Lovelock on his way home East. He played the one-armed bandit with a passion, his mouth opened, his eyes fixed on the fruit like a jackdaw bird. You could tell he was ready to pounce on his winnings. I could feel a stream of hot breath against the back of my hand. He must have noticed my chest swell when two

cherries and a gold brick caused the machine to cough up
five dollars in dimes. He smiled.

HARPER: Hot damned luck! Wha'cha think of that, girlie?

CASS: I said nothing.

HARPER: I'm goin' after the three watermelons.

CASS: Jackpot! He was going after the jackpot.

HARPER: If the odds are in my favor, girlie, I'm gonna buy you
a Hershey bar.

CASS: My chest swelled up good now. I figured he must have
some kind of magic.

(*The sound of the one-armed bandit giving up jackpot. Harper places
his hat at the mouth of the machine as if collecting winnings. Cass
becomes excited.*)

HARPER: Whooooeeeeeeeeee! . . . Hot damned luck!

CASS: He did it! He actually did it! It had to be a miracle. I got
so excited.

(*Cass, with childlike glee, rushes forth and kisses Harper on the
cheek. Before she can withdraw, Harper holds on and kisses her
firmly on the mouth. He summarily produces a Hershey bar from
within his hat, which she accepts with a bewildered expression.*)

It was the first time anybody ever gave me anything.
Daddy wouldn't allow me to accept gifts from strangers,
but I accepted anyway.

(*Hat in place, Harper gestures to her to follow him upstage to the
back of the chairs.*)

It seemed only righteous, though, to give something
back in return. We went out to the shed, out back of the
motel.

(*Harper sinks down behind a chair.*)

And I give him my cherry!

(*Cass sinks down as Harper rises and goes to the totebag to remove the soldier's hat. Cass rises slowly and observes him.*)

He got up . . . and left. Took my cherry with him, and not a word of thanks.

(*As lights return to normal, Cass slowly crosses to the trunk to put the apron inside while Harper gazes at her curiously.*)

He just slipped away in the dust. I guess I could've said thanks, but I didn't. Maybe should've! . . . My life has been one big blundering assault after another ever since.

HARPER: Did you love the fella?

CASS: You're disgusted, aren't you, Harper?

HARPER: I just wanna know if you loved him!

CASS: What makes you so disgusted, Harper?

HARPER: I have no respect for loose women!

CASS: Look, I gave it my best shot at fourteen. And I'm not the least bit ashamed of it. The rest has been a string of assaults!

(*Cass is drawn to the sound of the "Pilgrim Invitational Hymn" coming from the jukebox. She calmly sits and sings along with the music as the agitated Harper paces back and forth.*)

HARPER: That's what they all say when the chips fall. Diana was like that, too. With all her class, you wouldn't think she'd be so loose. She even jumped in bed with her shrink and called it assault. Said she was being treated for fertility repression, now that's pretty goddamned fantastic! And when her belly started to blow up, she called it a traumatized pregnancy. Hell, the woman was having more of a treat than a treatment!

CASS (*softly through Harper's rage*):
　　I thought his love would weaken
　　　　As more and more He knew me;

But it burneth like a beacon,
    And its light and heat go through me;
And I ever hear Him say,
As He goes along His way:
    "O wandering souls! come near me
    My sheep should never fear me
    I am the Shepherd true
    I am the Shepherd true."
Inspirational, isn't it, Harper? Every now and then, they play something other than trash on that jukebox. I used to sing that song for my Daddy until . . . until I told him about the colored G.I.!

HARPER: I thought you loved your Daddy!

CASS: Like to killed him. Poor man wept for days. He said God would punish me if I brought an unhallowed baby into this world.

HARPER: Don't tell me! . . . Another traumatized pregnancy.

CASS: I don't rightly know, but Daddy swore up and down that if I was with child, we'd have to get rid of it.

HARPER: You disgust me! (*He crosses upstage and examines the locks on the door with a disgusted expression.*)

CASS (*stoically*): I did it for my Dad. He was such a sanctified man. I had let the demons in his house, and his body was wracked with pain. Hot stones beat against his breast. I hated to see him suffer, so I went along with him to the back room of the local pharmacist. (*She props herself up on the table and leans backward.*) Daddy said I had nothing to be afraid of since God was witnessing this mournful testimony. He held my hand, then stroked my brow. The pharmacist now leveled his razor. I didn't even bat an eyelash as I reared back on my haunches with a stiff upper lip, my rump tilted at just the right angle! . . .

(*Cass screams loudly, distracting Harper from the door to allay her grave sense of disconsolation.*)

HARPER: Calm down! . . . Calm down, now. No more of that!

(*Cass slowly gains control of herself. Harper releases her and returns to the door.*)

CASS: They cleaned me out, Harper, took everything in one fell swoop. I've been living in cold storage ever since.

HARPER: Maybe it was a blessing!

CASS (*irately*): I was only fourteen, you bastard!

HARPER: I don't have to take that!

CASS (*comes to her feet abruptly*): And neither do I! Let's just stick to the facts. I was fourteen and long blessed, just like I said. I ran away from Lovelock, hitched a ride with a trucker who delivered me to the City of Saints, where I bathed away my sins in the Great Salt Lake. And for the first time in my life, I understood the feeling of being sanctified. I was clean on the outside, and clean on the inside, too, praise Jesus. The spirit must've got the best of me, 'cause, the next thing I knew, the water was over my head. I was going under for the third time when the heavenly figure of a beautiful, sun-baked man with golden hair streaming through his beard reached out to me. He looked like an angel in his strange longjohns, which I later was to learn were his celestial underwear. His eyes were pale and watery blue. He carried me safely to shore. When I came to my senses, my Saviour was gone. But right there on that salt bed, I knew I had discovered love everlasting!

(*Telephone rings. Harper responds alertly. Both stare at the ringing phone.*)

HARPER: Don't you wanna answer it?

(*Cass does not respond.*)

Maybe it's your Saviour in his celestial drawers!

(*Cass crosses circumspectly and picks up the receiver: sound of a click and dial tone.*)

CASS: Hello? . . . (*She hangs up the receiver.*) Somebody is tryin' to spook me!

HARPER: Could just be the pigment of your imagination.

CASS: Don't get cute with me, Harper! I think you're givin' me the runaround. I never should've paid you in advance. Now you wanna take advantage of me!

HARPER: Not a damned thing happened here!

CASS (*insistently*): I was assaulted!

(*Cass turns away from him and faces downstage. Harper crosses briskly to the totebag and removes a small tape recorder.*)

HARPER: We're gonna get down to the bottom of this mess! . . .

(*As he crosses back to the table, he touches Cass on the shoulder. Startled, she turns around with a defensive demeanor. They stare at each other apprehensively for a beat.*)

You wanna give me some straight facts?

(*He moves to a chair, sits, and sets up the tape recorder. Cass slowly finds her way to other chair.*)

Let's take it from the top! . . .

CASS: Top of what?

HARPER: The beginnin'! . . .

CASS: That's too far gone.

HARPER: Then bring it up to date.

CASS: What do you wanna know?

HARPER: Whatever you've got to say. Tell me about those spirits dwellin' in the underworld.

CASS: The shadows? . . .

HARPER: Yeah! . . . And speak clearly.

(*He holds the tape recorder in her direction. She does not respond.*)

I'm waitin'! . . .

CASS: I don't know what to say.

HARPER: Say anything! We're only testin'.

CASS: Shadows are spirits that dwell in the underworld.

HARPER: Hold it! . . . (*He rewinds the tape and replays.*)

CASS'S VOICE: Shadows are spirits that dwell in the underworld.

HARPER: Good! (*He stops tape and resets.*) Ready? . . . Go! . . .

(*The sound of "After Hours" from the jukebox as lights shift to focus Cass's private moment.*)

CASS: I was leaving that department store on Main Street where the old Gayoso Hotel used to be. And I thought to myself, what a shame that so much garbage should be heaped upon the spot where the finest hotel between New Orleans and Chicago used to be. It was the pride of the Cotton Kings. I passed through the debris and made my way to Beale Street, where my ears were assaulted by that wretched race music. And right there on the corner of Beale and Main was an old colored woman selling love potions. She seemed quite agitated, whooping and hollering as she talked to a large peacock called Juno that fanned out its tail in a mass of evil eyes. The woman turned toward me with her eyes rolled back in her head. I thought she was having a seizure, but she extended her hand to make an offering. I wanted that love potion dearly, but I was frightened by so many evil eyes. I turned away and ran home, leaving a five-block trail of rubbish behind me. And on my heels was a shadow. It followed me up the stairs. I dashed into my room, bolted the door, and being worn out by the whole ordeal, took off my clothes and went to bed. When I awoke, a man's hand was around my throat.

HARPER: Hold it! . . . Let's back it up!

(*Lights return to normal as Harper rewinds the tape, and presses "play." No sound.*)

Maybe a bit further.

(*He stops the tape, rewinds, and still no sound as Cass sits patiently on the edge of the bed. They stare at each other quizzically.*)

Just hold tight!

(*He repeats the procedure, and still no sound. Confounded, he stops the tape.*)

Nothin'!

CASS: What happened? . . .

HARPER: We lost it!

CASS (*approaches him curiously*): Did we ever have it?

HARPER: The truth don't move, Cass! (*He stands, crosses to the totebag, and places the tape recorder inside.*)

CASS: I can start from the beginning.

HARPER: Don't bother. All that mumbo-jumbo stuff gets pretty hard to follow. Who's gonna believe it anyway?

CASS: You think I'm foolish, don't you, Harper? Don't deny it, it's written all over your face. You think I'm some kind of hysterical broad getting her rocks off on some dream!

HARPER: Show me some material evidence!

CASS: I've got fingerprints on my throat, God damn you!

(*Harper crosses to her, starts to place his hand near her throat for closer inspection, but it is slapped away.*)

HARPER: Okay, so you've got a few bruises! . . . You gonna tell me how he got in? . . . (*He examines the door once more.*) The door surface is clean. No broken moldings, not the slightest sign of break 'n entry. And it would take a jackhammer to bust these locks.

CASS: What are you, a cop or a carpenter?

HARPER: I'm a professional! And I'm thorough! When you're caught up in the thick of some mess, there are only two ways to find a solution! . . . The right way and the which-a-way! I do it the right way!

CASS: I feel like a fly stuck in a bowl of gumbo soup!

HARPER (*crosses from the door to the window*): Then stay outta my way and let me find a solution.

CASS: I thought leaving New Orleans was gonna be a solution. I guess my sins were piling up over my head, so I decided to come to Memphis to join the Christian Cavalcade.

(*Lights shift for Cass's private moment as Harper removes a red-cap porter hat from totebag, places it on his head, and crosses downstage to the trunk.*)

I knew this trip was headed for trouble the moment I got down to the station and ran into a red-cap porter.

HARPER (*tilts his hat and smiles; rhythmically*): Pardon me, ma'am! . . . This is the Chattanooga choo-choo! . . . Track twenty-nine! . . . Ma'am, don't you waste any time! (*He places hat on his head and begins a strenuous effort to lift the trunk. He fails.*)

CASS: He tried to lift the trunk. My whole life was stored away in that trunk. There was no way he could lift it to his shoulders. And I was running out of time. The train loaded up and slowly pulled out of the station. I was gonna miss the train.

(*The sound of train pulling out of station, gaining speed, and ultimately exiting with a harrowing rattle.*)

I missed the train.

(*Harper discontinues his effort, turns toward Cass with a smile, tips his hat, and summarily crosses left to place the hat into the totebag as the lights return to normal.*)

I was certain that the red-cap, for some devilish reason, deliberately tried to detain me.

HARPER: How do you know that? Did the man touch you? Did he even come near you?

CASS: No, but I could read it in his evil eyes.

HARPER: What made you think the red-cap's eyes were evil?

CASS: They were bloodshot!

HARPER: The man was just probably worn out from tryin' to shoulder your burden!

CASS: That red-cap had a distinctly jaundiced gaze in his eyes. He frightened me!

HARPER (*crosses to her slowly with a glacial gaze*): Do I frighten you? . . .

CASS (*stares at him curiously for a beat*): You don't scare me, Harper. Besides, you don't have bloodshot eyes.

HARPER: But, I *am* black, you know!

CASS: That might just be the pigment of *your* imagination! (*She summarily crosses down left to the dress form.*)

HARPER (*appears flustered*): You know nothin' about me, Cass Pruitt! . . . Not one damn thing!

CASS: But the jackdaw knows! . . . (*She removes the sheet draping the dress form to unveil her wedding dress—a Mormon-inspired ceremonial dress with several layers of white chiffon and a green apron built in.*) How do you like my wedding dress? I've been saving it for that righteous day when my lover comes back to me.

HARPER: Don't try to evade the issue, Cass.

CASS: This dress is the issue. It took me seven years to make it. I've worn it only once, the day I left New Orleans to come to Memphis. Good thing I was wearing a spring coat, or that red-cap would've soiled it with his dreadful eyes. He came mighty close, though. (*She crosses down right and sits on the edge of the trunk.*) So, while waiting for the next train, I purified my mission with a good scrub-down with a pumice stone.

(*The muted sound of "Pilgrim Invitational Hymn" is heard from jukebox.*)

The Christian Cavalcade promised a glorious day in Memphis. So, I came to Memphis in search of God, and found Death lurking in the crossbars of the tent.

(*Lights shift for Cass's private moment as she crosses upstage. Harper removes a pastor's black bib and white collar from the totebag and dons them. He crosses downstage reverently with a small black Bible.*)

High above the head of the Evangelist, there in the roof of the tent, hovered a jackdaw. The Evangelist didn't even see the little black bird, but I did. I recognized its thievish eyes and that frightful cry which signaled danger. (*She crosses left and stands before the chest of drawers, which appears as an altar.*) But Christ was near, and I had nothing to fear. Christ had come to witness my wedding dress. I could hear the Evangelist saying . . .

HARPER: Give yourself to Jesus!

CASS: . . . and I was full of Christ. I had nothing to fear.

HARPER (*begins to sermonize in the tone and attitude of a used-car salesman*): Now, my friends, I know that some of you are thinking that you've gotta have luck to get along in this world. Many of you, right this very moment, are carry-ing a rabbit's foot in your purses or wearing a four-leaf clover in your hair. Some of you even have significant numbers written on your sleeves, while others sleep at night with a special button, a stickpin, some kinda lode-stone under their pillows. Well, you wouldn't need to covet all that junk, friends, if you'd come into the ministry and give yourself to Jesus. You can turn it all in, right here, like you would an old Chevy, then walk outta here with a spankin' new soul. You can't play Jesus cheap, friends. He's got a better deal for each and every man or woman, rich or poor. I'm reminded of that old invitational anthem . . .

(*He turns around to face Cass upstage as she sings the chorus section of the "Pilgrim Invitational Hymn"—now highly audible.*)

CASS (*greatly animated*):
O wandering souls! come near me
My sheep should never fear me
I am the Shepherd true
I am the Shepherd true.

(*Harper resumes the sermon as Cass mutters responses intermittently. The "Invitational Hymn" ends.*)

HARPER: Now, such a little daughter is on her way to becoming a godly woman. We can hear about a beautiful woman anytime. Even a smart woman. Or a career woman. Maybe even a talented woman. But we seldom ever hear the good news about a godly woman. I'm talkin' about the true Keepers of the Spring.

(*Cass slaps her hands joyously above her head, clasps them, and slowly brings them down, making a transition from joy to sorrow.*)

Now, I'm sure all of you remember the story about our Spiritual Leader's walk down a desolate street to meet his ministry. Amidst the crowd was a woman with acute sufferin'. Her beautiful face was lined with agony, her body wracked with pain. I wanna tell you, that gal was a mess! Each dawn promised a hopeless day, and every sunset was stained with her misery. Now, where in the world could this woman find a physician to cure such a malady.

(*Cass begins to cross upstage right sorrowfully.*)

She was lackin' spiritual exercise, and her soul had become soft and flabby. This gal needed help badly. So when she heard about the wonderful power of our Spiritual Leader, she decided to come amongst the crowd and test him. Folks always wanna test a good product before they use it. Now, as the Spiritual Leader came down that desolate street and through that massive crowd, this woman, with tears in her eyes, and his righteous name on her lips, reached out to touch him.

(*Cass gestures toward him, then throws herself down at his feet.*)

But where? . . . On his head would be too irreverent, and his hand, much too familiar. She angled down at the hem of his robe.

(*Cass touches Harper at the ankle and reacts with spontaneous bliss while kneeling. Harper turns around suddenly.*)

Who touched me? . . . Remember, he said, who touched me? Then looked down at his hemline to witness the magnetic effects of faith.

(*Harper helps Cass to her feet. She turns around, slowly walks to the bed, allowing her housecoat to fall to the floor, then climbs onto the bed and rocks back and forth on her knees reverently. The muted sound of the "Pilgrim Invitational Hymn" is heard from jukebox.*)

He reached down and touched the woman benevolently 'side her cheek. And lo and behold, grace had come to that woman. The lines that marred her beauty were gone, and her body was released from pain. New life had come to that woman's body. She was a sanctified woman. A godly woman. Let us pray! . . . Lord Jesus, we come to Thee now as little children. Dress us again in clean pinafores. Make us tidy once more with the tidiness of true remorse and confession. Oh, wash our hearts, that they may be clean again. Make us to know the strengthening joys of the Spirit, and the newness of life which only Thee can give. Amen!

(*Sound of the Transistor Voice as lights return to normal.*)

TRANSISTOR VOICE: Home to Harper! . . . Home callin' Harper! . . . Come on in, Harper! . . .

(*Harper crosses quickly to the totebag, places bib and collar in bag, and removes transistor. Cass remains transfixed in her reverie, rocking back and forth on her knees. The sound of rain. As Harper speaks, the sound of Martin Luther King's Memphis speech can be heard vaguely in the background over the transistor.*)

HARPER: Harper, here! . . .

KING'S VOICE: Well, I don't know what will happen now. We've got some difficult days ahead. But it really doesn't matter with me now. Because I've been to the mountaintop.

TRANSISTOR VOICE: Man, I been lookin' all over for you in this temple. Must be over two thousand people in here.

HARPER: Yeah! . . . And it's raining up a storm.

TRANSISTOR VOICE: The Reverend is wearin' 'em out in here. I wish you wouldn't be so slippery, Harper. You'd better stand by in case we need you.

(*Harper turns up the transistor so that the speech is more audible.*)

KING'S VOICE: I won't mind. Sure, I would like to live a long life. Longevity has its place. But I'm not concerned about that now. I just want to do God's will. And He's allowed me to go up to the mountain.

HARPER (*shouting*): If you need me, just holler, Home!

TRANSISTOR VOICE: Over and out!

KING'S VOICE: And I've looked over, and I've seen the promised land. I may not get there with you, but I want you to know tonight that we as a people will get to the promised land.

(*Harper, standing near the window listening to the speech, is distracted by Cass, who is on her knees mumbling, rocking back and forth frenetically.*)

CASS: Just to touch him! . . . One touch! . . . Oh, just one touch! . . .

(*As the throng at the temple responds with rhythmic clapping, Harper crosses toward her curiously and places the transistor on the table. He picks up her housecoat, examines it, and approaches.*)

HARPER: Cass! . . . You alright, Cass? . . . C'mon, come to yourself! . . .

KING'S VOICE: So I'm happy tonight. I'm not worried about anything. I'm not fearing any man. Mine eyes have seen the glory of the coming of the Lord!

(*Harper moves in to touch her. The sound of a loud clap of lightning and thunder.*)

HARPER (*forcefully*): I said, come to yourself, woman!!

CASS (*spins around abruptly and embraces him with blind passion*): Oh, Jesus! . . . Jesus! . . .

(*Lights fade out as Harper responds to the embrace.*)

ACT II

Open Curtain: Same setting. Late afternoon on the following day. The sound of footsteps on the other side of the upstage left wall. Also, the sound of the "Pilgrim Invitational Hymn" can be heard from the jukebox. The window drapes are opened to allow the late afternoon light to beam through.

Harper, nude under the sheet, lies upon the bed with an ungraceful attitude of exhaustion. His clothes are tidily folded on top of the trunk. Cass, wearing her wedding dress, sits in a chair fanning herself with a fan. In front of her is the undraped marble-topped table, upon which are two silver plates and two silver goblets. Upstage, on the hotplate, is a silver tea service. She sings the "Invitational Hymn" softly, her eyes gazing quizzically at the wall, her face expressing concern over the footsteps in the adjoining room.

CASS (*solemnly*):
  I was wandering and weary
    When my Saviour came unto me.
  For the ways of sin grew dreary,
    And the world had ceased to woo me;
  And I thought I heard Him say,
  As He came along His way:
    "O wandering souls! come near me;
    My sheep should never fear me;
    I am the Shepherd true,
    I am the Shepherd true."

(*Harper sits up abruptly as Cass had done earlier—with a wide-eyed, apprehensive look. He alertly directs his gaze toward the window, then inspects his nudity under the sheet before staring at Cass with a perplexed expression.*)

HARPER (*anxiously*): What did you do with my clothes?

(*Cass turns toward him, places a finger to her pursed lips as a sign to be quiet, then gestures toward the trunk as she stands, crosses to the wall, and listens attentively to the apparent footsteps on the other side of the wall. Harper, in the meantime, springs alertly from the*

486

bed with a sheet wrapped around his body and begins to dress himself with awkward anxiety.)

I know what you're thinkin'! . . . But it's not what you think! I wasn't plannin' on spendin' the night or nothin'. I don't do things like that! . . . Not on the job, anyway! But I can explain what happened, though. Even if you can't, I can. I had nothin' to do with what happened! It was an accident, that's all, an accident. Accidents happen! . . . Not to me, but they do happen. Somethin' just came over me last night that's hard to explain. I was kinda caught off guard, you know what I mean? It happens to the best of us, but that don't mean nothin'! . . . I just got too involved in my work. When you're moonlightin', those extra hours are bound to catch up with you, take you by surprise, and compromise your reputation. That's why I don't like to moonlight! Someone gets the wrong impression and you've blown a whole career. Can't explain it away with little truths 'cause they always sound like big lies in this sorta situation. And who needs it, you know what I mean, who needs all that grief over a minor accident? (*He adjusts his trousers while crossing to the sink to throw some water into his face and gargle. He glances over at Cass, who has been inattentive to his explanation.*) What time is it, anyway?

CASS (*gazes at him for a beat and crosses toward the window*): You're wearing the watch!

HARPER (*examines the watch as Cass peers out the window*): It must've stopped!

CASS: The sun is leaning toward the river.

HARPER (*spits water out of his mouth and into the sink, then quickly crosses to the totebag for his binoculars*): For Christ sakes, the day is practically gone!

CASS (*demurely*): Gone . . . but not wasted!

HARPER (*turns to her alertly*): Don't you start gettin' the wrong impression!!!

CASS: What impression do you want me to have? . . . It's just like you read about in those detective thrillers where the dick gets the girl in the end!

HARPER: It's that kind of trash that gives my profession a bad reputation. (*He turns to the window and peers out with his binoculars.*)

CASS: Believe me, Harper, you have nothin' to be ashamed of.

HARPER: Damn! . . . They've got the window draped. Can't see a damned thing!

CASS (*apologetically*): Oh, Harper, I almost forgot! . . . (*She sits in a chair and begins to rotate the tea service with her hands in order to stir the tea.*)

HARPER (*turns away from the window with a quizzical expression*): Forgot what? . . .

CASS: They tried to call you.

HARPER: They did? . . .

CASS: Yes, they did! . . .

HARPER: They, who? . . .

CASS: On the squawk box!

HARPER: Home! (*He quickly locates the transistor in the totebag, extends the antenna, and speaks urgently, as Cass calmly reflects on their episode.*) Harper to Home! . . . Harper to Home! . . . Come in, Home! . . .

CASS: No, Harper, you have nothing to be ashamed of. After the short night we spent, you still managed to work up a good lathery sweat this morning! . . .

HARPER: Come in, Home! . . . This is Harper callin'! . . .

CASS: Didn't have the heart to wake you. I guess you were just plumb fagged out!

HARPER: Harper to Home! . . . Harper to Home! . . . Come in, Home! . . .

CASS: Nothing unusual about a man being fagged out. Guess all that heat must've drained all the daylight outta your eyes.

HARPER: Home? . . . Dead!

CASS: You just kinda petered out, remember?

HARPER (*inattentively*): Remember what? . . .

CASS: Don't you wanna remember?

HARPER: Give me a clue! (*He places the transistor in totebag and crosses to search for shoes and socks under the bed.*)

CASS: Last night! . . . This morning! . . . We were very close this morning.

HARPER: I don't remember nothin'! I was dead to the world.

CASS: Exactly what I thought this morning when I saw a jackdaw perched on the windowsill. This man is dead to the world!

HARPER (*locates his shoes and socks and returns hastily to a chair to put them on*): Well, I'm back now, and I'm gettin' in the wind.

CASS: Just like one of those thievish jackdaws!

HARPER: Look, I've lost contact with Home. Anything could be happenin'!

CASS (*stands irately*): You can't just fly in here, pick the bones clean, and vanish like nothing ever happened!

HARPER (*anxiously*): What happened? . . .

CASS: Take the sleep outta your eyes!

HARPER (*wipes his eyes, leans back in the chair, and observes that the ceiling fan is not functioning*): Oh, I see! . . . The ventilation! The fan must've quit last night. No wonder I had a hard time gettin' outta bed this morning. Must've been suffocatin'.

CASS: Why are you tryin' to hurt me, Harper?

HARPER: How did I hurt you?

CASS: You've said nothin' about my dress!

(*Harper gazes at Cass quizzically. He glances over at the bare dress form for a beat, then returns his gaze to Cass, who stands downstage preening impatiently.*)

HARPER: Oh, yeah! . . . Turn around so I can have a good look! . . .

(*Cass responds with alacrity.*)

It sure is different.

CASS: Is that all this dress inspires in your mind?

HARPER: It's pretty, too.

CASS: I wore it for you, Harper.

HARPER: No kiddin'? . . . That's nice, real nice. But you didn't have to go through all that trouble for me. You oughta save somethin' like that for a special occasion.

CASS: It was an inspiration.

HARPER: Yeah, I can see that, too! (*He stands and crosses to the window to peer out.*)

CASS: And quite fitting for the occasion.

HARPER: What's the occasion?

CASS: Prenuptial! . . .

HARPER (*turns away from the window; circumspectly*): Prenuptial, huh? . . . And that's your wedding dress, right?

CASS: Last night, Harper . . . this morning! . . . You resurrected feelings in me I had not felt since I left the City of Saints.

HARPER: Uh-uh, you've gotta forget that, Cass. You've gotta bury all that deep in some hole in the back of your mind. Nothin' really happened, so forget it!

CASS: Forget it? . . . Sure, forget it! What part of it do you want me to forget, Harper? Maybe you want me to forget how everytime I called the Lord's name, you'd moan in my ear . . . "Yeeaaaah, baby! Yeeeaaaah, baby!"

HARPER: I said that? . . . You've gotta be kiddin'! I would never say nothin' like that. It's all in your mind, like those shadows that haunt you.

CASS: I'm not your tramp, Harper! You're treating me like some cheap little tramp. I've never been anybody's tramp!

HARPER: I know, I know! . . . You're a businesswoman!

CASS: That's right, buster! And I've paid for your time!

HARPER: Whoa . . . whoa, back up, Miss Pruitt. I've been through all that before. No woman could ever pay for my time. Not any more! You just can't afford that much time. (*He removes the watch from his wrist and places it on the table.*) So, take back your token. The case is closed! (*He summarily picks up his totebag and crosses upstage to the door.*)

CASS: You pledged yourself to me, Harper!!!

HARPER: Where'd you get that ridiculous notion?

CASS (*crosses briskly down to the bed*): Right here in these sweaty sheets where you promised to protect me. Come get a whiff of your handiwork, Harper. Your sweat stinks just like any other John!

HARPER (*becomes flustered*): What do you want me to do . . . burn some incense, maybe sprinkle some eau de cologne or somethin'? . . .

CASS: You can at least sit down and have a civilized breakfast before you quit on me! (*She crosses resignedly to refrigerator, raises the sheet, and removes pita bread and garlic pills, then returns to the table and places the morsels on two plates previously set for them.)*

HARPER (*indignantly*): I did not quit on you!

CASS: I know, you just wanna be let off the hook.

HARPER: I told you I've got priorities. Maybe you don't know about priorities, but I do! . . . I'm a prioritizer-er!

CASS: You wanna be let off the hook, or don't you?

HARPER (*emphatically*): I'm not a quitter, Cass!

CASS: Then, sit down and eat your breakfast so you can get on with your work.

(Harper acquiesces, drops his totebag near the door, then sits down in the chair as Cass ceremoniously arranges the table.)

Are you always so restless?

HARPER: I've got a lot on my mind.

CASS: I see! . . . Your wife, maybe.

HARPER (*sharply*): I don't have a wife!

CASS: Funny, you're as restless as any married man I've ever known.

HARPER: When you're married, there's no rest for the weary. You spend all your domestic hours in that labor of love tryin' to sweep sneakin' suspicions under the carpet. But, somehow, you never can vacuum all the skeletons out the closet.

CASS: How would you know?

HARPER: I used to be married.

CASS: Did you love her?

HARPER: You're gettin' too personal, Cass.

CASS: No wonder you're so restless.

HARPER: I don't wanna talk about it!

CASS: Might help your digestion.

HARPER (*reflecting bitterly*): I did everything in my power to win that woman's respect, and she showed me no more appreciation than a common whore! It was hard to understand how all that fine breedin' could make Diana like that.

CASS (*quizzically*): You were married to this Diana?

HARPER: Yeah! . . . And she supported me for a long time, too. She didn't want me to work, said she couldn't live with a man who worked as a carpenter. So I stayed home. I didn't like it none. Made me feel like her plaything. I wasn't used to bein' supported by a woman. Wasn't long before the plaything couldn't get up for the game. I mean, how can a man respect himself if he's gotta depend on a woman's wages? My union card wasn't comin', so I cashed in on my military police trainin' and got this job as a spook! And that's when she quit me. As soon as she saw me on my feet, she quit me! . . . Moved into a high-rise luxury building and had all kinds of creeps parading through her door. It was a regular circus up in there! Of course, I was never invited, but I still loved her. So one day I was in the neighborhood and stopped in to see how she was doin'. I didn't wanna tell the doorman we were married or nothin', so I showed him my credentials. The sonuvabitch directed me to the service entrance, can you imagine that? He then must've alerted her, 'cause soon as I get off the elevator, who do I see comin' outta her apartment but her pasty-faced shrink! He walked right past me, got on the elevator, and pretended like I wasn't even there. When I got inside, I took a look around. She looked like hell, but the furniture was pretty, I mean the place was laid out like a good-time house. I told her, "Baby, I know it's none of my business how you entertain, but you've gotta get outta this fast lane before you get in trouble. If you don't have any respect for yourself, at least have some respect for me. I love you, baby, I love you!" You know what she said? . . . "Get outta my face, you creep, and stop invadin' my privacy!" Can you imagine that? . . . She called me, her husband, who used to be her plaything . . . a creep! I grabbed her in the throat! . . .

(*Cass becomes suddenly tense and gazes at him circumspectly.*)

And kissed her!

CASS: What happened to the baby?

HARPER: What baby? . . .

CASS: You said there was a baby.

HARPER: I told you I don't wanna talk about it.

CASS: Too painful? . . .

HARPER: It's a fruitless discussion, Cass.

CASS: Then, why don't you eat your breakfast!

HARPER (*gazes at the bread and garlic pill on the plate with a perplexed expression*): Where's the breakfast?

CASS: On your plate!

HARPER: You call this breakfast? . . . I've been sittin' here waitin' for you to put some food on the plate.

CASS: Today is Thursday, a fast day.

HARPER: Yeah, it won't take more than a minute to get this down! (*He snatches up the bread, takes a generous bite, and chews voraciously. He now brings the goblet to his mouth.*)

CASS: You might show more reverence for that sacramental bread, Harper.

HARPER: Um-hm! . . . (*He takes a big swallow from the goblet, gags violently, and stands abruptly.*) Damn! . . . What the hell you tryin' to do, poison me?

CASS: Hot oil and lemon won't kill you. It's a purifying libation. Now, don't forget your garlic pill.

HARPER: Garlic pill? . . . You servin' garlic pills for breakfast?

CASS: Actually, we missed breakfast, Harper. We're now having a vespers meal. And that pill is gonna cleanse your blood good.

HARPER (*quizzically*): Is that what they do . . . cleanse?

CASS: Garlic is a natural antibiotic.

HARPER (*suspiciously*): I see! . . . But why would I be needin' an antibiotic? (*He sits down in the chair, picks up the garlic pill, and examines it.*) I don't have a cold or nothin'! . . .

CASS: You never know! . . .

HARPER: Do *you* know?

CASS: Know what, Harper?

HARPER: Why I might need an antibiotic?

CASS: I told you, it's a universal cleanser!

HARPER: Can you be more specific?

CASS: To tell you the truth, Harper . . .

HARPER (*uneasily*): That's exactly what I want, lady, the truth!

CASS: In your line of work, you know, spookin' around like you do, it's a wonder you don't pick up all kinds of germs.

HARPER: On strange toilet seats, maybe! . . .

CASS: Especially toilet seats.

HARPER: All I wanna know is what did I pick up in your bed?

CASS (*indignantly*): Certainly, you don't think I contaminated you!

HARPER: Did you?

CASS (*stands indignantly*): Harper, you are truly pitiful! I thought you had more guts than the average overgrown boy who gets horny, then climbs into a woman's bed like a miser who is afraid to empty his sack in the vault out of fear that he might lose his precious jewels! (*She summarily begins clearing the table, leaving a single goblet behind.*)

HARPER: It's better to be safe than sorry, if you get my meanin'.

CASS: Just what do you mean, Harper?

HARPER: I don't mess with professional women!

CASS: Try it, you might like it!

HARPER: Just did, and I hate it!! (*He stands and crosses to window.*)

CASS: Harper! . . . What happened here last night was the divine will of God. And if it wasn't, I'd have to call it one more nasty assault.

HARPER: It was an accident!

CASS: Okay, then I was assaulted.

HARPER: You makin' some kind of accusation?

CASS: You're a frightened man, Harper.

HARPER: I've got nothin' to be frightened about!

CASS: Don't you? . . . You oughta be. The police are funny in this town. What are they gonna think when they find you locked up in here with me?

HARPER: Don't start talkin' crazy. I'm here on an investigation.

CASS: What are you investigating?

HARPER: A case of assault!

CASS: Who's gonna believe that story?

HARPER: I've got credentials!

CASS (*picks up the watch from the table and handles it playfully*): You're off the hook, remember?

HARPER (*crosses briskly to the door*): Then open the door so I can get outta here!

CASS: Go on, bolt outta here. But you're gonna find that Memphis is no haven, Harper. I know this neck of the woods. I remember a colored G.I. coming through here with all kinds of campaign ribbons on him. He had just hijacked a Greyhound bus from Washington, D.C. The bus was loaded with a bunch of colored students on their way to a freedom march in Alabama. The soldier had just returned from overseas and went off his rocker when he discovered that his Scotch-Irish wife had abandoned their home in Maryland and returned to her roots in Memphis. He swore up and down the bus that he was gonna kill her. By the time he got to Memphis, those colored students had talked him out of it. He gave up peacefully. But it was just his rotten luck that among those freedom riders was one little Jewish girl, so the authorities locked up the soldier, charged him with one count of kidnapping, one count of attempted rape, and probably one count of just being there!

HARPER: Justice simply doesn't work that way, Cass. Not even in Memphis!

CASS: Who said anything about justice? When you get what you deserve . . . (*She gestures toward him with the watch and places it on the table*) . . . that's justice. When you get more or less than you deserve, that's good or bad luck. And I doubt if your luck could be any better than that soldier's, Harper.

HARPER (*intrepidly*): Call the police, Cass!

CASS (*stares at Harper for a beat, then crosses to the telephone*): I bet they're gonna be tickled pink to find you here.

HARPER: Just call 'em!!

CASS (*begins to dial the telephone*): I'm not just gonna call 'em! . . . I'm gonna scream!!

HARPER (*moves toward her alertly*): Hang up, Cass! . . . I said, hang up!!!

CASS (*complies and saunters over to the chair, sits and sips from goblet*): You scare easily, don't you, Harper?

HARPER (*agitated*): Do I look scared, huh, do I? . . . I'm just a bit worried 'bout not locatin' Home. (*He crosses to the window warily.*)

CASS: Oh, I thought you might be worried about the creep next door.

HARPER (*turns toward her alertly*): What creep? . . .

CASS: On the other side of the wall. Didn't you hear him pacing around?

HARPER (*moves to the wall and places his ear to it*): I didn't hear nothin'! . . .

CASS: He like to scared me to death.

HARPER: Somebody you know?

CASS: I don't know every drifter that gets a bed in this dump. But anybody who spends an hour in the bathroom has got to be creepy!

HARPER: How do you know that?

CASS: We share the bathroom down the hall. When you were sleeping, I stepped out to the toilet.

HARPER (*turns toward her with a quizzical expression and crosses down*): You mean, you actually left this room?

CASS: I had to relieve myself. I must've stood outside that bathroom door for at least an hour. It was hot. The old boozer across the hall had his door open for ventilation. I pretended not to notice him sitting on the edge of his bed with a gin bottle in one hand, and snapping his suspenders with the other. There he sat, licking his lips and calling out to me . . . "Here, kitty-kitty-kitty . . . here, kitty!" I don't know if it was the catcalls or that fella creeping around in the bathroom that made my skin crawl the most. I decided to hold my water, return to the room, and give myself the once-over with the pumice stone.

HARPER: Very peculiar! . . . I checked out the rooms on this floor yesterday. You and the old boozer across the hall were the only ones occupyin' any rooms. And the room next door was most certainly empty.

CASS: That room has been empty for weeks. I've been hoping that somebody more congenial than that old lush would come along and take it.

HARPER: Very peculiar, indeed.

CASS: Folks come and go around here.

HARPER: Yeah, but when I asked the manager if I could rent a room, she said she wouldn't be rentin' any more rooms for a while. I had to show her my credentials to get up here.

CASS: She don't truck with strangers much.

HARPER: Then it must be a familiar face. Maybe somebody you even know.

CASS: All I saw this morning was a jackdaw on the windowsill. It gave me a fright. So I put on my wedding dress. And soon past midday, I heard footsteps in the next room.

HARPER: I'd better call the manager! (*As he approaches the telephone, it rings. They both stare at the phone for a beat, then Harper quickly picks up the receiver before Cass can get to it. Sharply:*) Hello!!! . . . (*The sound of a phone being hung up, followed by a dial tone.*) They hung up!

(*He hangs up the receiver with a perplexed expression. Cass picks it up to listen for a beat, then hangs up irately.*)

CASS: And rightly so! It could've been one of my gentleman callers. Now you've gone and chased the rascal away.

HARPER: How would I know you were expectin' a call?

CASS: I wasn't! . . . But that doesn't give you the right to come in here and take such liberties with me, answering my phone as if my gentleman caller should reveal himself to you.

HARPER: So you do know who called.

(*The sound of "Flat Foot Floogie" can be heard on the jukebox.*)

CASS: I most certainly do not! I get all kinds of calls. Some are friendly, some are rude. Sometimes I get hot, lathery, labored breathing. Even had a few monumental offers most ladies would be hard pressed to refuse. But they don't usually hang up on me. Hell, my number is scrawled above the urinals of every bar in Memphis!

HARPER: And you wonder why you've got trouble? You oughta have that number changed.

CASS: And go out of existence? At least when those jokers call, I know somebody cares if I'm living or dead!

(*The music from the jukebox becomes more audible than usual as Harper crosses to the window with a sense of grave agitation, peers out for a beat, and returns to center.*)

HARPER: You should've waken me, Cass. Why didn't you wake me up? I've gotta know who's comin' and goin' around here. Can't afford to have nobody slippin' up on me. It could be important. How do you expect me to do my job if you're gonna withhold information from me? (*He suddenly stomps his foot three times against the floor.*) Why don't they turn down that goddamned jukebox!

(*Jukebox sound stops. And so do the footsteps next door.*)

CASS: No point gettin' all heated up about it, Harper. (*She quickly approaches with a serviette and wipes his brow.*)

Harper (*subdued*): I guess it is kinda close in this room. You know, stuffy! Hot and stuffy! Not enough ventilation in here.

Cass: Just relax! . . .

Harper: How do you expect me to relax?

(*Cass begins to open his shirt. He grabs her hand firmly, resisting for a beat, then releases it.*)

Cass: Just open your shirt and let some of that steam outta your collar! . . . Then, relax!

(*Harper acquiesces, opening up his shirt as he crosses to sit in a chair. Cass goes to the chest of drawers to fetch a pumice stone.*)

Harper: I guess I can sit for a minute. At least until I hear from Home.

Cass: You've simply gotta have faith, Harper.

Harper: I've got plenty of faith in Home. I depend on him.

Cass: And God? . . . Do you have faith in God? (*She crosses with the pumice stone and begins helping Harper out of his shirt, revealing his bare chest.*)

Harper: I doubt if I could recognize him if I saw him. But Home keeps the faith. One time I was in trouble and needed some peace of mind. Home said I should seek out God, who is on everybody's Most Wanted list in the world. I had given him up for dead, but Home said I'd find him alive and well in California. Guess you could say Home is a better than average crapshooter than I am!

Cass: Is Home colored?

Harper: Can't tell you! . . . I'd blow his cover!

(*She starts to rub his chest with the pumice stone. He grabs her hand.*)

What in hell are you doin'?

CASS: Relax, Harper. It's only pumice stone.

HARPER: Felt more like an assault with a deadly weapon!

CASS: A little rubdown won't hurt you.

HARPER: As long as you don't take the skin off my back. I
don't go for that rough stuff.

CASS: Harper, you're so conventional, I could scream.

(*Harper reclines in the chair. She begins massaging his brow with
her hand. The muted sound of "Just a Gigolo" is heard coming from
the jukebox. Harper, in an effort to relax, casually sings a few bars of
the song.*)

HARPER:
> Just a gigolo,
> > everywhere I go
> Nobody hears
> > me cryin' . . .

(*He chuckles.*) You know what I really think, Cass? . . . I
think you're way off the track. I mean, gone! You're so far
out I doubt if you have much chance of gettin' back.

CASS: Just sit still while I work these kinks outta your head.
(*She begins to massage his head.*)

HARPER (*reflectively*): I mean it, Cass. You have no sense of
urgency. Home used to say, if somebody is on your trail,
and you don't know who it is, you've gotta stay way out
in front of him. Home knows all about survival. There'll
be no slippin' up on Home. He stays on the move. Even
an unknown assailant has got to keep movin'. In a funny
way, the assailant gets caught up in his own momentum.
As long as he stalks his prey down some dark corridor on
Beale Street, he's okay. But as soon as he turns down
Main Street, he takes a chance of blowin' his cover. He
must move quickly and decisively on his momentum
before the prey turns around for an unguarded glimpse
and simply asks . . . "Haven't we met somewhere

before?" The prey never had a chance, catching only a brief peek at the sudden stroke of horror.

(*Cass, who is preoccupied with the pumice stone rubdown of his body, is only marginally attentive to the story.*)

CASS (*calmly*): Are you tryin' to frighten me, Harper?

HARPER: No, I'm tryin' to tell you somethin' for your own good.

CASS: Well, let me tell you something! . . . You oughta take better care of your body.

HARPER: Cass, I'm serious!

CASS: I'm serious, too. When I was growin' up, I was told that colored people were the victims of a curse placed on their bodies for sinful transgressions. But, if they would only repent, and return to the teachings of goodness, they would once again become a white and delightsome people.

HARPER (*impatiently*): You don't wanna be serious, do you?

CASS: It would be a blessing, Harper.

HARPER: I'm talkin' about survival!

CASS: You would be saved, Harper. One day, a prophet will come and collect your bones and say . . .

HARPER (*stands impatiently and begins putting on his shirt*): Don't tell me! . . . I know! . . . Before us . . . is a man . . . who in mortal life . . . was actually a white Lamanite. A large, thick-set man . . . but a man of God. His name is . . . Zelf. He was a warrior and chieftain . . . under the great prophet . . . Onandagus, who was known from the eastern sea to the Rocky Mountains. Notice how the curse of his skin has been lifted!

(*Harper summarily removes the binoculars from the totebag left upstage by the door, and quickly crosses to the window to peer out. Cass crosses to the chest of drawers to return the pumice stone.*)

CASS: Everybody would delight in being delightsome, if they could. If you had faith in God, Harper, you too could be delightful.

HARPER: Don't count on it!

CASS: But it's not easy to have faith. Faith slipped away from me on my wedding day.

(*Harper turns away from the window and gazes at her quizzically as he crosses upstage to the totebag and puts the binoculars inside.*)

HARPER: I thought you never married.

CASS: I was supposed to marry, but it was never consummated. You see, soon after my Saviour abandoned me, a Prophet found me adrift in the City of Saints. He took me to live in his household, which included not one but six wives. And that's the God-honest truth!

(*Lights shift to focus Cass's private moment. She crosses downstage left as Harper removes a Mormon prophet's mantle from the totebag and dons it.*)

It was there that I began working on my dress. Those gals tried to teach me everything about being a wife and a mother. After several years in the prophet's benevolent care, he came to my room one night.

HARPER (*stentorian*): My dear, I have a message for you. I have been commanded by God to take another wife. And you are that woman. What have you to say?

CASS: Nothing! I didn't know what to say. And I wasn't sure if I should confess the humiliating fact that I was not equipped to bare him a progeny.

(*Harper crosses down slowly as Cass begins to kneel downstage.*)

HARPER: You must pray for light and understanding, daughter, so that you may receive testimony on the wisdom of His command.

CASS (*anguished*): I got down on my knees, clasped my hands over the bed, bowed my head, and prayed. I prayed that

God would show me how I could possibly become the Prophet's wife without benefit of grace to fertilize his Kingdom. And the more I prayed, the more my soul seemed engulfed in darkness. It was tormenting, oh, how very tormenting! . . . I wept!

HARPER: Though I have no reassuring words to offer, little daughter, you must not weep. It is not I that makes this command of you, but God. And you will have only until tomorrow to decide. If you should reject His message, the gate shall be closed against you forever.

CASS (*greatly agitated*): No! . . . No! . . . I can't accept! I won't accept without God's word. I'd rather die!

HARPER (*strokes her head benevolently*): One step at a time, daughter. May God Almighty bless you. In this night of lonely trepidation, a testimony shall manifest itself unto you. It shall come in the form of unusual joy and peace, more than you have ever known before. (*He crosses upstage and begins a reverent vigil by the wall, pacing back and forth a few times, ending the action with a quizzical gaze toward the wall.*)

CASS (*turbulently*): I prayed, oh, how I prayed. I could hear the Prophet pacing like a sentinel in the next room. I prayed till my knees bled and my clutched fingers began to blister. I prayed all through the night and into the next morning while the Prophet kept his vigil. And still, the veil never parted. (*She screams hysterically.*) Oh, God! . . . Oh, God! Where is your sign, Father? Have mercy on me, Father, have mercy!

(*Lights return to normal as Harper quickly removes mantle, stuffs it into the totebag, and moves closer to the wall to investigate the sound of pacing footsteps now heard in the next room. Cass slowly rises to her feet with a forlorn expression.*)

The word never came down to me. So I ran off to New Orleans, hoping to find my Saviour in the clutches of sin.

You do understand, don't you, Harper? I had to find hope somewhere!

HARPER: That creep is on the prowl again!

CASS (*dejectedly*): I know! . . .

HARPER: I'd better go check out that room.

CASS (*anxiously*): Don't leave me here alone!

HARPER: I'm only goin' next door.

CASS: I don't wanna be left alone!

HARPER: Your life might depend on it, Cass.

CASS: I'm afraid to be alone, Harper.

HARPER: What are you afraid of? . . . You've got all these locks on the door! . . . Nobody can get in here.

CASS: You got in, didn't you?

HARPER: You unlocked the door, remember?

CASS (*plaintively*): Don't leave me alone with no creep, Harper.

(*Harper, disgruntled, goes to the totebag and removes the transistor. He manipulates the antenna desperately to get rid of the static as Cass nervously sits on a chair.*)

HARPER: Harper to Home! . . . Harper callin' Home! . . . Come in, Home! . . . (*He receives only static.*)

CASS: Sit down, Harper, you're making me nervous.

HARPER: You oughta be nervous.

CASS: You're making me nervous!

HARPER: I'm makin' you nervous? . . .

CASS: All that fidgeting around! . . .

HARPER: You expect me to be calm?

CASS: I'm calm!

HARPER: A moment ago you were nervous.

CASS: You were making me nervous.

HARPER: Okay, I'll try to be calm. (*He sits in a chair and manipulates the transistor.*)

CASS (*forcefully*): Will you stop it!!!

HARPER: What's buggin' you now?

CASS: You're getting on my nerves with that damned machine!

HARPER: Your life might be in danger.

CASS: And you expect me to sit here calm!

(*They pause for a beat to listen to the footsteps.*)

HARPER (*circumspectly*): You sure you don't know the fella?

CASS: How could I know?

HARPER: You must've thought about it!

CASS: Probably just ole Jack Mormon.

HARPER: Can you give me a description?

CASS: Yeah . . . long ears, an elongated face that ends in a snout, and you've gotta give 'im a swift kick in the balls to get his attention.

HARPER: What kinda jackass let you do a thing like that?

CASS: A Jack Mormon ain't nothing but a jackass, Harper!

HARPER: Well, in the meantime that fella next door is gettin' restless.

CASS: A familiar pattern with these jackasses.

HARPER: So what do you wanna do about it?

CASS: What can I do about it?

HARPER: We can't just sit here!

CASS: Let's just wait it out!

HARPER: Wait for what?

CASS: Something to happen.

HARPER: What do you expect to happen?

CASS: Nothing!

(*Harper stands abruptly, moves quickly upstage, places his transistor in the totebag, and removes the binoculars before crossing with purpose to the window, where he peers out.*)

HARPER: In that case, you don't need me here!

CASS (*turns toward the window to get his attention*): Harper! . . .

HARPER: Nothin' is more deadly than waitin'!

CASS: . . . why can't you be more delightsome?

HARPER (*remains focused out the window; cryptically*): Because I was born to raise Cain, okay? . . . I'm a regular hell-raiser! . . . (*He turns away from the window and focuses the binoculars on Cass.*) You oughta know that by now, don't you?

(*Cass gazes at him curiously for a beat, then chuckles, picks up the fan on the table, pops it open, and sits in the chair in an ungracefully alluring posture, exposing her bare legs inadvertently. Harper lowers the binoculars.*)

What's funny?

CASS: Just now . . . a most wicked thought just bullied its way into my mind!

HARPER: Wicked? . . .

(*Cass manipulates the fan for seductive insinuation.*)

CASS: When you spied me with your glasses, I had the strangest sensation you could see clear through my dress.

HARPER: And you felt wicked! . . .

CASS: It was kinda exciting, too. Your nose was tucked in my navel, and your eyes roamed wildly over my whole naked body. I felt helpless, you know, as if I had surrendered myself to the rapturous gaze of God.

HARPER: You done taken leave of your cotton-pickin' mind, haven't you?

CASS: Isn't that how you're supposed to feel when someone's got your body pinned down with binoculars?

HARPER: I only used these glasses for professional reasons, not amusement. You could be runnin' around here bare-butt ravin' mad and you wouldn't get my attention. So butt out while I take care my business. (*He resumes peering out the window with the binoculars.*)

CASS: Don't play me cheap, Harper. I bet if that creep next door had a good look at me, he wouldn't have been foolin' around in the john for an hour.

HARPER: If you're lookin' for amusement, why don't you go next door and try that fella on for size.

CASS: Who you kiddin', Harper? It's not my fault an ole peep specialist like you can't get turned on. I guess I'd have to be colored to turn your head to a magazine centerfold.

HARPER: I damn sure wouldn't be amused! . . .

CASS: You'd be ashamed! . . .

HARPER: I'd be embarrassed! . . .

CASS: Why, Harper, too close to home?

HARPER: I don't owe you any explanation!

CASS (*calculatingly*): You ever hear the Aesop tale about the great cock fight, Harper?

(*Harper ignores her and continues to peer out the window with binoculars as she reclines and calmly fans herself.*)

These two cocks were fighting over the hens. One cock took a beating and ran off to hide in a dark corner, while the victor climbed up on a high wall and crowed at the top of his voice. Cock-a-doodle-doo! . . . Cock-a-doodle-doo! It didn't take long to attract the attention of an eagle, who swooped down and snatched him up. The lame cock came out from his safe dark hiding place and was now able to mount the hens without interruption. Just goes to show you, Harper, that God resists the proud but gives grace to the humble.

HARPER (*excitedly*): They opened up the curtains! . . .

(*Cass snaps the fan closed and alertly turns her gaze to the wall, where the sound of footsteps had just stopped. She stands and crosses to the wall to listen curiously.*)

They must've had a meetin' or somethin'. I can see the Reverend. He's still got some of his cronies with him. Must've been a pretty good meetin' from the way they're laughin' it up. But somebody had better give the Reverend a towel. He's stumbling around with soap on his face.

(*The sound of an automobile pulling up outside and honking the horn. Cass is distracted from the wall by the sound. She slowly crosses to the chest of drawers to put down the fan and pick up the watch, which she raises to her ear and begins to wind as she slowly crosses to the window with a self-possessed attitude.*)

Let's see, now, who's that drivin' up? . . . Could be Home! No! . . . It's the local pastor. I guess he came to pick up the Reverend. Probably gonna take him to his house for dinner before goin' down to the rally. Home tells me that pastor has a young wife that looks like Amazin' Grace. And to hear Home talk about it, she puts on the finest pot of chicken 'n dumplins in Memphis. But the Reverend is gonna have to eat in a hurry if he plans to get down to Claiborne Temple in time to hear "Precious Lord, Take My Hand" . . .

(*He turns away from the window and is surprised to discover Cass standing directly behind him with a solemn deportment, the watch up to her ear.*)

That's his favorite song!

CASS (*somberly*): I'm not scared of dyin', Harper! . . . I'm just afraid of bein' alone! . . .

(*Harper gazes at her quizzically for a beat, then retreats upstage to place the binoculars in the totebag and locate the transistor.*)

HARPER: I've gotta find Home! . . .

CASS (*crosses to the table with watch*): I learned how to die at an early age. I was always alone on the desert. Alone, lonely, waiting for each tick to tock! . . . (*She raises the watch to her ear.*) Tick . . . Tock! . . . (*She offers the watch to Harper, who is manipulating the transistor antenna.*) You wanna listen? . . .

HARPER: Harper to Home! Harper callin' Home! . . . Come in, Home, come in! This is Harper, callin', I. W. Harper!

(*No response, only static, as Cass places the watch on the table and crosses over to the one-armed bandit.*)

CASS: You can't reach God on a transistor radio!

HARPER: I've lost contact with Home! . . .

CASS: The divine will of God! (*She begins to manipulate the one-armed bandit.*)

HARPER (*anxiously*): It's a technical failure. Bad equipment! . . . Domestic! I should've bought Japanese when I had a chance.

CASS: Now we're lost!

HARPER: Who said anything about bein' lost?

CASS: We're lost, and you know it, Harper.

HARPER: Don't talk crazy, woman! . . . You think I don't know what I'm doin'? As soon as I find Home, I'm gettin' the hell outta here!

CASS: All you can do is flounder in the dark, Harper. You have no faith, your unrepentant soul roaming restlessly in your own shadow, lost without vision, unable to even see if God follows his Reverend. And if you can't see that far, Harper, I have no confidence that you can see who's following me.

HARPER: You don't know what you're talkin' 'bout, lady. I've been in much deeper and darker holes than this one.

CASS: And did you see God?

HARPER: I got lucky! . . . I found Home! . . . He got me outta that mess . . . said I'd find peace of mind in California.

CASS: And you expect me to trust a man whose only weapon is luck?

HARPER (*reflects anxiously for a beat*): Suppose I did see God, I mean, at least once! . . . Would you say I was shootin' crap?

CASS: I don't believe you, Harper.

HARPER (*removes a pith helmet from the totebag and dons it*): What else could it have been?

(*Lights shift to focus Harper's private moment as he removes binoculars from totebag, turns around, and gazes downstage through the glasses.*)

I was crossin' the desert in a Land Rover, trackin' a man who was supposed to be dead. A case of fraud. He was the Most Wanted Man in the world. I had traveled the entire country searchin' for this man, who was last seen on the burnin' plains of Nevada. I eluded the temptations of Reno and headed for Boomtown near the California border, where I stopped at a shelter for gas and repast. (*He crosses downstage toward Cass at the one-armed bandit.*) The shelter was filled with Jack Mormons and one-armed bandits. A young girl who appeared like a Lily in the Valley was mannin' one of those tormentin' machines. I decided to pump her with questions. I smiled. She smiled. I put a dime in the machine and it came up cherries. What do you think of that, girlie? I asked. She smiled. I'm goin' after three watermelons!

CASS: Jackpot!

HARPER: I'm in town on an urgent mission.

CASS: I could tell! . . .

HARPER: How so? . . .

CASS: You look like a Great White Hunter!

HARPER: I was pleased that my cover was workin'. She didn't find me the least bit peculiar. No alarm whatsoever. I was now free to probe further, givin' her a description of the man I sought as bein' tall, lean, with fair complexion, a gaunt, withery face concealed with a scruffy blond beard, and long tresses of crownin' glory. His eyes are said to be pale and watery blue.

CASS: Christ, mister, if such a wonderful man had passed this way, I would've tucked him under my skirt. He sounds like a logger from Eureka!

(*Sound of jackpot emptying.*)

HARPER: I hit the jackpot, collected my winnings, and tipped the girl with a Hershey bar. (*He crosses to center stage.*) I then boarded my Land Rover, opened up the throttle, and moved on into California against a magenta sky, passin' through the august Sierras. It was here that it happened. I was struck by the awesome majesty of these mountains. It was a sight to behold. I had never seen anything so beautiful, yet forbiddin'. I was overwhelmed by a sense of solitude, touched by a feelin' of peace and joy. But somehow, I knew I was not alone. I could not be alone with such a wonder. I was consumed with the joy of life when a deer ran across my path and I struck him dead!

(*Lights return to normal as Harper removes the pith helmet and stares downstage with a vacant expression. Cass crosses toward him.*)

CASS (*bewildered*): You killed one of God's creatures! . . .

HARPER: It was an accident! (*He quickly dispatches himself upstage, retreating from her indictment, and places the pith helmet in the totebag.*)

CASS: Did you repent?

HARPER: I picked up a stone and threw it at the mountain!

CASS: Who else knows about this? . . . Does your Reverend know?

HARPER: I told Home. He said life is like a crap game! . . . You get a good roll most of the time, but God knows, snake eyes are bound to catch up with you.

(*Cass tries to take Harper in tow toward the chest of drawers, which is now used as an altar.*)

CASS (*anxiously*): Come, Harper, we must pray. Come on, now!

HARPER (*withdraws violently*): I don't wanna pray, woman!

CASS (*frantically lights the candles*): You've gotta pray! You killed an innocent creature. It is said in Revelations that the blood of the lamb! . . .

HARPER (*interrupting*): Stop harpin' on it, Cass! If you know somethin' about these things, just tell me! . . . Did I witness God, or didn't I?

CASS: You're a killer, Harper!

HARPER: I told you, it was an accident!

CASS: Accidents don't happen by accident!

HARPER: I can swear on it!

CASS: No, don't swear! . . . Just pray! . . . Come, Harper, pray with me. (*She kneels before the chest.*)

CASS: No, don't swear! . . . Just pray! . . . Come, Harper, pray with me. (*She kneels before the chest.*)

HARPER (*insistently*): Can't you just tell me what I saw out there?

CASS (*in grave agitation*): Please, Harper, please pray with me!

HARPER (*greatly agitated*): I had nothin' to do with it! That was God's work, wasn't it?

CASS: You're a killer, Harper. And we're lost!

(*He crosses to her bitterly and attempts to pull her to her feet. Cass withdraws.*)

HARPER: Just stop all that crazy talk! Nobody's lost, and I'm no killer, you understand? Killers carry weapons, and I don't, remember? I protect the innocent, so on your feet, come on, on your feet!

CASS: Go 'way! . . . Please, go 'way! . . .

HARPER: You've gotta trust me, Cass! . . .

(*As they struggle, Cass resists him desperately. She pushes away from him, causing Harper to accidentally strip away the high-necked bodice of her dress, slightly exposing her breasts. Cass covers up with alarm and moves desperately downstage with a shocked expression on her face. Harper pursues her with an embittered disposition as he holds out the bodice toward her.*)

See what you made me do? . . . I didn't mean to do it, but you won't listen! You act like I'm some kind of creep or somethin'. You think I don't know what's goin' on around here? You've got creeps comin' through here like Grand Central Station! Well, I ain't no creep! But I'm gonna tell you somethin' for your own good. Keep them outta here! I only came back to pick up my Longine Wittnauer, Diana! . . .

(*He stops in mid-thought with the sudden awareness that he has been ranting uncontrollably at a past episode with Diana. Cass also becomes aware of his unconscious lapse.*)

CASS: Jesus, save me!

(*Flustered, Harper turns and throws the bodice violently upstage, goes quickly to the totebag, removes the transistor, and crosses to the window.*)

HARPER: Good God, Home, where in hell are you?

(*Cass stealthily moves to the door and attempts to unlock the locks with her keys. Harper turns around suddenly and catches her in the act.*)

What are you tryin' to do? . . .

(*He approaches her slowly. Cass retreats fearfully to the downstage side of the table. Harper pursues her slowly, knocking the chair to one side as he advances to the table.*)

CASS: Go 'way! . . . Please, just go 'way!

HARPER: Can't you see I'm tryin' to help you?

CASS: I don't want your help. Here, take the keys and go!

(*She removes the chain of keys from around her neck and drops them on the table. As Harper reaches down to pick them up, she makes a dash for the window. Harper alertly intercepts her as she is about to scream. He places his hand over her mouth and forcefully shoves her upstage. Terrified, she picks up the fallen chair to hold Harper off as he slowly approaches, backing her toward the bed.*)

HARPER: I don't understand you! . . . My work isn't done here yet. What are you tryin' to do, take the pride outta my work?

(*He snatches the chair out of her hands and places it gingerly to one side as she backs into the bed.*)

It's the only thing I get paid to do. So, I ain't quittin' till the job is through.

(*He pushes her forcefully onto the bed. She gasps with an open mouth as if to scream.*)

Don't you do it! . . . Don't start that screamin' shit in here! All you're gonna do is give me some real facts, little lady!

(*She quickly grabs a pillow to place between them protectively.*)

Now, I want a true description of that fella who's been followin' you!

CASS (*terrified*): I . . . I don't know!

HARPER (*intimidatingly*): You do know the fella! He came to keep you company!

CASS: It was dark. He was in the shadows.

HARPER: On Beale Street, right? . . .

CASS: I think so! . . .

HARPER: You recognized your gentleman caller on Beale Street.

CASS: I never saw his face.

HARPER: He followed you home.

CASS: In the shadows! . . .

HARPER: He knocked at the door! . . .

CASS: I was sleeping! . . .

HARPER: You opened the door! . . .

CASS (*indignantly*): I *won't* swear on it!

(*She hits him violently in the face with the pillow and makes a desperate effort to retreat. Harper alertly grabs her and slaps her forcefully down to the bed.*)

HARPER: You're lyin', Cass! You want me to go crazy on you? I could go crazy on you, you know. I don't wanna hurt you! But you've gotta stop lyin'! Who is the fella?

CASS (*subdued*): I was sleeping! . . . It was dark. I was awakened by a shadow . . .

CASS: Please, go away! . . . Please? . . .

(*Harper raises his hand to slap her once again. She cowers fearfully. He withdraws the threat as the sound of an automobile blares its horn. He quickly crosses to the window. As he looks out the window, Cass climbs out of the bed slowly in disarray, crosses to the sink, rinses her mouth, and wipes her face with a towel.*)

HARPER: See what I mean, Cass? . . . I told you I didn't have all day to mess around with you. The Reverend is fixin' to leave. He's standin' out there on the balcony in his shirt sleeves . . . got his cronies waitin' down by the car. Looks like they're tryin' to tell him to put on his jacket so they can go!

(*He turns away from the window to confront Cass as she slowly crosses and sits on the edge of the bed with a vacant expression on her face.*)

I can't waste any more time over a dream, Cass! (*He blows out the candle.*)

CASS (*vacantly*): His hand was on my throat!

HARPER (*crosses to her with great deliberation*): Let's settle this once and for all! . . . Show me the evidence!

(*Cass reflexly rubs her neck, with a stunned, vacant expression. Harper touches her shoulder. She turns toward him submissively. He gently touches her throat. She reacts guardedly, clutching his hand as he inspects.*)

What are you frightened about, I'm not gonna hurt you. Now, show me, is it here? . . . Over here? . . . How 'bout, here! . . .

(*He clutches her throat with sudden firmness. She attempts to withdraw, but he holds on tightly. She grimaces and makes a gagging sound as he forces her down to the bed.*)

Was he chokin' you . . . or was he tryin' to kiss you? He leaned over your body and you saw his face, right? You recognized him! . . . Look at me!!! He was a rejected lover! . . . And you tried to scream. Go on, try to scream! . . . He had to shut you up! . . . (*He picks up the pillow and places it over Cass's head. He presses firmly.*) You struggled for a while, but he was too heavy. All you could hear were his distant cries . . . I love you! . . . I love you! . . . I swear on it, Diana, I love you! . . .

(*The loud, piercing sound of a rifle shot. Harper is startled. He alertly races over to the window and peers out with an incredulous expression as Cass lays limply on the bed. Stridently:*)

Good God! . . . He's been shot!

(*He is distracted by the sudden sound of footsteps racing down a squeaky staircase. He runs to the door but is unable to get out. He then removes the transistor from the totebag.*)

They got 'im, Cass, the Reverend, they shot him! Get on the phone, Cass, and call the manager! . . . I gotta call Home!

(*He glances at the limp body of Cass quizzically as the distant sound of a police siren can be heard approaching, along with the intrusion of a sense of general chaos outside the window.*)

Get up off your ass, woman, this is an emergency! Somethin' terrible has happened . . . terrible, terrible!

(*Telephone rings. Harper turns abruptly toward it with a bewildered expression, perplexed by Cass's lack of response. He gazes at her limp and lifeless body with sudden horror as the sound of increased commotion can be heard outside the window. Lights fade out slowly.*)

CURTAIN

ABOUT THE AUTHORS

WOLE SOYINKA, a Nigerian poet, novelist, and dramatist, is one of the most original thinkers and writers in world literature. Included among his plays are *The Road, The Lion and the Jewel, Kongi's Harvest, Madmen and Specialists, The Trials of Brother Jero, Jero's Metamorphosis*, an adaptation of *The Bacchae* of Euripides, and *Death and the King's Horseman*. His play *The Strong Breed* was first performed in the United States in 1967 at the Greenwich Mews Theatre in New York. A distinguished scholar and professor of literature at the University of Ife, Nigeria, he was the 1986 recipient of the Nobel Prize for Literature.

PEPE CARRIL is artistic director of the Teatro Guiñol, Havana, Cuba. *Shango de Ima*, a Yoruba mystery play, was first adapted from Spanish and performed by the La Mama Dance Drama Theatre in New York in 1970.

DEREK WALCOTT, a native of St. Lucia, is an internationally acclaimed poet whose work has been collected in several volumes. His name is normally associated with Trinidad, where he developed the Trinidad Workshop Theatre over a period of nine years. As a dramatist, his works include *The Sea at Dauphin, Malcochon, or The Six in the Rain, O Babylon, The Joker of Seville*, and the Obie Award–winning play *Dream on Monkey Mountain*. His play *Ti-Jean and His Brothers* enjoyed its first successful production in the United States in 1972 at the Public Theatre in New York. Recipient of a MacArthur Foundation Fellowship, he currently teaches poetry at Boston University.

ZAKES MOFOKENG is an actor, cultural activist, and one of the vital new dramatists to emerge out of the township theatre movement of South Africa. Born in Soweto, he was forced into exile in 1984. He began to develop his talents

521

in the sixties as a member of an experimental theatre group, The Rehearsal Room. His first play, *The Train*, was produced by the group in 1974. *A New Song* won critical acclaim after its 1982 production at the Culture and Resistance Festival in Botswana. He is currently writing, performing, and living out his exile in Zurich, Switzerland.

NTOZAKE SHANGE is a poet and novelist. She is the author of the book *Nappy Edges and Sassafras*. Included among her plays are *A Photograph: A Still Life with Shadows/A Photograph: A Study in Cruelty* and *Spell #7*, both presented at the Public Theatre in New York. Prior to its Broadway debut, her Obie Award–winning play *for colored girls who have considered suicide/when the rainbow is enuf* enjoyed wide national acclaim for its impact on feminist consciousness.

CHARLES FULLER is a prominent contributor to the repertory of the Negro Ensemble Company. His significant plays include the epic cycle *In My Many Names and Days*, *The Brownsville Raid*, and the 1982 Pulitzer Prize–winning work *A Soldier's Play*. His play *Zooman and the Sign* was awarded an Obie in 1981. He is also a Guggenheim recipient. *Sally*, the first part of his new epic cycle of plays, *We*, was produced by the Negro Ensemble Company at the 1988 Black Arts Festival in Atlanta.

AUGUST WILSON is a poet whose work had been published in the anthology *Black Poets of the Twentieth Century*. His dramaturgy has been nurtured by the Yale Repertory Company. *Ma Rainey's Black Bottom* was voted Best New Play of 1984–85 by the New York Drama Critics Circle; the following year, he was the recipient of the Pulitzer Prize for *Fences*, and he is also a Guggenheim recipient. His newest work is *Joe Turner's Come and Gone*. He is an associate playwright with the Playwright's Center in Minneapolis, Minnesota, where he lives.

PAUL CARTER HARRISON is a playwright/director; the author of *The Drama of Nommo*, which essays the African foundations of Afro-American aesthetics; and the editor of *Kuntu Drama*, a collection of African diaspora plays, and *Chuck Stewart's Jazz File*, a photodocumentary. Included among his plays are *Tabernacle*, *Tophat*, *The Death of Boogie Woogie*, *Ameri/Cain Gothic*, and the Obie Award–winning *The Great MacDaddy*. His blues operetta, *Anchorman*, was produced in the 1987–88 season by the American Folk Theatre. A 1985 recipient of the Rockefeller Fellowship for American Playwriting, he is currently writer-in-residence at Columbia College in Chicago.